Rock Inscriptions and Graffiti Project

SOCIETY OF BIBLICAL LITERATURE
Resources for Biblical Study

Edited by
Marvin A. Sweeney

Number 28
Rock Inscriptions and Graffiti Project
Volume 1

Edited by
MICHAEL E. STONE

ROCK INSCRIPTIONS AND GRAFFITI PROJECT

Catalogue of Inscriptions

Volume 1

Inscriptions 1-3000

Edited by

MICHAEL E. STONE

Editorial Assistant

Leslie Avital Kobayashi

Scholars Press

Atlanta, Georgia

Rock Inscriptions and Graffiti Project

Library of Congress Cataloging-in-Publication Data

Rock inscriptions and graffiti project: catalogue of inscriptions/
compiled and edited by Michael E. Stone; editorial assistant,
Leslie Avital Kobayashi.

p. cm. — (Resources for biblical study; no. 28-<29 >)

Includes bibliographical references and index.

Contents: v. 1. Inscriptions 1-3000 — v. 2. Inscriptions 3001-6000.

ISBN 1-55540-790-0 (v. 1) (alk. paper). — ISBN 1-55540-791-9 (v. 1) (pbk.: alk. paper). — ISBN 1-55540-792-7 (v. 2) (alk. paper). -- ISBN 1-55540-793-5 (v. 2) (pbk.: alk. paper)

1. Inscriptions—Palestine—Catalogs. 2. Inscriptions—Egypt--Sinai—Catalogs. 3. Bible—Antiquities—Catalogs. 4. Graffiti--Palestine—Antiquities—Catalogs. 7. Sinai (Egypt)—Antiquities-Catalogs. I. Stone, Michael E., 1938- . II. Series.

CN753.P19R6 1992

933—dc20

92-33418

CIP

Printed in the United States of America
on acid-free paper

Julius Stone

in memoriam

TABLE OF CONTENTS

LIST OF MAPS

PREFACE

The editor's thanks must be expressed to many persons who have helped in the production of this volume. First and foremost, the contribution of the Project staff must be acknowledged; Hannah Sirkis, Yigal Dorfmann, and Nicole Sotto had a particular hand in the preparation of the data for this volume. A special debt is owed to Leslie Kobayashi, the editorial assistant, who contributed in many, many aspects of the work of the Project and in the production of this volume. Oron Joffe and Leslie Kobayashi have worked wonders with the computer.

The Israel Academy of Sciences and Humanities through its Basic Research Fund has consistently supported the work of the project over the years. James D. Wolfensohn made a donation in memory of the late Julius Stone that enabled the data for this book to be prepared. A grant from the A.G.B.U. Alex Manoogian Cultural Fund was devoted to the photographic work of the Project.

The Antiquities Authority of the State of Israel offered its full co-operation in initiating this project and has proffered practical help from time to time. We wish to express our thanks and appreciation to the Research and Development Authority of the Hebrew University of Jerusalem for their support. A number of scholars and researchers have been generous enough to make photographs available to the Project. A. Goren, U. Avner, I. Finkelstein and Y. Tzafrir are particularly to be mentioned in this respect.

Michael E. Stone
Jerusalem 1992

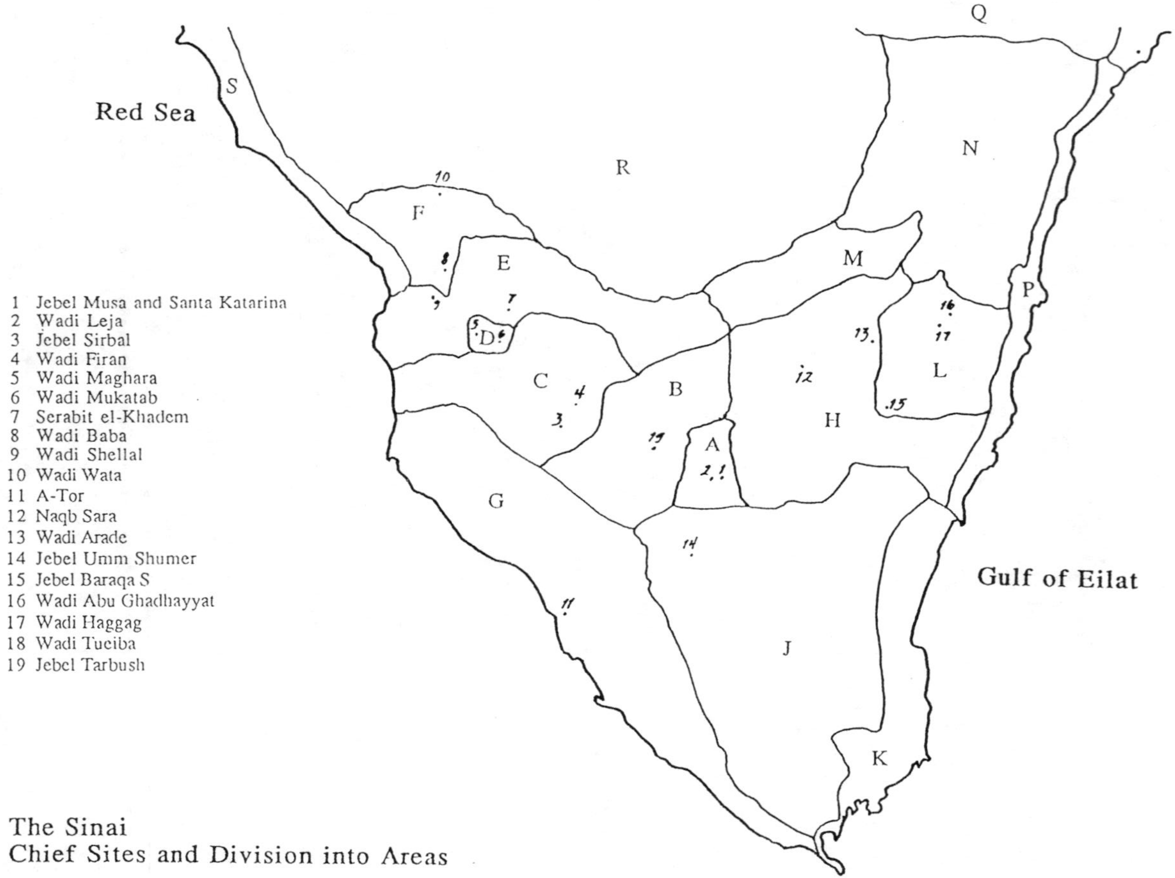

The Sinai
Chief Sites and Division into Areas

INTRODUCTION

The Character of the Catalogue

The Rock Inscriptions and Graffiti Project of the Institute of African and Asian Studies of the Hebrew University of Jerusalem has as its first aim the assembly, cataloguing and processing of rock inscriptions and graffiti from the Sinai, the Negev desert, the Christian holy places, and the Judean Desert. Its ultimate purpose is to create an integrated instrument for scholars, combining on-line data files, photographic documentation of the inscriptions, maps, and printed bibliography. The Project files contain both published and unpublished graffiti and rock inscriptions, for it is clearly of great advantage for research to have all known material in one data resource, whether that material has been published or not. Moreover, since our interests extend to routes of travel, we have felt it to be appropriate to record all markings observed on rocks, as far as available, including rock drawings and crosses. After the preparation of the integrated data resource, the Project will proceed to encourage the publication of various of the inscriptions. It is hoped that this will be undertaken by qualified scholars, in cooperation with the Project and utilizing the resources so carefully prepared. This catalogue is to be viewed, therefore, as an invitation to scholars to pursue further research on these epigraphs.

The chief part of the present volume is a catalogue of the first 3000 inscriptions in the files of the Project. It is not itself the publication of the inscriptions, nor is it intended to be an exhaustive presentation of all the data available about them in the Project files. Rather, its purpose is to present the chief information about the inscriptions to scholars, by way of initial indication of the holdings of the Project. The second part of the volume is a list providing information about the sites at which the inscriptions included in this volume were found. It should be stressed that this printed volume cannot substitute for actual on-line files, photographs, maps and bibliographical resources to be found in the Project headquarters. Those are available to all qualified scholars.

The use of on-line files, in combination with the photographs, enables the retrieval of information selected by combinations of criteria such as language and geographical area, coordinates and dates, as well as by the text of the inscriptions. It is impossible, of course, fully to present all such possible lists of the combinations of data in printed form, but those judged to be most useful are given in the "Indexes and Lists" section at the end of the book.

Presentation of the Inscriptions

Each inscription is described according to a number of categories, designated here as "fields." An explanation of the fields and their notation and contents follows:

Inscription	9
Site	Wadi Haggag, rock 3, #125
Dating	9th to 10th century
Technique	incised
Condition	fair
Dimensions	? x 6.5 cm.
Content	Armenian inscription *Ս* *ՏՐԴԱՏ*
Comment	*L.1: 3 x ? cm.; L.2: 1.7 x 6.5 cm.*
Access	AAb08 (photograph, M. Stone); *see also* AR31, AR32, AZ03, AZ04, Negev 1977 fig. 95
Corpus	H Arm 25

Inscription: The first item in the description is a serial number. Each epigraph in the Project is assigned a single, unique serial number and it is kept in the Project files according to this number. Epigraphs in the present list should be referred to as "Rock Inscriptions and Graffiti Project Inscription no. *nn*."

Site: The general location where the inscription was found and the specific place in this location, if known. Details concerning the sites may be found in the companion List of Sites. If the specific site is not known, only the general location will be given. If the location of origin of an inscription is not known, it is marked "unknown." The number at the end of each site entry is that of the site in the List of Sites.

Dating: All dates are C.E. unless otherwise indicated. Many inscriptions are undated or undatable.

Technique: Indicates the mode of execution of the inscription. Most inscriptions are incised, others are scratched, punched, painted or produced in relief.

Condition: Indicates the state of preservation of the inscription.

Dimensions: Given in cms, width first. A question mark stands for an unknown measurement. Frequently the dimensions are not available.

Content: A verbal description of the contents of the epigraph, e.g., "Greek inscription," "Nabatean inscription," "Rock drawing," etc. This is followed by the transcription of the epigraph if one is available either from publication or from authoritative decipherment. As far as possible we have verified all such decipherments and on occasion our reading has differed from the published one.[1] If there is only a working transcription in the Project files, that is indicated by the entry "Tentative decipherment only." If this field remains blank it means that the inscription was not deciphered. "Study only" indicates that while the owner of the negative has permitted it to be copied and stored, permission has not been granted for publication of the text of the inscription.

Comment: This item, given in italics following the text of the inscription, contains additional observations on the inscription or other supplementary data.

Access: This field supplies information as to where the inscription may be seen in photographic form. It contains the code indicating where the material form of the inscription is stored in the Project headquarters. In parentheses will follow the description of the medium and the name of the person or institution to whom the negative belongs. "Photograph" usually indicates a black and white photograph which is the preferred form of storage. Usually the Project also holds negatives and contact prints of epigraphs. Sometimes color transparencies are available. In the case of inscriptions which have already been published, wherever possible we have identified these inscriptions on our own negatives and have noted this in addition to giving a reference to the published form. If an inscription appears in more than one negative, then the additional access codes are to be found at the end of this field.

Corpus: If the inscription has been published, then under Corpus the number of the inscription in the definitive edition is given. The absence of this item indicates that the inscription has not previously been published. Below, a list of all abbreviations may be found.

Presentation of the Sites

The sites are presented in the following fashion:

Site Number	5
Site Name	Bir Ramhan
Location	Jebel Umm Shumer
Area Code	J
UTM	59351379
ITM	04707537
Geology	granite
Comment	*In Wadi Ramhan, Greek inscriptions and crosses on route to Santa Katarina which continues via Wadi Rahba to which access is gained from A-Tur via Wadi Isla or via Wadi Thanan.*

Site Number: This is the number of the site in the Project files.

[1] For technical reasons, supralinear marks in editions, indicating various levels of uncertainty of reading, have not been reproduced.

Site Name: This is the name of the specific site at which the inscription is to be found, if that information is available. If it is not available, the entry for this field is the same as the entry for the location.

Area Code: Project code for the particular area in which the site is found. These areas are divided up by topographical and geographical criteria. They are indicated on a Map of Areas of the Sinai given below.

UTM: The coordinates of the site on the Mercator grid.

ITM: The coordinates of the site on the Israel grid.

Location: This indicates the general area at which the inscription is found. This is usually known.

Geology: Here we record the type of rock in the particular site, if known.

Comment: Below the record, comments are sometimes included. These are usually drawn from the field notes made by Project surveys or from other oral or written sources. These comments are episodic and not systematic, but contain much data that might otherwise not be available. All abbreviations used in the comments are included in the list below.

Since many of the inscriptions reached our hands from private individuals and not as the result of systematic surveys, often the site name is unknown, only the general location. In such instances, the words "General site designator" are entered in the **Comment** field and the coordinates are related to the general location of the inscription, but not necessarily to its specific site.

There is much uncertainty about site and location names and their spellings. Many are known only orally through Beduin usage. No systematic, scholarly transliteration has been attempted. Where the names are available on the 1:100,000 and 1:50,000 maps, those forms of the names have been used. The letter "j" is used in all relevant transcriptions of names from Arabic, except for the name "Haggag," which has become embedded in scholarly usage.

Glossary

In site descriptions the following terms are sometimes used:

Bir	well
Deir	monastery
Hadbe	a large, free-standing boulder or monolith
Jebel	mountain
Naqb	a pass through a mountainous area or ridge
Wadi	valley

Alphabetic List of Special Abbreviations

Ann Arbor in the Access entry indicates the records of the University of Michigan-Princeton expedition to St. Catherine's monastery deposited at the University of Michigan, Ann Arbor.

CIS indicates *Corpus Inscriptionum Semiticarum*. In **Corpus** it is cited by volume, part, page and inscription number.

D.O.P. 1966 refers to: I. Ševčenko, "The Early Period of the Sinai Monastery in Light of Its Inscriptions," *Dumbarton Oaks Papers* 20 (1966) 258-263.

H Arm, M Arm, H Georg, etc., quoted by number in **Corpus** field. These are the inscriptions published by M.E. Stone, *The Armenian Inscriptions from the Sinai* (Harvard Armenian Texts and Studies 6; Cambridge, MA: Harvard University, 1982). A supplement to this publication is M.E. Stone, "Four Further Armenian Epigraphs from the Sinai," *Journal of the Society of Armenian Studies* 2 (1985-1986) 73-83.

Negev 1977, quoted by number and "fig." = figure in **Corpus** field. This is A. Negev, *The Inscriptions of Wadi Haggag, Sinai* (Qedem 6; Jerusalem: Institute of Archeology, 1977).

Bibliography

U. Avner, "New Evidence of Nabatean Presence in the Sinai," *South Sinai Researches 1967-1982*, ed. I. Lachish and Z. Meshel (Tel-Aviv: South Sinai Administration and Nature Protection Society, 1982) 25-32 (in Hebrew).

I. Finkelstein, "Relics of the Period of Byzantine Monasticism in Jebel Ṣafṣafa," *Antiquities of Sinai*, ed. Z. Meshel and I. Finkelstein (Tel-Aviv: HaKibbutz HeMeuhad, 1980) 385-410 (in Hebrew).

S. Levi, *Belief and Cult of the Beduin of Southern Sinai* (Tel-Aviv: Nature Protection Society, 1980) (in Hebrew).

A. Negev, "South Sinai Inscriptions," *Antiquities of Sinai*, ed. Z. Meshel and I. Finkelstein (Tel-Aviv: HaKibbutz HaMeuhad, 1980) 340-379 (in Hebrew).

Z. Meshel, "Were the Rock Inscriptions of the Sinai Really Written by Nabateans?," *Antiquities of Sinai*, ed. Z. Meshel and I. Finkelstein (Tel-Aviv: HaKibbutz HaMeuhad, 1980) 379-383 (in Hebrew).

E.H. Palmer, *The Desert of the Exodus* (Cambridge: Deighton, Bell & Co., 1871).

D. Rabinovitz, *Mt. Sirbal* (Tzukei David Field School: Nature Protection Society, 1979) (in Hebrew).

M.E. Stone, *The Armenian Inscriptions from the Sinai with Appendixes on the Georgian and Latin Inscriptions by Michel van Esbroeck and W. Adler* (Harvard Armenian Texts and Studies 6; Cambridge: Harvard University, 1982).

M.E. Stone, *Sinai Diary*: typescript of this work may be found in the Project rooms.

M.E. Stone, *Notebooks*: six volumes of field notes deposited in the Project rooms.

CATALOGUE OF INSCRIPTIONS

Inscription 1
Site Wadi Haggag, #118
Technique incised
Condition poor
Content unidentified inscription
Comment *Armenian?*
Access AAa02 (photograph, M. Stone)

Inscription 2
Site Wadi Haggag, #118
Technique incised
Condition good
Content Greek inscription

KE ΣΩΣΟΝ

Access AAa04 (photograph, M. Stone); *see also* AAa05, FE16, Negev 1977 fig. 73
Corpus Negev 1977 102

Inscription 3
Site Wadi Maghara, #72
Technique incised
Condition poor
Content Egyptian hieroglyphs
Access AEa13-14 (photograph, M. Stone); *see also* AEb15-16

Inscription 4
Site Wadi Haggag, rock 3, #125
Technique incised
Condition poor
Dimensions 4.3 x 6 cm.
Content Armenian inscription

ՅՄԵ

Access AAa06 (photograph, M. Stone); *see also* ABd23, ADg31, BK56, BK57, Negev 1977 fig. 90
Corpus H Arm 5

Inscription 5
Site Wadi Haggag, rock 3, #125
Technique incised
Condition fair
Dimensions 4.5 x 35 cm.
Content Armenian inscription

ԱՆԱՆԻԱ

Access AAa06 (photograph, M. Stone); *see also* ABd23, ADg31, BK56, BK57, Negev 1977 fig. 90
Corpus H Arm 6

Inscription 6
Site Wadi Haggag, rock 3, #125
Technique incised
Condition fair
Dimensions 4 x 7 cm.
Content Armenian inscription

ՆԵՐՍ

Access AAb07 (photograph, M. Stone); *see also* AQ01, AZ02, BG85, BG86, BM33, BM34
Corpus H Arm 21

Inscription 7
Site Wadi Haggag, rock 3, #125
Technique incised
Condition good
Content Greek inscription
Limitation *Tentative decipherment only*
Access AAb08 (photograph, M. Stone)

Inscription 8
Site Wadi Haggag, rock 3, #125
Dating 7th to 9th century
Technique incised
Condition good
Dimensions 2 x 10.5 cm.
Content Armenian inscription

......ՎԱՍԱԿ

Access AAb08 (photograph, M. Stone); *see also* AR31, AR32, AZ03, AZ04, Negev 1977 fig. 95
Corpus H Arm 24

Inscription 9
Site Wadi Haggag, rock 3, #125
Dating 9th to 10th century
Technique incised
Condition fair
Dimensions ? x 6.5 cm.
Content Armenian inscription

Ս

ՏՐԴԱՏ

Comment *L.1: 3 x ? cm.; L.2: 1.7 x 6.5 cm.*
Access AAb08 (photograph, M. Stone); *see also* AR31, AR32, AZ03, AZ04, Negev 1977 fig. 95
Corpus H Arm 25

Inscription 10
Site Wadi Haggag, #118
Technique incised
Condition poor
Content Greek inscription
Limitation *Tentative decipherment only*
Access AAb09 (photograph, M. Stone)

Inscription 11
Site Ein Hudra, #117
Technique incised
Condition excellent
Dimensions 45 x 37 cm.
Content rock drawing
Comment *camel*
Access EX17 (photograph, Project); see also EX18

Inscription 12
Site Wadi Haggag, #118
Technique incised
Condition good
Dimensions 4-5 x 15 cm.
Content Armenian inscription

ՈՐ ՈՔ

ՄՈԻԾ

Access AAb09 (photograph, M. Stone); *see also* Negev 1977 fig. 163
Corpus H Arm 27

Inscription 13
Site Wadi Haggag, rock 3, #125
Technique incised
Condition fair
Dimensions ? x 24 cm.
Content Armenian inscription

ՐԱԿՈՍ ԵՍ ԿԻԻ

Ա ՐԱՐԻ

ԽԱՉՍ

Comment *Preservation of L.1 fair, 3 x 24 cm.; L.2-3 poor. Parts of the name are reversed; upsilon is transcribed as iw.*
Access AAb10 (photograph, M. Stone); *see also* BP47, Negev 1977 figs. 163 and 164
Corpus H Arm 29

Inscription 14
Site Wadi Haggag, rock 3, #125
Technique incised
Condition fair
Content unidentified inscription
Access AAb10 (photograph, M. Stone); *see also* Negev 1977 fig. 163

Inscription 15
Site Wadi Haggag, rock 3, #125
Dating 9th to 11th century
Technique scratched
Condition good
Content Georgian inscription

grigol

Access ADf26 (photograph, M. Stone); *see also* ADh34, ADh35, AX14, AX15,
Corpus H Georg 6

Inscription 16
Site Wadi Haggag, rock 3, #125
Dating 7th to 9th century
Technique incised
Condition good
Dimensions 10 x 14 cm.
Content Armenian inscription

ԵՍ ԵՓՐԻՄ

ԵԻ ԹԱԹԱՆՈՅԾ

Comment *The letters are 3-4.5 cm.*
Access AAb12 (photograph, M. Stone); *see also* ABd22, ADe20, AS33, AS34, BQ62, BQ63
Corpus H Arm 34

Inscription 17
Site Wadi Haggag, rock 3, #125
Technique scratched
Condition poor
Content unidentified inscription
Access AAb12 (photograph, M. Stone); *see also* ABd22, ADe20, AS33, AS34, BQ62, BQ63

Inscription 18
Site Wadi Haggag, rock 3, #125
Dating 9th to 11th century
Technique incised
Condition good
Dimensions 1.7 x 10 cm.
Content Georgian inscription

ed gnjw

Access AAc13 (photograph, M. Stone); *see also* ABc16, BF64, BF65, Negev 1977 fig. 119
Corpus H Georg 4

Inscription 19
Site Wadi Haggag, rock 3, #125
Technique incised
Condition good
Dimensions 4 x 33 cm.
Content Armenian inscription

ՆԱԹԱՆ

Access AAc14 (photograph, M. Stone); *see also* ABc17, AW81, AW82, BQ74, BQ75
Corpus H Arm 59

Inscription 20
Site Wadi Haggag, rock 5, #131
Technique incised
Condition good
Content Nabatean inscription
Limitation *Tentative decipherment only*
Access AAc15 (photograph, M. Stone); *see also* AAc19, AW93, AW94, BA31, CP54

Inscription 21
Site Wadi Haggag, rock 5, #131
Technique scratched
Condition good
Content Armenian inscription

ՈՐԲՈԻՈ

Comment *The letters are large and readily legible from the ground. The meaning is enigmatic.*
Access AAc15 (photograph, M. Stone); *see also* AAc19, AW93, AW94, BA30, BA31, Negev 1977 fig. 193
Corpus H Arm 63

Inscription 22
Site Wadi Haggag, rock 3, #125
Technique incised
Condition poor
Content rock drawing
Comment *ibex pursued by hunter*
Access AAc16 (photograph, M. Stone); *see also* AAd20, BP50, BP51, CP65

Inscription 23
Site Wadi Haggag, rock 3, #125
Dating 6th to 7th century
Technique incised
Condition good
Dimensions 4-8 x 57 cm.
Content Armenian inscription

ԷՂ

ՋՎԱՆԻԿ ՅԻՇԵ

ԾԷՔ

Comment *L.1: 4-8 x 12 cm.; L.2: 4-8 x 57 cm.; L..3: 4-8 x 23 cm.*
Access AAc16 (photograph, M. Stone); *see also* AAd20, BP50, BP51, CP65
Corpus H Arm 64

Inscription 24
Site Wadi Haggag, rock 3, #125
Technique incised
Condition good
Content unidentified signs
Comment *two signs*
Access AAc16 (photograph, M. Stone); *see also* AAd20, BP50, BP51, CP65

Inscription 25
Site Wadi Haggag, rock 5, #131
Dating 7th to 8th century
Technique incised
Condition fair
Dimensions 8 x 25.5 cm.
Content Armenian inscription

]-- ՎԱԵՆ ՄՆԱ -Մ[

].- ՔՈՎԻ [ ] ՎԱՋԳԵՆ[]-[

ՄՈՎՍԷՍԻԿ

Comment *Each line is 2 cm. high.*
Access AAc17 (photograph, M. Stone); *see also* AAc18, ABf36, BC52, BC53, CP56
Corpus H Arm 66

Inscription 26
Site Wadi Haggag, rock 5, #131
Dating 8th to 9th century
Technique incised
Condition fair
Dimensions 7 x 20 cm.
Content Armenian inscription

ՅԱԿՈՎԲ

ՄԵՂԱՎՈՐ

Comment *L.1: 1.5-3.5 x 17 cm.; L.2: 2.5-3.5 x 20 cm.*
Access AAd21 (photograph, M. Stone); *see also* ACa01, AO15, AO16, BC54, BC55, Negev 1977 fig. 191
Corpus H Arm 67

Inscription 27
Site Wadi Haggag, rock 5, #131
Dating 9th to 10th century
Technique incised
Condition good
Dimensions 4 x 24 cm.
Content Georgian inscription

oo še miski

še ḫlni

gbl

Comment *L.1: 24 cm. long; L.2: 17 cm. long; L.3: 20 cm. long*
Access AAd22 (photograph, M. Stone); *see also* AO21, AO22, AX97, AX98
Corpus H Georg 9

Inscription 28
Site Wadi Haggag, rock 5, #131
Technique incised
Condition good
Dimensions 3.5-4 x 25 cm.
Content Armenian inscription

ԱԴՐԻՆԷ

Access AAd23 (photograph, M. Stone); *see also* ACa05, AP20, AP21, AY99, AY100, Negev 1977 fig. 186
Corpus H Arm 70

Inscription 29
Site Wadi Haggag, rock 5, #131
Dating 8th to 10th century
Technique incised
Condition good
Dimensions 8-4 x 38 cm.
Content Armenian inscription

ՄՈԻՍ

ԷՄՆ ՊԱՏԱԾԻ

Access AAd24 (photograph, M. Stone); *see also* ACa06, AP25, BG79, BG80, CJ04
Corpus H Arm 71

Inscription 30
Site Wadi Haggag, rock 5, #131
Dating 9th to10th century
Technique incised
Condition poor
Dimensions 11 x 17 cm.
Content Armenian inscription

ՏՐԴ

ԱՏ

Access AAe25 (photograph, M. Stone); *see also* ACa04, AO23, AO24, BG77, BG78, CR05
Corpus H Arm 72

Inscription 31
Site Wadi Haggag, rock 5, #131
Technique incised
Condition poor
Content unidentified signs
Access AAe25 (photograph, M. Stone)

Inscription 32
Site Jebel Baraqa S, #139
Technique incised
Condition fair
Content Nabatean inscription
Limitation *Tentative decipherment only*
Access AAe27 (photograph, M. Stone); *see also* AAe28, AAf36, CK19

Inscription 33
Site Jebel Baraqa S, #139
Technique incised
Condition good
Content Nabatean inscription
Limitation *Tentative decipherment only*
Access AAe29 (photograph, M. Stone); *see also* AAe30, AAf36, CK19

Inscription 34
Site Jebel Baraqa S, #139
Technique incised
Condition fair
Content Nabatean inscription
Limitation *Tentative decipherment only*
Access AAf31 (photograph, M. Stone); *see also* AAf32, AAf36, CJ01

Inscription 35
Site Jebel Baraqa S, #139
Technique incised
Condition good
Content rock drawing
Comment *camels and wolves*
Access AAf33 (photograph, M. Stone)

Inscription 36
Site Jebel Baraqa S, #139
Technique incised
Condition good
Content rock drawing
Comment *camels, ibex and wolves*
Access AAf34 (photograph, M. Stone)

Inscription 37
Site Jebel Baraqa S, #139
Technique incised
Condition good
Content rock drawing
Comment *humans and camels*
Access AAf35 (photograph, M. Stone)

Inscription 38
Site Wadi Haggag, rock 3, #125
Dating 9th to 11th century
Technique incised
Condition excellent
Dimensions 3 x 90 cm.
Content Armenian inscription

ՋՅԱԿՈՎ ՄԵՂԱԻՈՐ ՅԻՇԵՍՋԻՔ

Access ABa02 (photograph, M. Stone); *see also* ABa03, ABa04, ABb12, AM99, AN00, AT61, AU62
Corpus H Arm 39

Inscription 39
Site Wadi Haggag, rock 3, #125
Dating 9th to 11th century
Technique incised
Condition excellent
Dimensions 8 x 100 cm.
Content Armenian inscription

ԵՍ ՊԱԻՂՈՍ ԳՐԵՑԻ ՋԱՅՍ ԳԻՐ

ՈՐ ՋԱՅՍ ԿԱՐԴԱՍՑԷ ՋԻՍ ՅԻՇԵՑԷՔ

Access ABa02 (photograph, M. Stone); *see also* ABa03, ABa04, ABb12, AM99, AN00, AV89, AV90
Corpus H Arm 40

Inscription 40
Site Wadi Haggag, rock 3, #125
Dating 9th to 11th century
Technique incised
Condition fair
Dimensions 40 x 50 cm.
Content Armenian inscription

ԱՅ

ԵՍ ՊԵՏՐՈՍ-Ն-ՆԼ ՅԱ--ԳԵՂ

ԲՈՔ--ԱԼ

Ի ՍՈԻՐԲ ԿԱՏԱՐԼ

ՅԱՂԱԻԹՍ ԿԱԼ ՅԱԼ

ԵՍ ՅՈՀԱՆ ԵԻ ԿԱՂԵՆ

ԱՆ ՀՆԱԶԱՆԴ

Access ABa05 (photograph, M. Stone); *see also* ABf31, AR43, AS44, BJ99, BJ00, Negev 1977 fig. 57
Corpus H Arm 42

Inscription 41
Site Wadi Haggag, rock 3, #125
Technique incised
Condition good
Dimensions 15 x 15 cm.
Content Armenian inscription

ԵՂ ԻԹ

Access ABa05 (photograph, M. Stone); *see also* ABf31, AS45, AS46, BI01, BI02, Negev 1977 fig. 57
Corpus H Arm 41

Inscription 42
Site Wadi Haggag, rock 3, #125
Dating 9th to 10th century
Technique incised
Condition poor
Content Georgian inscription

d e a m

Access ABa05 (photograph, M. Stone); *see also* ABf31, AT47, AT48, BI03, BJ04
Corpus H Georg 8

Inscription 43
Site Wadi Haggag, rock 3, #125
Technique incised
Condition fair
Content Greek inscription
Limitation *Tentative decipherment only*
Access ABa05 (photograph, M. Stone); *see also* ABf31, AS45, AS46, BI01, BI02, Negev 1977 fig. 73

Inscription 44
Site Wadi Haggag, rock 3, #125
Technique incised
Condition good
Content crosses alone
Access ABa05 (photograph, M. Stone); *see also* ABf31, AT47, AT48, BI03, BJ04

Inscription 45
Site Wadi Biraq, #79
Technique incised
Condition excellent
Content rock drawing
Comment *camels mating; man holding reins of female camel*
Access EZ36 (photograph, Project)

Inscription 46
Site Wadi Biraq, #79
Technique incised
Condition poor
Content unidentified inscription
Access EZ36 (photograph, Project)

Inscription 47
Site Wadi Haggag, rock 3, #125
Technique incised
Condition good
Content Greek inscription
Limitation *Tentative decipherment only*
Access ABa05 (photograph, M. Stone); *see also* ABb09

Inscription 48
Site Wadi Haggag, rock 3, #125
Dating 7th to 8th century
Technique incised
Condition good
Dimensions 3.5 x 30 cm.
Content Armenian inscription

ԵՍ ՅՈՀԱՆ

Ի ՀՈԻԻՄԱՐԴԷ

Access ABa06 (photograph, M. Stone); *see also* AM91, AM92, AU63, AU64, BG73, BH74
Corpus H Arm 44

Inscription 49
Site Wadi Haggag, #118
Technique incised
Condition good
Content Latin inscription
Limitation *Tentative decipherment only*
Access ABb09 (photograph, M. Stone); *see also* ABb10, ABb11, Negev 1977 fig. 57

Inscription 50
Site Wadi Haggag, rock 3, #125
Dating 9th to 10th century
Technique incised
Condition fair
Dimensions 23 x 28 cm.
Content Armenian inscription

ԳՐԻԳՈՐ ՀԱՐԱԻ

ՍԱ [Ք]ՅԱՐ

Access ABc13 (photograph, M. Stone); *see also* ABc15, AM97, AM98, BL60, BQ64, BR65
Corpus H Arm 47

Inscription 51
Site Wadi Haggag, rock 3, #125
Technique incised
Condition poor
Content unidentified inscription
Access BO42 (photograph, Z. Radovan); *see also* ABc13

Inscription 52
Site Wadi Haggag, rock 3, #125
Technique incised
Condition good
Content crosses alone
Access ABc13 (photograph, M. Stone); *see also* BO42

Inscription 53
Site Wadi Haggag, rock 3, #125
Technique incised
Condition poor
Content Greek inscription
Limitation *Tentative decipherment only*
Comment *illegible*
Access ABc14 (photograph, M. Stone); *see also* AW87, AW88, BC67, BD68, Negev 1977 fig. 130

Inscription 54
Site Wadi Haggag, rock 3, #125
Technique incised
Condition poor
Content unidentified signs
Access ABc14 (photograph, M. Stone); *see also* AW87, AW88, BC67, BD68, Negev 1977 fig. 130

Inscription **55**
Site Wadi Haggag, rock 3, #125
Technique incised
Condition poor
Content unidentified signs
Access ABc14 (photograph, M. Stone); *see also* AW87, AW88, BC67, BD68

Inscription **56**
Site Wadi Haggag, rock 3, #125
Technique incised
Condition good
Content rock drawing
Comment *five-pointed star*
Access ABc14 (photograph, M. Stone); *see also* AW87, AW88, BC67, BD68

Inscription **57**
Site Wadi Haggag, rock 3, #125
Dating 9th to 10th century
Technique incised
Condition good
Content Armenian inscription

ՏԵՌՆԱՏՈՒՐ

ԱՏԴԵՆՈՅ

Access ABc14 (photograph, M. Stone); *see also* ADd13, AW87, AW88, BC67, BD68
Corpus H Arm 50

Inscription **58**
Site Wadi Haggag, rock 3, #125
Technique incised
Condition good
Content crosses alone
Access ABc14 (photograph, M. Stone); *see also* ADd13, AW87, AW88, BC67, BD68

Inscription **59**
Site Wadi Haggag, rock 3, #125
Technique incised
Condition good
Content crosses alone
Access ABc14 (photograph, M. Stone); *see also* ADd13, AW87, AW88, BC67, BD68

Inscription **60**
Site Wadi Haggag, #118
Technique incised
Condition good
Content crosses alone
Access ABc17 (photograph, M. Stone); *see also* AAc14, BQ74, BQ75

Inscription **61**
Site Wadi Haggag, rock 3, #125
Dating 10th to 11th century
Technique incised
Condition poor
Content Armenian inscription

ԻՈԱՆՆԷ

Access ABc15 (photograph, M. Stone); *see also* AM97, BP45
Corpus H Arm 48

Inscription **62**
Site Wadi Haggag, rock 3, #125
Technique incised
Condition good
Dimensions 7.8 x 13 cm.
Content Armenian inscription

ԵԱՅԻ

Ս

Comment *L.1: 4.5 x 13 cm.; L.2: 3.3 x 2 cm.*
Access ABc15 (photograph, M. Stone); *see also* AM97, BQ64, BR65
Corpus H Arm 49

Inscription **63**
Site Wadi Haggag, rock 3, #125
Technique incised
Condition good
Content crosses alone
Access ABc15 (photograph, M. Stone); *see also* AM97, BO42, BQ64, BR65

Inscription **64**
Site Wadi Haggag, #118
Technique incised
Condition good
Content crosses alone
Access AM97 (photograph, U. Avner); *see also* AM98

Inscription **65**
Site Wadi Haggag, rock 3, #125
Technique incised
Condition good
Content crosses with inscription
Comment *precedes insc. 50*
Access BP45 (photograph, Z. Radovan); *see also* BO42, BP43, BP44

Inscription **66**
Site Wadi Haggag, rock 3 area 3, #128
Technique incised
Condition good
Content varied crosses
Access ABc18 (photograph, M. Stone); *see also* AR35, AR36

Inscription **67**
Site Wadi Haggag, rock 3 area 3, #128
Dating 11th century
Technique incised
Condition poor
Dimensions 3 x 15 cm.
Content Armenian inscription

ԱՆՏՈ

Access ABc18 (photograph, M. Stone); *see also* AR35, AR36
Corpus H Arm 38

Inscription **68**
Site Wadi Haggag, rock 3 area 3, #128
Technique incised
Condition fair
Content Greek inscription
Limitation *Tentative decipherment only*
Access ABc18 (photograph, M. Stone)

Inscription **69**
Site Wadi Haggag, rock 3, #125
Technique incised
Condition good
Dimensions 1.7 x 20 cm.
Content Armenian inscription

ԹՈՒՄԱ ԱՐՂԱ

Access ABd19 (photograph, M. Stone); *see also* ABd24, AR37, AS38
Corpus H Arm 36

Inscription **70**
Site Wadi Haggag, rock 3, #125
Technique incised
Condition good
Dimensions 2.3 x 15 cm.
Content Armenian inscription

ՄԵՆԱՍ

Access ABd19 (photograph, M. Stone); *see also* ABd24, AN01, AN02, AS39, AS40
Corpus H Arm 37

Inscription **71**
Site Wadi Haggag, rock 3, #125
Technique incised
Condition poor
Content Greek inscription
Limitation *Tentative decipherment only*
Access ABd19 (photograph, M. Stone); *see also* ABd24, AN01, AN02

Inscription **72**
Site Wadi Haggag, rock 3 area 1, #126
Technique incised
Condition good
Content crosses alone
Access ABd20 (photograph, M. Stone); *see also* AX22, AY23, BG83, BG84, BJ05, BJ06

Inscription **73**
Site Wadi Haggag, rock 3 area 1, #126
Technique incised
Condition good
Content encircled crosses
Access ABd20 (photograph, M. Stone); *see also* AX22, AY23, BG83, BG84, BJ05, BJ06

Inscription **74**
Site Wadi Haggag, rock 3 area 1, #126
Technique incised
Condition good
Dimensions 4-5 x ? cm.
Content Armenian inscription

ԵՐԱՄ

Access ABd20 (photograph, M. Stone); *see also* AX22, AY23, BG83, BG84, BJ05, BJ06
Corpus H Arm 16

Inscription **75**
Site Wadi Haggag, rock 3 area 1, #126
Technique scratched
Condition poor
Content unidentified inscription
Access ABd20 (photograph, M. Stone); *see also* AX22, AY24, BJ05, BJ06

Inscription **76**
Site Wadi Haggag, rock 3 area 1, #126
Dating 8th to 9th century
Technique incised
Condition fair
Dimensions 3.5-4 x 26 cm.
Content Armenian inscription

ՅՀՆ ՁԱՅԼ

ՅԱ-ՈՐ ԱՍՏԼ

ՅՅԱ

Access ABd21 (photograph, M. Stone); *see also* AT53, AT54, BH81, BH82, BK07, BK08
Corpus H Arm 15

Inscription **77**
Site Wadi Haggag, rock 3 area 1, #126
Technique incised
Condition good
Content crosses alone
Access ABd22 (photograph, M. Stone); *see also* AAb12, ADe20, AS33, AS34, BQ62, BQ63

Inscription **78**
Site Wadi Haggag, rock 3 area 1, #126
Technique scratched
Condition poor
Content unidentified inscription
Access ABd22 (photograph, M. Stone); *see also* AAb12, ADe20, AS33, AS34, BQ62, BQ63

Inscription **79**
Site Santa Katarina, #10
Technique incised
Condition fair
Dimensions 1.2 x 15.5 cm.
Content Armenian inscription

ԿԱՄՊԱՐ ՅԻՇ(ԵԱ)

Access CL01 (photograph, Ann Arbor)
Corpus S Arm 28

Inscription 80
Site Santa Katarina, #10
Technique scratched
Condition fair
Content Armenian inscription
ՍԻՄԷՈՆ
Access CL01 (photograph, Ann Arbor)
Corpus S Arm 32

Inscription 81
Site Wadi Haggag, #118
Technique incised
Condition poor
Content Greek inscription
Limitation *Tentative decipherment only*
Access ABd23 (photograph, M. Stone)

Inscription 82
Site Wadi Haggag, #118
Technique incised
Condition fair
Content Greek inscription
Limitation *Tentative decipherment only*
Comment *fragment*
Access ABd23 (photograph, M. Stone)

Inscription 83
Site Wadi Haggag, rock 3, #125
Technique incised
Condition good
Content crosses with inscription
Access AAb09 (photograph, M. Stone)

Inscription 84
Site Wadi Haggag, #118
Technique incised
Condition fair
Content crosses with inscription
Comment *Maltese cross below insc. 25*
Access AAc17 (photograph, M. Stone); *see also* AAc18, BC52, BC53, CP56

Inscription 85
Site Wadi Haggag, #118
Technique incised
Condition good
Content crosses with inscription
Access AAd24 (photograph, M. Stone); *see also* AP25

Inscription 86
Site Wadi Haggag, #118
Technique incised
Condition good
Content crosses with inscription
Access ABa05 (photograph, M. Stone); *see also* BI01, BI02

Inscription 87
Site Wadi Haggag, #118
Technique incised
Condition good
Content varied crosses
Comment *Maltese and forked crosses*
Access ABa05 (photograph, M. Stone); *see also* ABb09, ABb10, ABb11

Inscription 88
Site Wadi Haggag, #118
Technique incised
Condition fair
Content Nabatean inscription
Limitation *Tentative decipherment only*
Access ABa06 (photograph, M. Stone); *see also* AM91, AM92, AU63, AU64, BG73, BH74

Inscription 89
Site Wadi Haggag, #118
Technique incised
Condition good
Content varied crosses
Access ABa06 (photograph, M. Stone); *see also* AM91, AM92, AU63, AU64, BG73, BH74

Inscription 90
Site Wadi Haggag, #118
Technique incised
Condition poor
Content unidentified inscription
Comment *Arabic or Syriac*
Access ABd20 (photograph, M. Stone); *see also* AX22, AY23, BG83, BG84, BJ05, BJ06

Inscription 91
Site Wadi Haggag, rock 3, #125
Dating 7th to 9th century
Technique incised
Condition good
Content Georgian inscription
evsebi
Comment *too high to measure*
Access ABe25 (photograph, M. Stone)
Corpus H Georg 5

Inscription 92
Site Wadi Haggag, rock 3, #125
Technique incised
Condition good
Content rock drawing
Comment *camel*
Access ABe25 (photograph, M. Stone)

Inscription **117**
Site Wadi Haggag, rock 3, #125
Technique incised
Condition fair
Dimensions 15 x 20 cm.
Content Armenian inscription

ԱԲՐ[ԱՀԱՄ ԱՆՅԱՐԺԱՆՆ

Access AY18 (photograph, Z. Radovan); *see also* AY19, BM40, Negev 1977 figs. 56 and 91
Corpus H Arm 9

Inscription **118**
Site Santa Katarina, #10
Technique incised
Condition good
Content varied crosses
Access CL01 (photograph, Ann Arbor); *see also* ADf24

Inscription **119**
Site Wadi Haggag, rock 3, #125
Technique incised
Condition good
Dimensions 6 x ? cm.
Content Armenian inscription

ԲԱԳՐԱՏ

Comment *The length could not be measured.*
Access BN30 (photograph, Z. Radovan); *see also* ACc13, ADf24, BN29
Corpus H Arm 10

Inscription **120**
Site Wadi Haggag, rock 3, #125
Dating 8th century
Technique incised
Condition fair
Dimensions 3 x 14 cm.
Content Armenian inscription

ԱՀԱՐՈՎՆ

Access BN30 (photograph, Z. Radovan); *see also* ACc13, ADf24, BN29
Corpus H Arm 11

Inscription **121**
Site Wadi Haggag, rock 3, #125
Technique incised
Condition fair
Dimensions 4 x ? cm.
Content Armenian inscription

ԱՆ

Access ACc16 (photograph, M. Stone)
Corpus H Arm 12

Inscription **122**
Site Wadi Haggag, rock 3, #125
Technique incised
Condition fair
Dimensions 20 x 10 cm.
Content Armenian inscription

ՄՈ[Վ]

ՍԷ[Ս]

Access ACc15 (photograph, M. Stone); *see also* ADg30, BD62, BD63
Corpus H Arm 13

Inscription **123**
Site Wadi Haggag, rock 3, #125
Technique incised
Condition good
Content crosses alone
Comment *group of crosses*
Access ACc15 (photograph, M. Stone); *see also* ADg30, BD62, BD63

Inscription **124**
Site Wadi Haggag, rock 3, #125
Technique incised
Condition fair
Dimensions 10 x 60 cm.
Content Armenian inscription

Ի ՆՂՐՑՐ

Access BK09 (photograph, Z. Radovan); *see also* ADf23, ADg30, AY24, AY25, Negev 1977 fig. 108
Corpus H Arm 14

Inscription **125**
Site Wadi Haggag, rock 3, #125
Technique incised
Condition fair
Content Greek inscription

ΣΘΗ ΜΝΗ

ΣΤΕΦΑ[ΝΟΥ]

Access BK09 (photograph, Z. Radovan); *see also* ADg30, AY24, AY25
Corpus Negev 1977 150

Inscription **126**
Site Wadi Haggag, rock 3, #125
Technique incised
Condition fair
Content Greek inscription

ΚΕ ΒΟΗΘΙ ΘΕΟΦΙ

ΛΟΝ ΕΠΙ...

Access BK09 (photograph, Z. Radovan); *see also* ADg30, AY24, AY25
Corpus Negev 1977 149

Inscription **127**
Site Wadi Haggag, rock 3, #125
Technique incised
Condition good
Content crosses alone
Comment *line of crosses*
Access BK09 (photograph, Z. Radovan); *see also* ADg30, AY24, AY25

Inscription **128**
Site Wadi Haggag, rock 3, #125
Technique incised
Condition fair
Dimensions 10 x 37 cm.
Content Armenian inscription

ՆՈՍ ԵԱԿ

Access ACc17 (photograph, M. Stone); *see also* ACb11, AX20, AX21, Negev 1977 figs. 114 and 115
Corpus H Arm 17

Inscription **129**
Site Wadi Haggag, rock 3, #125
Dating 11th to 12th century
Technique incised
Condition poor
Content Armenian inscription

ՍԻԱԼ ՅՄՔ

Comment *impossible to measure accurately*
Access BL54 (photograph, Z. Radovan); *see also* ACb10, ACb12
Corpus H Arm 18 (1)

Inscription **130**
Site Wadi Haggag, rock 3, #125
Dating 11th to 12th century
Technique incised
Condition poor
Content Armenian inscription

ՇԱՔԵՆՆԼ ՅԱՄՔ

ԱՔՔԱԼ

-Լ Յ

Comment *impossible to measure accurately*
Access BL55 (photograph, Z. Radovan); *see also* ACb10, ACb12, AU56
Corpus H Arm 18 (2)

Inscription **131**
Site Wadi Haggag, rock 3, #125
Technique incised
Condition poor
Dimensions 4 x 15 cm.
Content Armenian inscription

ՅՂ Դ ՆԼ Յ-Լ

Access BI90 (photograph, Z. Radovan); *see also* BH87, BH88, BI89, BI90
Corpus H Arm 19

Inscription **132**
Site Wadi Haggag, rock 3, #125
Technique incised
Condition poor
Content Armenian inscription
Limitation *Tentative decipherment only*
Access BI90 (photograph, Z. Radovan)

Inscription **133**
Site Wadi Haggag, rock 3 area 2, #127
Technique incised
Condition poor
Dimensions 12 x 20 cm.
Content Armenian inscription

ԱԿԱԿ

-Ա-ԱԿ

Access BN35 (photograph, Z. Radovan)
Corpus H Arm 20

Inscription **134**
Site Wadi Haggag, rock 2, #119
Technique incised
Condition good
Content Greek inscription

Ο Ω Υ

Comment *monogram*
Access CK09 (photograph, U. Avner)
Corpus Negev 1977 119

Inscription **135**
Site Wadi Haggag, rock 3, #125
Technique incised
Condition fair
Content Armenian inscription

ՊԵՏՐՈՍ

Comment *small letters, exact dimensions not available*
Access ADe22 (photograph, M. Stone); *see also* BN42, BN43
Corpus H Arm 22

Inscription **136**
Site Wadi Haggag, rock 3, #125
Technique incised
Condition good
Content crosses alone
Comment *lines of crosses*
Access ADe22 (photograph, M. Stone); *see also* BN42, BN43

Inscription **137**
Site Wadi Haggag, rock 3, #125
Technique incised
Condition fair
Content Greek inscription
Limitation *Tentative decipherment only*
Access ADe22 (photograph, M. Stone); *see also* BN42, BN43

Inscription **138**
Site Wadi Haggag, rock 3, #125
Technique incised
Condition poor
Dimensions 2.7 x ? cm. (L. 2)
Content Armenian inscription

ՆԼ

ՅԼ

Յ-Ե--

Comment *below H Arm 24*
Access BP49 (photograph, Z. Radovan)
Corpus H Arm 23

Inscription **139**
Site Wadi Haggag, rock 3, #125
Technique incised
Condition poor
Dimensions Approx. 3.5 x 15 cm.
Content Armenian inscription

ՔՍ

ԲԱՐԳԵՆ

Access BL53 (photograph, Z. Radovan); *see also* BK52
Corpus H Arm 26

Inscription **140**
Site Wadi Haggag, rock 3, #125
Technique incised
Condition fair
Dimensions 2 x 8 cm.
Content Armenian inscription

ԹԱԹ

Access BK51 (photograph, Z. Radovan); *see also* BK50
Corpus H Arm 28

Inscription **141**
Site Wadi Haggag, rock 3, #125
Technique incised
Condition poor
Dimensions 2 x 3 cm.
Content Armenian inscription

ՂՍԻԼ

Access BP(5)49 (photograph, Z. Radovan)
Corpus H Arm 30

Inscription **142**
Site Wadi Haggag, rock 3, #125
Dating 10th century
Technique incised
Condition poor
Dimensions 2.3 x 5.3 cm.
Content Armenian inscription

ՂՐԼ

ՂԻԼ

ՂԵՋՆԼ

Comment *The dimensions are of the smaller letters.*
Access AQ27 (photograph, Z. Radovan); *see also* ACc18, AQ28
Corpus H Arm 31

Inscription **143**
Site Wadi Haggag, rock 3, #125
Technique incised
Condition good
Dimensions 3.5 x 18 cm.
Content Armenian inscription

ՄՈԻՍԵՍ

Access AEa11-12 (photograph, M. Stone); *see also* AR30
Corpus H Arm 32

Inscription **144**
Site Wadi Haggag, rock 3, #125
Dating 9th to 10th century
Technique incised
Condition poor
Dimensions 7 x 15 cm.
Content Armenian inscription

ՅԱԿՈՎԲ

ՐՆԼ

Comment *L.1: 4 x 15 cm. L.2: 3 x 2.7 cm.*
Access AU58 (photograph, Z. Radovan); *see also* AEa07-08, AEa09-10, AU57
Corpus H Arm 33

Inscription **145**
Site Wadi Haggag, rock 3, #125
Technique incised
Condition poor
Dimensions 2.6 x 30.5 cm.
Content Armenian inscription

ՆԱՍ-ՈԼ ՂԻԿ

Access BR78 (photograph, Z. Radovan); *see also* BR79
Corpus H Arm 35

Inscription 146
Site Wadi Haggag, rock 3, #125
Technique incised
Condition poor
Dimensions 2.5 x 12 cm.
Content Armenian inscription

ԵՍ ԱՐ - - Ա Ղ --

Access BH75 (photograph, Z. Radovan); *see also* ADc10, ADc11, BG73, BH74, BH76
Corpus H Arm 43

Inscription 147
Site Wadi Haggag, rock 3, #125
Technique incised
Condition good
Content crosses alone
Access BH75 (photograph, Z. Radovan); *see also* ADc10, ADc11, BG73, BH74, BH76

Inscription 148
Site Wadi Haggag, rock 3, #125
Dating 10th century
Technique incised
Condition poor
Dimensions 3.5 x ? cm.
Content Armenian inscription

ԻՍՐ - - - ԾՀ

ԱՋ[ԱՅՐ[Ի]Ա ՏՈ -[

Access AU63 (photograph, Z. Radovan); *see also* ABa06, AM91, AM92, AV64, BG73, BH74
Corpus H Arm 45

Inscription 149
Site Wadi Haggag, rock 3, #125
Technique incised
Condition poor
Dimensions 1.5 x 10 cm.
Content Armenian inscription

ԵՍ ՍԻՄՈ[Ն]

Access AN95 (photograph, Z. Radovan); *see also* AM93, AN94, AN96
Corpus H Arm 46

Inscription 150
Site Wadi Haggag, rock 3 area 3, #128
Technique incised
Condition good
Content crosses alone
Access AN95 (photograph, Z. Radovan); *see also* AM93, AN94, AN96

Inscription 151
Site Wadi Haggag, rock 3 area 4, #129
Technique scratched
Condition poor
Dimensions 3.5 x 17 cm.
Content Armenian inscription

ԴՈՔԱ--Դ

Access BG71 (photograph, Z. Radovan); *see also* BG72
Corpus H Arm 53

Inscription 152
Site Wadi Haggag, rock 3 area 4, #129
Dating 10th to 11th century
Technique scratched
Condition fair
Dimensions 6 x 58 cm.
Content Armenian inscription

ԱՏԴԻՆՈՅ

ԱՅ ՏԵՌՆ

Comment *L.1: 3 x 58 cm.; L.2: 3 x 30 cm.*
Access BE67 (photograph, Z. Radovan); *see also* ADd15, ADd16, BF66
Corpus H Arm 54

Inscription 153
Site Wadi Haggag, rock 3 area 4, #129
Dating 8th to 9th century
Technique incised
Condition good
Dimensions 9 x 25 cm.
Content Armenian inscription

ԵՋԵԿԻԷՂ

ՅՈՎԱՆՆԷՍ

ԾՈԻԾՈԻՏ ---Ջ

Comment *The letters are about 3 cm. high.*
Access BC64 (photograph, Z. Radovan); *see also* BC65, BE68, BE69
Corpus H Arm 55

Inscription 154
Site Wadi Haggag, rock 3 area 4, #129
Technique scratched
Condition poor
Dimensions 1.5 x 15 cm.
Content Armenian inscription

ՆԱ-ՐՏ---

Access BR77 (photograph, Z. Radovan); *see also* BQ76
Corpus H Arm 57

Inscription 155
Site Wadi Haggag, rock 3 area 4, #129
Dating 10th century
Technique incised
Condition poor
Dimensions 10 x 22 cm.
Content Armenian inscription

ՅՐՈՏ

-ԻԻ[ ]--Ր

Access AV77 (photograph, Z. Radovan); *see also* AV78
Corpus H Arm 58

Inscription **156**
Site Wadi Haggag, rock 3 area 4, #129
Dating 10th to 11th century
Technique incised
Condition good
Dimensions 3 x 25 cm.
Content Armenian inscription

ՎԱՆԽԱՅՐ ՅՈՀՆԻԿ

Access AV83 (photograph, Z. Radovan); *see also* ADd17, ADe18, AV84
Corpus H Arm 61

Inscription **158**
Site Wadi Haggag, rock 5, #131
Technique incised
Condition poor
Dimensions 3 x 12 cm.
Content Armenian inscription

ԲԱԲԳԵՆ

Access ABf35 (photograph, M. Stone)
Corpus H Arm 65

Inscription **159**
Site Wadi Haggag, rock 5, #131
Technique incised
Condition fair
Dimensions 4.6 x 11 cm.
Content Armenian inscription

ԳՈ - -Ա

ԹՈՄԱՍ

ՈԲԴԵ

Comment *L.1: 1.8 x 10 cm.; L.2: 1.8 x 11 cm.; L.3: 2 x 8 cm.*
Access AP18 (photograph, Z. Radovan); *see also* ADd17, AX95, AX96
Corpus H Arm 68

Inscription **160**
Site Wadi Haggag, rock 5, #131
Technique incised
Condition good
Dimensions 20 x 70 cm.
Content Armenian inscription

ՄԱՆԱՍԷ

ԳՐԻԳՈՐ

Comment *L.1: 10 x 70 cm.; L.2: 10 x 51 cm.*
Access ACa02 (photograph, M. Stone); *see also* ACa03
Corpus H Arm 69

Inscription **161**
Site Wadi Haggag, rock 5, #131
Technique incised
Condition good
Content crosses with inscription
Comment *Two crosses enclose both lines of insc. 160.*
Access ACa02 (photograph, M. Stone); *see also* ACa03

Inscription **162**
Site Wadi Haggag, rock 5, #131
Technique incised
Condition poor
Dimensions 9.5 x 32 cm.
Content Armenian inscription

ՄԵՍՐ[ՈՊ]

Access ALc56-57 (photograph, M. Stone); *see also* ALb44-45, ALb46-47, ALb48-49, ALb50-51, ALc52-53, ALc54-55
Corpus H Arm 73

Inscription **163**
Site Wadi Leja, Leja 1, #22
Dating 11th to 12th century
Technique scratched
Condition good
Dimensions 10 x 21 cm.
Content Armenian inscription

ԴԱ

ԻԻԹ

Access AEd54-55 (photograph, M. Stone); *see also* AEf56-57
Corpus L Arm 1

Inscription **164**
Site Wadi Leja, Leja 1, #22
Technique scratched
Condition good
Content crosses with inscription
Comment *There is one cross before the letter "d" of insc. 167.*
Access AEd54-55 (photograph, M. Stone); *see also* AEf56-57

Inscription **165**
Site Wadi Leja, Leja 2, #23
Dating 9th to 10th century
Technique scratched
Condition good
Dimensions 10 x 69 cm.
Content Armenian inscription

Յ[ԱԿ]ՈԲ

Access AEf58-59 (photograph, M. Stone); *see also* AEf60-61
Corpus L Arm 2

Inscription **166**
Site Wadi Leja, Leja 2, #23
Dating 9th to 10th century
Technique scratched
Condition good
Content crosses with inscription
Access AEf58-59 (photograph, M. Stone); *see also* AEf60-61

Inscription **167**
Site Wadi Leja, Leja 3, #24
Technique scratched
Condition poor
Dimensions 18 x 40 cm.
Content Armenian inscription

ՏԵՍԱ

ԷՂ

Comment *L.1: 9 x 40 cm.; L.2: 9 x 11 cm.*
Access AEg65-66 (photograph, M. Stone); *see also* AEg67-68, AFe69-70
Corpus L Arm 3

Inscription **168**
Site Wadi Leja, Leja 3, #24
Technique scratched
Condition good
Dimensions 10 x ? cm.
Content crosses with inscription
Comment *One cross precedes the inscription.*
Access AEg65-66 (photograph, M. Stone); *see also* AEg67-68, AFe69-70, AFe71-72, AFe67-68

Inscription **169**
Site Wadi Leja, Leja 4, #25
Technique scratched
Condition poor
Dimensions 6 x 20 cm.
Content Armenian inscription

ՅԼԱԿՒՈԲ

Access AFd63-64 (photograph, M. Stone); *see also* AFd65-66
Corpus L Arm 4

Inscription **170**
Site Wadi Leja, Leja 4, #25
Technique scratched
Condition good
Dimensions ? x 6 cm.
Content crosses with inscription
Access AFd63-64 (photograph, M. Stone); *see also* AFd65-66

Inscription **171**
Site Wadi Maghara, #72
Technique incised
Condition excellent
Dimensions 2.5 x 11 cm.
Content Armenian inscription

ԹՈՎՄԱ

Access AEb17-18 (photograph, M. Stone); *see also* AEb21-22
Corpus M Arm 1

Inscription **172**
Site Wadi Mukatab, Mukatab 1, #65
Technique scratched
Condition good
Dimensions 6 x 15 cm.
Content Armenian inscription

ԷԱԾ

Access AE35 (photograph, M. Stone)
Corpus M Arm 2

Inscription **173**
Site Wadi Mukatab, Mukatab 2, #228
Technique incised
Condition good
Dimensions 7 x 27 cm.
Content Armenian inscription

Կ(Ա)ՄՊ(ԱՐ) ՅԻՇ(ԵԱ)

Comment *written by the same hand as insc. 79*
Access AEc42-43 (photograph, M. Stone)
Corpus M Arm 3

Inscription **174**
Site Wadi Mukatab, Mukatab 2, #228
Technique incised
Condition good
Content crosses alone
Access AEc42-43 (photograph, M. Stone)

Inscription **175**
Site Wadi Mukatab, Mukatab 2, #228
Technique incised
Condition poor
Dimensions 2 x 2 cm.
Content Armenian inscription

Ւ Ն Լ

Access AEc40-41 (photograph, M. Stone)
Corpus M Arm 4

Inscription **176**
Site Wadi Mukatab, Mukatab 3, #229
Technique incised
Condition poor
Content Armenian inscription

ՒՂՐԼ

Access AEd52-53 (photograph, M. Stone)
Corpus M Arm 5

Inscription **177**
Site Jebel Musa, steps above Elijah, #15
Technique scratched
Condition poor
Dimensions 3 x 5 cm.
Content Armenian inscription

ՒԴՐԼ

Access AIc42-43 (photograph, M. Stone)
Corpus S Arm 1

Inscription **178**
Site Jebel Musa, peak flat rock, #11
Dating 1463
Technique scratched
Condition excellent
Dimensions 20 x 50 cm.
Content Armenian inscription

ՏԱԻԻԼ ՄԱՐՏԻՐՈՍ

ՏՕՆԱԿԱՆ Ա(ՍՏՈՒԱ)ԾԱՏՈՒՐ

ՋԺԲ

Comment *L.1: 5.5-9 x 38 cm.; L.2: 5.5-9 x 50 cm.; L.3: 11 x 18 cm.*
Access AIc44-45 (photograph, M. Stone)
Corpus S Arm 2

Inscription **179**
Site Jebel Musa, peak flat rock, #11
Technique scratched
Condition excellent
Dimensions 27 x 49 cm.
Content Armenian inscription

ՏՐ ԱԾ ՅԻՇԵԱ

Ջ

ԹՈՐՈՍ

Comment *L.1: 10 x 49 cm.; L.2: 12 x 19 cm.; L.3: 5 x 13 cm.*
Access AId50-51 (photograph, M. Stone)
Corpus S Arm 3

Inscription **180**
Site Jebel Musa, peak flat rock, #11
Technique scratched
Condition fair
Dimensions 16.5 x 52 cm.
Content Armenian inscription

ԳՐԻԳՈՐ

ԵՂԻՍ[Է]

Վ

Comment *L.1: 9.5 x 52 cm.; L.2: 7 x 42 cm.*
Access AId58-59 (photograph, M. Stone); *see also* AId54-55, AId56-57
Corpus S Arm 4

Inscription **181**
Site Jebel Musa, #19
Technique scratched
Condition fair
Content Greek inscription
Limitation *Tentative decipherment only*
Access AId58-59 (photograph, M. Stone); *see also* AId54-55, AId56-57

Inscription **182**
Site Jebel Musa, peak behind mosque, #14
Technique scratched
Condition poor
Dimensions 6 x 12.1 cm.
Content Armenian inscription

ՏՐ ՅՍ ՔՍ ՍՐ

ՂՐ

Comment *The letters are 3 cm. high.*
Access AIe68-69 (photograph, M. Stone)
Corpus S Arm 5

Inscription **183**
Site Jebel Musa, peak behind mosque, #14
Technique scratched
Condition good
Content crosses with inscription
Comment *cross after "QS" superimposed on "SR" of insc. 182*
Access AIe68-69 (photograph, M. Stone)

Inscription **184**
Site Jebel Musa, peak behind mosque, #14
Technique scratched
Condition poor
Dimensions 3 x 27 cm.
Content Armenian inscription
Comment *illegible*
Access AIe70-71 (photograph, M. Stone)
Corpus S Arm 6

Inscription **185**
Site Jebel Musa, peak behind mosque, #14
Technique scratched
Condition poor
Dimensions 6 x 12.1 cm.
Content Armenian inscription

ՃՓՈՐ

ՏՐ ՔՍ

Comment *The letters are 3 cm. high.*
Access AIe72-73 (photograph, M. Stone)
Corpus S Arm 7

Inscription **186**
Site Jebel Musa, peak grotto, #12
Technique scratched
Condition good
Dimensions 2.5 x 33 cm.
Content Armenian inscription

ՏԱՂԱՆ ԹՈՄ

Comment *It is not certain that the inscription has been preserved completely.*
Access AHb03-04 (photograph, M. Stone); *see also* AHa01-02, AHg69-70, AHg67-68
Corpus S Arm 8

Inscription 187
Site Jebel Musa, peak grotto, #12
Technique incised
Condition good
Dimensions 2 x 35 cm.
Content Armenian inscription

ՏՐ ՈՂՈՐՄԵԱՑ

ԿԱՄԷՂԻ ԵՒ ԽՈԴԷԳՈՍԻ

Comment *L.1: 1 x 27 cm.; L.2: 1 x 35 cm.*
Access AHd31-32 (photograph, M. Stone); *see also* AHa01-02, AHb09-10, AHb11-12, AHe39-40, AHe45-46, AHg67-68, AHg69-70, D.O.P. 1966, pl.13-1
Corpus S Arm 9

Inscription 188
Site Jebel Musa, peak grotto, #12
Technique incised
Condition good
Dimensions 5 x 36 cm.
Content Armenian inscription

ՏՐ ՅՍ

ՈՂՈՐՄ ԵԱՑ

ԿԼԵՄԱՅ ԵՂԻԱԲԱ

ՏԻՐԱՆԱՅ ԵՂԻՇԱԻ

ԱՆԱՏՈՂՈՅ ՀԱԲԵՂԻ

Comment *L.2: 2 x 36 cm.; L.3: 2 x 35 cm.; L.4: 3 x 35 cm.; L.5: 3 x 36 cm.*
Access AHd29-30 (photograph, M. Stone)
Corpus S Arm 10

Inscription 189
Site Jebel Musa, peak grotto, #12
Dating 6th to 7th century
Technique incised
Condition good
Dimensions 2 x 45.1 cm.
Content Armenian inscription

ՎԱՐԱՋԴՈՒԽ[Տ]

Access AHc15-16 (photograph, M. Stone); *see also* AHb13-14, AHc17-18, AHg67-68, D.O.P 1966, pl.13-14
Corpus S Arm 11

Inscription 190
Site Jebel Musa, peak grotto, #12
Technique scratched
Condition poor
Content Armenian inscription

ՊԵՏՐՈՍ

Comment *The inscription is small in size.*
Access AHb13-14 (photograph, M. Stone); *see also* AHc15-16, AHc17-18, AHe45-46, AHg67-68, D.O.P 1966, pl.13-14
Corpus S Arm 13

Inscription 191
Site Jebel Musa, peak grotto, #12
Technique incised
Condition good
Dimensions 5.5 x 9 cm.
Content Armenian inscription

ԱՋՈՏ

ԴՈԴ

Comment *L.1: 2-3.5 x 9 cm.; L.2: 2 x 5 cm.*
Access AHb11-12 (photograph, M. Stone); *see also* AHa01-02, AHc15-16, AHc17-18, AHc19-20, AHe45-46, AHg67-68, AHg69-70, D.O.P 1966 pl.13-14
Corpus S Arm 14

---

nscription 192
Site Jebel Musa, peak grotto, #12
Technique scratched
Condition good
Content crosses with inscription
Comment *precedes insc. 191*
Access AHb13-14 (photograph, M. Stone); *see also* AHa01-02, AHb11-12, AHc15-16, AHc17-18, AHc19-20, AHe45-46, AHg67-68, AHg69-70

Inscription 193
Site Jebel Musa, peak grotto, #12
Technique scratched
Condition poor
Dimensions 2 x 9 cm.
Content Armenian inscription

ՍԱՀԱԿ

Access AHe43-44 (photograph, M. Stone); *see also* AHc19-20
Corpus S Arm 15

Inscription 194
Site Jebel Musa, peak grotto, #12
Technique scratched
Condition poor
Dimensions 2 x 9 cm.
Content Armenian inscription

ՄՈՒՍԵՍ

Comment *L.1: 2 x 9 cm.*
Access AHe43-44 (photograph, M. Stone); *see also* AHc19-20
Corpus S Arm 16

Inscription 195
Site Jebel Musa, peak grotto, #12
Dating 7th to 8th century
Technique scratched
Condition fair
Content Armenian inscription

ՎԱՍԱ[Կ]

Comment *The inscription is small; exact size is not available.*
Access AHe45-46 (photograph, M. Stone); *see also* AHc17-18, AHg67-68
Corpus S Arm 17

Inscription **196**
Site Jebel Musa, peak grotto, #12
Technique scratched
Condition poor
Content Armenian inscription

ՄԱԹԻ

Comment *The inscription is small; exact size is not available.*
Access AHe45-46 (photograph, M. Stone); *see also* AHb13-14, AHc17-18, AHg67-68
Corpus S Arm 18

Inscription **197**
Site Jebel Musa, peak grotto, #12
Dating 9th to 10th century
Technique incised
Condition fair
Dimensions 2.3 x 12.5 cm.
Content Armenian inscription

ՋԱՎԷՆ

Access AHb11-12 (photograph, M. Stone); *see also* AHa1-2, AHc15-16, AHc17-18, AHc19-20, AHe43-44, AHg67-68, AHg69-70, BTc21
Corpus S Arm 12

Inscription **198**
Site Jebel Musa, peak grotto, #12
Dating 9th to 10th century
Technique scratched
Condition poor
Dimensions 1.3 x 7 cm.
Content Armenian inscription

Ն[Ա]ԹԱՆ

Access AHe43-44 (photograph, M. Stone); *see also* AHa1-2, AHc21-22, AHe41-42, AHg67-68
Corpus S Arm 19

Inscription **199**
Site Jebel Musa, peak grotto, #12
Technique scratched
Condition fair
Dimensions 9-10 x 52 cm.
Content Armenian inscription

ՍՏԵՓԱՆՈՍ

Access AHg69-70 (photograph, M. Stone); *see also* AHc23-24, AHd33-34, AHe39-40, AHe43-44, D.O.P. 20, 1966 pl.14
Corpus S Arm 20

Inscription **200**
Site Jebel Musa, peak grotto, #12
Technique incised
Condition good
Content English inscription
Limitation *Tentative decipherment only*
Access AHg69-70 (photograph, M. Stone); *see also* AHc23-24, AHd33-34, AHe43-44

Inscription **201**
Site Jebel Musa, peak grotto, #12
Technique incised
Condition fair
Content Greek inscription
Limitation *Tentative decipherment only*
Access AHg69-70 (photograph, M. Stone); *see also* AHc23-24, AHd33-34, AHe43-44

Inscription **202**
Site Jebel Musa, peak grotto, #12
Technique incised
Condition fair
Dimensions 6 x 12 cm.
Content Armenian inscription

]ԵԱԼ

Access AHd35-36 (photograph, M. Stone); *see also* AHd27-28, AHd37-38, AHc25-26
Corpus S Arm 21

Inscription **203**
Site Jebel Musa, peak mosque, #16
Technique scratched
Condition fair
Dimensions 5 x 18 cm.
Content Armenian inscription

ՇՄԱԻՈՆ

ՏԻՏՈՍ ԱՄ

Comment *L.1: ? x 14 cm.; L.2: ? x 18 cm.*
Access AHe49-50 (photograph, M. Stone); *see also* AHe47-48
Corpus S Arm 22

Inscription **204**
Site Jebel Musa, peak behind mosque, #14
Dating 1351-1450
Technique scratched
Condition poor
Dimensions 4 x 11 cm.
Content Armenian inscription

]Կ Ա[ ]Կ[ ] Ն[

]Ն Ր[ ]ՊՈ

]-[]--

--Ն[]-ՊԵՏՐՈՍ

-Ն[ ]Ջ--

ՔՍ--ԱԾ

Comment *The height 2-4 cm.; length of the complete word in L.4 is 11 cm.*
Access AHf55-56 (photograph, M. Stone); *see also* AHf57-58
Corpus S Arm 23

Inscription **205**
Site Jebel Musa, peak behind mosque, #14
Technique scratched
Condition poor
Dimensions 7.6 x 26 cm.
Content Armenian inscription
ՏԱՑԷ
Comment *The inscription is obviously incomplete.*
Access AHf59-60 (photograph, M. Stone)
Corpus S Arm 24

Inscription **206**
Site Jebel Musa, peak behind mosque, #14
Technique scratched
Condition poor
Content crosses with inscription
Comment *precedes insc. 205*
Access AHf59-60 (photograph, M. Stone)

Inscription **207**
Site Jebel Musa, peak behind mosque, #14
Technique scratched
Condition good
Dimensions 5 x 12 cm.
Content Armenian inscription
ՅՍ
Access AHf61-62 (photograph, M. Stone)
Corpus S Arm 25

Inscription **208**
Site Jebel Musa, peak behind mosque, #14
Technique scratched
Condition good
Content crosses with inscription
Comment *large cross above insc. 207*
Access AHf61-62 (photograph, M. Stone)

Inscription **209**
Site Jebel Musa, stairs from upper gate, #18
Technique scratched
Condition poor
Dimensions 7.5 x 100 cm.
Content Armenian inscription
Հ- ՃՈՀԱԿ
Access BTa01-02 (photograph, M. Stone)
Corpus S Arm 26

Inscription **210**
Site Jebel Musa, steps from lower gate, #31
Dating 9th to 10th century
Technique scratched
Condition good
Dimensions 29.7 x ? cm.
Content Armenian inscription
ՍԱՐԳԻՍ
Comment *average height of letters is 2.7 cm.*
Access BTb07-08 (photograph, M. Stone)
Corpus S Arm 27

Inscription **211**
Site Jebel Musa, steps from lower gate, #31
Dating 9th to 10th century
Technique scratched
Condition good
Content crosses with inscription
Comment *cross preceding insc. 210*
Access BTb07-08 (photograph, M. Stone)

Inscription **212**
Site Jebel Musa, steps from lower gate, #31
Dating 9th to 10th century
Technique incised
Condition good
Content rock drawing
Comment *hand*
Access BTb07-08 (photograph, M. Stone)

Inscription **213**
Site Wadi Haggag, rock 1, #160
Dating 13th to 14th century
Technique incised
Condition good
Dimensions 12 x 130 cm.
Content Georgian inscription
k'e še cdli gi ǰoarli an
Access ABf32 (photograph, M. Stone); *see also* CL04
Corpus H Georg 1

Inscription **214**
Site Wadi Haggag, rock 1, #160
Dating 14th century
Technique incised
Condition good
Content crosses with inscription
Comment *precedes insc. 214*
Access ABf32 (photograph, M. Stone); *see also* CL04

Inscription **215**
Site Wadi Haggag, rock 1, #160
Dating 14th century
Technique incised
Condition good
Dimensions 6 x 72 cm.
Content Georgian inscription
k'e še gi an
Access ABf33 (photograph, M. Stone)
Corpus H Georg 2

Inscription **216**
Site Wadi Haggag, rock 1, #160
Dating 13th to 14th century
Technique incised
Condition good
Content crosses with inscription
Access ABf33 (photograph, M. Stone)

Inscription 217
Site Wadi Haggag, rock 1, #160
Technique incised
Condition good
Content Square Arabic inscription
Limitation *Tentative decipherment only*
Access ABf36 (photograph, M. Stone); *see also* AAc17, AAc18

Inscription 218
Site Wadi Haggag, rock 3 area 2, #127
Technique incised
Condition good
Content Greek inscription
Limitation *Tentative decipherment only*
Access BO44 (photograph, Z. Radovan); *see also* AR31, AS32, AZ03, AZ04, Negev 1977 fig. 95

Inscription 219
Site Santa Katarina, Justinian doors rt, #9
Technique incised
Condition fair
Dimensions 1-1.6 x 10.1 cm.
Content Armenian inscription

Մ Հ Կ -

Access CL02 (photograph, Ann Arbor)
Corpus S Arm 29

Inscription 220
Site Wadi Haggag, rock 3 area 1, #126
Technique incised
Condition good
Content varied crosses
Access BN30 (photograph, Z. Radovan); *see also* ACc13, ADf24, BN29

Inscription 221
Site Wadi Haggag, rock 3 area 2, #127
Technique incised
Condition fair
Content Nabatean inscription
Limitation *Tentative decipherment only*
Access ACd19 (photograph, M. Stone)

Inscription 222
Site Wadi Arade Lesser, Arade 1, #140
Technique incised
Condition excellent
Content rock drawing
Comment *camels*
Access ACd20 (photograph, M. Stone)

Inscription 223
Site Wadi Arade Lesser, Arade 1, #140
Technique incised
Condition excellent
Content rock drawing
Comment *camels*
Access ACd21 (photograph, M. Stone)

Inscription 224
Site Wadi Arade Lesser, Arade 1, #140
Technique incised
Condition excellent
Content rock drawing
Comment *horses with riders; two persons facing, holding round objects*
Access ACd23 (photograph, M. Stone)

Inscription 225
Site Wadi Arade Lesser, Arade 1, #140
Technique incised
Condition excellent
Content rock drawing
Comment *hunter pursuing wolf*
Access ACd24 (photograph, M. Stone)

Inscription 226
Site Wadi Arade Lesser, Arade 1, #140
Technique incised
Condition good
Content rock drawing
Comment *three hunters with bows; one hunter on horseback; large unidentified animal*
Access ACe25 (photograph, M. Stone)

Inscription 227
Site Santa Katarina, Justinian doors rt, #9
Dating 11th to 12th century
Technique incised
Condition poor
Dimensions 1 x 6.5 cm.
Content Armenian inscription

ՄԷԴԱՏ

Access CL03 (photograph, Ann Arbor)
Corpus S Arm 30

Inscription 228
Site Santa Katarina, Justinian doors rt, #9
Technique scratched
Condition poor
Dimensions 0.6 x 1.4 cm.
Content Armenian inscription

ՅԵՆԼ

Comment *no photo*
Corpus S Arm 31

Inscription 229
Site Wadi Haggag, rock 3, #125
Dating 13th to 14th century
Technique incised
Condition poor
Dimensions 4 x 7 cm.
Content Georgian inscription

k‘ šē mp‘[e] davt

Comment *Each line is 2 cm. high.*
Access AR41 (photograph, Z. Radovan); *see also* AAb11, ADe21, AM03, AM04, AR42
Corpus H Georg 3

Inscription	**230**
Site	Wadi Haggag, rock 3, #125
Technique	incised
Condition	fair
Content	Greek inscription
Limitation	*Tentative decipherment only*
Access	AR41 (photograph, Z. Radovan); *see also* AAb11, ADe21

Inscription	**231**
Site	Wadi Haggag, rock 3, #125
Technique	incised
Condition	good
Content	crosses alone
Comment	*line of crosses*
Access	AR41 (photograph, Z. Radovan); *see also* AAb11, ADe21

Inscription	**232**
Site	Wadi Haggag, rock 3, #125
Dating	14th century
Technique	incised
Condition	fair
Content	Georgian inscription oo šqale šeicqale
Access	BE74 (photograph, Z. Radovan); *see also* BF73
Corpus	H Georg 7

Inscription	**233**
Site	Wadi Haggag, rock 3, #125
Technique	incised
Condition	fair
Content	varied crosses
Access	BE74 (photograph, Z. Radovan); *see also* BF73

Inscription	**234**
Site	Wadi Haggag, rock 13, #202
Dating	7th to 8th century
Technique	incised
Condition	excellent
Dimensions	3.5 x 28 cm.
Content	Georgian inscription co sina še me co
Access	ALc60-61 (photograph, M. Stone)
Corpus	H Georg 10

Inscription	**235**
Site	Wadi Haggag, rock 13, #202
Dating	7th to 8th century
Technique	incised
Condition	good
Content	crosses with inscription
Comment	*cross encloses insc. 264 on both sides.*
Access	ALc60-61 (photograph, M. Stone)

Inscription	**236**
Site	Wadi Mukatab, Mukatab 5, #69
Dating	8th to 9th century
Technique	scratched
Condition	good
Dimensions	12 x 60 cm.
Content	Georgian inscription k'e .zosime še
Access	AE25-26 (photograph, M. Stone)
Corpus	M Georg 1

Inscription	**237**
Site	Wadi Mukatab, Mukatab 5, #69
Dating	8th to 9th century
Technique	scratched
Condition	good
Content	crosses with inscription
Comment	*precedes insc. 236*
Access	AE25-26 (photograph, M. Stone); *see also* DN32, DN36

Inscription	**238**
Site	Wadi Mukatab, Mukatab 4, #68
Dating	10th century
Technique	incised
Condition	good
Dimensions	8 x 25 cm.
Content	Georgian inscription k'e šc'qle mny šni gsli ǰbrnis jē vin caikitḫot qavt
Comment	*L.1: 2 x 20 cm.; L.2: 2 x 25 cm.; L.3: 2 x 19 cm.; L.4; 2 x 11 cm. Line 4 is poorly preserved.*
Access	AEc38-39 (photograph, M. Stone)
Corpus	M Georg 2

Inscription	**239**
Site	Wadi Mukatab, Mukatab 4, #68
Dating	10th century
Technique	incised
Condition	good
Content	crosses with inscription
Comment	*precedes insc. 238*
Access	AEc38-39 (photograph, M. Stone)

Inscription	**240**
Site	Jebel Musa, stairs from upper gate, #18
Technique	scratched
Condition	poor
Content	rock drawing
Comment	*animal*
Access	BTa01-02 (photograph, M. Stone)

Inscription 241
Site Wadi Mukatab, Mukatab 4, #68
Technique incised
Condition good
Content Latin inscription
FACTUS
SENATUS ID
PQ
ROMANUS
EX IMP
Access AE30 (photograph, M. Stone)
Corpus M Lat 2

Inscription 242
Site Wadi Haggag, rock 3, #125
Technique scratched
Condition fair
Content Nabatean inscription
Limitation *Tentative decipherment only*
Access ADa03 (photograph, M. Stone)

Inscription 243
Site Wadi Haggag, rock 3, #125
Technique scratched
Condition fair
Content rock drawing
Comment *people riding camels and horses*
Access ADa03 (photograph, M. Stone); *see also* ADb06

Inscription 244
Site Wadi Haggag, rock 3, #125
Technique scratched
Condition fair
Content Nabatean inscription
Limitation *Tentative decipherment only*
Access ADb07 (photograph, M. Stone); *see also* ADb06

Inscription 245
Site Wadi Haggag, rock 3, #125
Technique scratched
Condition fair
Content rock drawing
Comment *animal*
Access ADb07 (photograph, M. Stone)

Inscription 246
Site Wadi Haggag, rock 3, #125
Technique scratched
Condition fair
Content rock drawing
Comment *animals*
Access ADc08 (photograph, M. Stone)

Inscription 247
Site Wadi Haggag, rock 3, #125
Technique scratched
Condition poor
Content Nabatean inscription
Limitation *Tentative decipherment only*
Access ADc08 (photograph, M. Stone)

Inscription 248
Site Wadi Haggag, rock 3, #125
Technique scratched
Condition poor
Content Nabatean inscription
Limitation *Tentative decipherment only*
Access ADc09 (photograph, M. Stone)

Inscription 249
Site Wadi Maghara, #72
Technique incised
Condition good
Content wasems & other Bedouin marks
Access AEa13-14 (photograph, M. Stone)

Inscription 250
Site Jebel Musa, peak grotto, #12
Technique incised
Condition fair
Content unidentified inscription
Access AHg71-72 (photograph, M. Stone); *see also* AHg73-74

Inscription 251
Site Wadi Haggag, rock 2, #119
Technique incised
Condition good
Content crosses alone
Access ADf25 (photograph, M. Stone); *see also* AX16, AY17, BM40, Negev 1977 fig. 56

Inscription 252
Site Wadi Haggag, rock 3 area 2, #127
Technique incised
Condition good
Content crosses alone
Access BN35 (photograph, Z. Radovan)

Inscription 253
Site Wadi Haggag, rock 3 area 2, #127
Technique incised
Condition good
Content Greek inscription
Limitation *Tentative decipherment only*
Access BN35 (photograph, Z. Radovan)

Inscription 254
Site Wadi Haggag, rock 3 area 1, #126
Technique incised
Condition good
Content Greek inscription
ΝΟΝΝΟΣ ΑΦΘΟΝΙΣ
Access ADf25 (photograph, M. Stone); *see also* AY18, AY19
Corpus Negev 1977 68

Inscription 255
Site Wadi Mukatab, Mukatab 2, #228
Technique incised
Condition good
Content crosses with inscription
Comment *below insc. 175*
Access AEc40-41 (photograph, M. Stone)

Inscription 256
Site Wadi Haggag, rock 3, #125
Technique scratched
Condition good
Content Greek inscription
Limitation *Tentative decipherment only*
Access ADf26 (photograph, M. Stone); *see also* ADh34, ADh35, AX14, AX15

Inscription 257
Site Wadi Haggag, rock 3, #125
Technique incised
Condition poor
Content Syriac inscription
Limitation *Tentative decipherment only*
Access ADg29 (photograph, M. Stone); *see also* AV91, AW92

Inscription 258
Site Wadi Haggag, rock 3, #125
Technique incised
Condition fair
Content Greek inscription
ΚΑΣΙΣ
ΑΒΤΙΡΩΝ
Access ADg29 (photograph, M. Stone)
Corpus Negev 1977 196

Inscription 259
Site Wadi Haggag, rock 3 area 1, #126
Technique incised
Condition good
Content unidentified signs
Access ADg30 (photograph, M. Stone); *see also* ACc15

Inscription 260
Site Wadi Haggag, rock 3 area 1, #126
Technique incised
Condition good
Content crosses with inscription
Comment *precedes insc. 117*
Access ADg32 (photograph, M. Stone); *see also* Negev 1977 figs. 56 and 91

Inscription 261
Site Wadi Haggag, rock 3, #125
Technique scratched
Condition good
Content crosses with inscription
Comment *cross following a drawing*
Access ADh34 (photograph, M. Stone); *see also* ADh35

Inscription 262
Site Wadi Haggag, rock 3 area 2, #127
Technique incised
Condition good
Content crosses with inscription
Comment *precedes insc. 262*
Access BK51 (photograph, Z. Radovan); *see also* BK50

Inscription 263
Site Wadi Haggag, rock 3 area 2, #127
Technique incised
Condition good
Content crosses alone
Access BR78 (photograph, Z. Radovan)

Inscription 264
Site Wadi Haggag, rock 3 area 2, #127
Technique incised
Condition poor
Content Syriac inscription
Limitation *Tentative decipherment only*
Access ACd19 (photograph, M. Stone)

Inscription 265
Site Wadi Haggag, rock 3 area 2, #127
Technique incised
Condition good
Content crosses alone
Comment *line of crosses*
Access ACd19 (photograph, M. Stone)

Inscription 266
Site Wadi Haggag, rock 3 area 3, #128
Technique incised
Condition fair
Content Greek inscription
Limitation *Tentative decipherment only*
Access ABa06 (photograph, M. Stone); *see also* AM91, AM92, BF73, BH74

Inscription 267
Site Wadi Haggag, rock 13, #202
Technique incised
Condition good
Content Greek inscription
Limitation *Tentative decipherment only*
Access ALc62-63 (photograph, M. Stone)

Inscription 268
Site Wadi Haggag, rock 13, #202
Technique incised
Condition good
Content rock drawing
Comment *fox or wolf*
Access ALc62-63 (photograph, M. Stone)

Inscription 269
Site Wadi Haggag, rock 13, #202
Technique incised
Condition good
Content Nabatean inscription
Limitation *Tentative decipherment only*
Access ALd64-65 (photograph, M. Stone)

Inscription 270
Site Wadi Haggag, rock 13, #202
Technique scratched
Condition fair
Content unidentified signs
Access ALd74-75 (photograph, M. Stone); *see also* ALd68-69, FE9

Inscription 271
Site Wadi Haggag, rock 13, #202
Technique incised
Condition fair
Content rock drawing
Comment *animal*
Access ALd74-75 (photograph, M. Stone); *see also* ALd68-69, FE9

Inscription 272
Site Wadi Haggag, rock 3 area 2, #127
Technique incised
Condition fair
Content Greek inscription
Limitation *Tentative decipherment only*
Access ACd19 (photograph, M. Stone)

Inscription 273
Site Wadi Haggag, rock 3 area 2, #127
Technique scratched
Condition fair
Content Nabatean inscription
Limitation *Tentative decipherment only*
Access ACd19 (photograph, M. Stone)

Inscription 274
Site Wadi Haggag, rock 3 area 2, #127
Technique incised
Condition good
Content rock drawing
Comment *ibex*
Access ACd19 (photograph, M. Stone)

Inscription 275
Site Wadi Maghara, #72
Technique incised
Condition fair
Content Old North Arabic inscription
Limitation *Tentative decipherment only*
Access AEb19-20 (photograph, M. Stone)

Inscription 276
Site Wadi Maghara, #72
Technique incised
Condition good
Content Latin inscription
Limitation *Tentative decipherment only*
Access AEa13-14 (photograph, M. Stone); *see also* AEb15-16

Inscription 277
Site Wadi Maghara, #72
Dating 1850
Technique incised
Condition good
Content Russian inscription
Limitation *Tentative decipherment only*
Access AEa13-14 (photograph, M. Stone); *see also* AEb15-16

Inscription 278
Site Wadi Maghara, #72
Dating 1805
Technique incised
Condition fair
Content crosses with inscription
Access AEa13-14 (photograph, M. Stone); *see also* AEb15-16

Inscription 279
Site Wadi Mukatab, Mukatab 2, #228
Technique incised
Condition good
Content crosses alone
Access AEc42-43 (photograph, M. Stone)

Inscription 280
Site Wadi Maghara, #72
Technique scratched
Condition good
Content Arabic inscription
Limitation *Tentative decipherment only*
Access AEa13-14 (photograph, M. Stone); *see also* AEb15-16

Inscription 281
Site Wadi Haggag, rock 13, #202
Technique scratched
Condition poor
Content unidentified inscription
Access ALd64-65 (photograph, M. Stone)

Inscription 282
Site Wadi Haggag, rock 13, #202
Technique scratched
Condition fair
Content crosses alone
Access ALd74-75 (photograph, M. Stone); *see also* FE09

Inscription 283
Site Wadi Haggag, rock 3 area 1, #126
Technique incised
Condition good
Content crosses with inscription
Access BI90 (photograph, Z. Radovan); *see also* BH87, BH88, BI89

Inscription 284
Site Wadi Maghara, #72
Technique incised
Condition good
Content crosses with inscription
Access AEb15-16 (photograph, M. Stone); *see also* AEa13-14

Inscription 285
Site Wadi Maghara, #72
Technique incised
Condition poor
Content Russian inscription
Limitation *Tentative decipherment only*
Access AEb15-16 (photograph, M. Stone); *see also* AEa13-14

Inscription **286**
Site Wadi Haggag, rock 13, #202
Technique incised
Condition good
Content Greek inscription
Limitation *Tentative decipherment only*
Access ALd66-67 (photograph, M. Stone)

Inscription **287**
Site Wadi Haggag, rock 13, #202
Technique incised
Condition good
Content rock drawing
Access ALd66-67 (photograph, M. Stone)

Inscription **288**
Site Wadi Haggag, rock 3, #125
Technique incised
Condition good
Content varied crosses
Access BI95 (photograph, Z. Radovan); *see also* BI96, Negev 1977 fig. 63

Inscription **289**
Site Wadi Abu Ghadhayyat, Ghadhayyat 1, #36
Technique incised
Condition good
Content Greek inscription
Limitation *Tentative decipherment only*
Access ALa30-31 (photograph, M. Stone)

Inscription **290**
Site Wadi Abu Ghadhayyat, Ghadhayyat 1, #36
Technique incised
Condition good
Content crosses with inscription
Comment *cross between the two words of insc. 289*
Access ALa30-31 (photograph, M. Stone)

Inscription **291**
Site Wadi Abu Ghadhayyat, Ghadhayyat 1, #36
Technique incised
Condition good
Content rock drawing
Access ALa30-31 (photograph, M. Stone)

Inscription **292**
Site Wadi Shellal, #90
Technique scratched
Condition good
Dimensions 4.5 x 11 cm.
Content Greek inscription
Limitation *Tentative decipherment only*
Access AFa33-34 (photograph, M. Stone); *see also* AFa35-36

Inscription **293**
Site Wadi Shellal, #90
Technique scratched
Condition good
Content footsteps
Access AFa33-34 (photograph, M. Stone); *see also* AFa35-36

Inscription **294**
Site Wadi Mukatab, Mukatab 2, #228
Technique incised
Condition fair
Content Greek inscription
Limitation *Tentative decipherment only*
Access AEc44-45 (photograph, M. Stone)

Inscription **295**
Site Wadi Mukatab, Mukatab 2, #228
Technique incised
Condition good
Content crosses alone
Comment *line of crosses*
Access AEc44-45 (photograph, M. Stone)

Inscription **296**
Site Wadi Haggag, rock 5, #131
Technique incised
Condition fair
Content rock drawing
Access CP65 (photograph, Z. Radovan); *see also* AAc16, AAd20, BP50, BP51

Inscription **297**
Site Wadi Mukatab, #64
Technique incised
Condition good
Content Nabatean inscription
¢lm wºlw hnyºw
Access CM56 (photograph, Z. Radovan)
Corpus CIS 1110

Inscription **298**
Site Wadi Mukatab, #64
Technique incised
Condition good
Content Nabatean inscription
Limitation *Tentative decipherment only*
Access CO27 (photograph, Z. Radovan)

Inscription **299**
Site Wadi Haggag, #118
Technique incised
Condition excellent
Content rock drawing
Comment *many camels*
Access EX35 (photograph, Project); *see also* EX36, EX36a

Inscription **300**
Site Wadi Baba, Baba 1, #190
Technique incised
Condition fair
Content Nabatean inscription
Limitation *Tentative decipherment only*
Access DJ50-51 (photograph, A. Goren)

Inscription 301
Site Wadi Haggag, rock 5, #131
Dating 626
Technique incised
Condition fair
Content Arabic inscription
Limitation *Tentative decipherment only*
Access ABf36 (photograph, M. Stone); *see also* AAc17, AAc18

Inscription 302
Site Wadi Haggag, rock 5, #131
Technique scratched
Condition poor
Content Greek inscription
Comment *illegible*
Access ABf36 (photograph, M. Stone)

Inscription 303
Site Wadi Mukatab, Mukatab 1, #65
Technique incised
Condition excellent
Content crosses alone
Access AEc36-37 (photograph, M. Stone)

Inscription 304
Site Wadi Mukatab, Mukatab 2, #228
Technique incised
Condition fair
Content unidentified inscription
Access AEc38-39 (photograph, M. Stone)

Inscription 305
Site Wadi Haggag, rock 3 area 1, #126
Technique incised
Condition fair
Content Greek inscription
Limitation *Tentative decipherment only*
Access ACc17 (photograph, M. Stone); *see also* ACb11, AX20, AX21, Negev 1977 fig. 115

Inscription 306
Site Jebel Musa, Vale of Elijah, #29
Technique scratched
Condition fair
Content unidentified inscription
Access BTa03-04 (photograph, M. Stone); *see also* BTb05-06

Inscription 307
Site Wadi Leja, Deir el Arbain, #26
Technique scratched
Condition good
Content Coptic inscription
Limitation *Tentative decipherment only*
Comment *possibly Greek*
Access BTc23-24 (photograph, M. Stone)

Inscription 308
Site Wadi Mukatab, Mukatab 6, #70
Technique incised
Condition good
Content Greek inscription
Limitation *Tentative decipherment only*
Comment *monogrammed cross*
Access AEd46-47 (photograph, M. Stone)

Inscription 309
Site Wadi Mukatab, Mukatab 7, #71
Technique punched
Condition good
Content Nabatean inscription
bryk wdw br
šrmʿrd
Access AEd48-49 (photograph, M. Stone); *see also* CI18, CM64
Corpus CIS 923

Inscription 310
Site Wadi Mukatab, Mukatab 7, #71
Technique incised
Condition good
Content Nabatean inscription
Limitation *Tentative decipherment only*
Access AEd48-49 (photograph, M. Stone); *see also* CI18, CM64

Inscription 311
Site Wadi Mukatab, Mukatab 7, #71
Technique incised
Condition poor
Content rock drawing
Comment *clothed woman*
Access CM64 (photograph, Z. Radovan); *see also* AEd48-49, CI18

Inscription 312
Site Wadi Mukatab, Mukatab 7, #71
Technique incised
Condition good
Content Nabatean inscription
Limitation *Tentative decipherment only*
Access CM64 (photograph, Z. Radovan); *see also* CI18

Inscription 313
Site Wadi Mukatab, Mukatab 7, #71
Technique scratched
Condition fair
Dimensions 35 x 9 cm.
Content Nabatean inscription
Limitation *Tentative decipherment only*
Access AEd50-51 (photograph, M. Stone)

Inscription 314
Site Wadi Mukatab, Mukatab 7, #71
Technique scratched
Condition poor
Content Nabatean inscription
Limitation *Tentative decipherment only*
Access AEd50-51 (photograph, M. Stone)

Inscription **315**
Site Wadi Mukatab, #64
Technique scratched
Condition fair
Content Greek inscription
Limitation *Tentative decipherment only*
Access AEf63-64 (photograph, M. Stone)

Inscription **316**
Site Wadi Leja, #27
Technique scratched
Condition poor
Content Greek inscription
Limitation *Tentative decipherment only*
Comment *language uncertain*
Access AEf58-59 (photograph, M. Stone); *see also* AEf60-61

Inscription **317**
Site Wadi Leja, #27
Technique scratched
Condition good
Content crosses with inscription
Access AEf58-59 (photograph, M. Stone); *see also* AEf60-61

Inscription **318**
Site Wadi Mukatab, #64
Technique scratched
Condition good
Content crosses with inscription
Comment *cross following insc. 315*
Access AEf63-64 (photograph, M. Stone)

Inscription **319**
Site Wadi Leja, Leja 1, #22
Technique scratched
Condition good
Content crosses alone
Access AEg65-66 (photograph, M. Stone); *see also* AEg67-68, AFe67-68, AFe69-70, AFe71-72

Inscription **320**
Site Wadi Shellal, Shellal 1, #91
Technique punched
Condition fair
Content Nabatean inscription
Limitation *Tentative decipherment only*
Access AFa31-32 (photograph, M. Stone)

Inscription **321**
Site Wadi Shellal, Shellal 1, #91
Technique punched
Condition good
Content Greek inscription
Limitation *Tentative decipherment only*
Access AFa31-32 (photograph, M. Stone)

Inscription **322**
Site Wadi Shellal, Shellal 1, #91
Technique punched
Condition fair
Content Greek inscription
Limitation *Tentative decipherment only*
Access AFa31-32 (photograph, M. Stone)

Inscription **323**
Site Wadi Shellal, Shellal 1, #91
Technique incised
Condition poor
Dimensions 4.5 x 11 cm.
Content Greek inscription
Limitation *Tentative decipherment only*
Access AFa37-38 (photograph, M. Stone)

Inscription **324**
Site Wadi Shellal, Shellal 1, #91
Technique incised
Condition fair
Content rock drawing
Comment *figure*
Access AFa37-38 (photograph, M. Stone)

Inscription **325**
Site Wadi Shellal, Shellal 1, #91
Technique scratched
Condition poor
Content Greek inscription
Limitation *Tentative decipherment only*
Access AFa37-38 (photograph, M. Stone)

Inscription **326**
Site Wadi Shellal, Shellal 1, #91
Technique incised
Condition good
Content footsteps
Access AFa37-38 (photograph, M. Stone)

Inscription **327**
Site Wadi Shellal, Shellal 1, #91
Technique scratched
Condition poor
Dimensions 6 x 21 cm.
Content Greek inscription
Limitation *Tentative decipherment only*
Access AFb39-40 (photograph, M. Stone)

Inscription **328**
Site Wadi Shellal, Shellal 1, #91
Technique scratched
Condition fair
Content rock drawing
Comment *squares*
Access AFb39-40 (photograph, M. Stone)

Inscription **329**
Site Wadi Shellal, Shellal 1, #91
Technique scratched
Condition fair
Content footsteps
Access AFb39-40 (photograph, M. Stone)

Inscription 330
Site Wadi Shellal, Shellal 1, #91
Technique punched
Condition fair
Content Greek inscription
Limitation *Tentative decipherment only*
Access AFb41-42 (photograph, M. Stone)

Inscription 331
Site Wadi Shellal, Shellal 1, #91
Technique punched
Condition fair
Content Greek inscription
Limitation *Tentative decipherment only*
Access AFb41-42 (photograph, M. Stone)

Inscription 332
Site Wadi Shellal, Shellal 1, #91
Technique scratched
Condition fair
Dimensions 5 x 30 cm.
Content Greek inscription
Limitation *Tentative decipherment only*
Access AFb41-42 (photograph, M. Stone)

Inscription 333
Site Wadi Shellal, Shellal 1, #91
Technique punched
Condition good
Content footsteps
Access AFb41-42 (photograph, M. Stone)

Inscription 334
Site Wadi Shellal, Shellal 1, #91
Technique punched
Condition good
Content Greek inscription
Limitation *Tentative decipherment only*
Access AFb41-42 (photograph, M. Stone)

Inscription 335
Site Wadi Shellal, Shellal 1, #91
Technique punched
Condition fair
Content Greek inscription
Limitation *Tentative decipherment only*
Access AFb43-44 (photograph, M. Stone); *see also* FE6

Inscription 336
Site Wadi Shellal, Shellal 1, #91
Technique punched
Condition good
Content footsteps
Access AFb43-44 (photograph, M. Stone); *see also* FE6

Inscription 337
Site Wadi Shellal, Shellal 2, #92
Technique incised
Condition good
Content rock drawing
Comment *people, camels and ibex*
Access AFb45-46 (photograph, M. Stone); *see also* AFb47-48

Inscription 338
Site Wadi Haggag, rock 3 area 1, #126
Technique incised
Condition fair
Content Greek inscription
Limitation *Tentative decipherment only*
Access ACc17 (photograph, M. Stone); *see also* ACb11, AX20, AX21, Negev 1977 fig. 115

Inscription 339
Site Wadi Shellal, Shellal 2, #92
Technique incised
Condition fair
Content unidentified signs
Access AFb45-46 (photograph, M. Stone); *see also* AFb47-48

Inscription 340
Site Wadi Haggag, rock 3 area 1, #126
Technique incised
Condition poor
Content Greek inscription
Limitation *Tentative decipherment only*
Access ACc17 (photograph, M. Stone); *see also* ACb11, AX20, AX21, Negev 1977 fig. 115

Inscription 341
Site Wadi Shellal, Shellal 5, #96
Technique scratched
Condition fair
Dimensions 4 x 74 cm.
Content Greek inscription
Limitation *Tentative decipherment only*
Access AFc49-50 (photograph, M. Stone); *see also* AFc51-52

Inscription 342
Site Wadi Mukatab, #64
Technique incised
Condition good
Content Greek inscription
Limitation *Tentative decipherment only*
Access CM35 (photograph, Z. Radovan)

Inscription 343
Site Wadi Mukatab, #64
Technique incised
Condition fair
Content Greek inscription
Limitation *Tentative decipherment only*
Access CM35 (photograph, Z. Radovan)

Inscription 344
Site Wadi Mukatab, #64
Technique incised
Condition good
Content crosses with inscription
Comment *cross following insc. 342*
Access CM35 (photograph, Z. Radovan)

Inscription **345**
Site Wadi Haggag, rock 3 area 1, #126
Technique scratched
Condition poor
Content Greek inscription
Limitation *Tentative decipherment only*
Access ADg28 (photograph, M. Stone); *see also* Negev 1977 fig. 90

Inscription **346**
Site Wadi Mukatab, Mukatab 4, #68
Technique incised
Condition good
Content Nabatean inscription
Limitation *Tentative decipherment only*
Access AE32 (photograph, M. Stone)

Inscription **347**
Site Wadi Mukatab, Mukatab 4, #68
Technique scratched
Condition good
Content Latin inscription
CESSENTI SYRI
ANTE LATINOS
ROMANOS
Access AE32 (photograph, M. Stone)
Corpus M Lat 1

Inscription **348**
Site Wadi Mukatab, Mukatab 4, #68
Technique scratched
Condition fair
Content crosses alone
Access AE32 (photograph, M. Stone)

Inscription **349**
Site Wadi Mukatab, Mukatab 4, #68
Technique incised
Condition good
Content Nabatean inscription
Limitation *Tentative decipherment only*
Access AE32 (photograph, M. Stone)

Inscription **350**
Site Wadi Mukatab, Mukatab 4, #68
Technique incised
Condition poor
Content crosses alone
Access AE32 (photograph, M. Stone)

Inscription **351**
Site Wadi Mukatab, #64
Technique incised
Condition good
Content rock drawing
Comment *camel*
Access CM49 (photograph, Z. Radovan)

Inscription **352**
Site Wadi Mukatab, #64
Technique incised
Condition good
Content rock drawing
Access CM49 (photograph, Z. Radovan)

Inscription **353**
Site Wadi Haggag, rock 3 area 1, #126
Technique incised
Condition fair
Content Greek inscription
Limitation *Tentative decipherment only*
Access ACc17 (photograph, M. Stone); *see also* ACb11, AX20, AX21, Negev 1977 fig. 115

Inscription **354**
Site Jebel Musa, peak grotto, #12
Technique incised
Condition poor
Content Greek inscription
Limitation *Tentative decipherment only*
Access AHg69-70 (photograph, M. Stone); *see also* AHg67-68

Inscription **355**
Site Jebel Musa, peak grotto, #12
Technique incised
Condition good
Content crosses with inscription
Access AHg69-70 (photograph, M. Stone); *see also* AHc23-24, AHd33-34, AHe43-44

Inscription **356**
Site Wadi Shellal, Shellal 5, #96
Technique incised
Condition fair
Content rock drawing
Access AFc49-50 (photograph, M. Stone); *see also* AFc51-52

Inscription **357**
Site Wadi Shellal, Shellal 5, #96
Technique incised
Condition fair
Content Greek inscription
Limitation *Tentative decipherment only*
Comment *a monogram*
Access AFc51-52 (photograph, M. Stone); *see also* AFc49-50

Inscription **358**
Site Wadi Shellal, Shellal 5, #96
Technique incised
Condition fair
Content crosses with inscription
Access AFc51-52 (photograph, M. Stone); *see also* AFc49-50

Inscription **359**
Site Wadi Shellal, Shellal 5, #96
Technique incised
Condition fair
Content Greek inscription
Limitation *Tentative decipherment only*
Access AFc51-52 (photograph, M. Stone); *see also* AFc49-50

Inscription **360**
Site Wadi Shellal, Shellal 5, #96
Technique incised
Condition good
Content crosses with inscription
Access AFc51-52 (photograph, M. Stone); *see also* AFc49-50

Inscription **361**
Site Wadi Leja, Leja 2, #23
Technique scratched
Condition good
Content unidentified inscription
Access AFd63-64 (photograph, M. Stone); *see also* AFd65-66

Inscription **362**
Site Jebel Musa, peak grotto, #12
Technique incised
Condition good
Content Greek inscription
Limitation *Tentative decipherment only*
Access AHb05-06 (photograph, M. Stone); *see also* AHa01-02, AHb03-04, AHb07-08, AHg69-70

Inscription **363**
Site Wadi Haggag, rock 1, #160
Technique incised
Condition good
Content Arabic inscription
Limitation *Tentative decipherment only*
Access CL04 (photograph, Ann Arbor); *see also* ABf32

Inscription **364**
Site Wadi Haggag, rock 3 area 2, #127
Technique incised
Condition fair
Content Latin inscription
Limitation *Tentative decipherment only*
Access BP49 (photograph, Z. Radovan); *see also* BO48

Inscription **365**
Site Jebel Musa, peak grotto, #12
Technique incised
Condition poor
Content Greek inscription
Limitation *Tentative decipherment only*
Access AHb07-08 (photograph, M. Stone); *see also* AHa01-02

Inscription **366**
Site Jebel Musa, peak grotto, #12
Technique incised
Condition good
Content crosses alone
Comment *large cross*
Access AHb09-10 (photograph, M. Stone); *see also* AHa01-02, AHb03-04, AHb07-08, AHg69-70

Inscription **367**
Site Jebel Musa, peak grotto, #12
Technique incised
Condition good
Content Greek inscription
Limitation *Tentative decipherment only*
Access AHb11-12 (photograph, M. Stone); *see also* AHa01-02, AHc15-16, AHc19-20, AHe39-40, AHe41-42, AHe45-46, AHg67-68, AHg69-70

Inscription **368**
Site Jebel Musa, peak grotto, #12
Technique incised
Condition good
Content crosses with inscription
Access AHb11-12 (photograph, M. Stone); *see also* AHa01-02, AHc15-16, AHc19-20, AHe39-40, AHe41-42, AHe45-46, AHg67-68, AHg69-70

Inscription **369**
Site Jebel Musa, peak grotto, #12
Technique incised
Condition fair
Content Greek inscription
Limitation *Tentative decipherment only*
Access AHd27-28 (photograph, M. Stone); *see also* AHd37-38

Inscription **370**
Site Jebel Musa, peak grotto, #12
Technique incised
Condition good
Content crosses with inscription
Access AHd29-30 (photograph, M. Stone)

Inscription **371**
Site Jebel Musa, peak grotto, #12
Technique scratched
Condition fair
Content unidentified inscription
Access AHe43-44 (photograph, M. Stone); *see also* AHa01-02, AHc21-22, AHe41-42, AHg67-68

Inscription **372**
Site Wadi Mukatab, Mukatab 1, #65
Technique incised
Condition good
Content footsteps
Access AE35 (photograph, M. Stone)

Inscription **373**
Site Jebel Musa, peak behind mosque, #14
Technique scratched
Condition fair
Content crosses with inscription
Comment *cross following insc. 204*
Access AHf55-56 (photograph, M. Stone); *see also* AHf57-58

Inscription 374
Site Wadi Abu Ghadhayyat, Ghadhayyat 1, #36
Technique incised
Condition good
Content varied crosses
Access ALa28-29 (photograph, M. Stone)

Inscription 375
Site Wadi Abu Ghadhayyat, Ghadhayyat 1, #36
Technique incised
Condition good
Content rock drawing
Comment *elephant carrying a canopy*
Access ALa28-29 (photograph, M. Stone)

Inscription 376
Site Wadi Abu Ghadhayyat, Ghadhayyat 1, #36
Technique incised
Condition good
Content rock drawing
Comment *people, wolves, ibex and camels*
Access ALa32-33 (photograph, M. Stone)

Inscription 377
Site Wadi Abu Ghadhayyat, Ghadhayyat 1, #36
Technique incised
Condition good
Content Greek inscription
Limitation *Tentative decipherment only*
Access ALa32-33 (photograph, M. Stone)

Inscription 378
Site Wadi Abu Ghadhayyat, Ghadhayyat 1, #36
Technique scratched
Condition fair
Content unidentified inscription
Access ALa32-33 (photograph, M. Stone)

Inscription 379
Site Wadi Abu Ghadhayyat, Ghadhayyat 1, #36
Technique incised
Condition good
Content rock drawing
Comment *dancing couple*
Access ALa36-37 (photograph, M. Stone)

Inscription 380
Site Wadi Abu Ghadhayyat, Ghadhayyat 1, #36
Technique incised
Condition poor
Content unidentified inscription
Access ALa36-37 (photograph, M. Stone)

Inscription 381
Site Jebel Musa, peak grotto, #12
Technique scratched
Condition poor
Content unidentified inscription
Comment *perhaps Syriac*
Access AHb11-12 (photograph, M. Stone)

Inscription 382
Site Santa Katarina, Justinian doors rt, #9
Technique incised
Condition good
Content crosses with inscription
Access CL01 (photograph, Ann Arbor)

Inscription 383
Site Santa Katarina, Justinian doors rt, #9
Technique scratched
Condition poor
Content Greek inscription
Limitation *Tentative decipherment only*
Access CL01 (photograph, Ann Arbor)

Inscription 384
Site Santa Katarina, Justinian doors rt, #9
Technique scratched
Condition poor
Content unidentified inscription
Access CL01 (photograph, Ann Arbor)

Inscription 385
Site Santa Katarina, Justinian doors rt, #9
Technique scratched
Condition good
Content unidentified signs
Access CL02 (photograph, Ann Arbor)

Inscription 386
Site Wadi Haggag, rock 13, #202
Technique incised
Condition good
Content rock drawing
Comment *wolf and horse*
Access ALc62-63 (photograph, M. Stone)

Inscription 387
Site Wadi Haggag, rock 13, #202
Technique incised
Condition good
Content rock drawing
Comment *ibex and horses*
Access ALd68-69 (photograph, M. Stone); *see also* ALd74-75

Inscription 388
Site Wadi Haggag, rock 13, #202
Technique incised
Condition fair
Content unidentified inscription
Access ALd68-69 (photograph, M. Stone); *see also* ALd74-75

Inscription 389
Site Santa Katarina, #10
Technique incised
Condition good
Content Latin inscription
Limitation *Tentative decipherment only*
Access BTd31-32 (photograph, M. Stone); *see also* BTd35-36, BTg65-66

Inscription 390
Site Santa Katarina, #10
Technique incised
Condition fair
Content Latin inscription
Limitation *Tentative decipherment only*
Access BTd33-34 (photograph, M. Stone); *see also* BTd35-36, BTg65-66

Inscription 391
Site Wadi Haggag, rock 13, #202
Technique incised
Condition fair
Content unidentified inscription
Access ALd68-69 (photograph, M. Stone)

Inscription 392
Site Wadi Haggag, rock 13, #202
Dating 7th to 9th century
Technique incised
Condition good
Content Georgian inscription
A
Access ALd70-71 (photograph, M. Stone)
Corpus H Georg 10

Inscription 393
Site Wadi Haggag, rock 13, #202
Technique incised
Condition good
Content unidentified signs
Access ALd70-71 (photograph, M. Stone)

Inscription 394
Site Wadi Haggag, rock 13, #202
Technique incised
Condition poor
Content rock drawing
Access ALd72-73 (photograph, M. Stone)

Inscription 395
Site Wadi Haggag, rock 13, #202
Technique incised
Condition poor
Content unidentified inscription
Access ALd72-73 (photograph, M. Stone)

Inscription 396
Site Santa Katarina, #10
Technique incised
Condition good
Content Greek inscription
Limitation *Tentative decipherment only*
Comment *monogrammed cross*
Access BTd33-34 (photograph, M. Stone); *see also* BTg65-66

Inscription 397
Site Santa Katarina, #10
Technique scratched
Condition poor
Content Latin inscription
Limitation *Tentative decipherment only*
Access BTd33-34 (photograph, M. Stone); *see also* BTd35-36, BTg65-66

Inscription 398
Site Santa Katarina, #10
Technique incised
Condition good
Content crosses with inscription
Access BTd33-34 (photograph, M. Stone); *see also* BTd35-36, BTg65-66

Inscription 399
Site Santa Katarina, #10
Technique incised
Condition good
Content crosses alone
Access BTd33-34 (photograph, M. Stone); *see also* BTg65-66

Inscription 400
Site Santa Katarina, #10
Technique incised
Condition poor
Content Latin inscription
Limitation *Tentative decipherment only*
Access BTd33-34 (photograph, M. Stone); *see also* BTg65-66

Inscription 401
Site Santa Katarina, #10
Technique incised
Condition unknown
Content rock drawing
Access BTd33-34 (photograph, M. Stone); *see also* BTd35-36, BTg65-66

Inscription 402
Site Santa Katarina, #10
Technique incised
Condition poor
Content Latin inscription
Limitation *Tentative decipherment only*
Access BTd33-34 (photograph, M. Stone); *see also* BTd35-36, BTg65-66

Inscription 403
Site Santa Katarina, #10
Technique incised
Condition good
Content crosses alone
Access BTe45-46 (photograph, M. Stone); *see also* BTe41-42

Inscription **404**
Site Santa Katarina, #10
Technique incised
Condition good
Content crosses alone
Access BTe45-46 (photograph, M. Stone); *see also* BTe41-42

Inscription **405**
Site Santa Katarina, #10
Technique incised
Condition good
Content masons' marks
Access BTe45-46 (photograph, M. Stone); *see also* BTe41-42

Inscription **406**
Site Wadi Shellal, Shellal 1, #91
Technique scratched
Condition fair
Content crosses alone
Comment *similar cross found in Wadi Mukatab*
Access AFa33-34 (photograph, M. Stone); *see also* AFa35-36

Inscription **407**
Site Wadi Mukatab, #64
Technique scratched
Condition fair
Content Greek inscription
Limitation *Tentative decipherment only*
Access CM35 (photograph, Z. Radovan)

Inscription **408**
Site Wadi Shellal, Shellal 2, #92
Technique incised
Condition good
Content footsteps
Access AFb45-46 (photograph, M. Stone); *see also* AFb47-48

Inscription **409**
Site Wadi Shellal, Shellal 5, #96
Technique incised
Condition poor
Content rock drawing
Access AFc49-50 (photograph, M. Stone); *see also* AFc51-52

Inscription **410**
Site Wadi Haggag, rock 3 area 4, #129
Technique incised
Condition fair
Content Nabatean inscription
Limitation *Tentative decipherment only*
Access AN06 (photograph, Z. Radovan); *see also* AM05, Negev 1977 fig. 159

Inscription **411**
Site Wadi Haggag, rock 3 area 4, #129
Technique incised
Condition fair
Content Greek inscription
Limitation *Tentative decipherment only*
Access AN06 (photograph, Z. Radovan); *see also* AM05, Negev 1977 fig. 159

Inscription **412**
Site Wadi Haggag, rock 3 area 4, #129
Technique incised
Condition poor
Content Greek inscription
Limitation *Tentative decipherment only*
Access AN06 (photograph, Z. Radovan); *see also* AM05, Negev 1977 fig. 159

Inscription **413**
Site Wadi Haggag, rock 3 area 1, #126
Technique incised
Condition good
Content encircled crosses
Access ADg30 (photograph, M. Stone); *see also* Negev 1977 figs. 107 and 108

Inscription **414**
Site Wadi Haggag, rock 3 area 1, #126
Technique incised
Condition poor
Content unidentified inscription
Access ADg30 (photograph, M. Stone); *see also* Negev 1977 figs. 107 and 108

Inscription **415**
Site Wadi Haggag, rock 3 area 1, #126
Technique incised
Condition good
Content wasems & other Bedouin marks
Access ADg30 (photograph, M. Stone)

Inscription **416**
Site Wadi Haggag, rock 3 area 1, #126
Technique incised
Condition fair
Content rock drawing
Comment *ibex*
Access ADg30 (photograph, M. Stone)

Inscription **417**
Site Wadi Haggag, rock 3 area 1, #126
Technique incised
Condition fair
Content Greek inscription
Limitation *Tentative decipherment only*
Access ADg30 (photograph, M. Stone)

Inscription **418**
Site Wadi Haggag, rock 13, #202
Technique incised
Condition good
Content rock drawing
Access ALc58-59 (photograph, M. Stone)

Inscription 419
Site Wadi Haggag, rock 13, #202
Technique incised
Condition good
Content rock drawing
Access ALc58-59 (photograph, M. Stone)

Inscription 420
Site Wadi Haggag, rock 13, #202
Technique incised
Condition good
Content rock drawing
Comment *camels*
Access ALc58-59 (photograph, M. Stone)

Inscription 421
Site Wadi Haggag, rock 13, #202
Technique incised
Condition good
Content rock drawing
Comment *schematic figure*
Access ALc58-59 (photograph, M. Stone)

Inscription 422
Site Wadi Haggag, rock 13, #202
Technique incised
Condition fair
Content rock drawing
Comment *animals*
Access ALc58-59 (photograph, M. Stone)

Inscription 423
Site Wadi Haggag, rock 13, #202
Technique incised
Condition good
Content rock drawing
Comment *camel*
Access ALc58-59 (photograph, M. Stone)

Inscription 424
Site Wadi Haggag, rock 13, #202
Technique incised
Condition fair
Content wasems & other Bedouin marks
Access ALc58-59 (photograph, M. Stone)

Inscription 425
Site Wadi Haggag, rock 13, #202
Technique incised
Condition good
Content rock drawing
Comment *camels with riders*
Access ALc58-59 (photograph, M. Stone)

Inscription 426
Site Wadi Haggag, rock 13, #202
Technique incised
Condition good
Content rock drawing
Comment *ibexes*
Access ALc58-59 (photograph, M. Stone)

Inscription 427
Site Wadi Haggag, rock 13, #202
Technique incised
Condition good
Content rock drawing
Comment *large, stylized drawing; identification uncertain*
Access ALc58-59 (photograph, M. Stone)

Inscription 428
Site Wadi Haggag, rock 13, #202
Technique incised
Condition good
Content rock drawing
Comment *animals*
Access ALc58-59 (photograph, M. Stone)

Inscription 429
Site Wadi Haggag, rock 13, #202
Technique incised
Condition good
Content rock drawing
Comment *human figures*
Access ALc58-59 (photograph, M. Stone)

Inscription 430
Site Wadi Haggag, rock 13, #202
Technique incised
Condition good
Content rock drawing
Access ALc58-59 (photograph, M. Stone)

Inscription 431
Site Wadi Haggag, rock 13, #202
Technique incised
Condition good
Content rock drawing
Access ALc58-59 (photograph, M. Stone)

Inscription 432
Site Santa Katarina, #10
Technique incised
Condition poor
Content Latin inscription
Limitation *Tentative decipherment only*
Access BTd31-32 (photograph, M. Stone)

Inscription 433
Site Santa Katarina, #10
Technique incised
Condition poor
Content Latin inscription
Limitation *Tentative decipherment only*
Access BTd31-32 (photograph, M. Stone)

Inscription 434
Site Santa Katarina, #10
Technique incised
Condition poor
Content Latin inscription
Limitation *Tentative decipherment only*
Access BTd31-32 (photograph, M. Stone)

Inscription 435
Site Santa Katarina, #10
Technique incised
Condition good
Content rock drawing
Comment *fish*
Access BTd33-34 (photograph, M. Stone); *see also* BTg65-66

Inscription 436
Site Wadi Mukatab, Mukatab 5, #69
Technique incised
Condition good
Content rock drawing
Comment *human figures and animals*
Access AE25-26 (photograph, M. Stone); *see also* DN32, DN36

Inscription 437
Site Ein Hudra, #117
Technique incised
Condition good
Content Hebrew inscription
Limitation *Tentative decipherment only*
Access CI8 (photograph, U. Avner); *see also* BL60, BL61, CQ98, FF2

Inscription 438
Site Wadi Leja, #27
Technique scratched
Condition fair
Content Nabatean inscription
Limitation *Tentative decipherment only*
Access CV27 (photograph, A. Goren)

Inscription 439
Site Wadi Leja, #27
Technique scratched
Condition poor
Content Nabatean inscription
Comment *illegible*
Access CV29 (photograph, A. Goren)

Inscription 440
Site Wadi Haggag, rock 3, #125
Technique scratched
Condition fair
Content unidentified signs
Access ADc08 (photograph, M. Stone)

Inscription 441
Site Wadi Leja, #27
Technique scratched
Condition fair
Content Arabic inscription
Limitation *Tentative decipherment only*
Access CV29 (photograph, A. Goren)

Inscription 442
Site Jebel Tarbush, #315
Technique incised
Condition good
Content rock drawing
Comment *human figures and ibexes*
Access CY05 (photograph, A. Goren)

Inscription 443
Site Jebel Tarbush, #315
Technique scratched
Condition good
Content unidentified signs
Access CY05 (photograph, A. Goren)

Inscription 444
Site Jebel Tarbush, #315
Technique scratched
Condition good
Content rock drawing
Comment *frame of cross*
Access CY06 (photograph, A. Goren)

Inscription 445
Site Jebel Tarbush, #315
Technique scratched
Condition good
Content unidentified signs
Access CY06 (photograph, A. Goren)

Inscription 446
Site Naqb Sara, #309
Technique incised
Condition good
Content Nabatean inscription
Limitation *Tentative decipherment only*
Access CY20 (photograph, A. Goren); *see also* CY32

Inscription 447
Site Naqb Sara, #309
Technique incised
Condition fair
Content Nabatean inscription
Limitation *Tentative decipherment only*
Access CY20 (photograph, A. Goren); *see also* CY32

Inscription 448
Site Naqb Sara, #309
Technique incised
Condition fair
Content Nabatean inscription
Limitation *Tentative decipherment only*
Access CY20 (photograph, A. Goren); *see also* CY32

Inscription 449
Site Naqb Sara, #309
Technique incised
Condition good
Content Nabatean inscription
Limitation *Tentative decipherment only*
Access CY23 (photograph, A. Goren); *see also* CY28

Inscription 450
Site Naqb Sara, #309
Technique incised
Condition fair
Content Nabatean inscription
Limitation *Tentative decipherment only*
Access CY23 (photograph, A. Goren)

Inscription 451
Site Naqb Sara, #309
Technique incised
Condition fair
Content rock drawing
Comment *schematic figure*
Access CY23 (photograph, A. Goren); *see also* CY28

Inscription 452
Site Naqb Sara, #309
Technique scratched
Condition poor
Content Nabatean inscription
Limitation *Tentative decipherment only*
Access CY23 (photograph, A. Goren); *see also* CY28

Inscription 453
Site Naqb Sara, #309
Technique incised
Condition poor
Content Nabatean inscription
Limitation *Tentative decipherment only*
Access CY24 (photograph, A. Goren); *see also* CY25, CY27

Inscription 454
Site Naqb Sara, #309
Technique incised
Condition fair
Content Nabatean inscription
Limitation *Tentative decipherment only*
Access CY24 (photograph, A. Goren); *see also* CY25, CY27

Inscription 455
Site Naqb Sara, #309
Technique incised
Condition fair
Content Nabatean inscription
Limitation *Tentative decipherment only*
Access CY21 (photograph, A. Goren); *see also* CY30

Inscription 456
Site Naqb Sara, #309
Technique incised
Condition fair
Content rock drawing
Comment *human figures and animals*
Access CY21 (photograph, A. Goren); *see also* CY30

Inscription 457
Site Naqb Sara, #309
Technique incised
Condition fair
Content Nabatean inscription
Limitation *Tentative decipherment only*
Access CY29 (photograph, A. Goren)

Inscription 458
Site Naqb Sara, #309
Technique incised
Condition fair
Content rock drawing
Comment *animals and horses with riders*
Access CY36 (photograph, A. Goren)

Inscription 459
Site Naqb Sara, #309
Technique incised
Condition fair
Content Nabatean inscription
Limitation *Tentative decipherment only*
Access CY34 (photograph, A. Goren)

Inscription 460
Site Jebel Tarbush, #315
Technique incised
Condition fair
Content Nabatean inscription
Limitation *Tentative decipherment only*
Access CY19 (photograph, A. Goren); *see also* CY18

Inscription 461
Site Naqb Sara, #309
Technique incised
Condition poor
Content Nabatean inscription
Limitation *Tentative decipherment only*
Access CY31 (photograph, A. Goren)

Inscription 462
Site Naqb Sara, #309
Technique scratched
Condition poor
Content Nabatean inscription
Limitation *Tentative decipherment only*
Access CY33 (photograph, A. Goren)

Inscription 463
Site Naqb Sara, #309
Technique incised
Condition fair
Content Nabatean inscription
Limitation *Tentative decipherment only*
Access CY35 (photograph, A. Goren)

Inscription 464
Site Naqb Sara, #309
Technique incised
Condition good
Content rock drawing
Comment *animals*
Access CY35 (photograph, A. Goren)

Inscription 465
Site Wadi Firan, #53
Technique scratched
Condition good
Content wasems & other Bedouin marks
Access CW68-69 (photograph, A. Goren)

Inscription 466
Site Wadi Firan, #53
Technique scratched
Condition good
Content Nabatean inscription
Limitation *Tentative decipherment only*
Access CW68-69 (photograph, A. Goren)

Inscription 467
Site Wadi Firan, #53
Technique scratched
Condition fair
Content Nabatean inscription
Limitation *Tentative decipherment only*
Access CW70-71 (photograph, A. Goren)

Inscription 468
Site Wadi Firan, #53
Technique scratched
Condition good
Content wasems & other Bedouin marks
Access CW70-71 (photograph, A. Goren)

Inscription 469
Site Wadi Firan, #53
Technique scratched
Condition good
Content unidentified signs
Access CW70-71 (photograph, A. Goren)

Inscription 470
Site Wadi Wata, #225
Technique incised
Condition poor
Content Nabatean inscription
Limitation *Tentative decipherment only*
Access CZ62-63 (photograph, A. Goren); *see also* CZ66-67

Inscription 471
Site Wadi Wata, #225
Technique incised
Condition poor
Content Nabatean inscription
Limitation *Tentative decipherment only*
Access CZ62-63 (photograph, A. Goren); *see also* CZ66-67

Inscription 472
Site Wadi Wata, #225
Technique incised
Condition fair
Content Nabatean inscription
Limitation *Tentative decipherment only*
Access CZ62-63 (photograph, A. Goren); *see also* CZ66-67

Inscription 473
Site Wadi Wata, #225
Technique incised
Condition good
Content Latin inscription
Limitation *Tentative decipherment only*
Access CZ62-63 (photograph, A. Goren); *see also* CZ66-67

Inscription 474
Site Wadi Wata, #225
Technique incised
Condition poor
Content Nabatean inscription
Limitation *Tentative decipherment only*
Access CZ62-63 (photograph, A. Goren); *see also* CZ66-67

Inscription 475
Site Wadi Wata, #225
Technique incised
Condition fair
Content Nabatean inscription
Limitation *Tentative decipherment only*
Access CZ62-63 (photograph, A. Goren); *see also* CZ66-67

Inscription 476
Site Wadi Wata, #225
Technique incised
Condition good
Content Nabatean inscription
Limitation *Tentative decipherment only*
Access CZ62-63 (photograph, A. Goren); *see also* CZ66-67

Inscription 477
Site Wadi Wata, #225
Technique incised
Condition fair
Content Nabatean inscription
Limitation *Tentative decipherment only*
Access CZ62-63 (photograph, A. Goren); *see also* CZ66-67

Inscription 478
Site Wadi Wata, #225
Technique incised
Condition good
Content rock drawing
Comment *ibex*
Access CZ62-63 (photograph, A. Goren); *see also* CZ66-67

Inscription 479
Site Wadi Wata, #225
Technique incised
Condition good
Content Greek inscription
Limitation *Tentative decipherment only*
Access CZ66-67 (photograph, A. Goren)

Inscription 480
Site Wadi Wata, #225
Technique incised
Condition good
Content Nabatean inscription
Limitation *Tentative decipherment only*
Access CZ66-67 (photograph, A. Goren)

Inscription **481**
Site Wadi Wata, #225
Technique incised
Condition good
Content Nabatean inscription
Limitation *Tentative decipherment only*
Access CZ66-67 (photograph, A. Goren)

Inscription **482**
Site Wadi Wata, #225
Technique incised
Condition fair
Content Nabatean inscription
Limitation *Tentative decipherment only*
Access CZ66-67 (photograph, A. Goren)

Inscription **483**
Site Jebel Sirbal, Wadi Alayat, #187
Technique incised
Condition good
Content Nabatean inscription
Limitation *Tentative decipherment only*
Access DE22a-23 (photograph, A. Goren)

Inscription **484**
Site Jebel Sirbal, Wadi Rim, #186
Technique incised
Condition fair
Content Nabatean inscription
Limitation *Tentative decipherment only*
Access DD14-15 (photograph, A. Goren)

Inscription **485**
Site Jebel Sirbal, Wadi Rim, #186
Technique scratched
Condition good
Content Nabatean inscription
Limitation *Tentative decipherment only*
Access DD18-19 (photograph, A. Goren)

Inscription **486**
Site Jebel Sirbal, Wadi Rim, #186
Technique scratched
Condition fair
Content Nabatean inscription
Limitation *Tentative decipherment only*
Access DD20-21 (photograph, A. Goren)

Inscription **487**
Site Jebel Sirbal, Wadi Rim, #186
Technique scratched
Condition good
Content Nabatean inscription
Limitation *Tentative decipherment only*
Access DD22-23 (photograph, A. Goren)

Inscription **488**
Site Jebel Sirbal, Wadi Rim, #186
Technique scratched
Condition poor
Content Nabatean inscription
Limitation *Tentative decipherment only*
Access DD22-23 (photograph, A. Goren)

Inscription **489**
Site Wadi Mukatab, #64
Technique incised
Condition good
Content Nabatean inscription
šlm klbw br zydw bṭb
Access CM55 (photograph, Z. Radovan)
Corpus CIS 1104

Inscription **490**
Site Wadi Mukatab, #64
Technique incised
Condition good
Content Nabatean inscription
šlm ʿwdw br
wʾlw bṭb
Access CM55 (photograph, Z. Radovan)
Corpus CIS 1105

Inscription **491**
Site Wadi Mukatab, #64
Technique incised
Condition fair
Content Nabatean inscription
bryk wdw
br ...
Access CM55 (photograph, Z. Radovan)
Corpus CIS 1106

Inscription **492**
Site Wadi Mukatab, #64
Technique incised
Condition good
Content rock drawing
Comment *horse*
Access CM55 (photograph, Z. Radovan)

Inscription **493**
Site Wadi Mukatab, #64
Technique incised
Condition good
Content Nabatean inscription
šlm gdyw br bḥgh
Access CM53 (photograph, Z. Radovan)
Corpus CIS 1138

Inscription **494**
Site Wadi Mukatab, #64
Technique incised
Condition fair
Content Nabatean inscription
Limitation *Tentative decipherment only*
Access CM53 (photograph, Z. Radovan)

Inscription	**495**
Site	Wadi Mukatab, #64
Technique	incised
Condition	good
Content	Nabatean inscription
	šlm ᵓwšlhy
	br ᵓᶜlᵓ
Access	CM53 (photograph, Z. Radovan)
Corpus	CIS 1144

Inscription	**496**
Site	Wadi Mukatab, #64
Technique	incised
Condition	good
Content	Nabatean inscription
	...
	...
	bryk ᶜmmw
	brᶜtw mᶜnw
	ᵓlwᵓlt šᶜdw bkl šlm
Access	CM53 (photograph, Z. Radovan)
Corpus	CIS 1142, 1143

Inscription	**497**
Site	Wadi Mukatab, #64
Technique	incised
Condition	poor
Content	Greek inscription
Limitation	*Tentative decipherment only*
Access	CM43 (photograph, Z. Radovan)

Inscription	**498**
Site	Wadi Mukatab, #64
Technique	incised
Condition	poor
Content	Nabatean inscription
Comment	*illegible*
Access	CM43 (photograph, Z. Radovan)

Inscription	**499**
Site	Wadi Mukatab, #64
Technique	incised
Condition	good
Content	Greek inscription
Limitation	*Tentative decipherment only*
Access	CM45 (photograph, Z. Radovan)

Inscription	**500**
Site	Wadi Sreij, ascent, #381
Technique	incised
Condition	fair
Content	Greek inscription
Limitation	*Tentative decipherment only*
Access	GL17 (photograph, Project)

Inscription	**501**
Site	Wadi Mukatab, #64
Technique	incised
Condition	poor
Content	Nabatean inscription
Limitation	*Tentative decipherment only*
Access	CM45 (photograph, Z. Radovan)

Inscription	**502**
Site	Wadi Mukatab, #64
Technique	incised
Condition	good
Content	Greek inscription
Limitation	*Tentative decipherment only*
Access	CM49 (photograph, Z. Radovan)

Inscription	**503**
Site	Wadi Mukatab, #64
Technique	incised
Condition	good
Content	Nabatean inscription
Limitation	*Tentative decipherment only*
Access	CM49 (photograph, Z. Radovan)

Inscription	**504**
Site	Wadi Mukatab, #64
Technique	incised
Condition	good
Content	Nabatean inscription
Limitation	*Tentative decipherment only*
Access	CM49 (photograph, Z. Radovan)

Inscription	**505**
Site	Vale of John, Jebel Ṣafṣafa, #379
Technique	incised
Condition	fair
Content	Greek inscription
Limitation	*Tentative decipherment only*
Access	GL26 (photograph, Project)

Inscription	**506**
Site	Wadi Mukatab, #64
Technique	incised
Condition	fair
Content	Nabatean inscription
Limitation	*Tentative decipherment only*
Access	CM49 (photograph, Z. Radovan)

Inscription	**507**
Site	Wadi Mukatab, #64
Technique	incised
Condition	good
Content	rock drawing
Comment	*fragment of drawing of camel*
Access	CM49 (photograph, Z. Radovan)

Inscription 508
Site Wadi Mukatab, #64
Technique incised
Condition good
Content Nabatean inscription
šlm ʾšw br klbw wklbw brh .bṭb
Access CM56 (photograph, Z. Radovan)
Corpus CIS 1108

Inscription 509
Site Wadi Mukatab, #64
Technique incised
Condition good
Content Nabatean inscription
šlm ʿmnw br ʿwdw
Access CM56 (photograph, Z. Radovan)
Corpus CIS 1109

Inscription 510
Site Wadi Mukatab, #64
Technique incised
Condition good
šlm ʿbdʾlbʿly br ʾwšʾlh(y)
Content Nabatean inscription
Access CM56 (photograph, Z. Radovan)
Corpus CIS 1111

Inscription 511
Site Wadi Mukatab, #64
Technique incised
Condition good
Content Nabatean inscription
šlm ʿmyrt br ʾwšw
Access CM56 (photograph, Z. Radovan)
Corpus CIS 1111

Inscription 512
Site Wadi Mukatab, #64
Technique incised
Condition good
Content Nabatean inscription
šlm wtyqt br nʿrt
Access CM56 (photograph, Z. Radovan)
Corpus CIS 1114

Inscription 513
Site Wadi Mukatab, #64
Technique incised
Condition fair
Content Nabatean inscription
nʿrt br ʾbʾ..šlm
Access CM56 (photograph, Z. Radovan)
Corpus CIS 1113

Inscription 514
Site Wadi Mukatab, #64
Technique incised
Condition fair
Content Nabatean inscription
dkyrn zydw w
...wʾl.
...
bṭb
Access CM56 (photograph, Z. Radovan)
Corpus CIS 1115

Inscription 515
Site Wadi Mukatab, #64
Technique incised
Condition fair
Content Nabatean inscription
Limitation *Tentative decipherment only*
Access CM56 (photograph, Z. Radovan)

Inscription 516
Site Wadi Mukatab, #64
Technique incised
Condition poor
Content Nabatean inscription
Limitation *Tentative decipherment only*
Access CM56 (photograph, Z. Radovan)

Inscription 517
Site Wadi Mukatab, Mukatab 6, #70
Technique incised
Condition poor
Content rock drawing
Comment *boat*
Access FL08-08a (photograph, Project)

Inscription 518
Site Wadi Mukatab, Mukatab 6, #70
Technique incised
Condition poor
Content rock drawing
Comment *ibex*
Access FL08-08a (photograph, Project)

Inscription 519
Site Wadi Mukatab, Mukatab 6, #70
Technique incised
Condition poor
Content rock drawing
Access FL08-08a (photograph, Project)

Inscription 520
Site Wadi Mukatab, Mukatab 6, #70
Technique incised
Condition poor
Content rock drawing
Comment *tree?*
Access FL08-08a (photograph, Project)

Inscription 521
Site Wadi Mukatab, Mukatab 6, #70
Technique incised
Condition poor
Content rock drawing
Access FL08-08a (photograph, Project)

Inscription 522
Site Wadi Mukatab, Mukatab 6, #70
Technique incised
Condition poor
Content unidentified signs
Access FL08-08a (photograph, Project)

Inscription 523
Site Ein Hudra, #117
Technique incised
Condition good
Dimensions 230 x 60 cm.
Content rock drawing
Comment *camels with riders*
Access EX29 (photograph, Project); *see also* EX30

Inscription 524
Site Wadi Mukatab, #64
Technique incised
Condition good
Content rock drawing
Comment *goat, wolf, horses with riders*
Access CM63 (photograph, Z. Radovan); *see also* CM62

Inscription 525
Site Wadi Mukatab, #64
Technique incised
Condition good
Content rock drawing
Comment *horse and rider*
Access CM63 (photograph, Z. Radovan); *see also* CM62

Inscription 526
Site Wadi Mukatab, #64
Technique incised
Condition good
Content wasems & other Bedouin marks
Access CM63 (photograph, Z. Radovan); *see also* CM62

Inscription 527
Site Wadi Abu Ghadhayyat, #149
Technique incised
Condition excellent
Content rock drawing
Comment *human figure drawing a bow*
Access EO13 (photograph, Project)

Inscription 528
Site Ein Hudra, #117
Technique incised
Condition good
Dimensions 215 x 60 cm.
Content rock drawing
Comment *two humans fighting, camel and palm tree*
Access EX31 (photograph, Project); *see also* EX32

Inscription 529
Site Wadi Mukatab, #64
Technique incised
Condition good
Content Nabatean inscription
Limitation *Tentative decipherment only*
Access CN72 (photograph, Z. Radovan)

Inscription 530
Site Wadi Mukatab, #64
Technique incised
Condition good
Content Nabatean inscription
Limitation *Tentative decipherment only*
Access CN72 (photograph, Z. Radovan)

Inscription 531
Site Wadi Mukatab, #64
Technique incised
Condition good
Content Nabatean inscription
Limitation *Tentative decipherment only*
Access CN72 (photograph, Z. Radovan)

Inscription 532
Site Wadi Mukatab, #64
Technique incised
Condition good
Content Nabatean inscription
Limitation *Tentative decipherment only*
Access CN76 (photograph, Z. Radovan)

Inscription 533
Site Wadi Mukatab, #64
Technique incised
Condition good
Content Nabatean inscription
Limitation *Tentative decipherment only*
Access CN76 (photograph, Z. Radovan)

Inscription 534
Site Wadi Mukatab, #64
Technique incised
Condition good
Content Arabic inscription
Limitation *Tentative decipherment only*
Access CN76 (photograph, Z. Radovan)

Inscription 535
Site Wadi Mukatab, #64
Technique incised
Condition good
Content Nabatean inscription
Limitation *Tentative decipherment only*
Access CN76 (photograph, Z. Radovan)

Inscription 536
Site Wadi Mukatab, #64
Technique incised
Condition good
Content rock drawing
Comment *human*
Access CN76 (photograph, Z. Radovan)

Inscription 537
Site Wadi Mukatab, #64
Technique incised
Condition good
Content Nabatean inscription
šlm ʿwdw br šʿdʾlhy
bṭb
Access CN84 (photograph, Z. Radovan)
Corpus CIS 2133

Inscription 538
Site Wadi Mukatab, #64
Technique incised
Condition poor
Content rock drawing
Comment *small animals*
Access CN84 (photograph, Z. Radovan)

Inscription 539
Site Wadi Mukatab, #64
Technique incised
Condition good
Content rock drawing
Access CN86 (photograph, Z. Radovan)

Inscription 540
Site Wadi Mukatab, #64
Technique incised
Condition poor
Content unidentified inscription
Access CN86 (photograph, Z. Radovan)

Inscription 541
Site Wadi Mukatab, #64
Technique incised
Condition good
Content Nabatean inscription
Limitation *Tentative decipherment only*
Access CN91 (photograph, Z. Radovan)

Inscription 542
Site Wadi Mukatab, #64
Technique incised
Condition good
Content Nabatean inscription
Limitation *Tentative decipherment only*
Access CN99 (photograph, Z. Radovan)

Inscription 543
Site Wadi Mukatab, #64
Technique scratched
Condition fair
Content Nabatean inscription
Limitation *Tentative decipherment only*
Access CO06 (photograph, Z. Radovan)

Inscription 544
Site Wadi Mukatab, #64
Technique scratched
Condition poor
Content Nabatean inscription
Limitation *Tentative decipherment only*
Access CO06 (photograph, Z. Radovan)

Inscription 545
Site Wadi Mukatab, #64
Technique incised
Condition good
Content Nabatean inscription
Limitation *Tentative decipherment only*
Access CO13 (photograph, Z. Radovan)

Inscription 546
Site Wadi Mukatab, #64
Technique incised
Condition good
Content Nabatean inscription
Limitation *Tentative decipherment only*
Access CO13 (photograph, Z. Radovan)

Inscription 547
Site Wadi Mukatab, #64
Technique incised
Condition fair
Content Nabatean inscription
Limitation *Tentative decipherment only*
Access CO13 (photograph, Z. Radovan)

Inscription 548
Site Wadi Mukatab, Mukatab 6, #70
Technique incised
Condition excellent
Content rock drawing
Comment *standing ibex*
Access FL54-54a (photograph, Project)

Inscription 549
Site Wadi Mukatab, Mukatab 6, #70
Technique incised
Condition excellent
Content rock drawing
Comment *walking ibex*
Access FL54-54a (photograph, Project)

Inscription 550
Site Wadi Mukatab, #64
Technique incised
Condition good
Content rock drawing
Comment *camel*
Access CO13 (photograph, Z. Radovan)

Inscription 551
Site Wadi Mukatab, #64
Technique incised
Condition good
Content unidentified inscription
Access CO13 (photograph, Z. Radovan)

Inscription **552**
Site Jebel Musa, #19
Technique incised
Condition poor
Content unidentified inscription
Access EM03 (photograph, Project)

Inscription **553**
Site Jebel Musa, #19
Technique incised
Condition poor
Content rock drawing
Access EM03 (photograph, Project)

Inscription **554**
Site Wadi Mukatab, #64
Technique incised
Condition good
Content Nabatean inscription
Limitation *Tentative decipherment only*
Access CO19 (photograph, Z. Radovan)

Inscription **555**
Site Wadi Mukatab, #64
Technique incised
Condition fair
Content Nabatean inscription
Limitation *Tentative decipherment only*
Access CO19 (photograph, Z. Radovan)

Inscription **556**
Site Wadi Mukatab, #64
Technique incised
Condition good
Content Nabatean inscription
Limitation *Tentative decipherment only*
Access CO19 (photograph, Z. Radovan)

Inscription **557**
Site Wadi Mukatab, #64
Technique incised
Condition good
Content Greek inscription
Limitation *Tentative decipherment only*
Access CO24 (photograph, Z. Radovan)

Inscription **558**
Site Wadi Mukatab, #64
Technique incised
Condition good
Content unidentified inscription
Access CO24 (photograph, Z. Radovan)

Inscription **559**
Site Wadi Mukatab, Mukatab 6, #70
Technique scratched
Condition poor
Content unidentified inscription
Access FL34-34a (photograph, Project)

Inscription **560**
Site Wadi Mukatab, #64
Technique punched
Condition poor
Content Nabatean inscription
Limitation *Tentative decipherment only*
Access CO26 (photograph, Z. Radovan)

Inscription **561**
Site Wadi Mukatab, Mukatab 6, #70
Technique incised
Condition fair
Content Arabic inscription
Limitation *Tentative decipherment only*
Access FL34-34a (photograph, Project)

Inscription **562**
Site Wadi Mukatab, Mukatab 6, #70
Technique incised
Condition fair
Content rock drawing
Comment *animals*
Access FL34-34a (photograph, Project)

Inscription **563**
Site Wadi Mukatab, Mukatab 6, #70
Technique incised
Condition fair
Content rock drawing
Access FL34-34a (photograph, Project)

Inscription **564**
Site Wadi Mukatab, #64
Technique incised
Condition fair
Content Nabatean inscription
Limitation *Tentative decipherment only*
Access CO27 (photograph, Z. Radovan)

Inscription **565**
Site Wadi Mukatab, #64
Technique incised
Condition poor
Content Nabatean inscription
Limitation *Tentative decipherment only*
Access CO27 (photograph, Z. Radovan)

Inscription **566**
Site Wadi Mukatab, #64
Technique incised
Condition good
Content unidentified signs
Access CO27 (photograph, Z. Radovan)

Inscription **567**
Site Wadi Mukatab, #64
Technique punched
Condition good
Content rock drawing
Comment *ibex and camel*
Access CO31 (photograph, Z. Radovan)

Inscription 568
Site Wadi Mukatab, #64
Technique incised
Condition fair
Content Greek inscription
Limitation *Tentative decipherment only*
Access CP39 (photograph, Z. Radovan); *see also* CP40

Inscription 569
Site Wadi Mukatab, #64
Technique incised
Condition fair
Content Greek inscription
Limitation *Tentative decipherment only*
Access CP39 (photograph, Z. Radovan); *see also* CP40

Inscription 570
Site Wadi Mukatab, #64
Technique incised
Condition fair
Content Nabatean inscription
Limitation *Tentative decipherment only*
Access CP45 (photograph, Z. Radovan); *see also* CP46

Inscription 571
Site Wadi Mukatab, #64
Technique incised
Condition good
Content rock drawing
Comment *animal*
Access CP49 (photograph, Z. Radovan)

Inscription 572
Site Wadi Mukatab, #64
Technique incised
Condition good
Content rock drawing
Comment *hunters on horseback*
Access CP50 (photograph, Z. Radovan)

Inscription 573
Site Wadi Mukatab, #64
Technique incised
Condition good
Content rock drawing
Comment *camels and other animals*
Access CP51 (photograph, Z. Radovan)

Inscription 574
Site Wadi Mukatab, #64
Technique incised
Condition good
Content unidentified signs
Access CP51 (photograph, Z. Radovan)

Inscription 575
Site Wadi Mukatab, #64
Technique incised
Condition poor
Content rock drawing
Comment *seven-branched candelabrum; person on horseback*
Access CP52 (photograph, Z. Radovan)

Inscription 576
Site Wadi Mukatab, #64
Technique incised
Condition good
Content rock drawing
Comment *wolf and ibex*
Access CP53 (photograph, Z. Radovan)

Inscription 577
Site Wadi Mukatab, #64
Technique incised
Condition fair
Content Nabatean inscription
Limitation *Tentative decipherment only*
Access CP64 (photograph, Z. Radovan)

Inscription 578
Site Wadi Haggag, rock 3, #125
Technique incised
Condition fair
Content Greek inscription
ΧΑΣΕΤΟΣ
Access CQ74 (photograph, Z. Radovan)
Corpus Negev 1977 197

Inscription 579
Site Wadi Haggag, rock 3, #125
Technique incised
Condition poor
Content Greek inscription
Limitation *Tentative decipherment only*
Access CQ74 (photograph, Z. Radovan)

Inscription 580
Site Wadi Haggag, rock 3, #125
Technique scratched
Condition poor
Content Greek inscription
Limitation *Tentative decipherment only*
Access CQ74 (photograph, Z. Radovan)

Inscription 581
Site Wadi Umm Sidra, #174
Technique incised
Condition fair
Content Arabic inscription
Limitation *Tentative decipherment only*
Access FL52-52a (photograph, Project)

Inscription 582
Site Wadi Haggag, rock 3, #125
Technique incised
Condition good
Content crosses with inscription
Access CQ76 (photograph, Z. Radovan)

Inscription **583**
Site Wadi Haggag, rock 3, #125
Technique scratched
Condition poor
Content Greek inscription
Limitation *Tentative decipherment only*
Access CQ76 (photograph, Z. Radovan)

Inscription **584**
Site Wadi Haggag, #118
Technique incised
Condition poor
Content Greek inscription
Limitation *Tentative decipherment only*
Access CP41 (photograph, Z. Radovan); *see also* CP42

Inscription **585**
Site Wadi Haggag, rock 3, #125
Technique incised
Condition good
Content crosses with inscription
Comment *accompanies insc. 584*
Access CQ97 (photograph, Z. Radovan); *see also* Negev 1977 fig. 74

Inscription **586**
Site Wadi Haggag, rock 3 area 3, #128
Technique incised
Condition poor
Content unidentified inscription
Access AM93 (photograph, Z. Radovan); *see also* AN94, AN95, AN96

Inscription **587**
Site Wadi Haggag, rock 3 area 3, #128
Technique incised
Condition poor
Content unidentified inscription
Access AM93 (photograph, Z. Radovan); *see also* AN94, AN95, AN96

Inscription **588**
Site Wadi Haggag, rock 3 area 3, #128
Technique incised
Condition poor
Content unidentified inscription
Access CR04 (photograph, Z. Radovan); *see also* AN94, AN95, AN96

Inscription **589**
Site Wadi Haggag, #118
Technique incised
Condition good
Content Greek inscription
Limitation *Tentative decipherment only*
Access CR04 (photograph, Z. Radovan)

Inscription **590**
Site Wadi Haggag, #118
Technique incised
Condition poor
Content Nabatean inscription
Limitation *Tentative decipherment only*
Access CP58 (photograph, Z. Radovan)

Inscription **591**
Site Wadi Haggag, rock 3, #125
Technique incised
Condition good
Content rock drawing
Comment *camels with riders*
Access EZ23 (photograph, Project); *see also* EZ24, EZ25, EZ26, EZ27

Inscription **592**
Site Wadi Haggag, rock 3, #125
Technique incised
Condition good
Content crosses with inscription
Comment *crosses accompanying insc. 591*
Access CQ78 (photograph, Z. Radovan); *see also* Negev 1977 fig. 75

Inscription **593**
Site Wadi Haggag, rock 3, #125
Technique incised
Condition good
Content unidentified signs
Access CQ78 (photograph, Z. Radovan)

Inscription **594**
Site Wadi Haggag, rock 3, #125
Technique incised
Condition good
Content crosses alone
Access CQ78 (photograph, Z. Radovan)

Inscription **595**
Site Wadi Haggag, rock 5, #131
Technique incised
Condition good
Content Nabatean inscription
Limitation *Tentative decipherment only*
Access CR05 (photograph, Z. Radovan)

Inscription **596**
Site Wadi Haggag, rock 5, #131
Technique incised
Condition good
Content rock drawing
Comment *ibex*
Access CR05 (photograph, Z. Radovan)

Inscription **597**
Site Wadi Haggag, rock 5, #131
Technique incised
Condition fair
Content Nabatean inscription
Limitation *Tentative decipherment only*
Access CR05 (photograph, Z. Radovan)

Inscription **598**
Site Wadi Haggag, rock 5, #131
Technique scratched
Condition poor
Content Nabatean inscription
Comment *illegible*
Access CR05 (photograph, Z. Radovan)

Inscription **599**
Site Wadi Haggag, rock 5, #131
Technique scratched
Condition poor
Content unidentified inscription
Access CR05 (photograph, Z. Radovan)

Inscription **600**
Site Wadi Haggag, rock 5, #131
Technique scratched
Condition poor
Content Nabatean inscription
Limitation *Tentative decipherment only*
Access CR05 (photograph, Z. Radovan)

Inscription **601**
Site Wadi Haggag, rock 5, #131
Technique incised
Condition poor
Content unidentified inscription
Access CR05 (photograph, Z. Radovan)

Inscription **602**
Site Wadi Haggag, rock 3, #125
Technique incised
Condition good
Content Greek inscription
ΜΝΗΣΘΗ
.ΑΔΙΣΟΣ
ΑΛΤΙΡΩΝ
Access CR17 (photograph, Z. Radovan)
Corpus Negev 1977 105

Inscription **603**
Site Wadi Haggag, #118
Technique incised
Condition good
Content rock drawing
Comment *palm branches*
Access CR27 (photograph, Z. Radovan)

Inscription **604**
Site Wadi Haggag, #118
Technique incised
Condition good
Content crosses alone
Comment *many crosses*
Access CR26 (photograph, Z. Radovan)

Inscription **605**
Site Wadi Haggag, #118
Technique scratched
Condition good
Content encircled crosses
Access CR26 (photograph, Z. Radovan)

Inscription **606**
Site Wadi Haggag, #118
Technique incised
Condition good
Content crosses alone
Comment *line of crosses*
Access CR26 (photograph, Z. Radovan)

Inscription **607**
Site Wadi Haggag, #118
Technique incised
Condition good
Content Greek inscription
Limitation *Tentative decipherment only*
Access CR26 (photograph, Z. Radovan)

Inscription **608**
Site Wadi Haggag, #118
Technique incised
Condition good
Content crosses alone
Access CR26 (photograph, Z. Radovan)

Inscription **609**
Site Sinai, unknown, #0
Technique incised
Condition good
Content rock drawing
Comment *ibexes*
Access EM5 (photograph, Project)

Inscription **610**
Site Wadi Haggag, rock 3, #125
Technique incised
Condition poor
Content Greek inscription
Comment *illegible*
Access CR32 (photograph, Z. Radovan)

Inscription **611**
Site Wadi Mukatab, #64
Technique punched
Condition fair
Content Nabatean inscription
Limitation *Tentative decipherment only*
Access CS35 (photograph, Z. Radovan)

Inscription **612**
Site Wadi Mukatab, #64
Technique punched
Condition good
Content Nabatean inscription
Limitation *Tentative decipherment only*
Access CS35 (photograph, Z. Radovan)

Inscription **613**
Site Wadi Mukatab, #64
Technique incised
Condition poor
Content Nabatean inscription
Comment *illegible*
Access CS35 (photograph, Z. Radovan)

Inscription **614**
Site Wadi Mukatab, #64
Technique scratched
Condition fair
Content Nabatean inscription
Limitation *Tentative decipherment only*
Access CS35 (photograph, Z. Radovan)

Inscription **615**
Site Wadi Mukatab, #64
Technique incised
Condition poor
Content Nabatean inscription
Limitation *Tentative decipherment only*
Access CS35 (photograph, Z. Radovan)

Inscription **616**
Site Wadi Mukatab, #64
Technique incised
Condition poor
Content Greek inscription
Limitation *Tentative decipherment only*
Access CQ66 (photograph, Z. Radovan)

Inscription **617**
Site Wadi Mukatab, #64
Technique scratched
Condition good
Content English inscription
Limitation *Tentative decipherment only*
Access CS41 (photograph, Z. Radovan)

Inscription **618**
Site Wadi Mukatab, #64
Technique incised
Condition good
Content Nabatean inscription
Limitation *Tentative decipherment only*
Access CS42 (photograph, Z. Radovan)

Inscription **619**
Site Wadi Mukatab, #64
Technique incised
Condition fair
Content Nabatean inscription
Limitation *Tentative decipherment only*
Access CS47 (photograph, Z. Radovan)

Inscription **620**
Site Wadi Mukatab, #64
Technique incised
Condition fair
Content Nabatean inscription
Limitation *Tentative decipherment only*
Access CS47 (photograph, Z. Radovan)

Inscription **621**
Site Wadi Mukatab, #64
Technique incised
Condition good
Content Nabatean inscription
Limitation *Tentative decipherment only*
Access CS48 (photograph, Z. Radovan)

Inscription **622**
Site Wadi Mukatab, Mukatab 6, #70
Technique incised
Condition good
Content rock drawing
Comment *camel*
Access FK74-75 (photograph, Project)

Inscription **623**
Site Wadi Mukatab, #64
Technique incised
Condition good
Content Nabatean inscription
Limitation *Tentative decipherment only*
Access CS56 (photograph, Z. Radovan)

Inscription **624**
Site Wadi Mukatab, Mukatab 6, #70
Technique incised
Condition poor
Content unidentified inscription
Access FK74-75 (photograph, Project); *see also* FK76-77

Inscription **625**
Site Wadi Mukatab, Mukatab 6, #70
Technique incised
Condition poor
Content rock drawing
Comment *animals*
Access FK74-75 (photograph, Project); *see also* FK76-77

Inscription **626**
Site Wadi Mukatab, Mukatab 6, #70
Technique incised
Condition fair
Content unidentified signs
Comment *circle within a square*
Access FK74-75 (photograph, Project); *see also* FK76-77

Inscription **627**
Site Wadi Mukatab, Mukatab 6, #70
Technique incised
Condition fair
Content Nabatean inscription
Limitation *Tentative decipherment only*
Access FK74-75 (photograph, Project); *see also* FK76-76

Inscription **628**
Site Wadi Mukatab, Mukatab 6, #70
Technique incised
Condition poor
Content unidentified signs
Access FK74-75 (photograph, Project); *see also* FK76-77

Inscription **629**
Site Wadi Umm Sidra, #174
Technique incised
Condition poor
Content Nabatean inscription
Limitation *Tentative decipherment only*
Access FL50-50a (photograph, Project)

Inscription **630**
Site Wadi Umm Sidra, #174
Technique incised
Condition poor
Content Greek inscription
Limitation *Tentative decipherment only*
Access FL50-50a (photograph, Project)

Inscription **632**
Site Wadi Mukatab, #64
Technique incised
Condition fair
Content rock drawing
Comment *animals*
Access CS61 (photograph, Z. Radovan)

Inscription **633**
Site Wadi Mukatab, #64
Technique incised
Condition good
Content unidentified signs
Access CS61 (photograph, Z. Radovan)

Inscription **634**
Site A-Tor, Bir Abu Sueira, #191
Technique incised
Condition good
Content Greek inscription
Limitation *Tentative decipherment only*
Access CT36 (photograph, A. Goren)

Inscription **635**
Site A-Tor, Bir Abu Sueira, #191
Technique incised
Condition fair
Content Greek inscription
Limitation *Tentative decipherment only*
Access CT36 (photograph, A. Goren)

Inscription **636**
Site A-Tor, Bir Abu Sueira, #191
Technique incised
Condition good
Content crosses with inscription
Access CT36 (photograph, A. Goren)

Inscription **637**
Site Ein Hudra, #117
Technique incised
Condition excellent
Content rock drawing
Comment *camel*
Access EX22 (photograph, Project); *see also* EX23

Inscription **638**
Site A-Tor, Bir Abu Sueira, #191
Technique incised
Condition good
Content Arabic inscription
Limitation *Tentative decipherment only*
Access CT36 (photograph, A. Goren)

Inscription **639**
Site A-Tor, Bir Abu Sueira, #191
Technique incised
Condition good
Content Arabic inscription
Limitation *Tentative decipherment only*
Access CT36 (photograph, A. Goren)

Inscription **640**
Site A-Tor, Bir Abu Sueira, #191
Technique incised
Condition good
Content Greek inscription
Limitation *Tentative decipherment only*
Access CT36 (photograph, A. Goren)

Inscription **641**
Site A-Tor, Bir Abu Sueira, #191
Technique incised
Condition poor
Content unidentified inscription
Access CT36 (photograph, A. Goren)

Inscription **642**
Site A-Tor, Bir Abu Sueira, #191
Technique scratched
Condition good
Content Greek inscription
Limitation *Tentative decipherment only*
Access CT08 (photograph, A. Goren)

Inscription **643**
Site A-Tor, Bir Abu Sueira, #191
Dating 1766
Technique scratched
Condition good
Content Greek inscription
Limitation *Tentative decipherment only*
Access CT08 (photograph, A. Goren)

Inscription **644**
Site A-Tor, Bir Abu Sueira, #191
Technique scratched
Condition good
Content Greek inscription
Limitation *Tentative decipherment only*
Comment *fragment*
Access CT08 (photograph, A. Goren)

Inscription **645**
Site A-Tor, Bir Abu Sueira, #191
Technique scratched
Condition fair
Content Greek inscription
Limitation *Tentative decipherment only*
Comment *written in cursive script*
Access CT08 (photograph, A. Goren)

Inscription **646**
Site Wadi Haggag, rock 3, #125
Technique incised
Condition poor
Content Nabatean inscription
Limitation *Tentative decipherment only*
Access ADa03 (photograph, M. Stone)

Inscription **647**
Site Wadi Haggag, rock 3, #125
Technique incised
Condition poor
Content Nabatean inscription
Limitation *Tentative decipherment only*
Access ADa03 (photograph, M. Stone)

Inscription **648**
Site A-Tor, Bir Abu Sueira, #191
Technique scratched
Condition good
Content varied crosses
Access CT08 (photograph, A. Goren)

Inscription **649**
Site A-Tor, Bir Abu Sueira, #191
Technique scratched
Condition fair
Content Greek inscription
Limitation *Tentative decipherment only*
Access CT08 (photograph, A. Goren)

Inscription **650**
Site A-Tor, Bir Abu Sueira, #191
Technique scratched
Condition fair
Content Greek inscription
Limitation *Tentative decipherment only*
Access CT08 (photograph, A. Goren)

Inscription **651**
Site A-Tor, Bir Abu Sueira, #191
Technique scratched
Condition fair
Content Greek inscription
Limitation *Tentative decipherment only*
Access CT08 (photograph, A. Goren)

Inscription **652**
Site A-Tor, Bir Abu Sueira, #191
Technique scratched
Condition good
Content Greek inscription
Limitation *Tentative decipherment only*
Access CT08 (photograph, A. Goren)

Inscription **653**
Site A-Tor, Bir Abu Sueira, #191
Technique scratched
Condition good
Content Arabic inscription
Limitation *Tentative decipherment only*
Access CT08 (photograph, A. Goren)

Inscription **654**
Site A-Tor, Bir Abu Sueira, #191
Technique scratched
Condition fair
Content Arabic inscription
Limitation *Tentative decipherment only*
Access CT06 (photograph, A. Goren)

Inscription **655**
Site Wadi Shellal, Shellal 1, #91
Technique incised
Condition fair
Content rock drawing
Access AFa31-32 (photograph, M. Stone)

Inscription **656**
Site A-Tor, Bir Abu Sueira, #191
Technique incised
Condition good
Content Greek inscription
Limitation *Tentative decipherment only*
Access CT06 (photograph, A. Goren)

Inscription **657**
Site Wadi Tueiba, #226
Technique scratched
Condition fair
Content Greek inscription
Limitation *Tentative decipherment only*
Access CU30a-31 (photograph, A. Goren); *see also* CF09, CU29a-30

Inscription **658**
Site Wadi Tueiba, #226
Technique scratched
Condition poor
Content Latin inscription
Limitation *Tentative decipherment only*
Access CU30a-31 (photograph, A. Goren); *see also* CF09, CF15, CU29a-30

Inscription **659**
Site Wadi Tueiba, #226
Technique scratched
Condition poor
Content Greek inscription
Limitation *Tentative decipherment only*
Access CU30a-31 (photograph, A. Goren); *see also* CF09, CF15, CU29a-30

Inscription **660**
Site Ostrakine, #208
Technique incised
Condition good
Content Coptic inscription
Limitation *Tentative decipherment only*
Access CU18a-19 (photograph, A. Goren); *see also* CU16a-17

Inscription **661**
Site Ostrakine, #208
Technique incised
Condition good
Content varied crosses
Access CU18a-19 (photograph, A. Goren); *see also* CU16a-17

Inscription 662
Site Ostrakine, #208
Technique incised
Condition good
Content rock drawing
Comment *face*
Access CU18a-19 (photograph, A. Goren); *see also* CU16a-17

Inscription 663
Site Wadi Firan, #53
Technique scratched
Condition fair
Content Nabatean inscription
Limitation *Tentative decipherment only*
Access DC69-70 (photograph, A. Goren); *see also* DC67-68

Inscription 664
Site Wadi Firan, #53
Technique scratched
Condition poor
Content Nabatean inscription
Limitation *Tentative decipherment only*
Access DC69-70 (photograph, A. Goren); *see also* DC67-68

Inscription 665
Site Ostrakine, #208
Technique incised
Condition poor
Content Greek inscription
Limitation *Tentative decipherment only*
Access CU06a-07 (photograph, A. Goren); *see also* DC67-68

Inscription 666
Site Ostrakine, #208
Technique incised
Condition good
Content crosses with inscription
Access CU06a-07 (photograph, A. Goren); *see also* CU05a-06

Inscription 667
Site Ostrakine, #208
Technique incised
Condition good
Content rock drawing
Comment *geometric forms*
Access CU06a-07 (photograph, A. Goren); *see also* CU05a-06

Inscription 668
Site Serabit el Khadem, #86
Technique incised
Condition good
Content Greek inscription
Limitation *Tentative decipherment only*
Access DO21 (photograph, A. Goren); *see also* DO20

Inscription 669
Site Serabit el Khadem, #86
Technique incised
Condition fair
Content crosses with inscription
Access DO21 (photograph, A. Goren); *see also* DO20

Inscription 670
Site Serabit el Khadem, #86
Technique incised
Condition good
Content Nabatean inscription
Limitation *Tentative decipherment only*
Access DO21 (photograph, A. Goren); *see also* DO20

Inscription 671
Site Serabit el Khadem, #86
Technique incised
Condition fair
Content Nabatean inscription
Limitation *Tentative decipherment only*
Access DO21 (photograph, A. Goren); *see also* DO20

Inscription 672
Site Serabit el Khadem, #86
Technique scratched
Condition poor
Content Nabatean inscription
Limitation *Tentative decipherment only*
Access DO21 (photograph, A. Goren); *see also* DO20

Inscription 673
Site Serabit el Khadem, #86
Technique scratched
Condition poor
Content Nabatean inscription
Limitation *Tentative decipherment only*
Access DO21 (photograph, A. Goren); *see also* DO20

Inscription 674
Site Serabit el Khadem, #86
Technique incised
Condition good
Content rock drawing
Comment *camels*
Access DO21 (photograph, A. Goren); *see also* DO20

Inscription 675
Site Serabit el Khadem, #86
Technique incised
Condition good
Content Egyptian hieroglyphs
Comment *stele*
Access DF13a-14 (photograph, A. Goren)

Inscription	**676**
Site	Serabit el Khadem, #86
Technique	incised
Condition	good
Content	rock drawing
Comment	*seated figure in Egyptian dress accompanying insc. 675*
Access	DF13a-14 (photograph, A. Goren)

Inscription	**677**
Site	Wadi Mukatab, #64
Technique	incised
Condition	poor
Content	Nabatean inscription
Limitation	*Tentative decipherment only*
Access	CP47 (photograph, Z. Radovan); *see also* CP48

Inscription	**678**
Site	Wadi Mukatab, #64
Technique	incised
Condition	good
Content	crosses with inscription
Access	CP47 (photograph, Z. Radovan); *see also* CP48

Inscription	**679**
Site	Wadi Mukatab, #64
Technique	incised
Condition	fair
Content	Nabatean inscription
Limitation	*Tentative decipherment only*
Access	CP47 (photograph, Z. Radovan); *see also* CP48

Inscription	**680**
Site	Ein Hudra, #117
Technique	incised
Condition	good
Dimensions	270 x 80 cm.
Content	rock drawing
Comment	*camels*
Access	EX14 (photograph, Project); *see also* EX15

Inscription	**681**
Site	Wadi Mukatab, #64
Technique	incised
Condition	good
Content	rock drawing
Comment	*schematic figure of a bird*
Access	CS51 (photograph, Z. Radovan)

Inscription	**682**
Site	Wadi Mukatab, #64
Technique	incised
Condition	fair
Content	Nabatean inscription
Limitation	*Tentative decipherment only*
Access	CS63 (photograph, Z. Radovan)

Inscription	**683**
Site	Wadi Mukatab, #64
Technique	incised
Condition	good
Content	Nabatean inscription šlm ...hršw br .ydw br šlm ʿyydw br ʾwšw bṭb
Access	CS63 (photograph, Z. Radovan)
Corpus	CIS 795b

Inscription	**684**
Site	Wadi Mukatab, #64
Technique	incised
Condition	fair
Content	Nabatean inscription
Limitation	*Tentative decipherment only*
Access	CS63 (photograph, Z. Radovan)

Inscription	**685**
Site	Wadi Mukatab, #64
Technique	incised
Condition	fair
Content	Nabatean inscription
Limitation	*Tentative decipherment only*
Access	CS63 (photograph, Z. Radovan)

Inscription	**686**
Site	Wadi Mukatab, #64
Technique	incised
Condition	fair
Content	Nabatean inscription
Limitation	*Tentative decipherment only*
Access	CS63 (photograph, Z. Radovan)

Inscription	**687**
Site	Wadi Mukatab, #64
Technique	incised
Condition	poor
Content	Nabatean inscription
Comment	*illegible*
Access	CS63 (photograph, Z. Radovan)

Inscription	**688**
Site	Wadi Mukatab, #64
Technique	incised
Condition	good
Content	rock drawing
Comment	*animals*
Access	DA68-69 (photograph, A. Goren)

Inscription	**689**
Site	Wadi Maghara, #72
Technique	incised
Condition	good
Content	Nabatean inscription
Limitation	*Tentative decipherment only*
Access	DO22 (photograph, A. Goren)

Inscription 690
Site Wadi Maghara, #72
Technique relief
Condition good
Content rock drawing
Comment *tableau of one man striking another who is drawing a bow, two men bearing weapons, and a fifth carrying a bow*
Access DO35 (photograph, A. Goren)

Inscription 691
Site Wadi Maghara, #72
Technique relief
Condition good
Content Egyptian hieroglyphs
Access DO35 (photograph, A. Goren); *see also* DI02-03

Inscription 692
Site Wadi Maghara, #72
Technique scratched
Condition fair
Content Nabatean inscription
Limitation *Tentative decipherment only*
Access DO19 (photograph, A. Goren)

Inscription 693
Site Wadi Sreij, ascent, #381
Technique incised
Condition good
Content varied crosses
Comment *numerous forked crosses*
Access GL20 (photograph, Project)

Inscription 694
Site Wadi Sreij, ascent, #381
Technique incised
Condition poor
Content Greek inscription
Limitation *Tentative decipherment only*
Comment *monogram?*
Access GL20 (photograph , Project)

Inscription 695
Site Wadi Maghara, #72
Technique scratched
Condition poor
Content unidentified inscription
Access DO19 (photograph, A. Goren)

Inscription 696
Site Wadi Maghara, #72
Technique relief
Condition excellent
Content rock drawing
Comment *fragmentary Egyptian relief*
Access DO14 (photograph, A. Goren)

Inscription 697
Site Wadi Maghara, #72
Technique relief
Condition good
Content Egyptian hieroglyphs
Access DO14 (photograph, A. Goren); *see also* DH20-21, DI04-05, DI34-35

Inscription 698
Site Wadi Maghara, #72
Technique incised
Condition good
Content Egyptian hieroglyphs
Access DO14 (photograph, A. Goren); *see also* DH18-19, DH22-23, DH24-25, DI04-05, DI06-07, DI08-09, DI32-33, DI34-35

Inscription 699
Site Qunteilat Ajrud, #211
Technique incised
Condition good
Content Greek inscription
Limitation *Tentative decipherment only*
Access DN29 (photograph, A. Goren)

Inscription 700
Site Qunteilat Ajrud, #211
Technique incised
Condition good
Content crosses with inscription
Access DN29 (photograph, A. Goren)

Inscription 701
Site Qunteilat Ajrud, #211
Technique scratched
Condition fair
Content Nabatean inscription
Limitation *Tentative decipherment only*
Access DN29 (photograph, A. Goren)

Inscription 702
Site Qunteilat Ajrud, #211
Technique incised
Condition fair
Content rock drawing
Access DN29 (photograph, A. Goren)

Inscription 703
Site Qunteilat Ajrud, #211
Technique incised
Condition good
Content Nabatean inscription
Limitation *Tentative decipherment only*
Access DN28 (photograph, A. Goren)

Inscription 704
Site Qunteilat Ajrud, #211
Technique incised
Condition good
Content rock drawing
Access DN28 (photograph, A. Goren)

Inscription 705
Site Qunteilat Ajrud, #211
Technique incised
Condition good
Content rock drawing
Access DN24 (photograph, A. Goren)

Inscription **706**
Site Qunteilat Ajrud, #211
Technique incised
Condition good
Content rock drawing
Access DN21 (photograph, A. Goren)

Inscription **707**
Site Sinai, unknown, #0
Technique scratched
Condition fair
Content Nabatean inscription
Limitation *Tentative decipherment only*
Access DM22a-23 (photograph, A. Goren)

Inscription **708**
Site Sinai, unknown, #0
Technique incised
Condition fair
Content rock drawing
Comment *animals*
Access DM22a-23 (photograph, A. Goren)

Inscription **709**
Site Sinai, unknown, #0
Technique scratched
Condition poor
Content Nabatean inscription
Limitation *Tentative decipherment only*
Access DM22a-23 (photograph, A. Goren)

Inscription **710**
Site Sinai, unknown, #0
Technique incised
Condition good
Content Nabatean inscription
Limitation *Tentative decipherment only*
Access DL01 (photograph, A. Goren)

Inscription **711**
Site Qunteilat Ajrud, #211
Technique incised
Condition good
Content unidentified signs
Access DL01 (photograph, A. Goren)

Inscription **712**
Site Sinai, unknown, #0
Technique incised
Condition good
Content rock drawing
Comment *group of humans mounted and on foot, bearing weapons*
Access DK25a-26 (photograph, A. Goren); *see also* DK26a-27

Inscription **713**
Site Sinai, unknown, #0
Technique incised
Condition good
Content rock drawing
Comment *camels with riders*
Access DK23a-24 (photograph, A. Goren)

Inscription **714**
Site Sinai, unknown, #0
Technique incised
Condition good
Content rock drawing
Comment *camels with riders*
Access DK22a-23 (photograph, A. Goren)

Inscription **715**
Site Sinai, unknown, #0
Technique incised
Condition good
Content rock drawing
Comment *man on horseback*
Access DK21a-22 (photograph, A. Goren)

Inscription **716**
Site Sinai, unknown, #0
Technique incised
Condition good
Content rock drawing
Comment *horse with rider*
Access DK20a-21 (photograph, A. Goren)

Inscription **717**
Site Sinai, unknown, #0
Technique incised
Condition poor
Content rock drawing
Comment *horse with rider*
Access DK18a-19 (photograph, A. Goren); *see also* FE07

Inscription **718**
Site Sinai, unknown, #0
Technique incised
Condition poor
Content rock drawing
Comment *animal with rider*
Access DK17a-18 (photograph, A. Goren)

Inscription **719**
Site Sinai, unknown, #0
Technique incised
Condition poor
Content rock drawing
Comment *animal*
Access DK15a-16 (photograph, A. Goren); *see also* DK20a-21

Inscription **720**
Site Sinai, unknown, #0
Technique incised
Condition poor
Content rock drawing
Comment *human figures*
Access DK16a-17 (photograph, A. Goren)

Inscription 721
Site Sinai, unknown, #0
Technique incised
Condition good
Content rock drawing
Comment *camel with rider*
Access DK14a-15 (photograph, A. Goren); *see also* DK20a-21

Inscription 722
Site Sinai, unknown, #0
Technique incised
Condition good
Content rock drawing
Comment *geese*
Access DK13a-14 (photograph, A. Goren); *see also* DK20a-21

Inscription 723
Site Sinai, unknown, #0
Technique incised
Condition fair
Content rock drawing
Comment *unclear*
Access DK11a-12 (photograph, A. Goren)

Inscription 724
Site Sinai, unknown, #0
Technique incised
Condition good
Content rock drawing
Comment *two camels, three men bearing weapons*
Access DK10a-11 (photograph, A. Goren)

Inscription 725
Site Sinai, unknown, #0
Technique incised
Condition fair
Content rock drawing
Comment *armed man on horseback*
Access DK09a-10 (photograph, A. Goren)

Inscription 726
Site Sinai, unknown, #0
Technique incised
Condition good
Content rock drawing
Comment *human figures*
Access DK07a-08 (photograph, A. Goren); *see also* DK08a-09

Inscription 727
Site Sinai, unknown, #0
Technique incised
Condition fair
Content rock drawing
Comment *horse with rider*
Access DK06a-07 (photograph, A. Goren)

Inscription 728
Site Sinai, unknown, #0
Technique incised
Condition fair
Content rock drawing
Comment *animals*
Access DK05a-06 (photograph, A. Goren)

Inscription 729
Site Sinai, unknown, #0
Technique incised
Condition poor
Content rock drawing
Comment *horses with riders*
Access DK04a-05 (photograph, A. Goren)

Inscription 730
Site Sinai, unknown, #0
Technique incised
Condition good
Content rock drawing
Comment *man on foot, leading a man on horseback*
Access DK02a-03 (photograph, A. Goren); *see also* DK03a-04

Inscription 731
Site Sinai, unknown, #0
Technique incised
Condition poor
Content rock drawing
Comment *humans*
Access DK01a-02 (photograph, A. Goren); *see also* DK0a-01

Inscription 732
Site Wadi Baba, Baba 1, #190
Technique incised
Condition good
Content Nabatean inscription
Limitation *Tentative decipherment only*
Access DJ52-53 (photograph, A. Goren)

Inscription 733
Site Wadi Baba, Baba 1, #190
Technique incised
Condition fair
Content Nabatean inscription
Limitation *Tentative decipherment only*
Access DJ52-53 (photograph, A. Goren)

Inscription 734
Site Wadi Baba, Baba 1, #190
Technique incised
Condition good
Content Nabatean inscription
Limitation *Tentative decipherment only*
Access DJ52-53 (photograph, A. Goren)

Inscription 735
Site Wadi Baba, Baba 1, #190
Technique incised
Condition fair
Content Nabatean inscription
Limitation *Tentative decipherment only*
Access DJ52-53 (photograph, A. Goren)

Inscription 736
Site Wadi Baba, Baba 1, #190
Technique scratched
Condition poor
Content Nabatean inscription
Limitation *Tentative decipherment only*
Access DJ52-53 (photograph, A. Goren)

Inscription 737
Site Wadi Baba, Baba 1, #190
Technique incised
Condition fair
Content Nabatean inscription
Limitation *Tentative decipherment only*
Access DJ52-53 (photograph, A. Goren)

Inscription 738
Site Wadi Baba, Baba 1, #190
Technique incised
Condition good
Content unidentified inscription
Access DJ52-53 (photograph, A. Goren)

Inscription 739
Site Wadi Baba, Baba 1, #190
Technique incised
Condition good
Content Nabatean inscription
Limitation *Tentative decipherment only*
Access DJ50-51 (photograph, A. Goren)

Inscription 740
Site Wadi Baba, Baba 1, #190
Technique incised
Condition good
Content Nabatean inscription
Limitation *Tentative decipherment only*
Access DJ50-51 (photograph, A. Goren)

Inscription 741
Site Wadi Baba, Baba 1, #190
Technique incised
Condition good
Content Nabatean inscription
Limitation *Tentative decipherment only*
Access DJ50-51 (photograph, A. Goren)

Inscription 742
Site Wadi Baba, Baba 1, #190
Technique incised
Condition good
Content Nabatean inscription
Limitation *Tentative decipherment only*
Access DJ50-51 (photograph, A. Goren)

Inscription 743
Site Wadi Baba, Baba 1, #190
Technique incised
Condition good
Content Nabatean inscription
Limitation *Tentative decipherment only*
Access DJ50-51 (photograph, A. Goren)

Inscription 744
Site Wadi Baba, Baba 1, #190
Technique incised
Condition fair
Content Nabatean inscription
Limitation *Tentative decipherment only*
Access DJ50-51 (photograph, A. Goren)

Inscription 745
Site Wadi Baba, Baba 1, #190
Technique incised
Condition fair
Content Nabatean inscription
Limitation *Tentative decipherment only*
Access DJ50-51 (photograph, A. Goren)

Inscription 746
Site Wadi Baba, Baba 1, #190
Technique incised
Condition good
Content Nabatean inscription
Limitation *Tentative decipherment only*
Access DJ50-51 (photograph, A. Goren)

Inscription 747
Site Wadi Baba, Baba 1, #190
Technique incised
Condition fair
Content Nabatean inscription
Limitation *Tentative decipherment only*
Access DJ50-51 (photograph, A. Goren)

Inscription 748
Site Wadi Baba, Baba 1, #190
Technique incised
Condition fair
Content rock drawing
Comment *ibexes*
Access DJ50-51 (photograph, A. Goren)

Inscription 749
Site Wadi Baba, Baba 1, #190
Technique incised
Condition good
Content rock drawing
Comment *camel*
Access DJ50-51 (photograph, A. Goren)

Inscription 750
Site Wadi Baba, Baba 1, #190
Technique incised
Condition good
Content unidentified sign
Access DJ50-51 (photograph, A. Goren)

Inscription 751
Site Wadi Mukatab, Mukatab 7, #71
Technique incised
Condition good
Content wasems & other Bedouin marks
Access CM64 (photograph, Z. Radovan)

Inscription **752**
Site Wadi Mukatab, Mukatab 7, #71
Technique incised
Condition good
Content Nabatean inscription
Limitation *Tentative decipherment only*
Access CM64 (photograph, Z. Radovan)

Inscription **753**
Site Wadi Mukatab, Mukatab 7, #71
Technique incised
Condition good
Content Nabatean inscription
Limitation *Tentative decipherment only*
Access CM64 (photograph, Z. Radovan)

Inscription **754**
Site Wadi Leja, #27
Technique scratched
Condition fair
Content Nabatean inscription
Limitation *Tentative decipherment only*
Access CV29 (photograph, A. Goren)

Inscription **755**
Site Wadi Baba, #216
Technique scratched
Condition good
Content rock drawing
Access CY06 (photograph, A. Goren)

Inscription **756**
Site Naqb Sara, #309
Technique incised
Condition fair
Content Nabatean inscription
Limitation *Tentative decipherment only*
Access CY20 (photograph, A. Goren)

Inscription **757**
Site Naqb Sara, #309
Technique incised
Condition fair
Content Nabatean inscription
Limitation *Tentative decipherment only*
Access CY20 (photograph, A. Goren)

Inscription **758**
Site Naqb Sara, #309
Technique incised
Condition good
Content unidentified signs
Access CY21 (photograph, A. Goren); *see also* CY30

Inscription **759**
Site Serabit el Khadem, #86
Technique scratched
Condition good
Content encircled crosses
Access DO17 (photograph, A. Goren)

Inscription **760**
Site Serabit el Khadem, #86
Technique scratched
Condition good
Content rock drawing
Comment *humans and animals*
Access DO17 (photograph, A. Goren)

Inscription **761**
Site Wadi Mukatab, #64
Technique incised
Condition fair
Content rock drawing
Comment *ibex and other animals*
Access DN37 (photograph, A. Goren)

Inscription **762**
Site Wadi Mukatab, #64
Technique incised
Condition fair
Content Nabatean inscription
Limitation *Tentative decipherment only*
Access DN32 (photograph, A. Goren); *see also* DN35

Inscription **763**
Site Wadi Mukatab, #64
Technique incised
Condition fair
Content Nabatean inscription
Limitation *Tentative decipherment only*
Access DN32 (photograph, A. Goren)

Inscription **764**
Site Wadi Mukatab, #64
Technique incised
Condition poor
Content Nabatean inscription
Limitation *Tentative decipherment only*
Access DN32 (photograph, A. Goren)

Inscription **765**
Site Wadi Haggag, rock 3 area 1, #126
Technique incised
Condition fair
Content rock drawing
Comment *ibexes*
Access ACc17 (photograph, M. Stone); *see also* AX20, AX21

Inscription **766**
Site Wadi Haggag, rock 3 area 1, #126
Technique incised
Condition poor
Content Greek inscription
Limitation *Tentative decipherment only*
Access ACc17 (photograph, M. Stone); *see also* AX20, AX21

Inscription **767**
Site Wadi Mukatab, #64
Technique incised
Condition fair
Content Nabatean inscription
Limitation *Tentative decipherment only*
Access DN32 (photograph, A. Goren); *see also* DN36

Inscription **768**
Site Wadi Mukatab, #64
Technique incised
Condition fair
Content rock drawing
Comment *human*
Access DN32 (photograph, A. Goren)

Inscription **769**
Site Wadi Mukatab, #64
Technique incised
Condition good
Content Greek inscription
Limitation *Tentative decipherment only*
Access DN32 (photograph, A. Goren)

Inscription **770**
Site Wadi Mukatab, #64
Technique incised
Condition good
Content rock drawing
Comment *figure with upraised hands*
Access DN32 (photograph, A. Goren); *see also* DN35

Inscription **771**
Site Wadi Mukatab, #64
Technique incised
Condition fair
Content rock drawing
Comment *wolf (?)*
Access DM09a-10 (photograph, A. Goren)

Inscription **772**
Site Wadi Mukatab, #64
Technique incised
Condition fair
Content Old North Arabic inscription
Limitation *Tentative decipherment only*
Access DM09a-10 (photograph, A. Goren)

Inscription **773**
Site Wadi Mukatab, #64
Technique scratched
Condition good
Content Nabatean inscription
Limitation *Tentative decipherment only*
Access DM06a-07 (photograph, A. Goren)

Inscription **774**
Site Wadi Mukatab, #64
Technique scratched
Condition fair
Content Nabatean inscription
Limitation *Tentative decipherment only*
Access DM07a-08 (photograph, A. Goren); *see also* DL05

Inscription **775**
Site Wadi Mukatab, #64
Technique scratched
Condition poor
Content Arabic inscription
Limitation *Tentative decipherment only*
Access DM07a-08 (photograph, A. Goren); *see also* DL05

Inscription **776**
Site Wadi Mukatab, #64
Technique incised
Condition good
Content rock drawing
Comment *warriors riding camels and horses*
Access DK28a-29 (photograph, A. Goren); *see also* DK29a-30

Inscription **777**
Site Wadi Mukatab, #64
Technique incised
Condition good
Content rock drawing
Comment *warriors riding camels and horses*
Access DK29a-30 (photograph, A. Goren); *see also* DK30a-31

Inscription **778**
Site Wadi Mukatab, #64
Technique incised
Condition good
Content rock drawing
Comment *warriors riding camels and horses*
Access DK30a-31 (photograph, A. Goren); *see also* DK31a-32

Inscription **779**
Site Wadi Mukatab, #64
Technique incised
Condition good
Content rock drawing
Comment *warriors riding camels and horses*
Access DK31a-32 (photograph, A. Goren); *see also* DK32a-33

Inscription **780**
Site Wadi Mukatab, #64
Technique incised
Condition good
Content rock drawing
Comment *warriors riding camels and horses*
Access DK32a-33 (photograph, A. Goren); *see also* DK33a-34, DK34a-35

Inscription **781**
Site Wadi Mukatab, #64
Technique incised
Condition good
Content rock drawing
Comment *warriors riding camels and horses*
Access DK34a-35 (photograph, A. Goren)

Inscription **782**
Site Wadi Haggag, rock 3, #125
Technique incised
Condition good
Content Greek inscription
ΜΝΗΣΘΗ
ΤΟ ΔΕΟΣ
ΜΑ ΣΟΥ ΔΟΥ
Access CQ66 (photograph, Z. Radovan)
Corpus Negev 1977 89

Inscription **783**
Site Wadi Haggag, rock 3, #125
Technique incised
Condition good
Content crosses with inscription
Comment *cross accompanying insc. 782*
Access CQ66 (photograph, Z. Radovan); *see also* Negev 1977 figs. 63 and 065

Inscription **784**
Site Wadi Haggag, rock 3, #125
Technique incised
Condition fair
Content Greek inscription
Limitation *Tentative decipherment only*
Access CQ66 (photograph, Z. Radovan)

Inscription **785**
Site Wadi Haggag, rock 3, #125
Technique incised
Condition fair
Content Arabic inscription
Limitation *Tentative decipherment only*
Access CQ66 (photograph, Z. Radovan)

Inscription **786**
Site Wadi Haggag, rock 3, #125
Technique incised
Condition good
Content Greek inscription
Limitation *Tentative decipherment only*
Access CQ66 (photograph, Z. Radovan)

Inscription **787**
Site Wadi Haggag, rock 3, #125
Technique incised
Condition good
Content crosses alone
Access CQ66 (photograph, Z. Radovan)

Inscription **788**
Site Jebel Umm Shumer, Bir Ramhan, #5
Technique scratched
Condition fair
Content Greek inscription
Limitation *Tentative decipherment only*
Access DQ01 (photograph, I. Finkelstein); *see also* DQ02

Inscription **789**
Site Jebel Umm Shumer, Bir Ramhan, #5
Technique scratched
Condition fair
Content Greek inscription
Limitation *Tentative decipherment only*
Access DQ01 (photograph, I. Finkelstein); *see also* DQ02

Inscription **790**
Site Jebel Umm Shumer, Bir Ramhan, #5
Technique scratched
Condition good
Content Greek inscription
Limitation *Tentative decipherment only*
Access DQ02 (photograph, I. Finkelstein)

Inscription **791**
Site Jebel Umm Shumer, Bir Ramhan, #5
Technique scratched
Condition good
Content Greek inscription
Limitation *Tentative decipherment only*
Access DQ02 (photograph, I. Finkelstein)

Inscription **792**
Site Wadi Haggag, #118
Technique scratched
Condition poor
Content Nabatean inscription
Limitation *Tentative decipherment only*
Access DD16-17 (photograph, A. Goren)

Inscription **793**
Site Wadi Haggag, #118
Technique scratched
Condition fair
Content Nabatean inscription
Limitation *Tentative decipherment only*
Access DD16-17 (photograph, A. Goren)

Inscription **794**
Site Wadi Haggag, #118
Technique scratched
Condition poor
Content Nabatean inscription
Limitation *Tentative decipherment only*
Access DD16-17 (photograph, A. Goren)

Inscription **795**
Site Wadi Wata, #225
Technique scratched
Condition poor
Content Nabatean inscription
Limitation *Tentative decipherment only*
Access CZ62-63 (photograph, A. Goren); *see also* CZ66-67

Inscription **796**
Site Wadi Wata, #225
Technique scratched
Condition good
Content Nabatean inscription
Limitation *Tentative decipherment only*
Access CZ62-63 (photograph, A. Goren); *see also* CZ66-67

Inscription **797**
Site Wadi Wata, #225
Technique scratched
Condition poor
Content Nabatean inscription
Limitation *Tentative decipherment only*
Access CZ62-63 (photograph, A. Goren)

Inscription **798**
Site Wadi Mukatab, #64
Technique incised
Condition good
Content Nabatean inscription
Limitation *Tentative decipherment only*
Access CM53 (photograph, Z. Radovan)

Inscription **799**
Site Wadi Haggag, #118
Technique incised
Condition excellent
Dimensions 105 x 65 cm.
Content rock drawing
Comment *three camels with riders*
Access EZ18 (photograph, Project); *see also* EZ19, EZ20

Inscription **800**
Site Wadi Mukatab, #64
Technique scratched
Condition poor
Content Nabatean inscription
Limitation *Tentative decipherment only*
Access CM45 (photograph, Z. Radovan)

Inscription **801**
Site Wadi Mukatab, #64
Technique incised
Condition fair
Content Nabatean inscription
Limitation *Tentative decipherment only*
Access CM53 (photograph, Z. Radovan)

Inscription **802**
Site Vale of John, Jebel Ṣafṣafa, #379
Technique scratched
Condition poor
Content Greek inscription
Limitation *Tentative decipherment only*
Access GL25 (photograph, Project)

Inscription **803**
Site Wadi Mukatab, #64
Technique incised
Condition good
Content Nabatean inscription
Limitation *Tentative decipherment only*
Comment *perhaps continuation of insc. 496*
Access CM53 (photograph, Z. Radovan)

Inscription **804**
Site Wadi Mukatab, #64
Technique scratched
Condition poor
Content Nabatean inscription
Limitation *Tentative decipherment only*
Access CM53 (photograph, Z. Radovan)

Inscription **805**
Site Wadi Mukatab, #64
Technique scratched
Condition poor
Content Nabatean inscription
Limitation *Tentative decipherment only*
Access CM53 (photograph, Z. Radovan)

Inscription **806**
Site Wadi Mukatab, #64
Technique scratched
Condition fair
Content Nabatean inscription
Limitation *Tentative decipherment only*
Access CM53 (photograph, Z. Radovan)

Inscription **807**
Site Wadi Mukatab, #64
Technique scratched
Condition poor
Content Nabatean inscription
Limitation *Tentative decipherment only*
Access CM53 (photograph, Z. Radovan)

Inscription **808**
Site Wadi Mukatab, #64
Technique scratched
Condition fair
Content Nabatean inscription
Limitation *Tentative decipherment only*
Access CM53 (photograph, Z. Radovan)

Inscription **809**
Site Wadi Mukatab, #64
Technique scratched
Condition fair
Content Nabatean inscription
Limitation *Tentative decipherment only*
Access CM53 (photograph, Z. Radovan)

Inscription	**810**
Site	Naqb Sara, #309
Technique	incised
Condition	fair
Content	Nabatean inscription
Limitation	*Tentative decipherment only*
Access	CY34 (photograph, A. Goren)

Inscription	**811**
Site	Naqb Sara, #309
Technique	scratched
Condition	poor
Content	unidentified inscription
Comment	*Nabatean?*
Access	CY33 (photograph, A. Goren)

Inscription	**812**
Site	Naqb Sara, #309
Technique	incised
Condition	fair
Content	unidentified inscription
Access	CY35 (photograph, A. Goren)

Inscription	**813**
Site	Jebel Sirbal, Wadi Rim, #186
Technique	scratched
Condition	poor
Content	Nabatean inscription
Limitation	*Tentative decipherment only*
Access	DD14-15 (photograph, A. Goren)

Inscription	**814**
Site	Wadi Mukatab, #64
Technique	incised
Condition	poor
Content	Nabatean inscription
Limitation	*Tentative decipherment only*
Access	CM56 (photograph, Z. Radovan)

Inscription	**815**
Site	Wadi Mukatab, #64
Technique	incised
Condition	good
Content	Nabatean inscription
Limitation	*Tentative decipherment only*
Access	CM56 (photograph, Z. Radovan)

Inscription	**816**
Site	Wadi Mukatab, #64
Technique	scratched
Condition	poor
Content	Nabatean inscription
Limitation	*Tentative decipherment only*
Access	CM56 (photograph, Z. Radovan)

Inscription	**817**
Site	Wadi Mukatab, #64
Technique	incised
Condition	poor
Content	Nabatean inscription
Limitation	*Tentative decipherment only*
Access	CM56 (photograph, Z. Radovan)

Inscription	**818**
Site	Wadi Mukatab, #64
Technique	incised
Condition	poor
Content	Nabatean inscription
Limitation	*Tentative decipherment only*
Access	CM63 (photograph, Z. Radovan); *see also* CM62

Inscription	**819**
Site	Wadi Mukatab, #64
Technique	incised
Condition	poor
Content	unidentified inscription
Comment	*Greek?*
Access	ACc17 (photograph, M. Stone); *see also* AX20, AX21

Inscription	**820**
Site	Wadi Mukatab, #64
Technique	incised
Condition	good
Content	rock drawing
Comment	*warrior riding a horse*
Access	CM63 (photograph, Z. Radovan); *see also* CM62

Inscription	**821**
Site	Wadi Mukatab, #64
Technique	incised
Condition	good
Content	Nabatean inscription
Limitation	*Tentative decipherment only*
Access	CN91 (photograph, Z. Radovan)

Inscription	**822**
Site	Wadi Mukatab, #64
Technique	incised
Condition	poor
Content	rock drawing
Comment	*unidentifiable traces of a drawing*
Access	CO06 (photograph, Z. Radovan)

Inscription	**823**
Site	Wadi Mukatab, #64
Technique	incised
Condition	fair
Content	rock drawing
Comment	*humans fighting*
Access	CO13 (photograph, Z. Radovan)

Inscription	**824**
Site	Wadi Mukatab, #64
Technique	incised
Condition	poor
Content	Nabatean inscription
Limitation	*Tentative decipherment only*
Access	CO29 (photograph, Z. Radovan)

Inscription	**825**
Site	Wadi Mukatab, #64
Technique	scratched
Condition	poor
Content	unidentified inscription
Access	CO27 (photograph, Z. Radovan)

Inscription **826**
Site Wadi Mukatab, #64
Technique incised
Condition fair
Content Nabatean inscription
Limitation *Tentative decipherment only*
Access CP45 (photograph, Z. Radovan); *see also* CP46

Inscription **827**
Site Wadi Haggag, rock 3, #125
Technique incised
Condition fair
Content unidentified inscription
Access CQ74 (photograph, Z. Radovan)

Inscription **828**
Site Wadi Haggag, rock 3, #125
Technique incised
Condition good
Content crosses alone
Access CQ74 (photograph, Z. Radovan)

Inscription **829**
Site Wadi Haggag, rock 3, #125
Technique incised
Condition good
Content rock drawing
Comment *triangle*
Access CQ74 (photograph, Z. Radovan)

Inscription **830**
Site Wadi Haggag, rock 3, #125
Technique incised
Condition fair
Content Greek inscription
Limitation *Tentative decipherment only*
Comment *fragment*
Access CQ76 (photograph, Z. Radovan)

Inscription **831**
Site Wadi Haggag, rock 3, #125
Technique scratched
Condition poor
Content Greek inscription
Limitation *Tentative decipherment only*
Access CR04 (photograph, Z. Radovan)

Inscription **832**
Site Wadi Haggag, rock 5, #131
Technique incised
Condition poor
Content Nabatean inscription
Limitation *Tentative decipherment only*
Access CR05 (photograph, Z. Radovan)

Inscription **833**
Site Wadi Haggag, rock 5, #131
Technique incised
Condition good
Content Nabatean inscription
Limitation *Tentative decipherment only*
Access CR05 (photograph, Z. Radovan)

Inscription **834**
Site Wadi Haggag, rock 3 area 1, #126
Technique scratched
Condition poor
Content Greek inscription
Limitation *Tentative decipherment only*
Access ACc17 (photograph, M. Stone); *see also* AX20, AX21

Inscription **835**
Site Wadi Haggag, rock 6, #135
Technique incised
Condition good
Content crosses with inscription
Comment *cross accompanying insc. 609*
Access CR32 (photograph, Z. Radovan)

Inscription **836**
Site Wadi Mukatab, #64
Technique incised
Condition poor
Content Nabatean inscription
Limitation *Tentative decipherment only*
Access CS59 (photograph, Z. Radovan)

Inscription **837**
Site A-Tor, Bir Abu Sueira, #191
Technique incised
Condition fair
Content Arabic inscription
Limitation *Tentative decipherment only*
Access CT06 (photograph, A. Goren)

Inscription **838**
Site A-Tor, Bir Abu Sueira, #191
Technique scratched
Condition fair
Content rock drawing
Access CT06 (photograph, A. Goren)

Inscription **839**
Site A-Tor, Bir Abu Sueira, #191
Technique scratched
Condition poor
Content Arabic inscription
Limitation *Tentative decipherment only*
Access CT06 (photograph, A. Goren)

Inscription **840**
Site Wadi Tueiba, #226
Technique scratched
Condition fair
Content Arabic inscription
Limitation *Tentative decipherment only*
Access CU30a-31 (photograph, A. Goren); *see also* CU29a-30

Inscription **841**
Site Wadi Firan, #53
Technique scratched
Condition poor
Content unidentified inscription
Comment *Latin?*
Access DC69-70 (photograph, A. Goren); *see also* DC67-68

Inscription 842
Site Serabit el Khadem, #86
Technique incised
Condition fair
Content Nabatean inscription
Limitation *Tentative decipherment only*
Access DO21 (photograph, A. Goren); *see also* DO20

Inscription 843
Site Serabit el Khadem, #86
Technique incised
Condition fair
Content Nabatean inscription
Limitation *Tentative decipherment only*
Access DO21 (photograph, A. Goren); *see also* DO20

Inscription 844
Site Wadi Mukatab, #64
Technique incised
Condition fair
Content Nabatean inscription
Limitation *Tentative decipherment only*
Access CP47 (photograph, Z. Radovan); *see also* CP48

Inscription 845
Site Wadi Mukatab, #64
Technique incised
Condition poor
Content Nabatean inscription
Limitation *Tentative decipherment only*
Access CP47 (photograph, Z. Radovan); *see also* CP48

Inscription 846
Site Wadi Maghara, #72
Technique incised
Condition good
Content unidentified signs
Access DO22 (photograph, A. Goren)

Inscription 847
Site Naqb Sara, #309
Technique incised
Condition fair
Content Nabatean inscription
Limitation *Tentative decipherment only*
Access CY34 (photograph, A. Goren)

Inscription 848
Site Sinai, unknown, #0
Technique scratched
Condition poor
Content unidentified inscription
Access DK14a-15 (photograph, A. Goren)

Inscription 849
Site Sinai, unknown, #0
Technique scratched
Condition poor
Content unidentified inscription
Access DK09a-10 (photograph, A. Goren)

Inscription 850
Site Wadi Baba, Baba 1, #190
Technique incised
Condition good
Content Nabatean inscription
Limitation *Tentative decipherment only*
Access DJ52-53 (photograph, A. Goren)

Inscription 851
Site Wadi Baba, Baba 1, #190
Technique scratched
Condition good
Content unidentified signs
Access DJ52-53 (photograph, A. Goren)

Inscription 852
Site Wadi Baba, Baba 1, #190
Technique incised
Condition good
Content Arabic inscription
Limitation *Tentative decipherment only*
Access DJ52-53 (photograph, A. Goren)

Inscription 853
Site Wadi Baba, Baba 1, #190
Technique scratched
Condition fair
Content Old North Arabic inscription
Limitation *Tentative decipherment only*
Access DJ52-53 (photograph, A. Goren)

Inscription 854
Site Sinai, unknown, #0
Technique incised
Condition fair
Content unidentified inscription
Access DM09a-10 (photograph, A. Goren)

Inscription 855
Site Sinai, unknown, #0
Technique scratched
Condition poor
Content Nabatean inscription
Comment *illegible*
Access DM09a-10 (photograph, A. Goren)

Inscription 856
Site Sinai, unknown, #0
Technique scratched
Condition poor
Content Nabatean inscription
Comment *illegible*
Access DM09a-10 (photograph, A. Goren)

Inscription 857
Site Sinai, unknown, #0
Technique scratched
Condition poor
Content Nabatean inscription
Limitation *Tentative decipherment only*
Access DM09a-10 (photograph, A. Goren)

Inscription **858**
Site Sinai, unknown, #0
Technique scratched
Condition poor
Content unidentified inscription
Access DM09a-10 (photograph, A. Goren)

Inscription **859**
Site Sinai, unknown, #0
Technique scratched
Condition fair
Content unidentified inscription
Access DM09a-10 (photograph, A. Goren)

Inscription **860**
Site Sinai, unknown, #0
Technique scratched
Condition fair
Content Nabatean inscription
Limitation *Tentative decipherment only*
Comment *fragment*
Access DM06a-07 (photograph, A. Goren)

Inscription **861**
Site Sinai, unknown, #0
Technique scratched
Condition fair
Content rock drawing
Comment *people riding camels*
Access DM06a-07 (photograph, A. Goren)

Inscription **862**
Site Sinai, unknown, #0
Technique scratched
Condition poor
Content Old North Arabic inscription
Limitation *Tentative decipherment only*
Access DM06a-07 (photograph, A. Goren)

Inscription **863**
Site Sinai, unknown, #0
Technique scratched
Condition poor
Content unidentified inscription
Access DM06a-07 (photograph, A. Goren)

Inscription **864**
Site Sinai, unknown, #0
Technique scratched
Condition poor
Content unidentified inscription
Access DM06a-07 (photograph, A. Goren)

Inscription **865**
Site Wadi Haggag, rock 3 area 1, #126
Technique incised
Condition poor
Content Greek inscription
Limitation *Tentative decipherment only*
Access ACc17 (photograph, M. Stone); *see also* AX20, AX21, Negev 1977 fig. 115

Inscription **866**
Site Wadi Haggag, rock 3 area 1, #126
Technique incised
Condition poor
Content Greek inscription
Limitation *Tentative decipherment only*
Comment *possibly Latin*
Access ACc17 (photograph, M. Stone); *see also* AX20, AX21

Inscription **867**
Site Wadi Arade Lesser, Arade 1, #140
Technique incised
Condition good
Content Nabatean inscription
Limitation *Tentative decipherment only*
Access ACd21 (photograph, M. Stone)

Inscription **868**
Site Wadi Haggag, rock 3, #125
Technique incised
Condition good
Content unidentified signs
Access ADc09 (photograph, M. Stone)

Inscription **869**
Site Wadi Haggag, rock 3, #125
Technique incised
Condition good
Content Nabatean inscription
Limitation *Tentative decipherment only*
Access ADa03 (photograph, M. Stone)

Inscription **870**
Site Jebel Musa, #19
Technique incised
Condition poor
Content Greek inscription
Limitation *Tentative decipherment only*
Access AHe43-44 (photograph, M. Stone); *see also* AHe43-44, AHg69-70

Inscription **871**
Site Jebel Musa, #19
Technique scratched
Condition poor
Content unidentified inscription
Access AHe43-44 (photograph, M. Stone)

Inscription **872**
Site Wadi Haggag, rock 3 area 1, #126
Technique incised
Condition poor
Content Greek inscription
Limitation *Tentative decipherment only*
Access ADg32 (photograph, M. Stone)

Inscription **873**
Site Wadi Haggag, rock 3 area 1, #126
Technique incised
Condition good
Content crosses with inscription
Access ADg32 (photograph, M. Stone)

Inscription 874
Site Wadi Shellal, Shellal 1, #91
Technique incised
Condition good
Content Nabatean inscription
Limitation *Tentative decipherment only*
Comment *Only part of the inscription appears in the photograph.*
Access AFa31-32 (photograph, M. Stone)

Inscription 875
Site Wadi Haggag, rock 3 area 3, #128
Technique incised
Condition fair
Content Nabatean inscription
Limitation *Tentative decipherment only*
Access ABd23 (photograph, M. Stone)

Inscription 876
Site Wadi Haggag, rock 3, #125
Technique incised
Condition poor
Content unidentified inscription
Access CQ66 (photograph, Z. Radovan)

Inscription 877
Site Wadi Haggag, rock 3, #125
Technique incised
Condition good
Content crosses with inscription
Access CQ66 (photograph, Z. Radovan)

Inscription 878
Site Wadi Haggag, rock 3, #125
Technique incised
Condition fair
Content Greek inscription
Limitation *Tentative decipherment only*
Access CQ66 (photograph, Z. Radovan)

Inscription 879
Site Wadi Haggag, rock 3, #125
Technique incised
Condition fair
Content Greek inscription
Limitation *Tentative decipherment only*
Access CQ66 (photograph, Z. Radovan)

Inscription 880
Site Wadi Haggag, rock 3, #125
Technique incised
Condition poor
Content Greek inscription
Limitation *Tentative decipherment only*
Access CQ66 (photograph, Z. Radovan)

Inscription 881
Site Wadi Haggag, rock 3, #125
Technique incised
Condition fair
Content crosses with inscription
Access CQ66 (photograph, Z. Radovan)

Inscription 882
Site Wadi Haggag, rock 3, #125
Technique incised
Condition good
Content Greek inscription
Limitation *Tentative decipherment only*
Access CQ66 (photograph, Z. Radovan)

Inscription 883
Site Wadi Mukatab, #64
Technique incised
Condition good
Content Nabatean inscription
Limitation *Tentative decipherment only*
Access CS44 (photograph, Z. Radovan)

Inscription 884
Site Wadi Mukatab, #64
Technique incised
Condition fair
Content Nabatean inscription
Limitation *Tentative decipherment only*
Access CS44 (photograph, Z. Radovan)

Inscription 885
Site Wadi Mukatab, #64
Technique incised
Condition good
Content unidentified signs
Access CS44 (photograph, Z. Radovan)

Inscription 886
Site Wadi Mukatab, #64
Technique incised
Condition poor
Content Nabatean inscription
Limitation *Tentative decipherment only*
Access CS44 (photograph, Z. Radovan)

Inscription 887
Site Wadi Mukatab, #64
Technique incised
Condition poor
Content unidentified inscription
Access CS44 (photograph, Z. Radovan)

Inscription 888
Site Wadi Mukatab, #64
Technique incised
Condition good
Content wasems & other Bedouin marks
Access CS37 (photograph, Z. Radovan)

Inscription 889
Site Wadi Mukatab, #64
Technique incised
Condition poor
Content unidentified inscription
Access CS37 (photograph, Z. Radovan)

Inscription **890**
Site A-Tor, Bir Abu Sueira, #191
Technique incised
Condition fair
Content Nabatean inscription
Limitation *Tentative decipherment only*
Access DA72-73 (photograph, A. Goren)

Inscription **891**
Site A-Tor, Bir Abu Sueira, #191
Technique incised
Condition good
Content Nabatean inscription
Limitation *Tentative decipherment only*
Access DA72-73 (photograph, A. Goren)

Inscription **892**
Site A-Tor, Bir Abu Sueira, #191
Technique incised
Condition poor
Content rock drawing
Comment *animals*
Access DA72-73 (photograph, A. Goren)

Inscription **893**
Site Sinai, unknown, #0
Technique incised
Condition good
Content rock drawing
Comment *ibexes*
Access DN26 (photograph, A. Goren); *see also* FE08

Inscription **894**
Site Sinai, unknown, #0
Technique incised
Condition fair
Content Nabatean inscription
Limitation *Tentative decipherment only*
Comment *Only part of the inscription appears in the photograph.*
Access DN26 (photograph, A. Goren)

Inscription **895**
Site Serabit el Khadem, #86
Dating 1872
Technique incised
Condition fair
Content French inscription
Limitation *Tentative decipherment only*
Access DO15 (photograph, A. Goren)

Inscription **896**
Site Serabit el Khadem, #86
Technique incised
Condition good
Content rock drawing
Comment *relief of a horseman*
Access DO15 (photograph, A. Goren)

Inscription **897**
Site Sinai, unknown, #0
Technique incised
Condition fair
Content Nabatean inscription
Limitation *Tentative decipherment only*
Access DM10a-11 (photograph, A. Goren); *see also* DL16

Inscription **898**
Site Sinai, unknown, #0
Technique scratched
Condition poor
Content Arabic inscription
Limitation *Tentative decipherment only*
Access DM10a-11 (photograph, A. Goren); *see also* DL16

Inscription **899**
Site Wadi Maghara, #72
Technique relief
Condition good
Content rock drawing
Comment *Egyptian man, woman and child*
Access DH56-57 (photograph, A. Goren)

Inscription **900**
Site Wadi Maghara, #72
Technique incised
Condition good
Content Egyptian hieroglyphs
Access DH56-57 (photograph, A. Goren); *see also* DH54-55

Inscription **901**
Site Wadi Mukatab, #64
Technique incised
Condition good
Content Nabatean inscription
Limitation *Tentative decipherment only*
Access CS67 (photograph, Z. Radovan)

Inscription **902**
Site Wadi Mukatab, #64
Technique incised
Condition poor
Content Nabatean inscription
Limitation *Tentative decipherment only*
Access CS67 (photograph, Z. Radovan)

Inscription **903**
Site Wadi Mukatab, #64
Technique incised
Condition fair
Content Arabic inscription
Limitation *Tentative decipherment only*
Access CS67 (photograph, Z. Radovan)

Inscription **904**
Site A-Tor, #101
Dating 1461
Technique incised
Condition good
Content Greek inscription
Limitation *Tentative decipherment only*
Access DW01 (photograph, Y. Tsafrir)

Inscription **905**
Site A-Tor, #101
Technique incised
Condition good
Content unidentified signs
Access DW01 (photograph, Y. Tsafrir)

Inscription **906**
Site A-Tor, #101
Technique painted
Condition good
Content Greek inscription
Limitation *Tentative decipherment only*
Access DW04 (photograph, Y. Tsafrir)

Inscription **907**
Site A-Tor, #101
Dating 1889
Technique painted
Condition good
Content Greek inscription
Limitation *Tentative decipherment only*
Access DW04 (photograph, Y. Tsafrir)

Inscription **908**
Site Sinai, unknown, #0
Technique scratched
Condition poor
Content Nabatean inscription
Limitation *Tentative decipherment only*
Access DM07a-08 (photograph, A. Goren)

Inscription **909**
Site Sinai, unknown, #0
Technique scratched
Condition poor
Content rock drawing
Comment *traces*
Access DM07a-08 (photograph, A. Goren)

Inscription **910**
Site Sinai, unknown, #0
Technique scratched
Condition poor
Content rock drawing
Comment *animals*
Access DM07a-08 (photograph, A. Goren)

Inscription **911**
Site Sinai, unknown, #0
Technique punched
Condition poor
Content rock drawing
Access DM07a-08 (photograph, A. Goren)

Inscription **912**
Site Sinai, unknown, #0
Technique painted
Condition fair
Content rock drawing
Access DL06 (photograph, A. Goren)

Inscription **913**
Site Sinai, unknown, #0
Technique scratched
Condition good
Content unidentified signs
Access DL06 (photograph, A. Goren)

Inscription **914**
Site Sinai, unknown, #0
Technique scratched
Condition fair
Content rock drawing
Access DM20a-21 (photograph, A. Goren)

Inscription **915**
Site Sinai, unknown, #0
Technique scratched
Condition fair
Content rock drawing
Access DM19a-20 (photograph, A. Goren)

Inscription **916**
Site Sinai, unknown, #0
Technique scratched
Condition poor
Content unidentified inscription
Access DM19a-20 (photograph, A. Goren)

Inscription **917**
Site Wadi Mukatab, #64
Technique incised
Condition good
Content Armenian inscription
որ
Access CS39 (photograph, Z. Radovan)
Corpus M Arm 6

Inscription **918**
Site Wadi Mukatab, #64
Technique punched
Condition fair
Content rock drawing
Access CS39 (photograph, Z. Radovan)

Inscription **919**
Site Wadi Mukatab, #64
Technique incised
Condition poor
Content unidentified inscription
Access CS39 (photograph, Z. Radovan)

Inscription	**920**
Site	Wadi Mukatab, #64
Technique	scratched
Condition	poor
Content	Nabatean inscription
Comment	*illegible*
Access	CS39 (photograph, Z. Radovan)

Inscription	**921**
Site	Wadi Mukatab, #64
Technique	scratched
Condition	poor
Content	unidentified inscription
Access	CS39 (photograph, Z. Radovan)

Inscription	**922**
Site	Wadi Mukatab, #64
Technique	scratched
Condition	poor
Content	unidentified inscription
Access	CS39 (photograph, Z. Radovan)

Inscription	**923**
Site	Wadi Mukatab, #64
Technique	scratched
Condition	poor
Content	unidentified inscription
Access	CS39 (photograph, Z. Radovan)

Inscription	**924**
Site	Wadi Mukatab, #64
Technique	scratched
Condition	poor
Content	unidentified inscription
Access	CS39 (photograph, Z. Radovan)

Inscription	**925**
Site	Wadi Mukatab, #64
Technique	incised
Condition	poor
Content	Syriac inscription
Limitation	*Tentative decipherment only*
Access	CN85 (photograph, Z. Radovan)

Inscription	**926**
Site	Wadi Mukatab, #64
Technique	incised
Condition	good
Content	Nabatean inscription
Limitation	*Tentative decipherment only*
Comment	*fragment*
Access	CN85 (photograph, Z. Radovan)

Inscription	**927**
Site	Wadi Mukatab, Mukatab 6, #70
Technique	incised
Condition	good
Content	Arabic inscription
Limitation	*Tentative decipherment only*
Access	FL94-94a (photograph, Project)

Inscription	**928**
Site	Wadi Haggag, #118
Technique	incised
Condition	excellent
Dimensions	75 x 70 cm.
Content	rock drawing
Comment	*camel with rider*
Access	EX34 (photograph, Project); *see also* EX33

Inscription	**929**
Site	Wadi Haggag, rock 3, #125
Technique	incised
Condition	poor
Content	unidentified inscription
Access	CQ93 (photograph, Z. Radovan); *see also* Negev 1977 fig. 78

Inscription	**930**
Site	Wadi Haggag, rock 3, #125
Technique	incised
Condition	poor
Content	unidentified inscription
Access	CQ93 (photograph, Z. Radovan); *see also* Negev 1977 fig. 78

Inscription	**931**
Site	Wadi Haggag, rock 3, #125
Technique	incised
Condition	good
Content	crosses alone
Access	CQ93 (photograph, Z. Radovan)

Inscription	**932**
Site	Wadi Haggag, rock 3, #125
Technique	incised
Condition	good
Content	encircled crosses
Access	CQ93 (photograph, Z. Radovan)

Inscription	**933**
Site	Wadi Haggag, rock 3, #125
Technique	incised
Condition	fair
Content	unidentified inscription
Access	CQ93 (photograph, Z. Radovan)

Inscription	**934**
Site	Wadi Haggag, rock 3, #125
Technique	incised
Condition	good
Content	crosses alone
Access	CQ93 (photograph, Z. Radovan)

Inscription	**935**
Site	Wadi Haggag, rock 3, #125
Technique	incised
Condition	fair
Content	unidentified signs
Access	CQ93 (photograph, Z. Radovan)

Inscription **936**
Site Wadi Mukatab, #64
Technique incised
Condition fair
Content Nabatean inscription
Limitation *Tentative decipherment only*
Access CN88 (photograph, Z. Radovan)

Inscription **937**
Site Wadi Mukatab, #64
Technique incised
Condition good
Content crosses alone
Access CN88 (photograph, Z. Radovan)

Inscription **938**
Site Wadi Mukatab, #64
Technique scratched
Condition fair
Content Nabatean inscription
Limitation *Tentative decipherment only*
Access CN88 (photograph, Z. Radovan)

Inscription **939**
Site A-Tor, #101
Technique painted
Condition good
Content Armenian inscription

ԱԻՐՀՆԵԼ ԵՍ
ՅԱՎԻՏԵՆ ՈՂՈՐՄ
Է ՈՍԿԵԳՆԴԻ ԵՒ ԻՐ ԾՆ
ՈՂԱՑՆ ԵՒ ՈՐԴՋ ՎԱՐԴԱՆ
ԱՄԵՆ

Access DW10-11 (photograph, Y. Tsafrir)
Corpus A-T Arm 1

Inscription **940**
Site Wadi Mukatab, #64
Technique incised
Condition poor
Content Greek inscription
Limitation *Tentative decipherment only*
Access CP39 (photograph, Z. Radovan); *see also* CP40

Inscription **941**
Site Wadi Mukatab, #64
Technique incised
Condition good
Content crosses alone
Access CP39 (photograph, Z. Radovan); *see also* CP40

Inscription **942**
Site Wadi Haggag, rock 3, #125
Technique incised
Condition good
Dimensions 7 x 11 cm.
Content Armenian inscription

ՋԱՅՍ ԵՍ ԱՆԳԻ

Access EA01 (photograph, Project)
Corpus H Arm 74

Inscription **943**
Site Wadi Mukatab, #64
Technique incised
Condition good
Content rock drawing
Comment *camels*
Access CS64 (photograph, Z. Radovan)

Inscription **944**
Site Wadi Mukatab, #64
Technique scratched
Condition fair
Content unidentified inscription
Access CS64 (photograph, Z. Radovan)

Inscription **945**
Site Wadi Mukatab, #64
Technique incised
Condition fair
Content rock drawing
Comment *person riding a camel*
Access CO08 (photograph, Z. Radovan)

Inscription **946**
Site A-Tor, Bir Abu Sueira, #191
Technique incised
Condition good
Content Latin inscription
Limitation *Tentative decipherment only*
Access CT37 (photograph, A. Goren); *see also* DX01

Inscription **947**
Site A-Tor, Bir Abu Sueira, #191
Technique incised
Condition good
Content Arabic inscription
Limitation *Tentative decipherment only*
Access CT37 (photograph, A. Goren); *see also* DX01

Inscription **948**
Site A-Tor, Bir Abu Sueira, #191
Technique incised
Condition good
Content Arabic inscription
Limitation *Tentative decipherment only*
Access CT37 (photograph, A. Goren); *see also* DX01

Inscription **949**
Site A-Tor, Bir Abu Sueira, #191
Technique incised
Condition fair
Content Greek inscription
Limitation *Tentative decipherment only*
Access CT37 (photograph, A. Goren); *see also* DX01

Inscription **950**
Site A-Tor, Bir Abu Sueira, #191
Technique incised
Condition good
Content Greek inscription
Limitation *Tentative decipherment only*
Access CT37 (photograph, A. Goren); *see also* DX01, DX03

Inscription **951**
Site A-Tor, Bir Abu Sueira, #191
Technique incised
Condition good
Content crosses alone
Access CT37 (photograph, A. Goren); *see also* DX01, DX03

Inscription **952**
Site A-Tor, Bir Abu Sueira, #191
Technique incised
Condition poor
Content encircled crosses
Access CT37 (photograph, A. Goren); *see also* DX01, DX03

Inscription **953**
Site A-Tor, Bir Abu Sueira, #191
Technique scratched
Condition poor
Content encircled crosses
Access CT37 (photograph, A. Goren); *see also* DX01, DX03

Inscription **954**
Site A-Tor, Bir Abu Sueira, #191
Technique incised
Condition fair
Content Greek inscription
Limitation *Tentative decipherment only*
Access CT37 (photograph, A. Goren); *see also* DX01, DX03

Inscription **955**
Site A-Tor, Bir Abu Sueira, #191
Technique incised
Condition good
Content Latin inscription
Limitation *Tentative decipherment only*
Access CT37 (photograph, A. Goren); *see also* DX01, DX03

Inscription **956**
Site A-Tor, Bir Abu Sueira, #191
Technique incised
Condition good
Content crosses alone
Access CT37 (photograph, A. Goren); *see also* DX01, DX03

Inscription **957**
Site A-Tor, Bir Abu Sueira, #191
Technique scratched
Condition poor
Content unidentified inscription
Access CT37 (photograph, A. Goren); *see also* DX01

Inscription **958**
Site A-Tor, Bir Abu Sueira, #191
Technique scratched
Condition poor
Content unidentified inscription
Comment *Greek?*
Access CT37 (photograph, A. Goren)

Inscription **959**
Site A-Tor, Bir Abu Sueira, #191
Technique scratched
Condition fair
Content crosses with inscription
Access CT37 (photograph, A. Goren); *see also* DX01

Inscription **960**
Site A-Tor, Bir Abu Sueira, #191
Technique incised
Condition fair
Content rock drawing
Comment *ships*
Access CT37 (photograph, A. Goren); *see also* DX01, DX03

Inscription **961**
Site A-Tor, Bir Abu Sueira, #191
Technique scratched
Condition poor
Content unidentified inscription
Access CT37 (photograph, A. Goren); *see also* DX01, DX03

Inscription **962**
Site A-Tor, Bir Abu Sueira, #191
Technique scratched
Condition poor
Content unidentified inscription
Access CT37 (photograph, A. Goren); *see also* DX01, DX03

Inscription **963**
Site Wadi Mukatab, #64
Technique incised
Condition good
Content Nabatean inscription
Limitation *Tentative decipherment only*
Access CO09 (photograph, Z. Radovan); *see also* DX01, DX03

Inscription **964**
Site Wadi Mukatab, #64
Technique incised
Condition poor
Content Nabatean inscription
Limitation *Tentative decipherment only*
Access CO09 (photograph, Z. Radovan)

Inscription **965**
Site Wadi Mukatab, #64
Technique incised
Condition fair
Content crosses alone
Access CO09 (photograph, Z. Radovan)

Inscription **966**
Site A-Tor, Bir Abu Sueira, #191
Dating 1872
Technique incised
Condition good
Content Greek inscription
Limitation *Tentative decipherment only*
Access CT09 (photograph, A. Goren)

Inscription **967**
Site A-Tor, Bir Abu Sueira, #191
Technique incised
Condition fair
Content Greek inscription
Limitation *Tentative decipherment only*
Access CT09 (photograph, A. Goren)

Inscription **968**
Site Wadi Haggag, rock 3 area 2, #127
Technique incised
Condition fair
Content Greek inscription
Limitation *Tentative decipherment only*
Access AEa11-12 (photograph, M. Stone); *see also* AR29, AR30

Inscription **969**
Site A-Tor, Bir Abu Sueira, #191
Technique scratched
Condition fair
Content Greek inscription
Limitation *Tentative decipherment only*
Access CT09 (photograph, A. Goren)

Inscription **970**
Site A-Tor, Bir Abu Sueira, #191
Technique scratched
Condition fair
Content Greek inscription
Limitation *Tentative decipherment only*
Access CT09 (photograph, A. Goren)

Inscription **971**
Site A-Tor, Bir Abu Sueira, #191
Technique incised
Condition good
Content Greek inscription
Limitation *Tentative decipherment only*
Access CT09 (photograph, A. Goren)

Inscription **972**
Site A-Tor, Bir Abu Sueira, #191
Technique scratched
Condition poor
Content Greek inscription
Limitation *Tentative decipherment only*
Comment *almost illegible*
Access CT09 (photograph, A. Goren)

Inscription **973**
Site A-Tor, Bir Abu Sueira, #191
Technique scratched
Condition good
Content crosses with inscription
Access CT09 (photograph, A. Goren)

Inscription **974**
Site A-Tor, Bir Abu Sueira, #191
Technique scratched
Condition poor
Content unidentified inscription
Access CT09 (photograph, A. Goren)

Inscription **975**
Site A-Tor, Bir Abu Sueira, #191
Technique incised
Condition poor
Content Latin inscription
Limitation *Tentative decipherment only*
Access CT09 (photograph, A. Goren)

Inscription **976**
Site A-Tor, Bir Abu Sueira, #191
Technique scratched
Condition poor
Content Greek inscription
Limitation *Tentative decipherment only*
Access CT09 (photograph, A. Goren)

Inscription **977**
Site A-Tor, Bir Abu Sueira, #191
Technique incised
Condition poor
Content Greek inscription
Limitation *Tentative decipherment only*
Access CT09 (photograph, A. Goren)

Inscription **978**
Site A-Tor, Bir Abu Sueira, #191
Technique scratched
Condition good
Content Arabic inscription
Limitation *Tentative decipherment only*
Access CT09 (photograph, A. Goren)

Inscription **979**
Site A-Tor, Bir Abu Sueira, #191
Technique incised
Condition fair
Content Arabic inscription
Limitation *Tentative decipherment only*
Access CT09 (photograph, A. Goren)

Inscription 980
Site A-Tor, Bir Abu Sueira, #191
Technique incised
Condition good
Content crosses with inscription
Access CT09 (photograph, A. Goren)

Inscription 981
Site Wadi Mukatab, #64
Technique scratched
Condition poor
Content Greek inscription
Limitation *Tentative decipherment only*
Comment *inscription followed by a cross*
Access DA70-71 (photograph, A. Goren)

Inscription 982
Site Wadi Mukatab, #64
Technique incised
Condition good
Content crosses with inscription
Access DA70-71 (photograph, A. Goren)

Inscription 983
Site Wadi Mukatab, #64
Technique incised
Condition poor
Content Greek inscription
Limitation *Tentative decipherment only*
Access DA70-71 (photograph, A. Goren)

Inscription 984
Site Wadi Mukatab, #64
Technique incised
Condition good
Content crosses with inscription
Access DA70-71 (photograph, A. Goren)

Inscription 985
Site Wadi Mukatab, #64
Technique incised
Condition fair
Content rock drawing
Comment *camels and other animals*
Access DA70-71 (photograph, A. Goren)

Inscription 986
Site Jebel Salmon, Khorbat Seadim, #239
Technique incised
Condition poor
Content Greek inscription
Limitation *Tentative decipherment only*
Access DB72-73 (photograph, A. Goren)

Inscription 987
Site Jebel Salmon, Khorbat Seadim, #239
Technique incised
Condition poor
Content Greek inscription
Limitation *Tentative decipherment only*
Access DB72-73 (photograph, A. Goren)

Inscription 988
Site Jebel Salmon, Khorbat Seadim, #239
Technique incised
Condition good
Content crosses alone
Access DB72-73 (photograph, A. Goren)

Inscription 989
Site Jebel Salmon, Khorbat Seadim, #239
Technique incised
Condition poor
Content Greek inscription
Limitation *Tentative decipherment only*
Comment *monogram framed by cross*
Access DB72-73 (photograph, A. Goren)

Inscription 990
Site Jebel Salmon, Khorbat Seadim, #239
Technique incised
Condition fair
Content rock drawing
Comment *Two pairs of stars, the larger of which is located in the two sides of the cross, is encircled.*
Access DB72-73 (photograph, A. Goren)

Inscription 991
Site Sinai, unknown, #0
Technique incised
Condition poor
Content rock drawing
Access DK19a-20 (photograph, A. Goren)

Inscription 992
Site Wadi Mukatab, #64
Technique incised
Condition fair
Content Nabatean inscription
Limitation *Tentative decipherment only*
Access CP38 (photograph, Z. Radovan); *see also* CP37

Inscription 993
Site Wadi Mukatab, #64
Technique incised
Condition poor
Content unidentified inscription
Access CP38 (photograph, Z. Radovan)

Inscription 994
Site Wadi Mukatab, #64
Technique incised
Condition poor
Content unidentified inscription
Access CP38 (photograph, Z. Radovan)

Inscription 995
Site Wadi Mukatab, #64
Technique incised
Condition poor
Content Arabic inscription
Limitation *Tentative decipherment only*
Access CP38 (photograph, Z. Radovan)

Inscription 996
Site Sinai, unknown, #0
Technique incised
Condition good
Content Arabic inscription
Limitation *Tentative decipherment only*
Access DM11a-12 (photograph, A. Goren); *see also* DL18

Inscription 997
Site Sinai, unknown, #0
Technique scratched
Condition poor
Content Nabatean inscription
Limitation *Tentative decipherment only*
Access DL08 (photograph, A. Goren)

Inscription 998
Site Wadi Haggag, #118
Technique incised
Condition good
Content Greek inscription
Limitation *Tentative decipherment only*
Comment *monogram*
Access CR11 (photograph, Z. Radovan)

Inscription 999
Site Wadi Mukatab, #64
Technique incised
Condition poor
Content Greek inscription
Limitation *Tentative decipherment only*
Access CM59 (photograph, Z. Radovan)

Inscription 1000
Site Wadi Mukatab, #64
Technique incised
Condition fair
Content crosses with inscription
Access CM59 (photograph, Z. Radovan)

Inscription 1001
Site Wadi Mukatab, #64
Technique scratched
Condition good
Content Greek inscription
Limitation *Tentative decipherment only*
Access CM59 (photograph, Z. Radovan)

Inscription 1002
Site Wadi Mukatab, #64
Technique scratched
Condition fair
Content English inscription
Limitation *Tentative decipherment only*
Access CM59 (photograph, Z. Radovan)

Inscription 1003
Site Wadi Mukatab, #64
Technique scratched
Condition fair
Content crosses with inscription
Access CM59 (photograph, Z. Radovan)

Inscription 1004
Site Wadi Mukatab, #64
Technique incised
Condition poor
Content Greek inscription
Limitation *Tentative decipherment only*
Access CM59 (photograph, Z. Radovan)

Inscription 1005
Site Wadi Mukatab, #64
Technique scratched
Condition poor
Content unidentified signs
Access CM59 (photograph, Z. Radovan)

Inscription 1006
Site Wadi Mukatab, #64
Technique incised
Condition poor
Content unidentified signs
Access CM59 (photograph, Z. Radovan)

Inscription 1007
Site Wadi Mukatab, #64
Technique scratched
Condition good
Content Nabatean inscription
Limitation *Tentative decipherment only*
Access DE23a-24 (photograph, A. Goren)

Inscription 1008
Site Wadi Mukatab, #64
Technique scratched
Condition good
Content Nabatean inscription
Limitation *Tentative decipherment only*
Access DE23a-24 (photograph, A. Goren)

Inscription 1009
Site Church of the Nativity, well inside, #267
Technique incised
Condition good
Dimensions 40 x 18 cm.
Content Greek inscription
Limitation *Tentative decipherment only*
Access DSa05 (photograph, M. Stone)

Inscription 1010
Site Church of the Nativity, well inside, #267
Technique incised
Condition good
Content crosses with inscription
Access DSa05 (photograph, M. Stone)

Inscription 1011
Site Church of the Nativity, south door to crypt, #258
Technique incised
Condition good
Content Russian inscription
Limitation *Tentative decipherment only*
Access DUb58 (photograph, M. Stone)

Inscription **1012**
Site Church of the Nativity, south door to crypt, #258
Technique incised
Condition fair
Content Russian inscription
Limitation *Tentative decipherment only*
Access DUb58 (photograph, M. Stone)

Inscription **1013**
Site Church of the Nativity, south door to crypt, #258
Technique incised
Condition good
Content Italian inscription
Limitation *Tentative decipherment only*
Access DUb58 (photograph, M. Stone)

Inscription **1014**
Site Church of the Nativity, south door to crypt, #258
Technique incised
Condition good
Content crosses alone
Access DUb58 (photograph, M. Stone)

Inscription **1015**
Site Church of the Nativity, south door to crypt, #258
Technique incised
Condition fair
Content crosses alone
Access DUb58 (photograph, M. Stone)

Inscription **1016**
Site Church of the Nativity, south door to crypt, #258
Technique incised
Condition fair
Content encircled crosses
Access DUb58 (photograph, M. Stone)

Inscription **1017**
Site Church of the Nativity, south door to crypt, #258
Technique incised
Condition fair
Content Armenian inscription
Limitation *Tentative decipherment only*
Access DUb58 (photograph, M. Stone)

Inscription **1018**
Site Church of the Nativity, south door to crypt, #258
Technique incised
Condition fair
Content Armenian inscription
Limitation *Tentative decipherment only*
Access DUb58 (photograph, M. Stone)

Inscription **1019**
Site Church of the Nativity, south door to crypt, #258
Technique incised
Condition fair
Content crosses with inscription
Access DUb58 (photograph, M. Stone)

Inscription **1020**
Site Church of the Nativity, south door to crypt, #258
Technique incised
Condition fair
Dimensions 35 x 19 cm.
Content Latin inscription
Limitation *Tentative decipherment only*
Access DUb58 (photograph, M. Stone)

Inscription **1021**
Site Church of the Nativity, south door to crypt, #258
Dating 1666
Technique incised
Condition fair
Content Russian inscription
Limitation *Tentative decipherment only*
Access DUb58 (photograph, M. Stone)

Inscription **1022**
Site Church of the Nativity, south door to crypt, #258
Technique incised
Condition fair
Content Russian inscription
Limitation *Tentative decipherment only*
Access DUb58 (photograph, M. Stone)

Inscription **1023**
Site Church of the Nativity, south door to crypt, #258
Technique incised
Condition poor
Content Russian inscription
Limitation *Tentative decipherment only*
Access DUb58 (photograph, M. Stone)

Inscription **1024**
Site Church of the Nativity, south door to crypt, #258
Dating 1504
Technique incised
Condition poor
Content Greek inscription
Limitation *Tentative decipherment only*
Access DUb58 (photograph, M. Stone)

Inscription **1025**
Site Church of the Nativity, south door to crypt, #258
Technique incised
Condition good
Content crosses alone
Access DUb58 (photograph, M. Stone)

Inscription **1026**
Site Church of the Nativity, south door to crypt, #258
Technique incised
Condition fair
Content Greek inscription
Limitation *Tentative decipherment only*
Comment *Coptic?*
Access DUb60 (photograph, M. Stone)

Inscription **1027**
Site Church of the Nativity, south door to crypt, #258
Technique incised
Condition poor
Content Georgian inscription
Limitation *Tentative decipherment only*
Access DUb60 (photograph, M. Stone)

Inscription **1028**
Site Church of the Nativity, south door to crypt, #258
Technique incised
Condition poor
Content unidentified inscription
Comment *illegible*
Access DUb60 (photograph, M. Stone)

Inscription **1029**
Site Church of the Nativity, south door to crypt, #258
Technique scratched
Condition poor
Content Armenian inscription
Limitation *Tentative decipherment only*
Access DUb60 (photograph, M. Stone)

Inscription **1030**
Site Church of the Nativity, south door to crypt, #258
Technique scratched
Condition fair
Content crosses with inscription
Comment *large cross*
Access DUb60 (photograph, M. Stone)

Inscription **1031**
Site Church of the Nativity, south door to crypt, #258
Dating 1572
Technique scratched
Condition poor
Content Armenian inscription
Limitation *Tentative decipherment only*
Access DUb60 (photograph, M. Stone)

Inscription **1032**
Site Church of the Nativity, south door to crypt, #258
Technique incised
Condition good
Content unidentified signs
Access DUb58 (photograph, M. Stone)

Inscription **1033**
Site Church of the Nativity, south door to crypt, #258
Technique scratched
Condition poor
Content Greek inscription
Limitation *Tentative decipherment only*
Access DUb58 (photograph, M. Stone)

Inscription **1034**
Site Church of the Nativity, south door to crypt, #258
Technique scratched
Condition poor
Content unidentified inscription
Access DUb58 (photograph, M. Stone)

Inscription **1035**
Site Church of the Nativity, pillar C6, #245
Technique incised
Condition excellent
Dimensions 4.5 x 0.5 cm.
Content Italian inscription
Limitation *Tentative decipherment only*
Access DVa18 (photograph, M. Stone)

Inscription **1036**
Site Church of the Nativity, pillar C6, #245
Technique incised
Condition poor
Content Arabic inscription
Limitation *Tentative decipherment only*
Access DVa18 (photograph, M. Stone)

Inscription **1037**
Site Church of the Nativity, pillar C6, #245
Technique incised
Condition poor
Content unidentified inscription
Access DVa18 (photograph, M. Stone)

Inscription **1038**
Site Church of the Nativity, pillar C6, #245
Technique incised
Condition fair
Content English inscription
Limitation *Tentative decipherment only*
Access DVa18 (photograph, M. Stone)

Inscription **1039**
Site Church of the Nativity, pillar C6, #245
Technique incised
Condition poor
Content unidentified inscription
Access DVa18 (photograph, M. Stone)

Inscription **1040**
Site Church of the Nativity, south door to crypt, #258
Dating 18th century
Technique incised
Condition excellent
Dimensions 20 x 15 cm.
Content Italian inscription
Limitation *Tentative decipherment only*
Access DUb68 (photograph, M. Stone)

Inscription **1041**
Site Church of the Nativity, south door to crypt, #258
Technique incised
Condition excellent
Content Greek inscription
Limitation *Tentative decipherment only*
Comment *monogram*
Access DUb68 (photograph, M. Stone)

Inscription **1042**
Site Church of the Nativity, south door to crypt, #258
Technique incised
Condition excellent
Content crosses with inscription
Comment *cross surmounting insc. 1041*
Access DUb68 (photograph, M. Stone)

Inscription **1043**
Site Church of the Nativity, south door to crypt, #258
Technique incised
Condition poor
Content Latin inscription
Limitation *Tentative decipherment only*
Comment *monogram*
Access DUb68 (photograph, M. Stone)

Inscription **1044**
Site Church of the Nativity, south door to crypt, #258
Technique incised
Condition poor
Content rock drawing
Comment *crown surmounting insc. 1043*
Access DUb68 (photograph, M. Stone)

Inscription **1045**
Site Church of the Nativity, south door to crypt, #258
Technique incised
Condition good
Content crosses alone
Access DUb68 (photograph, M. Stone)

---

nscription **1046**
Site Church of the Nativity, pillar C11, #253
Technique incised
Condition good
Dimensions 16 x 2 cm.
Content Greek inscription
Limitation *Tentative decipherment only*
Access DUa15 (photograph, M. Stone)

Inscription **1047**
Site Church of the Nativity, pillar C11, #253
Technique incised
Condition good
Content varied crosses
Access DUa15 (photograph, M. Stone)

Inscription **1048**
Site Church of the Nativity, pillar C11, #253
Technique incised
Condition fair
Content varied crosses
Access DUa15 (photograph, M. Stone)

Inscription **1049**
Site Church of the Nativity, pillar C11, #253
Technique incised
Condition poor
Content Greek inscription
Limitation *Tentative decipherment only*
Access DUa15 (photograph, M. Stone)

Inscription **1050**
Site Church of the Nativity, pillar C11, #253
Technique incised
Condition poor
Content unidentified inscription
Access DUa15 (photograph, M. Stone)

Inscription **1051**
Site Church of the Nativity, pillar C11, #253
Technique incised
Condition fair
Content Arabic inscription
Limitation *Tentative decipherment only*
Access DUa15 (photograph, M. Stone)

Inscription **1052**
Site Church of the Nativity, pillar C11, #253
Technique incised
Condition poor
Content unidentified inscription
Access DUa15 (photograph, M. Stone)

Inscription **1053**
Site Church of the Nativity, pillar C11, #253
Technique incised
Condition fair
Content crosses with inscription
Access DUa15 (photograph, M. Stone)

Inscription 1054
Site Church of the Nativity, pillar B3, #268
Dating 1618
Technique incised
Condition good
Dimensions 12 x 13 cm.
Content Italian inscription
Limitation *Tentative decipherment only*
Access DSa08 (photograph, M. Stone)

Inscription 1055
Site Sinai, unknown, #0
Technique incised
Condition fair
Content Old North Arabic inscription
Limitation *Tentative decipherment only*
Access FU12 (photograph, A. Goren)

Inscription 1056
Site Church of the Nativity, pillar B3, #268
Technique incised
Condition poor
Content unidentified inscription
Access DSa08 (photograph, M. Stone)

Inscription 1057
Site Church of the Nativity, pillar B3, #268
Dating 1584
Technique incised
Condition fair
Dimensions 12 x 18 cm.
Content Armenian inscription
Limitation *Tentative decipherment only*
Access DSa08 (photograph, M. Stone)

Inscription 1058
Site Church of the Nativity, pillar B3, #268
Technique incised
Condition fair
Content Armenian inscription
Limitation *Tentative decipherment only*
Access DSa08 (photograph, M. Stone)

Inscription 1059
Site Church of the Nativity, pillar B3, #268
Technique incised
Condition fair
Content unidentified inscription
Access DSa08 (photograph, M. Stone)

Inscription 1060
Site Church of the Nativity, pillar B3, #268
Technique incised
Condition good
Content crosses alone
Access DSa08 (photograph, M. Stone)

Inscription 1061
Site Church of the Nativity, pillar B3, #268
Technique incised
Condition fair
Content Greek inscription
Limitation *Tentative decipherment only*
Access DSa08 (photograph, M. Stone)

Inscription 1062
Site Church of the Nativity, pillar B3, #268
Technique incised
Condition fair
Content crosses with inscription
Access DSa08 (photograph, M. Stone)

Inscription 1063
Site Church of the Nativity, pillar B3, #268
Technique incised
Condition fair
Content crosses alone
Access DSa08 (photograph, M. Stone)

Inscription 1064
Site Church of the Nativity, south door to crypt, #258
Technique incised
Condition good
Content crosses alone
Access DUb64 (photograph, M. Stone)

Inscription 1065
Site Church of the Nativity, south door to crypt, #258
Technique incised
Condition good
Content crosses alone
Access DUb64 (photograph, M. Stone)

Inscription 1066
Site Church of the Nativity, south door to crypt, #258
Technique incised
Condition poor
Content Arabic inscription
Limitation *Tentative decipherment only*
Access DUb64 (photograph, M. Stone)

Inscription 1067
Site Church of the Nativity, south door to crypt, #258
Technique incised
Condition fair
Content Greek inscription
Limitation *Tentative decipherment only*
Access DUb64 (photograph, M. Stone)

Inscription 1068
Site Church of the Nativity, south door to crypt, #258
Technique incised
Condition fair
Content Syriac inscription
Limitation *Tentative decipherment only*
Access DUb64 (photograph, M. Stone)

Inscription 1069
Site Church of the Nativity, south door to crypt, #258
Technique incised
Condition poor
Content Greek inscription
Limitation *Tentative decipherment only*
Access DUb64 (photograph, M. Stone)

Inscription **1070**
Site Church of the Nativity, south door to crypt, #258
Technique incised
Condition poor
Content crosses with inscription
Access DUb64 (photograph, M. Stone)

Inscription **1071**
Site Church of the Nativity, south door to crypt, #258
Technique incised
Condition poor
Content unidentified inscription
Access DUb64 (photograph, M. Stone)

Inscription **1072**
Site Church of the Nativity, south door to crypt, #258
Technique incised
Condition poor
Content unidentified signs
Access DUb64 (photograph, M. Stone)

Inscription **1073**
Site Church of the Nativity, south door to crypt, #258
Technique incised
Condition good
Content crosses alone
Comment *many decorative crosses*
Access DUb64 (photograph, M. Stone)

Inscription **1074**
Site Church of the Nativity, north door to crypt, #262
Dating 1528
Technique incised
Condition excellent
Dimensions 13 x 17 cm.
Content Latin inscription
Limitation *Tentative decipherment only*
Access DRa08 (photograph, M. Stone)

Inscription **1075**
Site Church of the Nativity, north door to crypt, #262
Technique incised
Condition fair
Content Arabic inscription
Limitation *Tentative decipherment only*
Comment *Arabic inscription?*
Access DRa08 (photograph, M. Stone)

Inscription **1076**
Site Church of the Nativity, north door to crypt, #262
Technique incised
Condition good
Content crosses alone
Comment *many single crosses*
Access DRa08 (photograph, M. Stone)

Inscription **1077**
Site Church of the Nativity, north door to crypt, #262
Technique incised
Condition poor
Content unidentified inscription
Access DRa08 (photograph, M. Stone)

Inscription **1078**
Site Church of the Nativity, north door to crypt, #262
Technique incised
Condition poor
Content Greek inscription
Comment *Illegible*
Access DRa08 (photograph, M. Stone)

Inscription **1079**
Site Church of the Nativity, north door to crypt, #262
Technique scratched
Condition poor
Content unidentified inscription
Access DRa08 (photograph, M. Stone)

Inscription **1080**
Site Church of the Nativity, north door to crypt, #262
Technique scratched
Condition good
Content crosses with inscription
Access DRa08 (photograph, M. Stone)

Inscription **1081**
Site Church of the Nativity, pillar C10, #252
Technique incised
Condition excellent
Dimensions 10 x 13 cm.
Content Polish inscription
Limitation *Tentative decipherment only*
Access DUa13 (photograph, M. Stone)

Inscription **1082**
Site Church of the Nativity, pillar C10, #252
Technique incised
Condition good
Content crosses alone
Access DUa13 (photograph, M. Stone)

Inscription **1083**
Site Church of the Nativity, pillar C10, #252
Technique incised
Condition fair
Content unidentified signs
Access DUa13 (photograph, M. Stone)

Inscription **1084**
Site Church of the Nativity, pier P, #263
Dating 1590
Technique scratched
Condition fair
Dimensions 22 x 2 cm.
Content Armenian inscription
Limitation *Tentative decipherment only*
Access DRa16 (photograph, M. Stone)

Inscription **1085**
Site Church of the Nativity, pier P, #263
Technique scratched
Condition fair
Content Armenian inscription
Limitation *Tentative decipherment only*
Access DRa16 (photograph, M. Stone)

Inscription **1086**
Site Church of the Nativity, pier P, #263
Technique incised
Condition fair
Content crosses with inscription
Access DRa16 (photograph, M. Stone)

Inscription **1087**
Site Church of the Nativity, pier P, #263
Technique incised
Condition fair
Content crosses alone
Access DRa16 (photograph, M. Stone)

Inscription **1088**
Site Church of the Nativity, pier P, #263
Technique incised
Condition fair
Content Arabic inscription
Limitation *Tentative decipherment only*
Access DRa16 (photograph, M. Stone)

Inscription **1089**
Site Church of the Nativity, pier P, #263
Technique incised
Condition poor
Content Armenian inscription
Limitation *Tentative decipherment only*
Access DRa16 (photograph, M. Stone)

Inscription **1090**
Site Church of the Nativity, pier P, #263
Technique scratched
Condition poor
Content unidentified inscription
Access DRa16 (photograph, M. Stone)

Inscription **1091**
Site Church of the Nativity, pillar B3, #268
Technique painted
Condition good
Content Arabic inscription
Limitation *Tentative decipherment only*
Access DSa13 (photograph, M. Stone)

Inscription **1092**
Site Church of the Nativity, pillar B3, #268
Technique painted
Condition good
Dimensions 30 x 10 cm.
Content Latin inscription
Limitation *Tentative decipherment only*
Access DSa13 (photograph, M. Stone)

Inscription **1093**
Site Church of the Nativity, pillar B3, #268
Technique painted
Condition good
Content rock drawing
Comment *decorated basin*
Access DSa13 (photograph, M. Stone)

Inscription **1094**
Site Church of the Nativity, pillar B3, #268
Technique painted
Condition poor
Content unidentified inscription
Access DSa13 (photograph, M. Stone)

Inscription **1095**
Site Church of the Nativity, pillar B4, #266
Dating 1620
Technique incised
Condition good
Dimensions 12 x 1 cm.
Content Armenian inscription
Limitation *Tentative decipherment only*
Access DSa04 (photograph, M. Stone)

Inscription **1096**
Site Wadi Haggag, #118
Technique incised
Condition excellent
Content rock drawing
Comment *hunters on camels*
Access EZ21 (, M. Stone); *see also* EZ22, EZ24, EZ25, EZ26, EZ27

Inscription **1097**
Site Church of the Nativity, pillar B4, #266
Technique incised
Condition poor
Content Greek inscription
Limitation *Tentative decipherment only*
Access DSa04 (photograph, M. Stone)

Inscription **1098**
Site Church of the Nativity, pillar B4, #266
Technique incised
Condition fair
Content crosses alone
Access DSa04 (photograph, M. Stone)

Inscription **1099**
Site Church of the Nativity, pillar B4, #266
Technique incised
Condition fair
Content Arabic inscription
Limitation *Tentative decipherment only*
Access DSa04 (photograph, M. Stone)

Inscription **1100**
Site Church of the Nativity, pillar B3, #268
Technique painted
Condition good
Content Armenian inscription
Limitation *Tentative decipherment only*
Access DSa10 (photograph, M. Stone)

Inscription 1101
Site Church of the Nativity, pillar B3, #268
Technique painted
Condition good
Content Arabic inscription
Limitation *Tentative decipherment only*
Access DSa10 (photograph, M. Stone)

Inscription 1102
Site Church of the Nativity, pillar B3, #268
Technique painted
Condition fair
Content Arabic inscription
Limitation *Tentative decipherment only*
Access DSa10 (photograph, M. Stone)

Inscription 1103
Site Church of the Nativity, pillar B3, #268
Technique painted
Condition poor
Content Latin inscription
Limitation *Tentative decipherment only*
Access DSa10 (photograph, M. Stone)

Inscription 1104
Site Church of the Nativity, pillar B3, #268
Dating 1051
Technique painted
Condition poor
Content Latin inscription
Limitation *Tentative decipherment only*
Access DSa10 (photograph, M. Stone)

Inscription 1105
Site Church of the Nativity, pillar B3, #268
Technique scratched
Condition poor
Content Arabic inscription
Limitation *Tentative decipherment only*
Access DSa10 (photograph, M. Stone)

Inscription 1106
Site Wadi Haggag, #118
Technique incised
Condition poor
Content Greek inscription
Limitation *Tentative decipherment only*
Access CR20 (photograph, Z. Radovan)

Inscription 1107
Site Wadi Haggag, #118
Technique incised
Condition fair
Content Nabatean inscription
Limitation *Tentative decipherment only*
Access CR20 (photograph, Z. Radovan)

Inscription 1108
Site Wadi Haggag, #118
Technique incised
Condition good
Content Greek inscription
Limitation *Tentative decipherment only*
Comment *monogrammed cross*
Access CR20 (photograph, Z. Radovan)

Inscription 1109
Site Wadi Haggag, #118
Technique incised
Condition good
Content Greek inscription
Limitation *Tentative decipherment only*
Access CR20 (photograph, Z. Radovan)

Inscription 1110
Site Wadi Haggag, #118
Technique incised
Condition poor
Content Greek inscription
Limitation *Tentative decipherment only*
Access CR20 (photograph, Z. Radovan)

Inscription 1111
Site Wadi Haggag, #118
Technique incised
Condition fair
Content crosses alone
Access CR20 (photograph, Z. Radovan)

Inscription 1112
Site Wadi Haggag, #118
Technique incised
Condition poor
Content Nabatean inscription
Limitation *Tentative decipherment only*
Access CR20 (photograph, Z. Radovan)

Inscription 1113
Site Wadi Haggag, #118
Technique incised
Condition fair
Content Greek inscription
Limitation *Tentative decipherment only*
Access CR20 (photograph, Z. Radovan)

Inscription 1114
Site Wadi Haggag, #118
Technique incised
Condition fair
Content unidentified signs
Access CR20 (photograph, Z. Radovan)

Inscription 1115
Site Wadi Haggag, #118
Technique incised
Condition good
Content crosses alone
Comment *monogrammed cross*
Access CR20 (photograph, Z. Radovan)

Inscription 1116
Site Wadi Haggag, #118
Technique incised
Condition poor
Content unidentified inscription
Access CR20 (photograph, Z. Radovan)

Inscription **1117**
Site Wadi Haggag, #118
Technique incised
Condition poor
Content Nabatean inscription
Comment *illegible*
Access CR20 (photograph, Z. Radovan)

Inscription **1118**
Site A-Tor, Bir Abu Sueira, #191
Dating 1672
Technique incised
Condition fair
Content Arabic inscription
Limitation *Tentative decipherment only*
Access CT24 (photograph, Z. Radovan)

Inscription **1119**
Site Wadi Firan, #53
Technique incised
Condition good
Content Arabic inscription
Limitation *Tentative decipherment only*
Access DC23-24 (photograph, A. Goren); *see also* DC23-24

Inscription **1120**
Site Wadi Firan, #53
Technique incised
Condition poor
Content unidentified signs
Access DC23-24 (photograph, A. Goren)

Inscription **1121**
Site Wadi Firan, #53
Technique incised
Condition good
Content Arabic inscription
Limitation *Tentative decipherment only*
Access CP43 (photograph, Z. Radovan); *see also* CP44

Inscription **1122**
Site Wadi Firan, #53
Technique incised
Condition poor
Content unidentified inscription
Access CP43 (photograph, Z. Radovan); *see also* CP44

Inscription **1123**
Site Wadi Firan, #53
Technique incised
Condition poor
Content unidentified signs
Access CP43 (photograph, Z. Radovan); *see also* CP44

Inscription **1124**
Site Sinai, unknown, #0
Technique scratched
Condition fair
Content Nabatean inscription
Limitation *Tentative decipherment only*
Access DD10-11 (photograph, A. Goren)

Inscription **1125**
Site Sinai, unknown, #0
Technique scratched
Condition good
Content Nabatean inscription
Limitation *Tentative decipherment only*
Access DD10-11 (photograph, A. Goren)

Inscription **1126**
Site Sinai, unknown, #0
Technique scratched
Condition poor
Content Nabatean inscription
Limitation *Tentative decipherment only*
Access DD10-11 (photograph, A. Goren)

Inscription **1127**
Site Sinai, unknown, #0
Technique scratched
Condition good
Content rock drawing
Access DD10-11 (photograph, A. Goren)

Inscription **1128**
Site Sinai, unknown, #0
Technique scratched
Condition poor
Content rock drawing
Access DD10-11 (photograph, A. Goren)

Inscription **1129**
Site Sinai, unknown, #0
Technique incised
Condition poor
Content Nabatean inscription
Limitation *Tentative decipherment only*
Access DD12-13 (photograph, A. Goren)

Inscription **1130**
Site Sinai, unknown, #0
Technique incised
Condition good
Content Greek inscription
Limitation *Tentative decipherment only*
Access CO21 (photograph, Z. Radovan)

Inscription **1131**
Site Sinai, unknown, #0
Technique incised
Condition good
Content crosses alone
Access CO21 (photograph, Z. Radovan)

Inscription **1132**
Site Church of the Nativity, pillar B6, #264
Dating 1723
Technique incised
Condition good
Content Armenian inscription
Limitation *Tentative decipherment only*
Access DRa18 (photograph, M. Stone)

Inscription 1133
Site Church of the Nativity, pillar B6, #264
Technique incised
Condition fair
Content crosses with inscription
Access DRa18 (photograph, M. Stone)

Inscription 1134
Site Church of the Nativity, pillar B6, #264
Technique incised
Condition good
Content English inscription
Limitation *Tentative decipherment only*
Access DRa18 (photograph, M. Stone)

Inscription 1135
Site Church of the Nativity, pillar B6, #264
Technique incised
Condition fair
Dimensions 15 x 1 cm.
Content Latin inscription
Limitation *Tentative decipherment only*
Access DRa18 (photograph, M. Stone)

Inscription 1136
Site Church of the Nativity, pillar B6, #264
Technique scratched
Condition fair
Content crosses alone
Access DRa18 (photograph, M. Stone)

Inscription 1137
Site Church of the Nativity, pillar B6, #264
Technique incised
Condition fair
Content Arabic inscription
Limitation *Tentative decipherment only*
Access DRa18 (photograph, M. Stone)

Inscription 1138
Site Church of the Nativity, pillar B6, #264
Technique scratched
Condition poor
Content Georgian inscription
Limitation *Tentative decipherment only*
Access DRa18 (photograph, M. Stone)

Inscription 1139
Site Church of the Nativity, pillar B6, #264
Technique incised
Condition fair
Content Arabic inscription
Limitation *Tentative decipherment only*
Access DRa18 (photograph, M. Stone)

Inscription 1140
Site Church of the Nativity, pillar B6, #264
Technique scratched
Condition poor
Content Armenian inscription
Limitation *Tentative decipherment only*
Access DRa18 (photograph, M. Stone)

Inscription 1141
Site Church of the Nativity, pillar B4, #266
Technique painted
Condition good
Content Latin inscription
Limitation *Tentative decipherment only*
Access DSa01 (photograph, M. Stone)

Inscription 1142
Site Church of the Nativity, pillar B4, #266
Technique painted
Condition good
Content Greek inscription
Limitation *Tentative decipherment only*
Access DSa01 (photograph, M. Stone)

Inscription 1143
Site Church of the Nativity, pillar B4, #266
Technique scratched
Condition poor
Content Arabic inscription
Limitation *Tentative decipherment only*
Access DSa01 (photograph, M. Stone)

Inscription 1144
Site Church of the Nativity, pillar C4, #243
Technique incised
Condition good
Dimensions 9 x 2 cm.
Content Latin inscription
Limitation *Tentative decipherment only*
Access DVa09 (photograph, M. Stone)

Inscription 1145
Site Church of the Nativity, pillar C4, #243
Technique incised
Condition fair
Content Arabic inscription
Limitation *Tentative decipherment only*
Access DVa09 (photograph, M. Stone)

Inscription 1146
Site Church of the Nativity, pillar C4, #243
Technique incised
Condition fair
Content crosses alone
Access DVa09 (photograph, M. Stone)

Inscription 1147
Site Church of the Nativity, pillar C4, #243
Technique incised
Condition fair
Content unidentified signs
Access DVa09 (photograph, M. Stone)

Inscription 1148
Site Church of the Nativity, pillar C4, #243
Technique incised
Condition good
Content crosses with inscription
Access DVa09 (photograph, M. Stone)

Inscription 1149
Site Church of the Nativity, pillar C4, #243
Technique incised
Condition poor
Content Arabic inscription
Limitation *Tentative decipherment only*
Access DVa09 (photograph, M. Stone)

Inscription 1150
Site Church of the Nativity, pillar C4, #243
Technique incised
Condition fair
Content crosses alone
Access DVa09 (photograph, M. Stone)

Inscription 1151
Site Church of the Nativity, pillar C5, #244
Dating 1601
Technique scratched
Condition fair
Dimensions 12 x 7 cm.
Content English inscription
Limitation *Tentative decipherment only*
Access DVa14 (photograph, M. Stone)

Inscription 1152
Site Church of the Nativity, pillar C5, #244
Technique scratched
Condition fair
Content crosses alone
Access DVa14 (photograph, M. Stone)

Inscription 1153
Site Church of the Nativity, pillar C5, #244
Technique incised
Condition poor
Content unidentified inscription
Access DVa14 (photograph, M. Stone)

Inscription 1154
Site Santa Katarina, #10
Technique incised
Condition good
Content encircled crosses
Access BTd33-34 (photograph, M. Stone)

Inscription 1155
Site Santa Katarina, #10
Technique incised
Condition fair
Content rock drawing
Access BTd33-34 (photograph, M. Stone)

Inscription 1156
Site Church of the Nativity, north door to crypt, #262
Technique incised
Condition fair
Dimensions 35 x 15 cm.
Content Arabic inscription
Limitation *Tentative decipherment only*
Access DRa02 (photograph, M. Stone)

Inscription 1157
Site Church of the Nativity, north door to crypt, #262
Technique incised
Condition excellent
Content crosses alone
Comment *two lines of crosses*
Access DRa02 (photograph, M. Stone)

Inscription 1158
Site Church of the Nativity, north door to crypt, #262
Technique incised
Condition poor
Content Arabic inscription
Limitation *Tentative decipherment only*
Access DRa02 (photograph, M. Stone)

Inscription 1159
Site Church of the Nativity, north door to crypt, #262
Technique incised
Condition fair
Content crosses alone
Access DRa02 (photograph, M. Stone)

Inscription 1160
Site Church of the Nativity, north door to crypt, #262
Technique incised
Condition poor
Content Armenian inscription
Comment *illegible*
Access DRa02 (photograph, M. Stone)

Inscription 1161
Site Church of the Nativity, north door to crypt, #262
Technique scratched
Condition poor
Content Latin inscription
Limitation *Tentative decipherment only*
Access DRa02 (photograph, M. Stone)

Inscription 1162
Site Church of the Nativity, north door to crypt, #262
Technique scratched
Condition poor
Content Arabic inscription
Limitation *Tentative decipherment only*
Access DRa02 (photograph, M. Stone)

Inscription 1163
Site Church of the Nativity, north door to crypt, #262
Technique incised
Condition good
Content Armenian inscription
Limitation *Tentative decipherment only*
Access DRa13 (photograph, M. Stone)

Inscription **1164**
Site Church of the Nativity, north door to crypt, #262
Technique scratched
Condition fair
Dimensions 13 x 5 cm.
Content Arabic inscription
Limitation *Tentative decipherment only*
Access DRa13 (photograph, M. Stone)

Inscription **1165**
Site Church of the Nativity, north door to crypt, #262
Technique scratched
Condition fair
Content Italian inscription
Limitation *Tentative decipherment only*
Access DRa13 (photograph, M. Stone)

Inscription **1166**
Site Church of the Nativity, north door to crypt, #262
Technique scratched
Condition poor
Content Greek inscription
Limitation *Tentative decipherment only*
Access DRa13 (photograph, M. Stone)

Inscription **1167**
Site Church of the Nativity, north door to crypt, #262
Technique scratched
Condition poor
Content English inscription
Limitation *Tentative decipherment only*
Access DRa13 (photograph, M. Stone)

Inscription **1168**
Site Church of the Nativity, north door to crypt, #262
Technique scratched
Condition poor
Content Arabic inscription
Limitation *Tentative decipherment only*
Access DRa13 (photograph, M. Stone)

Inscription **1169**
Site Santa Katarina, #10
Technique incised
Condition fair
Content Greek inscription
Limitation *Tentative decipherment only*
Access BTd31-32 (photograph, M. Stone)

Inscription **1170**
Site Santa Katarina, #10
Technique incised
Condition good
Content encircled crosses
Access BTd31-32 (photograph, M. Stone)

Inscription **1171**
Site Santa Katarina, #10
Technique incised
Condition good
Content rock drawing
Access BTd31-32 (photograph, M. Stone)

Inscription **1172**
Site Church of the Nativity, pillar B3, #268
Technique scratched
Condition fair
Content Greek inscription
Limitation *Tentative decipherment only*
Access DSa14 (photograph, M. Stone)

Inscription **1173**
Site Church of the Nativity, pillar B3, #268
Technique painted
Condition good
Dimensions 25 x 10 cm.
Content Arabic inscription
Limitation *Tentative decipherment only*
Access DSa14 (photograph, M. Stone)

Inscription **1174**
Site Church of the Nativity, pillar B3, #268
Technique painted
Condition good
Content Arabic inscription
Limitation *Tentative decipherment only*
Access DSa14 (photograph, M. Stone)

Inscription **1175**
Site Church of the Nativity, pillar B3, #268
Technique painted
Condition fair
Content Arabic inscription
Limitation *Tentative decipherment only*
Access DSa14 (photograph, M. Stone)

Inscription **1176**
Site Church of the Nativity, pillar B3, #268
Technique painted
Condition good
Content Arabic inscription
Limitation *Tentative decipherment only*
Access DSa14 (photograph, M. Stone)

Inscription **1177**
Site Church of the Nativity, pillar B3, #268
Technique scratched
Condition poor
Content Latin inscription
Limitation *Tentative decipherment only*
Access DSa14 (photograph, M. Stone)

Inscription **1178**
Site Church of the Nativity, pillar B3, #268
Technique scratched
Condition poor
Content unidentified inscription
Access DSa14 (photograph, M. Stone)

Inscription **1179**
Site Church of the Nativity, pillar B3, #268
Technique scratched
Condition poor
Content unidentified inscription
Access DSa14 (photograph, M. Stone)

Inscription **1180**
Site Church of the Nativity, pillar B3, #268
Technique scratched
Condition poor
Dimensions 30 x 7 cm.
Content Latin inscription
Limitation *Tentative decipherment only*
Access DSa15 (photograph, M. Stone)

Inscription **1181**
Site Church of the Nativity, pillar B3, #268
Technique painted
Condition fair
Content Latin inscription
Limitation *Tentative decipherment only*
Access DSa15 (photograph, M. Stone)

Inscription **1182**
Site Church of the Nativity, pillar B3, #268
Technique scratched
Condition fair
Content unidentified signs
Access DSa15 (photograph, M. Stone)

Inscription **1183**
Site Church of the Nativity, pillar B3, #268
Technique scratched
Condition poor
Content unidentified inscription
Access DSa15 (photograph, M. Stone)

Inscription **1184**
Site Church of the Nativity, pillar A4, #275
Dating 1832
Technique incised
Condition excellent
Dimensions 7 x 1 cm.
Content Arabic inscription
Limitation *Tentative decipherment only*
Access DTb59-60 (photograph, M. Stone)

Inscription **1185**
Site Church of the Nativity, pillar A4, #275
Technique incised
Condition good
Content crosses with inscription
Access DTb59-60 (photograph, M. Stone)

Inscription **1186**
Site Church of the Nativity, pillar A4, #275
Technique incised
Condition good
Content Armenian inscription
Limitation *Tentative decipherment only*
Access DTb59-60 (photograph, M. Stone)

Inscription **1187**
Site Church of the Nativity, pillar A4, #275
Technique incised
Condition good
Content crosses with inscription
Access DTb59-60 (photograph, M. Stone)

Inscription **1188**
Site Church of the Nativity, pillar A4, #275
Technique incised
Condition good
Content encircled crosses
Access DTb59-60 (photograph, M. Stone)

Inscription **1189**
Site Church of the Nativity, pillar A4, #275
Technique incised
Condition poor
Content Arabic inscription
Limitation *Tentative decipherment only*
Access DTb59-60 (photograph, M. Stone)

Inscription **1190**
Site Church of the Nativity, pillar A4, #275
Technique incised
Condition good
Content crosses alone
Access DTb59-60 (photograph, M. Stone)

Inscription **1191**
Site Church of the Nativity, pillar A4, #275
Technique incised
Condition fair
Content Armenian inscription
Limitation *Tentative decipherment only*
Access DTb59-60 (photograph, M. Stone)

Inscription **1192**
Site Church of the Nativity, pillar A4, #275
Technique incised
Condition fair
Content rock drawing
Access DTb59-60 (photograph, M. Stone)

Inscription **1193**
Site Church of the Nativity, pillar A4, #275
Technique incised
Condition fair
Content crosses alone
Access DTb59-60 (photograph, M. Stone)

Inscription **1194**
Site Church of the Nativity, pillar A4, #275
Technique incised
Condition fair
Content unidentified signs
Access DTb59-60 (photograph, M. Stone)

Inscription **1195**
Site Church of the Nativity, pillar A4, #275
Technique incised
Condition poor
Content Arabic inscription
Limitation *Tentative decipherment only*
Access DTb59-60 (photograph, M. Stone)

Inscription 1196
Site Church of the Nativity, pillar C11, #253
Technique incised
Condition fair
Dimensions 15 x 1 cm.
Content Greek inscription
Limitation *Tentative decipherment only*
Access DUa17 (photograph, M. Stone)

Inscription 1197
Site Church of the Nativity, pillar C11, #253
Technique scratched
Condition fair
Dimensions 15 x 1 cm.
Content Greek inscription
Limitation *Tentative decipherment only*
Access DUa17 (photograph, M. Stone)

Inscription 1198
Site Church of the Nativity, pillar C11, #253
Technique incised
Condition good
Dimensions 8 x 1 cm.
Content Syriac inscription
Limitation *Tentative decipherment only*
Access DUa17 (photograph, M. Stone)

Inscription 1199
Site Church of the Nativity, pillar C11, #253
Technique incised
Condition good
Content Armenian inscription
Limitation *Tentative decipherment only*
Access DUa17 (photograph, M. Stone)

Inscription 1200
Site Church of the Nativity, pillar C11, #253
Technique scratched
Condition good
Content Arabic inscription
Limitation *Tentative decipherment only*
Access DUa17 (photograph, M. Stone); *see also* DUa19

Inscription 1201
Site Church of the Nativity, pillar C11, #253
Technique scratched
Condition good
Content crosses alone
Access DUa17 (photograph, M. Stone)

Inscription 1202
Site Church of the Nativity, pillar C11, #253
Technique scratched
Condition poor
Content Arabic inscription
Limitation *Tentative decipherment only*
Access DUa17 (photograph, M. Stone); *see also* DUa19

Inscription 1203
Site Church of the Nativity, pillar C11, #253
Technique incised
Condition poor
Content unidentified inscription
Access DUa17 (photograph, M. Stone)

Inscription 1204
Site Church of the Nativity, pillar C11, #253
Technique scratched
Condition fair
Content Armenian inscription
Limitation *Tentative decipherment only*
Access DUa17 (photograph, M. Stone); *see also* DUa19

Inscription 1205
Site Church of the Nativity, pillar C11, #253
Technique scratched
Condition good
Content Greek inscription
Limitation *Tentative decipherment only*
Access DUa19 (photograph, M. Stone)

Inscription 1206
Site Church of the Nativity, pillar C11, #253
Technique scratched
Condition fair
Content Greek inscription
Limitation *Tentative decipherment only*
Access DUa19 (photograph, M. Stone)

Inscription 1207
Site Church of the Nativity, pillar C11, #253
Technique scratched
Condition fair
Content Syriac inscription
Limitation *Tentative decipherment only*
Access DUa19 (photograph, M. Stone)

Inscription 1208
Site Church of the Nativity, pillar C11, #253
Technique scratched
Condition fair
Content Italian inscription
Limitation *Tentative decipherment only*
Access DUa19 (photograph, M. Stone)

Inscription 1209
Site Church of the Nativity, pillar C11, #253
Technique scratched
Condition poor
Dimensions 10 x 1 cm.
Content Armenian inscription
Limitation *Tentative decipherment only*
Access DUa19 (photograph, M. Stone)

Inscription 1210
Site Church of the Nativity, pillar C11, #253
Technique scratched
Condition fair
Content crosses with inscription
Access DUa19 (photograph, M. Stone)

Inscription **1211**
Site Church of the Nativity, pillar C11, #253
Technique scratched
Condition good
Content crosses alone
Access DUa19 (photograph, M. Stone)

Inscription **1212**
Site Church of the Nativity, pillar C11, #253
Technique scratched
Condition poor
Content crosses alone
Access DUa19 (photograph, M. Stone)

Inscription **1213**
Site Church of the Nativity, pillar C11, #253
Technique scratched
Condition poor
Content unidentified inscription
Access DUa19 (photograph, M. Stone)

Inscription **1214**
Site Church of the Nativity, pillar B7, #257
Dating 1694
Technique incised
Condition good
Content Armenian inscription
Limitation *Tentative decipherment only*
Access DUb42 (photograph, M. Stone)

Inscription **1215**
Site Church of the Nativity, pillar B7, #257
Technique incised
Condition fair
Content Armenian inscription
Limitation *Tentative decipherment only*
Access DUb42 (photograph, M. Stone)

Inscription **1216**
Site Church of the Nativity, pillar B7, #257
Technique incised
Condition good
Content crosses alone
Access DUb42 (photograph, M. Stone); *see also* DUb48

Inscription **1217**
Site Church of the Nativity, pillar B7, #257
Technique incised
Condition poor
Content Arabic inscription
Limitation *Tentative decipherment only*
Access DUb42 (photograph, M. Stone)

Inscription **1218**
Site Church of the Nativity, pillar B7, #257
Technique incised
Condition poor
Content Armenian inscription
Limitation *Tentative decipherment only*
Access DUb42 (photograph, M. Stone)

Inscription **1219**
Site Church of the Nativity, pillar B7, #257
Technique incised
Condition poor
Content unidentified inscription
Access DUb42 (photograph, M. Stone)

Inscription **1220**
Site Church of the Nativity, pillar B7, #257
Technique incised
Condition good
Content crosses alone
Access DUb42 (photograph, M. Stone)

Inscription **1221**
Site Church of the Nativity, pillar B7, #257
Technique incised
Condition fair
Content Greek inscription
Limitation *Tentative decipherment only*
Access DUb44 (photograph, M. Stone); *see also* DUb46

Inscription **1222**
Site Church of the Nativity, pillar B7, #257
Technique incised
Condition fair
Content Armenian inscription
Limitation *Tentative decipherment only*
Access DUb44 (photograph, M. Stone); *see also* DUb46

Inscription **1223**
Site Church of the Nativity, pillar B7, #257
Technique incised
Condition fair
Dimensions 6 x 9 cm.
Content crosses with inscription
Access DUb44 (photograph, M. Stone); *see also* DUb46

Inscription **1224**
Site Church of the Nativity, pillar B7, #257
Technique incised
Condition poor
Content unidentified inscription
Access DUb44 (photograph, M. Stone); *see also* DUb46

Inscription **1225**
Site Church of the Nativity, pillar B7, #257
Technique incised
Condition poor
Content Arabic inscription
Limitation *Tentative decipherment only*
Access DUb44 (photograph, M. Stone)

Inscription **1226**
Site Church of the Nativity, pillar B7, #257
Dating 1523
Technique incised
Condition fair
Content crosses alone
Access DUb44 (photograph, M. Stone)

Inscription	**1227**
Site	Church of the Nativity, pillar B7, #257
Dating	1523
Technique	incised
Condition	good
Dimensions	40 x 20 cm.
Content	Armenian inscription
Limitation	*Tentative decipherment only*
Access	DUb46 (photograph, M. Stone)

Inscription	**1228**
Site	Sinai, unknown, #0
Dating	1888
Technique	incised
Condition	poor
Content	Greek inscription
Limitation	*Tentative decipherment only*
Access	FS09 (photograph, Project)

Inscription	**1229**
Site	Church of the Nativity, pillar B7, #257
Technique	scratched
Condition	poor
Content	unidentified inscription
Access	DUb46 (photograph, M. Stone)

Inscription	**1230**
Site	Church of the Nativity, pillar B7, #257
Technique	scratched
Condition	poor
Content	unidentified inscription
Access	DUb46 (photograph, M. Stone)

Inscription	**1231**
Site	Church of the Nativity, pillar B7, #257
Technique	scratched
Condition	fair
Content	crosses alone
Access	DUb46 (photograph, M. Stone)

Inscription	**1232**
Site	Church of the Nativity, pillar B7, #257
Technique	incised
Condition	fair
Content	Arabic inscription
Limitation	*Tentative decipherment only*
Access	DUb48 (photograph, M. Stone)

Inscription	**1233**
Site	Church of the Nativity, pillar B7, #257
Technique	incised
Condition	good
Content	crosses with inscription
Access	DUb48 (photograph, M. Stone)

Inscription	**1234**
Site	Church of the Nativity, pillar B7, #257
Dating	1711
Technique	scratched
Condition	fair
Content	Armenian inscription
Limitation	*Tentative decipherment only*
Access	DUb48 (photograph, M. Stone)

Inscription	**1235**
Site	Church of the Nativity, pillar B7, #257
Dating	16??
Technique	scratched
Condition	fair
Content	Armenian inscription
Limitation	*Tentative decipherment only*
Access	DUb48 (photograph, M. Stone)

Inscription	**1236**
Site	Church of the Nativity, pillar B7, #257
Technique	incised
Condition	poor
Content	Armenian inscription
Limitation	*Tentative decipherment only*
Access	DUb48 (photograph, M. Stone)

Inscription	**1237**
Site	Sinai, unknown, #0
Technique	incised
Condition	poor
Content	Greek inscription
Limitation	*Tentative decipherment only*
Access	FS09 (photograph, Project)

Inscription	**1238**
Site	Church of the Nativity, pillar B7, #257
Technique	scratched
Condition	poor
Content	Arabic inscription
Limitation	*Tentative decipherment only*
Access	DUb48 (photograph, M. Stone)

Inscription	**1239**
Site	Sinai, unknown, #0
Technique	incised
Condition	fair
Content	Arabic inscription
Limitation	*Tentative decipherment only*
Access	FS10 (photograph, Project)

Inscription	**1240**
Site	Church of the Nativity, pillar B7, #257
Dating	1641(?)
Technique	incised
Condition	good
Content	Latin inscription
Limitation	*Tentative decipherment only*
Access	DUb48 (photograph, M. Stone)

Inscription	**1241**
Site	Church of the Nativity, pillar B7, #257
Technique	scratched
Condition	poor
Content	Polish inscription
Limitation	*Tentative decipherment only*
Access	DUb48 (photograph, M. Stone)

Inscription	**1242**
Site	Church of the Nativity, pillar B7, #257
Technique	scratched
Condition	poor
Content	unidentified inscription
Access	DUb48 (photograph, M. Stone)

Inscription **1243**
Site Church of the Nativity, pillar B7, #257
Technique scratched
Condition fair
Content crosses alone
Access DUb48 (photograph, M. Stone)

Inscription **1244**
Site Church of the Nativity, pillar B9, #256
Dating 1741
Technique incised
Condition fair
Dimensions 9 x 3 cm.
Content Armenian inscription
Limitation *Tentative decipherment only*
Access DUa30 (photograph, M. Stone)

Inscription **1245**
Site Church of the Nativity, pillar B9, #256
Technique incised
Condition poor
Content unidentified signs
Access DUa30 (photograph, M. Stone)

Inscription **1246**
Site Church of the Nativity, pillar B9, #256
Technique incised
Condition good
Content crosses alone
Access DUa30 (photograph, M. Stone)

Inscription **1247**
Site Church of the Nativity, pillar C11, #253
Technique incised
Condition good
Dimensions 6 x 10 cm.
Content Armenian inscription
Limitation *Tentative decipherment only*
Access DUa32 (photograph, M. Stone)

Inscription **1248**
Site Church of the Nativity, pillar C11, #253
Technique incised
Condition poor
Dimensions 6 x 10 cm.
Content Arabic inscription
Limitation *Tentative decipherment only*
Access DUa32 (photograph, M. Stone)

Inscription **1249**
Site Wadi Shellal, #90
Condition good
Content Nabatean inscription
šlm ʿbdʾlbʿly br
[š]ʿdʾlhl[y] bṭb
Access II.2.358 (printed, CIS)
Corpus CIS 490

Inscription **1250**
Site Naqb Budra, #99
Condition good
Content Nabatean inscription
šlm p
ytʿw br wdw bryk lʿ[l]m
Access II.2.359 (printed, CIS)
Corpus CIS 491

---

nscription **1251**
Site Naqb Budra, #99
Condition poor
Content Nabatean inscription
gdyw br [bḥnh]
Access II.2.359 (printed, CIS)
Corpus CIS 492

Inscription **1252**
Site Naqb Budra, #99
Condition excellent
Content Nabatean inscription
dkyr hnyʾw br
ʾwšʾlḥy
šʾrʾ bṭb
Access II.2.359 (printed, CIS)
Corpus CIS 493

Inscription **1253**
Site Wadi Sih, #80
Condition excellent
Content Nabatean inscription
dkyr yʿly
br ʿmyw bṭb
Access II.2.360 (printed, CIS)
Corpus CIS 494

Inscription **1254**
Site Wadi Sih, #80
Condition fair
Content Nabatean inscription
dkyr ʿw
dw br zydw
... ṭ[b] w
šlm
Access II.2.360 (printed, CIS)
Corpus CIS 495

Inscription **1255**
Site Wadi Sih, #80
Condition excellent
Content Nabatean inscription
šlm dʾbw br
ʿmyw bṭb
Access II.2.360 (printed, CIS)
Corpus CIS 496

Inscription 1256
Site Wadi Sih, #80
Condition excellent
Content Nabatean inscription
šlm ʾʿlʾ br
ḥlṣt bṭb
Access II.2.361 (printed, CIS)
Corpus CIS 497

Inscription 1257
Site Wadi Sih, #80
Condition good
Content Nabatean inscription
šlm lmynw br
ʿbdʾl .. bṭb
Access II.2.361 (printed, CIS)
Corpus CIS 498

Inscription 1258
Site Wadi Sih, #80
Condition good
Content Nabatean inscription
dkyr ʾšw br ḥry
šw dy mqtry ʾšy
bw bṭb
Access II.2.361 (printed, CIS)
Corpus CIS 499

Inscription 1259
Site Wadi Sih, #80
Condition excellent
Content Nabatean inscription
šlm grmʾlyh br ʿbydw
Access II.2.361 (printed, CIS)
Corpus CIS 500

Inscription 1260
Site Wadi Sih, #80
Condition excellent
Content Nabatean inscription
šlm ʾwšw br
klbw bṭb
Access II.2.361 (printed, CIS)
Corpus CIS 501

Inscription 1261
Site Wadi Sih, #80
Condition fair
Content Nabatean inscription
ʾwyšw
dkyr ʾšw[dw]
br ʿbydw
bṭb
Access II.2.362 (printed, CIS)
Corpus CIS 502

Inscription 1262
Site Wadi Sih, #80
Condition excellent
Content Nabatean inscription
šlm ḥlyṣw br
ʾtmw bṭb
Access II.2.362 (printed, CIS)
Corpus CIS 503

Inscription 1263
Site Wadi Sih, #80
Condition excellent
Content Nabatean inscription
šlm grmʾlbʿly br ḥnṭlw
Access II.2.362 (printed, CIS)
Corpus CIS 504

Inscription 1264
Site Wadi Sih, #80
Condition good
Content Nabatean inscription
dkyr ḥryšw br wʾlw bṭb ʿ.mw
Access II.2.362 (printed, CIS)
Corpus CIS 505

Inscription 1265
Site Wadi Sih, #80
Condition fair
Content Nabatean inscription
dkyr ḥršw br ʿmyw khn tʾ
Access II.2.363 (printed, CIS)
Corpus CIS 506

Inscription 1266
Site Wadi Sih, #80
Condition excellent
Content Nabatean inscription
dkyr ḥnṭlw br ʾbn ʾlqynw bṭb
Access II.2.363 (printed, CIS)
Corpus CIS 507

Inscription 1267
Site Wadi Sih, #80
Condition good
Content Nabatean inscription
ʿbdʾlbʿly br yʿl[y]
Access II.2.363 (printed, CIS)
Corpus CIS 508

Inscription 1268
Site Wadi Sih, #80
Condition excellent
Content Nabatean inscription
dkyr zydw br zydw
wʿmyw brh bṭb wšlm
Access II.2.363 (printed, CIS)
Corpus CIS 509

Inscription 1269
Site Wadi Sih, #80
Condition good
Content Nabatean inscription
šlm ʾwšw br
ṣḥbw b[ṭb]
Access II.2.363 (printed, CIS)
Corpus CIS 510

Inscription 1270
Site Wadi Sih, #80
Condition fair
Content Nabatean inscription
šlm ʾtmw br ʿ[bdʾlhy]
Access II.2.363 (printed, CIS)
Corpus CIS 511

Inscription 1271
Site Wadi Sih, #80
Condition fair
Content Nabatean inscription
[ʾt]mw br ʿbdʾl[h]y šlm
Access II.2.364 (printed, CIS)
Corpus CIS 512

Inscription 1272
Site Wadi Sih, #80
Condition fair
Content Nabatean inscription
šlm ʾbʾwšw br
ḥryšw b[ṭb]
Access II.2.364 (printed, CIS)
Corpus CIS 513

Inscription 1273
Site Wadi Sih, #80
Condition good
Content Nabatean inscription
dkyr dʾbw
br ʾwšw b[ṭb]
Access II.2.364 (printed, CIS)
Corpus CIS 514

Inscription 1274
Site Wadi Sih, #80
Condition good
Content Nabatean inscription
dkyr ʿbdʾlbʿly
[br] ʿbydw bṭb
Access II.2.364 (printed, CIS)
Corpus CIS 515

Inscription 1275
Site Wadi Sih, #80
Condition good
Content Nabatean inscription
dkyr ḥryšw br tymʾlhy b[ṭb]
Access II.2.364 (printed, CIS)
Corpus CIS 516

Inscription 1276
Site Wadi Sih, #80
Condition fair
Content Nabatean inscription
dkyr ʿmyw br
ʾ... bṭ[b]
Access II.2.364 (printed, CIS)
Corpus CIS 517

Inscription 1277
Site Wadi Sih, #80
Condition good
Content Nabatean inscription
dkyr ḥryšw
[b]r bryʾw
Access II.2.364 (printed, CIS)
Corpus CIS 518

Inscription 1278
Site Wadi Sih, #80
Condition good
Content Nabatean inscription
šlm prʾn br
ʿnyšw b[ṭb]
Access II.2.365 (printed, CIS)
Corpus CIS 519

Inscription 1279
Site Wadi Sih, #80
Condition excellent
Content Nabatean inscription
šlm ʾʿlʾ br
zydw bṭb
Access II.2.365 (printed, CIS)
Corpus CIS 520

Inscription 1280
Site Wadi Sih, #80
Condition fair
Content Nabatean inscription
dkyr ʿbydw br
mg[d]yw b[ṭb]
Access II.2.365 (printed, CIS)
Corpus CIS 521

Inscription 1281
Site Wadi Sih, #80
Condition excellent
Content Nabatean inscription
šlm ḥršw br
šlmw bṭb
Access II.2.365 (printed, CIS)
Corpus CIS 522

Inscription 1282
Site Wadi Sih, #80
Condition fair
Content Nabatean inscription
šlm ʿmyw br n
rml[bʿly]
Access II.2.365 (printed, CIS)
Corpus CIS 523

Inscription 1283
Site Wadi Sih, #80
Condition good
Content Nabatean inscription
dkyr w[ʾ]lw br
ʾwšw
Access II.2.365 (printed, CIS)
Corpus CIS 524

Inscription 1284
Site Wadi Sih, #80
Condition fair
Content Nabatean inscription
[šlm] ṣhbw br grmʾlhy
šlm ʿw[dw br] ʾwšʾlhy
Access II.2.365 (printed, CIS)
Corpus CIS 525

Inscription 1285
Site Wadi Sih, #80
Condition good
Content Nabatean inscription
dkyr ʿbdʾlbʿly br
ʿbydw khn
ʾʾlhy bṭb
ʾlhʾ
Access II.2.366 (printed, CIS)
Corpus CIS 526

Inscription 1286
Site Wadi Sih, #80
Condition good
Content Nabatean inscription
šlm ḥryšw
br yʿly bṭ[b]
Access II.2.366 (printed, CIS)
Corpus CIS 527

Inscription 1287
Site Wadi Sih, #80
Condition good
Content Nabatean inscription
dkyr ḥnṭlw
br ʿwdw w[ʿ]wdw brh
Access II.2.366 (printed, CIS)
Corpus CIS 528

Inscription 1288
Site Wadi Sih, #80
Condition poor
Content Nabatean inscription
b]r dʾybw bṭb
Access II.2.366 (printed, CIS)
Corpus CIS 529

Inscription 1289
Site Wadi Sih, #80
Condition poor
Content Nabatean inscription
šʿrʾlh
Access II.2.366 (printed, CIS)
Corpus CIS 530

Inscription 1290
Site Wadi Sih, #80
Condition good
Content Nabatean inscription
dkyr ʿmyw
br ḥryšw
Access II.2.366 (printed, CIS)
Corpus CIS 531

Inscription 1291
Site Wadi Sih, #80
Condition poor
Content Nabatean inscription
šl[m] bryʾw br
...w br ʾwšʾl[hy]
Access II.2.366 (printed, CIS)
Corpus CIS 532

Inscription 1292
Site Wadi Sih, #80
Condition fair
Content Nabatean inscription
dkyr ḥnṭlw br zydw .... bṭb
Access II.2.366 (printed, CIS)
Corpus CIS 533

Inscription 1293
Site Wadi Sih, #80
Condition fair
Content Nabatean inscription
dkyr wb[r]yk ʾbn ʾlqyny br ʾʿlʾ bṭb
Access II.2.366 (printed, CIS)
Corpus CIS 534

Inscription 1294
Site Wadi Sih, #80
Condition fair
Content Nabatean inscription
šlm ʿmyw br p[ʾrn]
bṭb wpʾ[rn]
brh
Access II.2.367 (printed, CIS)
Corpus CIS 535

Inscription **1295**
Site Wadi Sih, #80
Condition excellent
Content Nabatean inscription
šlm šlm
šlm mḥlmw
br grmʾlh[y]
wbnyhy grmʾlhy
w ʿmmw bnyhw
Access II.2.367 (printed, CIS)
Corpus CIS 536

Inscription **1296**
Site Wadi Sih, #80
Condition poor
Content Nabatean inscription
Comment *illegible*
Access II.2.367 (printed, CIS)
Corpus CIS 537

Inscription **1297**
Site Wadi Sih, #80
Condition excellent
Content Nabatean inscription
ḥršw
br wʾlw
šlm wʾlw
Access II.2.367 (printed, CIS)
Corpus CIS 538

Inscription **1298**
Site Wadi Sih, #80
Condition excellent
Content Nabatean inscription
šlm ḥbrkn br ḥlṣt bṭb
Access II.2.367 (printed, CIS)
Corpus CIS 539

Inscription **1299**
Site Wadi Sih, #80
Condition excellent
Content Nabatean inscription
šlm wʾlw br ʾlʾbršw bṭb
Access II.2.367 (printed, CIS)
Corpus CIS 540

Inscription **1300**
Site Wadi Sih, #80
Condition fair
Content Nabatean inscription
dkyr .... br šʿdʾlh
Access II.2.367 (printed, CIS)
Corpus CIS 541

Inscription **1301**
Site Wadi Sih, #80
Condition fair
Content Nabatean inscription
šlm šʿdʾlhy br yʿ[ly]
dkyr ḥlyṣw br
ʿmyw bṭb
Access II.2.368 (printed, CIS)
Corpus CIS 542

Inscription **1302**
Site Wadi Sih, #80
Condition excellent
Content Nabatean inscription
dkyr bryʾw br
ḥršw w
ʿmrw brh bṭb
Access II.2.368 (printed, CIS)
Corpus CIS 543

Inscription **1303**
Site Wadi Sih, #80
Condition good
Content Nabatean inscription
dkyr [n]bhw br ʾlktyw bṭb
Access II.2.368 (printed, CIS)
Corpus CIS 544

Inscription **1304**
Site Wadi Sih, #80
Condition fair
Content Nabatean inscription
šlm ʾʿlʾ
br šnrḥ wʿmyw
.... bnyh bṭb
Access II.2.368 (printed, CIS)
Corpus CIS 545

Inscription **1305**
Site Wadi Sih, #80
Condition good
Content Nabatean inscription
dkyr wʾlt br ʿmyw bṭb
Access II.2.368 (printed, CIS)
Corpus CIS 546

Inscription **1306**
Site Wadi Sih, #80
Condition poor
Content Nabatean inscription
Comment *illegible*
Access II.2.368 (printed, CIS)
Corpus CIS 547

Inscription 1307
Site Wadi Sih, #80
Condition excellent
Content Nabatean inscription
šlm ʿmrw
br ḥryš
w bṭb
Access II.2.368 (printed, CIS)
Corpus CIS 548

Inscription 1308
Site Wadi Sih, #80
Condition poor
Content Nabatean inscription
Comment *illegible*
Access II.2.369 (printed, CIS)
Corpus CIS 549

Inscription 1309
Site Wadi Sih, #80
Condition fair
Content Nabatean inscription
šlm ḥršw ... šlm qynw br ṭ...
Access II.2.369 (printed, CIS)
Corpus CIS 550

Inscription 1310
Site Wadi Sih, #80
Condition excellent
Content Nabatean inscription
dkyr ʾwyšw
zydw br qynw bkl ṭb
dkyr
Access II.2.369 (printed, CIS)
Corpus CIS 551

Inscription 1311
Site Wadi Sih, #80
Condition fair
Content Nabatean inscription
ʿbdʾlbʿly [br]
ʾtmw .... ʿbydw
br ʿbdʾlbʿl[y]
Access II.2.369 (printed, CIS)
Corpus CIS 552

Inscription 1312
Site Wadi Sih, #80
Condition fair
Content Nabatean inscription
dkyr ḥwbn b[r]
Access II.2.369 (printed, CIS)
Corpus CIS 553

Inscription 1313
Site Wadi Sih, #80
Condition excellent
Content Nabatean inscription
šlm ʾlmbqrw
br ʿwdw
šlm ʾwšw
br ʿwdw
Access II.2.369 (printed, CIS)
Corpus CIS 554

Inscription 1314
Site Wadi Sih, #80
Condition poor
Content Nabatean inscription
]šʿdʾl [hy
Access II.2.370 (printed, CIS)
Corpus CIS 555

Inscription 1315
Site Wadi Sih, #80
Condition good
Content Nabatean inscription
šlm ʿwdw
br ʾlmbqrw
Access II.2.370 (printed, CIS)
Corpus CIS 556

Inscription 1316
Site Wadi Sih, #80
Condition good
Content Nabatean inscription
šlm ʾlmbqrw br wʾlw
Access II.2.370 (printed, CIS)
Corpus CIS 557

Inscription 1317
Site Wadi Sih, #80
Condition excellent
Content Nabatean inscription
šlm ʾmrʾyʿwt br ṣhbn
Access II.2.370 (printed, CIS)
Corpus CIS 558

Inscription 1318
Site Wadi Sih, #80
Condition excellent
Content Nabatean inscription
šlm šʿdw br drkw
Access II.2.370 (printed, CIS)
Corpus CIS 559

Inscription 1319
Site Wadi Sih, #80
Condition excellent
Content Nabatean inscription
šlm ʿwdw br šʿdʾlhy
Access II.2.370 (printed, CIS)
Corpus CIS 560

Inscription 1320
Site Wadi Sih, #80
Condition good
Content Nabatean inscription
šlm ʿbdʾl. w br lmynw bṭb wšlm
Access II.2.370 (printed, CIS)
Corpus CIS 561

Inscription 1321
Site Wadi Sih, #80
Condition fair
Content Nabatean inscription
[grmʾ]lhy br ʿbydw
Access II.2.370 (printed, CIS)
Corpus CIS 562

Inscription 1322
Site Wadi Sih, #80
Condition good
Content Nabatean inscription
dkyr ʾwšʾlh
Access II.2.371 (printed, CIS)
Corpus CIS 563

Inscription 1323
Site Wadi Sih, #80
Condition poor
Content Nabatean inscription
šlm...ʾb
...mʾlbʿly
Access II.2.371 (printed, CIS)
Corpus CIS 564

Inscription 1324
Site Wadi Sih, #80
Condition fair
Content Nabatean inscription
dkyr ḥw[bn]
br ʾlmbq[rw]
Access II.2.371 (printed, CIS)
Corpus CIS 565

Inscription 1325
Site Wadi Sih, #80
Condition good
Content Nabatean inscription
dkyr ʾṣlḥw
br yʿly
Access II.2.371 (printed, CIS)
Corpus CIS 566

Inscription 1326
Site Wadi Sih, #80
Condition good
Content Nabatean inscription
dkyr wʾlw
Access II.2.371 (printed, CIS)
Corpus CIS 567

Inscription 1327
Site Wadi Sih, #80
Condition fair
Content Nabatean inscription
dkyr ʿbdʾlhy br ....
Access II.2.371 (printed, CIS)
Corpus CIS 568

Inscription 1328
Site Wadi Sih, #80
Condition excellent
Content Nabatean inscription
šlm zydw br
wʾlw ʾmyrw
Access II.2.371 (printed, CIS)
Corpus CIS 569

Inscription 1329
Site Wadi Sih, #80
Condition fair
Content Nabatean inscription
dkyr ʾwyšw
br p[ṣyw]
Access II.2.371 (printed, CIS)
Corpus CIS 570

Inscription 1330
Site Wadi Sih, #80
Condition poor
Content Nabatean inscription
Comment *illegible*
Access II.2.371 (printed, CIS)
Corpus CIS 571

Inscription 1331
Site Wadi Sih, #80
Condition excellent
Content Nabatean inscription
šlm wdʿw wyʿly bny pṣy mn qdm
bwbk ʾlhʾ
bṭb
Access II.2.372 (printed, CIS)
Corpus CIS 572

Inscription 1332
Site Wadi Sih, #80
Condition fair
Content Nabatean inscription
šlm ...w br ʿwdw
Access II.2.372 (printed, CIS)
Corpus CIS 573

Inscription 1333
Site Wadi Sih, #80
Condition fair
Content Nabatean inscription
šlm zydw
br ...
Access II.2.372 (printed, CIS)
Corpus CIS 574

Inscription	1334
Site	Wadi Sih, #80
Condition	good
Content	Nabatean inscription
	dkyr ʿlyw br šʿdʾl[hy]
Access	II.2.372 (printed, CIS)
Corpus	CIS 575

Inscription	1335
Site	Wadi Sih, #80
Condition	excellent
Content	Nabatean inscription
	šlm ṭylt br dmnw
Access	II.2.372 (printed, CIS)
Corpus	CIS 576

Inscription	1336
Site	Wadi Sih, #80
Condition	poor
Content	Nabatean inscription
Comment	*illegible*
Access	II.2.372 (printed, CIS)
Corpus	CIS 577

Inscription	1337
Site	Wadi Sih, #80
Condition	good
Content	Nabatean inscription
	ʿbdʾlbʿly br ʿlht
Access	II.2.372 (printed, CIS)
Corpus	CIS 578

Inscription	1338
Site	Wadi Sih, #80
Condition	good
Content	Nabatean inscription
	šlm dʾbw br ʿmyw
Access	II.2.373 (printed, CIS)
Corpus	CIS 579

Inscription	1339
Site	Wadi Sih, #80
Condition	good
Content	Nabatean inscription
	šlm ʾwšw br
	ʿwd w
Access	II.2.373 (printed, CIS)
Corpus	CIS 580

Inscription	1340
Site	Wadi Sih, #80
Condition	good
Content	Nabatean inscription
	šlm grmʾlbʿly
	br wʾl[t]
Access	II.2.373 (printed, CIS)
Corpus	CIS 581

Inscription	1341
Site	Wadi Sih, #80
Condition	good
Content	Nabatean inscription
	š[l]m ʿwdw br ʿmrw
Access	II.2.373 (printed, CIS)
Corpus	CIS 582

Inscription	1342
Site	Wadi Sih, #80
Condition	poor
Content	Nabatean inscription
	ʿb]dʾlbʿly ...
Access	II.2.373 (printed, CIS)
Corpus	CIS 583

Inscription	1343
Site	Wadi Sih, #80
Condition	good
Content	Nabatean inscription
	dkyr ʿbdʾlbʿly ...
Access	II.2.373 (printed, CIS)
Corpus	CIS 584

Inscription	1344
Site	Wadi Sih, #80
Condition	excellent
Content	Nabatean inscription
	šlm hnʾw br šʿdʾlhy
Access	II.2.373 (printed, CIS)
Corpus	CIS 585

Inscription	1345
Site	Wadi Sih, #80
Condition	excellent
Content	Nabatean inscription
	dkyr wʾlw br zydw
	wzydw brh bṭb
Access	II.2.373 (printed, CIS)
Corpus	CIS 586

Inscription	1346
Site	Wadi Sih, #80
Condition	good
Content	Nabatean inscription
	šlm šʿdʾlhy
	br w[ʾ]lw
Access	II.2.373 (printed, CIS)
Corpus	CIS 587

Inscription	1347
Site	Wadi Sih, #80
Condition	good
Content	Nabatean inscription
	šlm ḥlyṣw br
	ʾtmw wʾt[mw brh]
	bṭb
Access	II.2.374 (printed, CIS)
Corpus	CIS 588

Inscription 1348
Site Wadi Sih, #80
Condition good
Content Nabatean inscription
dkyr wʾlt br zydw
Access II.2.374 (printed, CIS)
Corpus CIS 589

Inscription 1349
Site Wadi Sih, #80
Condition good
Content Nabatean inscription
bryk tntlw br ʾʿlʾ
Access II.2.374 (printed, CIS)
Corpus CIS 590

Inscription 1350
Site Wadi Sih, #80
Condition fair
Content Nabatean inscription
[šlm] grmʾlhy
[br] ʾlktyw
Access II.2.374 (printed, CIS)
Corpus CIS 591

Inscription 1351
Site Wadi Sih, #80
Condition excellent
Content Nabatean inscription
šlm bṭšw
br bkrw bṭb
Access II.2.374 (printed, CIS)
Corpus CIS 592

Inscription 1352
Site Wadi Sih, #80
Condition poor
Content Nabatean inscription
Comment *illegible*
Access II.2.374 (printed, CIS)
Corpus CIS 593

Inscription 1353
Site Wadi Sih, #80
Condition good
Content Nabatean inscription
dkyr ʾwšw
br zydw b[ṭb]
Access II.2.374 (printed, CIS)
Corpus CIS 594

Inscription 1354
Site Wadi Sih, #80
Condition poor
Content Nabatean inscription
Comment *illegible*
Access II.2.374 (printed, CIS)
Corpus CIS 595

Inscription 1355
Site Wadi Sih, #80
Condition fair
Content Nabatean inscription
ʾwšʾlhy
Access II.2.374 (printed, CIS)
Corpus CIS 596

Inscription 1356
Site Wadi Sih, #80
Condition excellent
Content Nabatean inscription
šlm ʿmyw br ṣwbw bṭb
Access II.2.374 (printed, CIS)
Corpus CIS 597

Inscription 1357
Site Wadi Sih, #80
Condition poor
Content Nabatean inscription
Comment *illegible*
Access II.2.375 (printed, CIS)
Corpus CIS 598

Inscription 1358
Site Wadi Sih, #80
Condition poor
Content Nabatean inscription
.ṭ...mn ʾl
Access II.2.375 (printed, CIS)
Corpus CIS 599

Inscription 1359
Site Wadi Sih, #80
Condition poor
Content Nabatean inscription
br grmlhy
Access II.2.375 (printed, CIS)
Corpus CIS 600

Inscription 1360
Site Wadi Sih, #80
Condition fair
Content Nabatean inscription
dkyr šʿdlhy br...
Access II.2.375 (printed, CIS)
Corpus CIS 601

Inscription 1361
Site Wadi Sih, #80
Condition poor
Content Nabatean inscription
...hʾ...ly
Access II.2.375 (printed, CIS)
Corpus CIS 602

Inscription **1362**
Site Wadi Sih, #80
Condition poor
Content Nabatean inscription
dkyr šʿr...
Access II.2.375 (printed, CIS)
Corpus CIS 603

Inscription **1363**
Site Wadi Sih, #80
Condition poor
Content Nabatean inscription
...rw.mw.
Access II.2.375 (printed, CIS)
Corpus CIS 604

Inscription **1364**
Site Wadi Sih, #80
Condition excellent
Content Nabatean inscription
šlm grmʾlbʿly br
ʾwšw
Access II.2.375 (printed, CIS)
Corpus CIS 605

Inscription **1365**
Site Wadi Sih, #80
Condition good
Content Nabatean inscription
šlm hnʾw
Access II.2.375 (printed, CIS)
Corpus CIS 606

Inscription **1366**
Site Wadi Sih, #80
Condition fair
Content Nabatean inscription
[šlm] šmrh br wʾlw bṭb
Access II.2.375 (printed, CIS)
Corpus CIS 607

Inscription **1367**
Site Wadi Sih, #80
Condition fair
Content Nabatean inscription
šlm
šmrw
br ʿmyw k[hn
bṭb
Access II.2.375 (printed, CIS)
Corpus CIS 608

Inscription **1368**
Site Wadi Sih, #80
Condition fair
Content Nabatean inscription
šlm ʾw
šw b]r whbl
ḥ br pʾrn
br ʿṣrw
Access II.2.375 (printed, CIS)
Corpus CIS 609

Inscription **1369**
Site Wadi Sih, #80
Condition fair
Content Nabatean inscription
šlm ʾʿlʾ qš[ṭw]
br ḥryšw bṭb
br ʾ. w
Access II.2.376 (printed, CIS)
Corpus CIS 610

Inscription **1370**
Site Wadi Sih, #80
Condition good
Content Nabatean inscription
šlm ʿmyw br ḥryšw khn ʿzyʾ
Access II.2.376 (printed, CIS)
Corpus CIS 611

Inscription **1371**
Site Wadi Sih, #80
Condition excellent
Content Nabatean inscription
ḥlṣt br ḥlṣt bṭb
Access II.2.376 (printed, CIS)
Corpus CIS 612

Inscription **1372**
Site Wadi Sih, #80
Condition good
Content Nabatean inscription
dkyr bṭb wšlm grmʾlbʿly
br ʿb[ydw]
ʾʿlʾ qšṭw
br ḥryšw bṭb
Access II.2.376 (printed, CIS)
Corpus CIS 613

Inscription **1373**
Site Wadi Sih, #80
Condition good
Content Nabatean inscription
ʿyydw br
ʾwšw br wd...
bṭb
Access II.2.376 (printed, CIS)
Corpus CIS 614

Inscription **1374**
Site Wadi Sih, #80
Condition good
Content Nabatean inscription
šlm ʿbydw br [q]štw bṭb
Access II.2.376 (printed, CIS)
Corpus CIS 615

Inscription **1375**
Site Wadi Sih, #80
Condition good
Content Nabatean inscription
šlm ḥwyḥw
Access II.2.377 (printed, CIS)
Corpus CIS 616

Inscription **1376**
Site Wadi Sih, #80
Condition excellent
Content Nabatean inscription
šlm ʾwšʾlbʿly
br grmʾlbʿly bṭb
Access II.2.377 (printed, CIS)
Corpus CIS 617

Inscription **1377**
Site Wadi Sih, #80
Condition excellent
Content Nabatean inscription
dkyr zydw
br ʾlmbqrw
bṭb mbṭh
Access II.2.377 (printed, CIS)
Corpus CIS 618

Inscription **1378**
Site Wadi Sih, #80
Content Nabatean inscription
Condition excellent
dkyr bṭb wšlm gdyw br bḥgh bṭb
Access II.2.377 (printed, CIS)
Corpus CIS 619

Inscription **1379**
Site Wadi Sih, #80
Content Nabatean inscription
Condition good
dkyr ʿmrw br gdyw grm[ʾl]bʿcly
br gdyw
Access II.2.377 (printed, CIS)
Corpus CIS 620

Inscription **1380**
Site Wadi Sih, #80
Condition good
Content Nabatean inscription
ʾwšw [br] klbw bṭb
Access II.2.377 (printed, CIS)
Corpus CIS 621

Inscription **1381**
Site Wadi Sih, #80
Condition poor
Content Nabatean inscription
šlm ʾ... ḥyw
Access II.2.377 (printed, CIS)
Corpus CIS 622

Inscription **1382**
Site Wadi Sih, #80
Condition poor
Content Nabatean inscription
šlm bryʾw br ...
šlm ʾwšw [br]
ʾbn ʾlqyn
Access II.2.378 (printed, CIS)
Corpus CIS 623

Inscription **1383**
Site Wadi Sih, #80
Condition poor
Content Nabatean inscription
Comment *illegible*
Access II.2.378 (printed, CIS)
Corpus CIS 624

Inscription **1384**
Site Wadi Sih, #80
Condition poor
Content Nabatean inscription
Comment *illegible*
Access II.2.378 (printed, CIS)
Corpus CIS 625

Inscription **1385**
Site Wadi Sih, #80
Condition fair
Content Nabatean inscription
šlm yʿly
Access II.2.378 (printed, CIS)
Corpus CIS 626

Inscription **1386**
Site Wadi Sih, #80
Condition poor
Content Nabatean inscription
Comment *illegible*
Access II.2.378 (printed, CIS)
Corpus CIS 627

Inscription **1387**
Site Wadi Sih, #80
Condition poor
Content Nabatean inscription
Comment *illegible*
Access II.2.378 (printed, CIS)
Corpus CIS 628

Inscription **1388**
Site Wadi Sih, #80
Condition excellent
Content Nabatean inscription
šlm šmrḥ br
ḥryšw bṭb w
šlm
Access II.2.378 (printed, CIS)
Corpus CIS 629

Inscription **1389**
Site Wadi Sih, #80
Condition fair
Content Nabatean inscription
wʾlw
Access II.2.378 (printed, CIS)
Corpus CIS 630

Inscription **1390**
Site Wadi Sih, #80
Condition poor
Content Nabatean inscription
grmʾlbʿly..
dkyr zydw br ʿmyw bṭb
Access II.2.378 (printed, CIS)
Corpus CIS 631

Inscription **1391**
Site Wadi Sih, #80
Condition poor
Content Nabatean inscription
Comment *illegible*
Access II.2.378 (printed, CIS)
Corpus CIS 632

Inscription **1392**
Site Wadi Sih, #80
Condition poor
Content Nabatean inscription
Comment *illegible*
Access II.2.378 (printed, CIS)
Corpus CIS 633

Inscription **1393**
Site Wadi Sih, #80
Condition poor
Content Nabatean inscription
Comment *illegible*
Access II.2.378 (printed, CIS)
Corpus CIS 634

Inscription **1394**
Site Wadi Sih, #80
Condition poor
Content Nabatean inscription
...]šlm ʿmrw
Access II.2.378 (printed, CIS)
Corpus CIS 635

Inscription **1395**
Site Wadi Maghara, #72
Condition fair
Content Nabatean inscription
dkyr ʿyydw br bryʾw
šl[m] w'[lw..]
Access II.2.379 (printed, CIS)
Corpus CIS 636

Inscription **1396**
Site Wadi Maghara, #72
Condition good
Content Nabatean inscription
dkyr ʾʿl wdmgw
wprpryw bnyṭ
ylʾ bṭb
Access II.2.379 (printed, CIS)
Corpus CIS 637

Inscription **1397**
Site Wadi Maghara, #72
Condition excellent
Content Nabatean inscription
dkyr ʾbʾwšw wʿyydw
wbryʾw bny ḥryšw
Access II.2.379 (printed, CIS)
Corpus CIS 638

Inscription **1398**
Site Wadi Maghara, #72
Condition good
Content Nabatean inscription
dkyr
ḥryšw br...
Access II.2.379 (printed, CIS)
Corpus CIS 639

Inscription **1399**
Site Wadi Maghara, #72
Condition good
Content Nabatean inscription
šlm šmrḥ
br ʿwd[w] wʾlw
brh
Access II.2.380 (printed, CIS)
Corpus CIS 640

Inscription **1400**
Site Wadi Maghara, #72
Condition good
Content Nabatean inscription
šlm wʾl[w]
br bkrw b[ṭb]
Access II.2.380 (printed, CIS)
Corpus CIS 641

Inscription 1401
Site Wadi Maghara, #72
Condition excellent
Content Nabatean inscription
dkyr ḥlṣt br
wʾlw
Access II.2.380 (printed, CIS)
Corpus CIS 642

Inscription 1402
Site Wadi Maghara, #72
Condition good
Content Nabatean inscription
šlm ḥryšw br
zydw
Access II.2.380 (printed, CIS)
Corpus CIS 643

Inscription 1403
Site Wadi Maghara, #72
Condition good
Content Nabatean inscription
šlm pʾrn br ʾwšw
Access II.2.380 (printed, CIS)
Corpus CIS 644

Inscription 1404
Site Wadi Maghara, #72
Condition good
Content Nabatean inscription
šlm kʿmw br ʿmrw
Access II.2.380 (printed, CIS); see also CN72
Corpus CIS 645

Inscription 1405
Site Wadi Maghara, #72
Condition good
Content Nabatean inscription
šlm ʾbn q[w]mw
Access II.2.380 (printed, CIS)
Corpus CIS 646

Inscription 1406
Site Wadi Maghara, #72
Condition good
Content Nabatean inscription
lʾ dkyr šrpyw br
ʿrbyw
Access II.2.380 (printed, CIS)
Corpus CIS 647

Inscription 1407
Site Wadi Maghara, #72
Condition poor
Content Nabatean inscription
[š]lm [w]...w br ʾšwdw bṭb
Access II.2.381 (printed, CIS)
Corpus CIS 648

Inscription 1408
Site Wadi Maghara, #72
Condition fair
Content Nabatean inscription
dkyr ʿwd[w br]
ʿbydw
bṭb
Access II.2.381 (printed, CIS)
Corpus CIS 649

Inscription 1409
Site Wadi Maghara, #72
Condition fair
Content Nabatean inscription
šl[m] šʿd'lhy
Access II.2.381 (printed, CIS)
Corpus CIS 650

Inscription 1410
Site Wadi Maghara, #72
Condition good
Content Nabatean inscription
dkyr ʾlmbqrw
br ʿwdw
Access II.2.381 (printed, CIS)
Corpus CIS 651

Inscription 1411
Site Wadi Maghara, #72
Condition fair
Content Nabatean inscription
...wdy wšlm
Access II.2.381 (printed, CIS)
Corpus CIS 652

Inscription 1412
Site Wadi Maghara, #72
Condition fair
Content Nabatean inscription
šlm ḥnṭlw b[r] ...
Access II.2.381 (printed, CIS)
Corpus CIS 653

Inscription 1413
Site Wadi Maghara, #72
Condition good
Content Nabatean inscription
šlm šlmw
br ʾšwdw bkl ṭ[b]
Access II.2.381 (printed, CIS)
Corpus CIS 654

Inscription 1414
Site Wadi Maghara, #72
Condition excellent
Content Nabatean inscription
šlm pṣy bryʾw
br ḥryšw
Access II.2.381 (printed, CIS)
Corpus CIS 655

Inscription 1415
Site Wadi Maghara, #72
Condition good
Content Nabatean inscription
dkyr zydw
[b]r ʾlmbqrw bṭb
mbṭḥ
Access II.2.382 (printed, CIS)
Corpus CIS 656

Inscription 1416
Site Wadi Maghara, #72
Condition good
Content Nabatean inscription
šlm ḥnṭlw
br zydw
Access II.2.382 (printed, CIS)
Corpus CIS 657

Inscription 1419
Site Wadi Maghara, #72
Condition good
Content Nabatean inscription
šlm ʿwdw br šʿdʾlhy
Access II.2.382 (printed, CIS)
Corpus CIS 660

Inscription 1420
Site Wadi Maghara, #72
Condition good
Content Nabatean inscription
šlm gdyw br bḥgh
Access II.2.382 (printed, CIS)
Corpus CIS 661

Inscription 1421
Site Wadi Maghara, #72
Condition good
Content Nabatean inscription
dkyr wʾlw br
hnyʾw bṭb
Access II.2.382 (printed, CIS)
Corpus CIS 662

Inscription 1422
Site Wadi Maghara, #72
Condition good
Content Nabatean inscription
šlm ḥnṭlw
br pṣy bṭb
Access II.2.382 (printed, CIS)
Corpus CIS 663

Inscription 1423
Site Wadi Maghara, #72
Condition good
Content Nabatean inscription
šlm kwšlw br
ʾlgršw bṭb
Access II.2.383 (printed, CIS)
Corpus CIS 664

Inscription 1424
Site Wadi Maghara, #72
Condition good
Content Nabatean inscription
šlm ʿwdw br
šlmw
Access II.2.383 (printed, CIS)
Corpus CIS 665

Inscription 1425
Site Wadi Maghara, #72
Condition good
Content Nabatean inscription
šlm ḥnṭlw br
ʿmyw
Access II.2.383 (printed, CIS)
Corpus CIS 666

Inscription 1426
Site Wadi Maghara, #72
Condition good
Content Nabatean inscription
šlm
ʿwdw br
ḥryšw
Access II.2.383 (printed, CIS)
Corpus CIS 667

Inscription 1427
Site Wadi Maghara, #72
Condition good
Content Nabatean inscription
šlm ḥryšw br wdʿw
Access II.2.383 (printed, CIS)
Corpus CIS 668

Inscription 1428
Site Wadi Maghara, #72
Condition good
Content Nabatean inscription
šlm ʿm[mw] br ʾbn ʾlqyn[w]
Access II.2.383 (printed, CIS)
Corpus CIS 669

Inscription 1429
Site Wadi Maghara, #72
Condition fair
Content Nabatean inscription
šlm ʿmy[w]
Access II.2.383 (printed, CIS)
Corpus CIS 670

Inscription 1430
Site Wadi Maghara, #72
Condition good
Content Nabatean inscription
šlm ʾlktryw
br hnyʾw bṭb
Access II.2.383 (printed, CIS)
Corpus CIS 671

Inscription 1431
Site Wadi Maghara, #72
Condition good
Content Nabatean inscription
šlm grmʾlbʿly br ʾwšʾlbʿly [b]ṭb
Access II.2.384 (printed, CIS)
Corpus CIS 672

Inscription 1432
Site Wadi Maghara, #72
Condition poor
Content Nabatean inscription
tymʾ[lhy] br ...
Access II.2.384 (printed, CIS)
Corpus CIS 673

Inscription 1433
Site Wadi Maghara, #72
Condition good
Content Nabatean inscription
šlm bryʾw br
wʾlw
Access II.2.384 (printed, CIS)
Corpus CIS 674

Inscription 1434
Site Wadi Maghara, #72
Condition good
Content Nabatean inscription
šlm ṯylt
Access II.2.384 (printed, CIS)
Corpus CIS 675

Inscription 1435
Site Wadi Maghara, #72
Condition poor
Content Nabatean inscription
šlm š[mrḥ]
Access II.2.384 (printed, CIS)
Corpus CIS 676

Inscription 1436
Site Wadi Maghara, #72
Condition good
Content Nabatean inscription
šlm ʿmyw br wdw
Access II.2.384 (printed, CIS)
Corpus CIS 677

Inscription 1437
Site Wadi Maghara, #72
Condition good
Content Nabatean inscription
dkyr ʿmrw
Access II.2.384 (printed, CIS)
Corpus CIS 678

Inscription 1438
Site Wadi Maghara, #72
Condition fair
Content Nabatean inscription
dkyr ʿmlh br ʾ...
Access II.2.384 (printed, CIS)
Corpus CIS 679

Inscription 1439
Site Wadi Maghara, #72
Condition fair
Content Nabatean inscription
[dky]r ḥgw br ʿmrw
Access II.2.384 (printed, CIS)
Corpus CIS 680

Inscription 1440
Site Wadi Maghara, #72
Condition good
Content Nabatean inscription
šlm ʿbdʾlbʿly
Access II.2.384 (printed, CIS)
Corpus CIS 681

Inscription 1441
Site Wadi Maghara, #72
Condition good
Content Nabatean inscription
šlm ʿbdʾlbʿly
Access II.2.384 (printed, CIS)
Corpus CIS 682

Inscription 1442
Site Wadi Maghara, #72
Condition good
Content Nabatean inscription
šlm [ty]mʾlhy
br ʿmmw
Access II.2.384 (printed, CIS)
Corpus CIS 683

Inscription 1443
Site Wadi Maghara, #72
Condition fair
Content Nabatean inscription
šlm šmrḥ...
Access II.2.385 (printed, CIS)
Corpus CIS 684

Inscription **1444**
Site Wadi Maghara, #72
Condition fair
Content Nabatean inscription
dkyr mʿnʾlhy
br ʿ.ʿ.yw
Access II.2.385 (printed, CIS)
Corpus CIS 685

Inscription **1445**
Site Wadi Maghara, #72
Condition good
Content Nabatean inscription
šlm šʿdʾlhy br bryʾw
Access II.2.385 (printed, CIS)
Corpus CIS 686

Inscription **1446**
Site Wadi Maghara, #72
Condition excellent
Content Nabatean inscription
šlm ʿlyw br šʿdʾlhy
bṭb
Access II.2.385 (printed, CIS)
Corpus CIS 687

Inscription **1447**
Site Wadi Maghara, #72
Condition good
Content Nabatean inscription
šlm bṭšw br zydw
Access II.2.385 (printed, CIS)
Corpus CIS 688

Inscription **1448**
Site Wadi Maghara, #72
Condition excellent
Content Nabatean inscription
dkyr ʾwšw br ʿbdʾlbʿly
Access II.2.385 (printed, CIS)
Corpus CIS 689

Inscription **1449**
Site Wadi Maghara, #72
Condition excellent
Content Nabatean inscription
šlm šʿdʾlhy br šmrḥw mšqy bṭb
Access II.2.385 (printed, CIS)
Corpus CIS 690

Inscription **1450**
Site Wadi Maghara, #72
Condition excellent
Content Nabatean inscription
šlm ʿbydw br qšṭw ʾʿlʾ
bṭb wšlm
Access II.2.385 (printed, CIS)
Corpus CIS 691

Inscription **1451**
Site Wadi Maghara, #72
Condition excellent
Content Nabatean inscription
šlm yʿly br ʿbdʾlbʿly
Access II.2.386 (printed, CIS)
Corpus CIS 692

Inscription **1452**
Site Wadi Maghara, #72
Condition good
Content Nabatean inscription
wʾlt
br zydw
Access II.2.386 (printed, CIS)
Corpus CIS 693

Inscription **1453**
Site Wadi Maghara, #72
Condition good
Content Nabatean inscription
šlm grmw br šmrḥ
Access II.2.386 (printed, CIS)
Corpus CIS 694

Inscription **1454**
Site Wadi Maghara, #72
Condition good
Content Nabatean inscription
šlm zydw br ʿmyw bṭb
Access II.2.386 (printed, CIS)
Corpus CIS 695

Inscription **1455**
Site Wadi Maghara, #72
Condition good
Content Nabatean inscription
šlm bṭšw br ḥbʾlhy
Access II.2.386 (printed, CIS)
Corpus CIS 696

Inscription **1456**
Site Wadi Maghara, #72
Condition good
Content Nabatean inscription
šlm ʿbdʾlbʿly br ḥryšw
Access II.2.386 (printed, CIS)
Corpus CIS 697

Inscription **1457**
Site Wadi Maghara, #72
Condition excellent
Content Nabatean inscription
šlm ʾbgr br šly mn qdm
kywbk ʾlhʾ bṭb
Access II.2.386 (printed, CIS)
Corpus CIS 698

Inscription 1458
Site Wadi Iqna, #74
Condition good
Content Nabatean inscription
šlm ḥršw
br' n
ʿw
Access II.2.387 (printed, CIS)
Corpus CIS 699

Inscription 1459
Site Wadi Iqna, #74
Condition fair
Content Nabatean inscription
šlm [ʿ]mnw br
Access II.2.387 (printed, CIS)
Corpus CIS 700

Inscription 1460
Site Wadi Iqna, #74
Condition fair
Content Nabatean inscription
šlm pṣy br
qšṭ[w]
[ʾ]ʿlʾ
Access II.2.387 (printed, CIS)
Corpus CIS 701

Inscription 1461
Site Wadi Iqna, #74
Condition excellent
Content Nabatean inscription
grmʾlbʿly br wʾlt br ʿmyw šlm
Access II.2.387 (printed, CIS)
Corpus CIS 702

Inscription 1462
Site Wadi Iqna, #74
Condition fair
Content Nabatean inscription
šlm ʾlm[b]qrw br wʾlw [bṭb]
Access II.2.387 (printed, CIS)
Corpus CIS 703

Inscription 1463
Site Wadi Iqna, #74
Condition good
Content Nabatean inscription
dkyr bṭb pṣyw br
wbnyh
Access II.2.387 (printed, CIS)
Corpus CIS 704

Inscription 1464
Site Wadi Iqna, #74
Condition good
Content Nabatean inscription
wʾlw br ḥnṭlw
Access II.2.387 (printed, CIS)
Corpus CIS 705

Inscription 1465
Site Wadi Iqna, #74
Condition fair
Content Nabatean inscription
šlm
grmʾlbʿly
br wʾlt...
Access II.2.388 (printed, CIS)
Corpus CIS 706

Inscription 1467
Site Wadi Haggag, rock 1, #160
Technique incised
Condition fair
Content Nabatean inscription
dkyr ʿmyw
... wʾwšw
Access Negev 1977 fig. 10 (printed, A. Negev)
Corpus Negev 1977 11

Inscription 1478
Site Wadi Haggag, rock 1, #160
Technique incised
Condition fair
Content Nabatean inscription
bryk zydw br ʾwšw ...šw bṭb
Access Negev 1977 fig. 10 (printed, A. Negev)
Corpus Negev 1977 12

Inscription 1479
Site Wadi Haggag, rock 1, #160
Technique incised
Condition good
Content Nabatean inscription
dkyr ʿwdw br ʿmyw bṭb
Comment *inscription preceded by a cornucopia*
Access Negev 1977 fig. 11 (printed, A. Negev)
Corpus Negev 1977 14

Inscription 1480
Site Wadi Haggag, rock 1, #160
Technique incised
Condition fair
Content Nabatean inscription
n. šlm (?)
Access Negev 1977 fig. 13 (printed, A. Negev)
Corpus Negev 1977 16

Inscription 1481
Site Wadi Haggag, rock 1, #160
Technique incised
Condition good
Content Nabatean inscription
šlm bḥgh br grmʾlbʿly br
ʿbdʾlbʿly bṭb
Access Negev 1977 fig. 14 (printed, A. Negev); *see also* Negev 1977 fig. 15
Corpus Negev 1977 17

Inscription **1482**
Site Wadi Haggag, rock 1, #160
Technique scratched
Condition good
Content Nabatean inscription
šlm qynw br ʾwyšw [bṭb]
Access Negev 1977 fig. 14 (printed, A. Negev); *see also* Negev 1977 fig. 15
Corpus Negev 1977 18

Inscription **1483**
Site Wadi Haggag, rock 1, #160
Technique scratched
Condition good
Content Nabatean inscription
šlm ʾwgm br ʿmrw
wʿmrw brh
bṭb
Access Negev 1977 fig. 14 (printed, A. Negev); *see also* Negev 1977 fig. 16
Corpus Negev 1977 19

Inscription **1484**
Site Wadi Haggag, rock 1, #160
Technique scratched
Condition good
Content Nabatean inscription
šlm ʾwšw br ʿbdʾlgyʾ bṭb
Access Negev 1977 fig. 14 (printed, A. Negev); *see also* Negev 1977 fig. 16
Corpus Negev 1977 20

Inscription **1485**
Site Wadi Haggag, rock 1, #160
Technique incised
Condition good
Content Nabatean inscription
šlm ʿnmw br ʾʿlʾ bṭb
Access Negev 1977 fig. 14 (printed, A. Negev); *see also* Negev 1977 fig. 16
Corpus Negev 1977 21

Inscription **1486**
Site Wadi Haggag, rock 1, #160
Technique incised
Condition good
Content Nabatean inscription
šlm ʿmyw br ʿmmw
Access Negev 1977 fig. 14 (printed, A. Negev); *see also* Negev 1977 fig. 16
Corpus Negev 1977 22

Inscription **1487**
Site Wadi Haggag, rock 2, #119
Technique scratched
Condition fair
Content Greek inscription
ΑΘΑ
ΝΑΣΙΟΣ
Access Negev 1977 fig. 17 (printed, A. Negev)
Corpus Negev 1977 23

Inscription **1488**
Site Wadi Haggag, rock 2, #119
Technique incised
Condition fair
Content Greek inscription
[Ε]ΥΧΗ
[ΑΜ]ΗΝ
ΝΟΝΝΟΣ
ΘΗΚΛΑ
.ΔΕΛΦΑ
ΣΩΣΑΝΝΑ
Access Negev 1977 fig. 18 (printed, A. Negev)
Corpus Negev 1977 24

Inscription **1489**
Site Wadi Haggag, rock 2, #119
Technique incised
Condition good
Content Greek inscription
ΜΝΗΣΘΗ
ΚΕ ΤΟΙΣ
ΔΟΥΛΟΙΣ ΣΟΥ
Access Negev 1977 fig. 18 (printed, A. Negev)
Corpus Negev 1977 25

Inscription **1490**
Site Wadi Haggag, rock 2, #119
Technique incised
Condition good
Content Greek inscription
ΑΒΔΑΓΗΣ
ΜΑΡΘΙΣ
ΘΑΝΟΥΜΑΣ
ΩΡΙΩΝ
ΚΑΣΣΙΣΑΣ
ΑΝΑΣΤΑΣΙΣ
ΜΟΥΣΗΟΣ
Access Negev 1977 fig. 18 (printed, A. Negev)
Corpus Negev 1977 26

Inscription **1491**
Site Wadi Haggag, rock 2, #119
Technique incised
Condition good
Content Greek inscription
ΑΔΑ
ΣΑΔΟΡΑ
ΦΕΧΕΡΑ
Access Negev 1977 fig. 18 (printed, A. Negev)
Corpus Negev 1977 27

Inscription 1492
Site Wadi Haggag, rock 2, #119
Technique incised
Condition good
Content Greek inscription
ΟΜΜΡΥΔΗΛΟΧ
ΜΑΡΘ
ΚΑΣΕΤΟΥ
ΣΤΕΦΑΝΟΣ
Κ ΑΝΑΣΤΑΣΙΑ
Access Negev 1977 fig. 19 (printed, A. Negev)
Corpus Negev 1977 28

Inscription 1493
Site Wadi Haggag, rock 2, #119
Technique incised
Condition fair
Content Greek inscription
ΚΕ ΒΟΗΘΗ ΚΑΣΙΣΟΝ
ΣΤΕΦΑΝΟΥ
Κ ΜΟΥΣΗ ΑΘΑΝΑΣΙΟΥ
Κ ΒΙΚΤΩΡΙΟΝ Α...
ΠΙΝΟΥ
Access Negev 1977 fig. 20 (printed, A. Negev)
Corpus Negev 1977 29

Inscription 1494
Site Wadi Haggag, rock 2, #119
Technique incised
Condition good
Content Greek inscription
ΙΩΑΝΝΗΣ ΝΟΝΝΑ
Access Negev 1977 fig. 21 (printed, A. Negev)
Corpus Negev 1977 30

Inscription 1495
Site Wadi Haggag, rock 2, #119
Technique incised
Condition good
Content Greek inscription
ΜΝΗΣΘΕ
ΙΣ
Access Negev 1977 fig. 22 (printed, A. Negev)
Corpus Negev 1977 31

Inscription 1496
Site Wadi Haggag, rock 2, #119
Technique incised
Condition good
Content Greek inscription
ΚΥ Α Κ Ω ΙΣ
Access Negev 1977 fig. 23 (printed, A. Negev)
Corpus Negev 1977 32

Inscription 1497
Site Wadi Haggag, rock 2, #119
Technique incised
Condition good
Content Greek inscription
ΓΕΩΡΓΙΣ
ΘΕΩΦΑΝΟΥ
Access Negev 1977 fig. 24 (printed, A. Negev)
Corpus Negev 1977 33

Inscription 1498
Site Wadi Haggag, rock 2, #119
Technique incised
Condition excellent
Content Greek inscription
ΑΝΟΥΝΑ
ΜΕΤΡΙ
Access Negev 1977 fig. 24 (printed, A. Negev)
Corpus Negev 1977 34

Inscription 1499
Site Wadi Haggag, rock 2, #119
Technique incised
Condition excellent
Content Greek inscription
ΙΟΥΒΙΝΟΣ
ΒΑΣΟ
Access Negev 1977 fig. 25 (printed, A. Negev)
Corpus Negev 1977 35

Inscription 1500
Site Wadi Haggag, rock 2, #119
Technique incised
Condition good
Content Greek inscription
ΕΛΕΗΣΟΝ
Ο ΘΣ ΤΟΝ ΔΟΥ
ΛΟ ΣΟΥ
ΔΑΜΙΑΤΙ
Access Negev 1977 fig. 26 (printed, A. Negev)
Corpus Negev 1977 36

Inscription 1501
Site Wadi Haggag, rock 2, #119
Technique incised
Condition good
Content Greek inscription
ΙΣ ΧΣ
ΔΑ Δ
ΔΟΥΛΟΣ
Access Negev 1977 fig. 27 (printed, A. Negev)
Corpus Negev 1977 37

Inscription **1502**
Site Wadi Haggag, rock 2, #119
Technique incised
Condition good
Content Greek inscription
ΖΗΣΕ
Ο ΓΡΑΥ
ΑΣ
Access Negev 1977 fig. 28 (printed, A. Negev)
Corpus Negev 1977 38

Inscription **1503**
Site Wadi Haggag, rock 2, #119
Technique incised
Condition fair
Content Greek inscription
ΣΤΕΦΑΝ
ΖΗΝΩΝ
ΜΑΓΔ
ΗΣ ΣΕ
Access Negev 1977 fig. 29 (printed, A. Negev)
Corpus Negev 1977 39

Inscription **1504**
Site Wadi Haggag, rock 2, #119
Technique incised
Condition fair
Content Greek inscription
ΙΩΑΝΝΗΣ
ΣΕΒΑΙΡΟΥ
ΕΥΧΑΡΙΣΤ
.ΒΟΥ
Access Negev 1977 fig. 30 (printed, A. Negev)
Corpus Negev 1977 40

Inscription **1505**
Site Wadi Haggag, rock 2, #119
Technique incised
Condition fair
Content Greek inscription
ΑΜΗΝ
Access Negev 1977 fig. 31 (printed, A. Negev)
Corpus Negev 1977 41

Inscription **1506**
Site Wadi Haggag, rock 2, #119
Technique incised
Condition fair
Content Greek inscription
ΘΑΝΑΣΙΣ ΝΟΝΝΑ
ΑΥΛΟΣ ΦΙΛΟΜΕΝ
ΕΙΣΑΡΟΥΣ ΝΑΖΟΜΜ Α
ΝΑΣΤΑΣΙΑ
...
ΑΒΔΑΛΛΑ
Access Negev 1977 fig. 32 (printed, A. Negev)
Corpus Negev 1977 42

Inscription **1507**
Site Wadi Haggag, rock 2, #119
Technique incised
Condition excellent
Content Greek inscription
ΙΩΒ ΚΟΠΡΟΣΕ
ΟΥ Κ ΕΥΦΥΜΙΣ
Access Negev 1977 fig. 33 (printed, A. Negev); *see also* Negev 1977 fig. 34
Corpus Negev 1977 43

Inscription **1508**
Site Wadi Haggag, rock 2, #119
Technique incised
Condition fair
Content Greek inscription
ΣΟΥΑΙ
Access Negev 1977 fig. 34 (printed, A. Negev)
Corpus Negev 1977 44

Inscription **1509**
Site Wadi Haggag, rock 2, #119
Technique incised
Condition good
Content Greek inscription
ΘΕΟΔΩΡΟΥ Ο ΤΟΥ ΦΕΩΣ
Access Negev 1977 fig. 34 (printed, A. Negev); *see also* Negev 1977 fig. 35
Corpus Negev 1977 45

Inscription **1510**
Site Wadi Haggag, rock 2, #119
Technique incised
Condition fair
Content Greek inscription
ΠΕΤΡΟΣ
ΣΩΕΟΥΕΡ
ΜΑΝΑΣΙΣ
ΜΑΡΤΥΡΙΑ
ΚΥΡΙΛΑ
Access Negev 1977 fig. 34 (printed, A. Negev); *see also* Negev 1977 fig. 36
Corpus Negev 1977 46

Inscription **1511**
Site Wadi Haggag, rock 2, #119
Technique incised
Condition good
Content Greek inscription
ΜΝΗΣΘΗ
ΜΑΧΙΜΟΣ
ΑΣΙΛΑΣ
Access Negev 1977 fig. 37 (printed, A. Negev)
Corpus Negev 1977 47

Inscription 1512
Site Wadi Haggag, rock 2, #119
Technique incised
Condition fair
Content Greek inscription
ΗΝΑΑΥΡΝΙΜΧΦ
Access Negev 1977 fig. 38 (printed, A. Negev)
Corpus Negev 1977 48

Inscription 1513
Site Wadi Haggag, rock 2, #119
Technique incised
Condition good
Content Greek inscription
ΑΒΡΑΜΗΟΣ
ΣΑΡΟΥΘΑ
Access Negev 1977 fig. 39 (printed, A. Negev)
Corpus Negev 1977 49

Inscription 1514
Site Wadi Haggag, rock 2, #119
Technique incised
Condition good
Content Greek inscription
ΙΩΒ ΣΤΕΦΑΝΟΥ
ΚΟΠΡΟΣΕΟΥ
Access Negev 1977 fig. 40 (printed, A. Negev)
Corpus Negev 1977 50

Inscription 1515
Site Wadi Haggag, rock 2, #119
Technique incised
Condition good
Content Greek inscription
ΑΑΡΩΝ
ΑΝΑΣΤΑΣΙΟΥ ΚΑΙ
ΑΛΑΦΑΛΛΑ ΑΔΕΛΦΩ
Access Negev 1977 fig. 41 (printed, A. Negev)
Corpus Negev 1977 51

Inscription 1516
Site Wadi Haggag, rock 2, #119
Technique scratched
Condition fair
Content Greek inscription
ΚΑΣΣΙΣΕΝΑΣ
ΙΑΤΡΟΣ
Access Negev 1977 fig. 42 (printed, A. Negev)
Corpus Negev 1977 52

Inscription 1517
Site Wadi Haggag, rock 2, #119
Technique incised
Condition fair
Content Greek inscription
ΛΟΝΝΔΙΑΤΡΙΒ
...ΘΥΑΝΟΝ
Access Negev 1977 fig. 43 (printed, A. Negev)
Corpus Negev 1977 53

Inscription 1518
Site Wadi Haggag, rock 2, #119
Technique incised
Condition good
Content Greek inscription
[Ε]ΛΕΗΣΟΝ ΤΟΝ ΔΟΥΛΟΝ ΣΟΥ
Comment *Negev has slightly different reading.*
Access Negev 1977 fig. 44 (printed, A. Negev)
Corpus Negev 1977 54

Inscription 1519
Site Wadi Haggag, rock 2, #119
Technique scratched
Condition fair
Content Greek inscription
ΠΡΟΤΕΡΑ
ΟΛΕΦΑ
Δ
Access Negev 1977 fig. 45 (printed, A. Negev)
Corpus Negev 1977 55

Inscription 1520
Site Wadi Haggag, rock 2, #119
Technique incised
Condition good
Content Greek inscription
ΜΑΡΘΑ ΑΒΔΑΙΟΣ
Comment *cross precedes each name*
Access Negev 1977 fig. 46 (printed, A. Negev)
Corpus Negev 1977 56

Inscription 1521
Site Wadi Haggag, rock 2, #119
Technique scratched
Condition good
Content Greek inscription
ΣΤΕΦΑΝΙΣ
ΚΥΡΑ
ΑΚΡΑΔΙΣ
ΝΟΝΝΑ
Access Negev 1977 fig. 47 (printed, A. Negev)
Corpus Negev 1977 57

Inscription 1522
Site Wadi Haggag, rock 2, #119
Technique scratched
Condition good
Content Greek inscription
ΔΟΜΕ
ΤΟΝΕ
Access Negev 1977 fig. 47 (printed, A. Negev)
Corpus Negev 1977 58

Inscription 1523
Site Wadi Haggag, rock 2, #119
Technique scratched
Condition fair
Content Greek inscription
ΛΕΟΝΤΙΣ
Access Negev 1977 fig. 48 (printed, A. Negev)
Corpus Negev 1977 59

Inscription 1524
Site Wadi Haggag, rock 2, #119
Technique scratched
Condition fair
Content Greek inscription
ΚΥΡΙΑΚΟ
...ΡΑΒΔ
Access Negev 1977 fig. 47 (printed, A. Negev)
Corpus Negev 1977 60

Inscription 1525
Site Wadi Haggag, rock 2, #119
Technique incised
Condition good
Content Greek inscription
ΕΝΤΚΕΤΕ
Access Negev 1977 fig. 49 (printed, A. Negev)
Corpus Negev 1977 61

Inscription 1526
Site Wadi Haggag, rock 2, #119
Technique incised
Condition fair
Content Greek inscription
ΑΛΕΝΤΙΝΟΣ ΑΝΟΥΒ
Access Negev 1977 fig. 50 (printed, A. Negev)
Corpus Negev 1977 62

Inscription 1527
Site Wadi Haggag, rock 2, #119
Technique incised
Condition good
Content Greek inscription
ΙΩΑΝΝ.
ΒΡΑΣΥ
Access Negev 1977 fig. 51 (printed, A. Negev)
Corpus Negev 1977 51

Inscription 1528
Site Wadi Haggag, rock 2, #119
Technique incised
Condition fair
Content Greek inscription
Χ.ΑΤΑΣ
ΛΕΔΑΙ
Access Negev 1977 fig. 52 (printed, A. Negev)
Corpus Negev 1977 64

Inscription 1529
Site Wadi Haggag, rock 2, #119
Technique scratched
Condition fair
Content Greek inscription
ΜΑΞΙΜΟΣ
ΣΟΦΙΑ
Access Negev 1977 fig. 53 (printed, A. Negev)
Corpus Negev 1977 65

Inscription 1530
Site Wadi Haggag, rock 2, #119
Technique scratched
Condition fair
Content Greek inscription
ΘΕΚΛΑ
ΑΒΑΣ...
ΜΟΣΑΔΙ
ΜΟΥΣΕ...
ΑΒΡΑ
...
Access Negev 1977 fig. 54 (printed, A. Negev)
Corpus Negev 1977 66

Inscription 1531
Site Wadi Haggag, rock 2, #119
Technique incised
Condition poor
Content Greek inscription
...
ΑΚ
...
ΑΝΑΣΤΑΣΙΑΣ
Access Negev 1977 fig. 55 (printed, A. Negev)
Corpus Negev 1977 67

Inscription 1532
Site Wadi Haggag, rock 2, #119
Technique incised
Condition good
Content Greek inscription
ΝΟΝΝΟΣ ΑΦΘΟΝΙΣ
Access Negev 1977 fig. 56 (printed, A. Negev); *see also* AY18, AY19, BM40, FU08
Corpus Negev 1977 68

Inscription 1533
Site Wadi Haggag, rock 3, #125
Technique incised
Condition good
Content Greek inscription
ΙΣΟΙΣ ΧΑΣΕΤΟΥ
ΜΟΥΣΗ
Access Negev 1977 fig. 57 (printed, A. Negev); *see also* ABa05, ABf31
Corpus Negev 1977 69

Inscription **1534**
Site Wadi Haggag, rock 3, #125
Technique incised
Condition good
Content Greek inscription
ΣΕΡΓΙΣ
Access Negev 1977 fig. 57 (printed, A. Negev); *see also* ABa05, FU07, FU08,
Corpus Negev 1977 70

Inscription **1535**
Site Wadi Haggag, rock 3, #125
Technique incised
Condition good
Content Greek inscription
ΚΕ ΙΕ ΧΕ ΜΕΓ
Access Negev 1977 fig. 57 (printed, A. Negev); *see also* ABa05
Corpus Negev 1977 71

Inscription **1536**
Site Wadi Haggag, rock 3, #125
Technique incised
Condition good
Content Greek inscription
ΚΕ ΒΟΗΘΙ ΤΩΝ ΔΟΥΛΩ ΣΟΥ
ΛΕΩΝΟΣ ΚΑΛΛΙΝΙΚΟΥ ΖΑΔΑΚΑ.
ΘΩΝ Κ[ΑΙ] ΤΟΥΣ ΦΙΛΟΥΣ ΑΥΤΟΥ ΑΜΕΝ
ΚΕ
Access Negev 1977 fig. 57 (printed, A. Negev); *see also* ABa05, ABf31
Corpus Negev 1977 72

Inscription **1537**
Site Wadi Haggag, rock 3, #125
Technique incised
Condition fair
Content Greek inscription
ΣΤΕΦΑΝΟΣ
Access Negev 1977 fig. 57 (printed, A. Negev); *see also* ABa05
Corpus Negev 1977 73

Inscription **1538**
Site Wadi Haggag, rock 3, #125
Technique incised
Condition good
Content crosses alone
Access Negev 1977 fig. 57 (printed, A. Negev); *see also* ABa05
Corpus Negev 1977 73

Inscription **1539**
Site Wadi Haggag, rock 3, #125
Technique incised
Condition good
Content Greek inscription
ΚΕ ΒΟΗΘΗΣΟΝ ΤΟΥ ΔΟΥ ΣΟΥ ΕΠΙΦΑΝΙΣ
ΚΑΙ ΣΟΥΑΙΡΟΣ ΚΑΙ ΜΟΥΣΗΣ ΚΑΙ ΙΩΑΝΝΗΣ
Access Negev 1977 fig. 58 (printed, A. Negev); *see also* CP69
Corpus Negev 1977 74

Inscription **1540**
Site Wadi Haggag, rock 3, #125
Technique incised
Condition good
Content Greek inscription
ΚΕ ΒΟΗΘΗΣΟΝ ΘΑΝΟΥΜΑΣ
Access Negev 1977 fig. 58 (printed, A. Negev)
Corpus Negev 1977 75

Inscription **1541**
Site Wadi Haggag, rock 3, #125
Technique incised
Condition fair
Content Greek inscription
ΘΕΟΦΙΛΟΣ
Access Negev 1977 fig. 58 (printed, A. Negev)
Corpus Negev 1977 76

Inscription **1542**
Site Wadi Haggag, rock 3, #125
Technique incised
Condition good
Content crosses with inscription
Access Negev 1977 fig. 58 (printed, A. Negev)
Corpus Negev 1977 76

Inscription **1543**
Site Wadi Haggag, rock 3, #125
Technique incised
Condition fair
Content Greek inscription
ΚΧΙ.ΜΕ.ΙΜΕ
.ΑΙΖΟΜΕΔΕΠ.
.ΚΕΑ...
Comment *Negev has different reading: KXRW...MAS*
Access Negev 1977 fig. 58 (printed, A. Negev)
Corpus Negev 1977 77

Inscription **1544**
Site Wadi Haggag, rock 3, #125
Technique incised
Condition good
Content crosses alone
Access Negev 1977 fig. 58 (printed, A. Negev)
Corpus Negev 1977 77

Inscription 1545
Site Wadi Haggag, rock 3, #125
Technique incised
Condition good
Content Greek inscription

ΚΕ ΒΟΗΘΙ ΤΟΝ ΔΟΥΛΟΝ

ΣΟΥ ΤΙΜΟΘΕΟΝ ΚΑΙ

ΤΗΣ ΑΥΤΟΥ ΟΡΜΑΣ

ΤΡΙΔΟΣ ΟΛΕΦΑΘΗΣ

Access Negev 1977 fig. 59 (printed, A. Negev)
Corpus Negev 1977 78

Inscription 1546
Site Wadi Haggag, rock 3, #125
Technique incised
Condition good
Content crosses with inscription
Access Negev 1977 fig. 59 (printed, A. Negev)
Corpus Negev 1977 78

Inscription 1547
Site Wadi Haggag, rock 3, #125
Technique incised
Condition good
Content Greek inscription

ΚΕ ΙΥ ΧΕ ΜΝΕΣΘΕΤΙ ΚΑΙ ΒΩΗΘΕΣΟΝ ΤΟΝ ΔΟΥ

ΛΟΝ ΣΟΥ ΣΑΜΑΣΣΑΣ ΑΒΡΑΑΜ Κ ΠΕΤΡΟΣ

ΑΝΑΣΤΑΣΙΑΣ

Access Negev 1977 fig. 59 (printed, A. Negev)
Corpus Negev 1977 79

Inscription 1548
Site Wadi Haggag, rock 3, #125
Technique incised
Condition excellent
Content Greek inscription

ΚΕ ΒΟΗΘΙ

ΘΕΟΔΩΡΑ

Ν

ΚΕ ΒΟΗΘΙ

ΦΙΛΑΔΕΛ

ΦΙΑΝ

Access Negev 1977 fig. 60 (printed, A. Negev); *see also* Negev 1977 fig. 128
Corpus Negev 1977 80

Inscription 1549
Site Wadi Haggag, rock 3, #125
Technique incised
Condition good
Content crosses with inscription
Access Negev 1977 fig. 60 (printed, A. Negev); *see also* Negev 1977 fig. 128
Corpus Negev 1977 80

Inscription 1550
Site Wadi Haggag, rock 3, #125
Technique scratched
Condition excellent
Content crosses with inscription
Comment *monogrammed cross flanked by letters 'A' and 'Ω*
Access Negev 1977 fig. 61 (printed, A. Negev)
Corpus Negev 1977 81

Inscription 1551
Site Wadi Haggag, rock 3, #125
Technique incised
Condition fair
Content Greek inscription

ΧΑΣΕΤΟΣ

ΔΙΟΝΥΣΟΣ

Access Negev 1977 fig. 61 (printed, A. Negev)
Corpus Negev 1977 82

Inscription 1552
Site Wadi Haggag, rock 3, #125
Technique scratched
Condition good
Content Greek inscription

ΑΒΒΑ

ΑΘΑΛΑΣ

ΣΟΦΡΟΝΗΣ

Access Negev 1977 fig. 62 (printed, A. Negev)
Corpus Negev 1977 83

Inscription 1553
Site Wadi Haggag, rock 3, #125
Technique scratched
Condition good
Content Greek inscription

ΑΓΙΕ ΣΤΕΦ

ΦΥΛΑΞΟΝ

ΔΟΥΛΟΝ ΣΟΥ ΘΕ

ΟΦΙΛΟΝ

Access Negev 1977 fig. 62 (printed, A. Negev)
Corpus Negev 1977 84

Inscription 1554
Site Wadi Haggag, rock 3, #125
Technique scratched
Condition fair
Content Greek inscription

ΚΩ...Α

ΞΙΓΟ...ΝΙΚΑ

ΜΝΗΣΘΗ ΤΗΝ

ΦΙΑΝΑ. ΤΟΥ

ΣΗΓΑΜΗ

Access Negev 1977 fig. 62 (printed, A. Negev)
Corpus Negev 1977 85

Inscription 1555
Site Wadi Haggag, rock 3, #125
Technique incised
Condition good
Content varied crosses
Access Negev 1977 fig. 62 (printed, A. Negev)
Corpus Negev 1977 85

Inscription 1556
Site Ein Hudra, #117
Technique incised
Condition good
Dimensions 35 x 40 cm.
Content rock drawing
Comment *animal with rider*
Access EX25 (photograph, Project); *see also* EX26

Inscription 1557
Site Wadi Haggag, rock 3, #125
Technique incised
Condition good
Content Greek inscription
ΧΣ ΝΙΚΑ
ΧΕ ΒΟΗΘΙ
ΜΑΡΚΕΛΛΟΝ
Access Negev 1977 fig. 63 (printed, A. Negev)
Corpus Negev 1977 87

Inscription 1558
Site Wadi Haggag, rock 3, #125
Technique incised
Condition fair
Content crosses with inscription
Comment *crosses enclosing 'ΧΣ ΝΙΚΑ'*
Access Negev 1977 fig. 63 (printed, A. Negev)
Corpus Negev 1977 87

Inscription 1559
Site Wadi Haggag, rock 3, #125
Technique incised
Condition fair
Content rock drawing
Comment *arches with varied crosses*
Access Negev 1977 fig. 63 (printed, A. Negev); *see also* Negev 1977 figs. 64 and 65
Corpus Negev 1977 86

Inscription 1560
Site Wadi Haggag, rock 3, #125
Technique incised
Condition fair
Content Greek inscription
ΚΕΑΓ...ΟΒΔ.ΑΚ
Access Negev 1977 fig. 63 (printed, A. Negev)
Corpus Negev 1977 88

Inscription 1561
Site Church of the Nativity, pillar C6, #245
Technique incised
Condition poor
Content Latin inscription
Limitation *Tentative decipherment only*
Access DVa18 (photograph, M. Stone)

Inscription 1562
Site Wadi Haggag, rock 3, #125
Technique incised
Condition good
Content crosses with inscription
Access Negev 1977 fig. 63 (printed, A. Negev); *see also* Negev 1977 fig. 65
Corpus Negev 1977 89

Inscription 1563
Site Wadi Haggag, rock 3, #125
Technique incised
Condition fair
Content rock drawing
Comment *tabula ansata surrounds the inscription*
Access Negev 1977 fig. 63 (printed, A. Negev); *see also* Negev 1977 fig. 65
Corpus Negev 1977 89

Inscription 1564
Site Wadi Haggag, rock 3, #125
Technique incised
Condition good
Content Greek inscription
ΦΥΛΑΡΧΟΣ ΠΡΟΚΟΠΙΟ
Access Negev 1977 fig. 63 (printed, A. Negev)
Corpus Negev 1977 90

Inscription 1565
Site Wadi Haggag, rock 3, #125
Technique incised
Condition good
Content Greek inscription
ΤΣΗΝΟΥΘΙΣ
Access Negev 1977 fig. 67 (printed, A. Negev)
Corpus Negev 1977 91

Inscription 1566
Site Wadi Haggag, rock 3, #125
Technique incised
Condition good
Content crosses with inscription
Access Negev 1977 fig. 67 (printed, A. Negev)
Corpus Negev 1977 91

Inscription 1567
Site Wadi Haggag, rock 3, #125
Technique incised
Condition good
Content Greek inscription
ΑΙΝΕΙΑΣ
Access Negev 1977 fig. 63 (printed, A. Negev); *see also* CK03
Corpus Negev 1977 92

Inscription **1568**
Site Wadi Haggag, rock 3, #125
Technique incised
Condition good
Content Greek inscription
ΜΝΗΣΘΗ
Access Negev 1977 fig. 63 (printed, A. Negev); *see also* CK03
Corpus Negev 1977 93

Inscription **1569**
Site Wadi Haggag, rock 3, #125
Technique incised
Condition good
Content Greek inscription
ΣΟΥ ΘΩΜΑ ΝΙΚΗΦΟΡΟΥ ΚΑΙ
ΤΟΥΣ ΦΙΛΟΥΣ Α...
Access Negev 1977 fig. 66 (printed, A. Negev)
Corpus Negev 1977 94

Inscription **1570**
Site Wadi Haggag, rock 3, #125
Technique incised
Condition good
Content crosses alone
Access Negev 1977 fig. 66 (printed, A. Negev)
Corpus Negev 1977 94

Inscription **1571**
Site Wadi Haggag, rock 3, #125
Technique incised
Condition excellent
Content crosses with inscription
Comment *monogrammed cross*
Access Negev 1977 fig. 66 (printed, A. Negev)
Corpus Negev 1977 95

Inscription **1572**
Site Wadi Haggag, rock 3, #125
Technique incised
Condition good
Content Greek inscription
ΙΩΑΝΝΗΣ
ΜΑΡΤΙΡΙΑΝΟΥ
Access Negev 1977 fig. 67 (printed, A. Negev)
Corpus Negev 1977 96

Inscription **1573**
Site Wadi Haggag, rock 3, #125
Technique incised
Condition good
Content crosses with inscription
Access Negev 1977 fig. 67 (printed, A. Negev)
Corpus Negev 1977 96

Inscription **1574**
Site Wadi Haggag, rock 3, #125
Technique incised
Condition good
Content Greek inscription
ΚΕ ΦΥΛΑΞΟΝ ΥΠΟ ΤΗΝ
ΣΚΕΠΗΝ ΣΟΥ ΤΟΝ ΔΟΥΛΟΝ
ΣΟΥ ΣΤΕΦΑΝΟΝ ΑΝΤΙΣΩ
ΝΟΣ ΜΕΤΑ ΣΥΜΒΙΟΥ
Κ ΤΕΚΝΩΝ
Access Negev 1977 fig. 68 (printed, A. Negev); *see also* Negev 1977 fig. 69
Corpus Negev 1977 97

Inscription **1575**
Site Wadi Haggag, rock 3, #125
Technique incised
Condition good
Content crosses with inscription
Access Negev 1977 fig. 68 (printed, A. Negev); *see also* Negev 1977 fig. 69
Corpus Negev 1977 97

Inscription **1576**
Site Wadi Haggag, rock 3, #125
Technique incised
Condition good
Content Greek inscription
ΜΝΗΣΘΗΤΙ ΚΕ ΤΟΥΣ
ΔΟΥΛΟ ΣΟΥ ΚΑΠΑΣ
ΔΟΥΑΙΔΑΙΟΥ ΑΝΑΣ
ΤΑΣΙΣ ΖΟΝΑΙΝΟΥ ΜΕΤΑ
ΣΥΜΒΙΟΥ ΚΑΙ ΤΕΚΝΟ
ΑΛΑΦΑΛΛΑΣ ΚΑΙ
ΑΑΡΩΝ ΚΑΙ ΣΕΡΓΙΣ
ΒΑΡΟΧΟΥ ΚΑΙ ΤΗΣ ΓΥΝΗ
ΚΟΣ ΑΥΤΟΥ ΘΕΚΛΑΣ
Access Negev 1977 fig. 68 (printed, A. Negev); *see also* Negev 1977 figs. 69 and 70
Corpus Negev 1977 98

Inscription **1577**
Site Wadi Haggag, rock 3, #125
Technique scratched
Condition good
Content Greek inscription
ΚΕ ΙΥ ΧΕ ΕΛΕΗΣΟΝ
ΤΟΝ ΔΟΥΛΟΝ ΣΟΥ
...ΑΝΑΣΤΑΣΙΑ
ΑΜΗΝ
Access Negev 1977 fig. 70 (printed, A. Negev)
Corpus Negev 1977 99

Inscription 1578
Site Wadi Haggag, rock 3, #125
Technique incised
Condition good
Content crosses with inscription
Access Negev 1977 fig. 70 (printed, A. Negev)
Corpus Negev 1977 99

Inscription 1579
Site Wadi Haggag, rock 3, #125
Technique incised
Condition good
Content Greek inscription
ΚΕ ΣΩΣΟΝ ΤΟΝ ΔΟΥΛΟΝ ΣΟΥ
ΘΕΟΦΙΛΟΝ Κ ΤΝ ΣΥΝΟΔΙΑΝ
ΑΥΤΟΥ ΑΜΗΝ
Access Negev 1977 fig. 71 (printed, A. Negev); *see also* CK07, Negev 1977 fig. 72
Corpus Negev 1977 100

Inscription 1580
Site Wadi Haggag, rock 3, #125
Technique incised
Condition good
Content crosses with inscription
Access Negev 1977 fig. 71 (printed, A. Negev); *see also* CK07, Negev 1977 fig. 72
Corpus Negev 1977 100

Inscription 1581
Site Wadi Haggag, rock 3, #125
Technique incised
Condition good
Content Greek inscription
ΚΕ ΕΥΛΟΓΗΣΟΝ ΤΟΝ ΔΟΥΛΟ ΣΟΥ
ΘΕΩΔΟΡΟΝ ΚΑΙ ΚΑΣΣΙΑ ΚΑΙ ΑΥΞΟΝ ΚΑΙ ΝΟΝΝΑ
ΚΑΙ ΣΤΕΦΑΝΟΝ ΚΑΙ ΙΩΑΝΝΗΝ
Access Negev 1977 fig. 72 (printed, A. Negev); *see also* CK05, CK07
Corpus Negev 1977 101

Inscription 1582
Site Wadi Haggag, rock 3, #125
Technique incised
Condition good
Content crosses with inscription
Access Negev 1977 fig. 72 (printed, A. Negev)
Corpus Negev 1977 101

Inscription 1583
Site Wadi Haggag, rock 3, #125
Technique incised
Condition good
Content crosses alone
Access FU12 (photograph, A. Goren)

Inscription 1584
Site Wadi Haggag, rock 3, #125
Technique incised
Condition good
Content crosses with inscription
Access Negev 1977 fig. 72 (printed, A. Negev); *see also* Negev 1977 fig. 73
Corpus Negev 1977 102

Inscription 1585
Site Wadi Haggag, rock 3, #125
Technique incised
Condition good
Content crosses with inscription
Comment *several monogrammed crosses*
Access Negev 1977 fig. 72 (printed, A. Negev); *see also* Negev 1977 fig. 73
Corpus Negev 1977 102

Inscription 1586
Site Wadi Haggag, rock 3, #125
Technique incised
Condition excellent
Content Greek inscription
ΚΥΡΙΕ ΙΣΟΥ ΧΡΙΣΤΗ
ΒΟΗΘ ΤΟΥ ΔΟΥΛΟΥ ΣΟΥ
ΘΕΟΔΟΥΛΟΥ
Access Negev 1977 fig. 74 (printed, A. Negev)
Corpus Negev 1977 103

Inscription 1587
Site Wadi Haggag, rock 3, #125
Technique incised
Condition good
Content crosses with inscription
Access Negev 1977 fig. 74 (printed, A. Negev)
Corpus Negev 1977 103

Inscription 1588
Site Wadi Haggag, rock 3, #125
Technique incised
Condition good
Content Greek inscription
ΚΑΣΤΡΟΥ ΖΑΔΑΚΑΘΑ
ΚΕ ΣΟΣΟΝ ΤΟΝ ΔΟΥΛΟΝ ΣΟΥ
ΣΕΡΓΙΟ ΣΤΕΦΑΝΟΥ
ΚΑΙ ΚΥΡΙΑΚΟΣ ΔΙΑΚΟΝΟΥ
ΚΑΙ ΘΕΟΔΟΡΟΣ
ΣΕΡΓΙΝΗΣ
Access Negev 1977 fig. 75 (printed, A. Negev); *see also* FU07
Corpus Negev 1977 104

Inscription 1589
Site Wadi Haggag, rock 3, #125
Technique incised
Condition good
Content crosses alone
Access Negev 1977 fig. 75 (printed, A. Negev); *see also* FU07
Corpus Negev 1977 104

Inscription **1590**
Site Wadi Haggag, rock 3, #125
Technique incised
Condition good
Content crosses alone
Access Negev 1977 fig. 75 (printed, A. Negev)
Corpus Negev 1977 104

Inscription **1591**
Site Wadi Haggag, rock 3, #125
Technique incised
Condition good
Content crosses alone
Access Negev 1977 fig. 75 (printed, A. Negev); *see also* FU07
Corpus Negev 1977 104

Inscription **1592**
Site Wadi Haggag, rock 3, #125
Technique incised
Condition good
Content Greek inscription
ΜΝΗΣΘΗ
ΑΔΙΣΟΣ
ΑΛΤΙΡΩΝ
Access Negev 1977 fig. 76 (printed, A. Negev)
Corpus Negev 1977 105

Inscription **1593**
Site Wadi Haggag, rock 3, #125
Technique incised
Condition fair
Content Greek inscription
ΚΕ ΙΥ ΧΕ ΧΕ ΚΑΙ ΛΩΓΕ
ΤΟΥ ΘΥ Ο ΘΣ ΣΥΝΟΔΕΥ
ΣΕΝ ΣΥ ΤΟΥ ΔΟΥΛΟΥ
ΣΟΥ ΣΕΡΗΒ ΑΜΗΝ
Access Negev 1977 fig. 77 (printed, A. Negev); *see also* FU02, FU03
Corpus Negev 1977 106

Inscription **1594**
Site Wadi Haggag, rock 3, #125
Technique incised
Condition good
Content crosses alone
Access Negev 1977 fig. 77 (printed, A. Negev); *see also* FU02, FU03
Corpus Negev 1977 106

Inscription **1595**
Site Wadi Haggag, rock 3, #125
Technique incised
Condition good
Content Greek inscription
ΚΕ Ο ΘΣ ΜΝΗ
ΔΟΥΛΟΝ ΣΟΥ
ΟΥΑΒΑΛΛΑΣ
ΑΜΗΝ ΚΕ
Access Negev 1977 fig. 78 (printed, A. Negev); *see also* FU02
Corpus Negev 1977 107

Inscription **1596**
Site Wadi Haggag, rock 3, #125
Technique incised
Condition good
Content crosses with inscription
Access Negev 1977 fig. 78 (printed, A. Negev)
Corpus Negev 1977 107

Inscription **1597**
Site Wadi Haggag, rock 3, #125
Technique scratched
Condition fair
Content Greek inscription
ΚΕ ΧΑΣΕΤΟΥ
ΑΒΔΑΛΛΑΣ
Access Negev 1977 fig. 79 (printed, A. Negev)
Corpus Negev 1977 108

Inscription **1598**
Site Wadi Haggag, rock 3, #125
Technique incised
Condition good
Content Greek inscription
ΕΥΧΗ
ΚΥΡΙΕ
ΧΡΙΣΤΕ
ΑΛΦΙΟΣ ΧΑΣΕΤΟΥ
ΒΙΔΑΤΡΙΟ ΑΜΑΒΙΟ
ΟΜΜΑΡΙΣΤΩΝ ΣΟΒΑΙΑ
ΑΒΙΣ
ΙΟΑΝΙΣ
ΟΥΑΡΙΘΑ
Access Negev 1977 fig. 80 (printed, A. Negev)
Corpus Negev 1977 110

Inscription **1599**
Site Wadi Haggag, rock 3, #125
Technique incised
Condition good
Content Greek inscription
Limitation *Tentative decipherment only*
Access Negev 1977 fig. 86 (printed, A. Negev)

Inscription 1600
Site Wadi Haggag, rock 3, #125
Technique incised
Condition good
Content Greek inscription
ΚΕ ΕΛΕΗΣ
ΜΟΥΣΟΣ
ΜΑΝΑΗΜ
ΑΛΑΦ
ΜΝΗ
Access Negev 1977 fig. 81 (printed, A. Negev)
Corpus Negev 1977 111

Inscription 1601
Site Wadi Haggag, rock 3, #125
Technique incised
Condition fair
Content Greek inscription
ΚΕ ΦΥΛΑΞΟΝ
ΤΟΝ ΣΕΥΗΡΟΝ
Access Negev 1977 fig. 82 (printed, A. Negev)
Corpus Negev 1977 112

Inscription 1602
Site Wadi Haggag, rock 3, #125
Technique incised
Condition fair
Content Greek inscription
ΚΥΡΙΕ ΕΛΕΗΣΟΝ
ΑΒΡΑΑΜ ΟΒΔ ΚΑΙ
ΕΛΕΥΘΕΡΑΝ
ΤΕΚΝΑ ΜΝΕ
Access Negev 1977 fig. 82 (printed, A. Negev)
Corpus Negev 1977 113

Inscription 1603
Site Wadi Haggag, rock 3, #125
Technique incised
Condition good
Content crosses with inscription
Access Negev 1977 fig. 82 (printed, A. Negev)
Corpus Negev 1977 113

Inscription 1604
Site Wadi Haggag, rock 3, #125
Technique incised
Condition good
Content crosses alone
Access Negev 1977 fig. 82 (printed, A. Negev)

Inscription 1605
Site Wadi Haggag, rock 3, #125
Technique incised
Condition poor
Content Greek inscription
Limitation *Tentative decipherment only*
Access Negev 1977 fig. 82 (printed, A. Negev)

Inscription 1606
Site Wadi Haggag, rock 3, #125
Technique incised
Condition fair
Content Greek inscription
.ΟΥΣ
.ΑΡΝ
.ΟΝΥ
Access Negev 1977 fig. 82 (printed, A. Negev)
Corpus Negev 1977 114

Inscription 1607
Site Wadi Haggag, rock 3, #125
Technique incised
Condition good
Content Greek inscription
ΜΟΥΝΟΝ
ΘΕΟΥ ΝΙΚΗΣ
Access Negev 1977 fig. 83 (printed, A. Negev)
Corpus Negev 1977 115

Inscription 1608
Site Wadi Haggag, rock 3, #125
Technique incised
Condition good
Content crosses with inscription
Access Negev 1977 fig. 82 (printed, A. Negev)
Corpus Negev 1977 115

Inscription 1609
Site Wadi Haggag, rock 3, #125
Technique incised
Condition good
Content Greek inscription
ΚΕ ΕΛΕΗΣΟΝ
ΤΟΝ ΔΟΥΛΟ...
ΠΡΟΚΟΠΙΟΝ ΑΜΗΝ
ΚΑΙ ΤΟΝ ΟΙ
ΚΟΝ ΑΥΤΟΥ
Access Negev 1977 fig. 84 (printed, A. Negev); *see also* CP66, Negev 1977 fig. 157
Corpus Negev 1977 116

Inscription 1610
Site Wadi Haggag, rock 3, #125
Technique incised
Condition fair
Content crosses with inscription
Comment *crosses enclosing 'ΚΕ...ΑΜΗΝ'*
Access Negev 1977 fig. 84 (printed, A. Negev); *see also* Negev 1977 fig. 157
Corpus Negev 1977 116

Inscription **1611**
Site Wadi Haggag, rock 3, #125
Technique incised
Condition good
Content Greek inscription
ΚΕ ΔΟΣ ΜΟΙ
ΑΦΕΣΙΝ
ΑΜΡΑΤΙΩΝ
ΚΥΡΙΑΚΟΣ
ΑΜΗΝ
Access Negev 1977 fig. 85 (printed, A. Negev)
Corpus Negev 1977 117

Inscription **1612**
Site Wadi Haggag, rock 3, #125
Technique incised
Condition fair
Content crosses with inscription
Access Negev 1977 fig. 85 (printed, A. Negev)
Corpus Negev 1977 117

Inscription **1613**
Site Wadi Haggag, rock 3, #125
Technique incised
Condition fair
Content Greek inscription
ΗΣ ΧΣ
ΑΩΡΑΤΩΣ
Comment *inscription surrounded by crosses*
Access Negev 1977 fig. 86 (printed, A. Negev)
Corpus Negev 1977 118

Inscription **1614**
Site Wadi Haggag, rock 3, #125
Technique incised
Condition fair
Content Greek inscription
ΑΠΑΜΙΑ
Access Negev 1977 fig. 86 (printed, A. Negev)
Corpus Negev 1977 118

Inscription **1615**
Site Wadi Haggag, rock 3, #125
Technique scratched
Condition fair
Content Greek inscription
ΜΝΗΣΘΕ
ΕΥΒΟΥΛΟΣ
ΝΟΜΕΡΙΑΣ
Access Negev 1977 fig. 88 (printed, A. Negev)
Corpus Negev 1977 120

Inscription **1616**
Site Wadi Haggag, rock 3, #125
Technique scratched
Condition good
Content crosses alone
Comment *line of crosses to the right of inscription*
Access Negev 1977 fig. 88 (printed, A. Negev)
Corpus Negev 1977 120

Inscription **1617**
Site Wadi Haggag, rock 3, #125
Technique scratched
Condition good
Content Greek inscription
ΤΟΝ ΔΟΥΛΟΝ ΣΟΥ ΟΥΑΛΗΣ
Access Negev 1977 fig. 88 (printed, A. Negev)
Corpus Negev 1977 121

Inscription **1618**
Site Wadi Haggag, rock 3, #125
Technique incised
Condition good
Content Greek inscription
ΓΕΟΡΓΙΣ
ΑΘΑΣ
ΣΤΕΦΑΝΟΣ
ΚΥΡΙΕ ΒΟΗΘΕΙ
Access Negev 1977 fig. 89 (printed, A. Negev)
Corpus Negev 1977 122

Inscription **1619**
Site Wadi Haggag, rock 3 area 1, #126
Technique scratched
Condition good
Content Greek inscription
ΓΑΙΣ
Access Negev 1977 fig. 90 (printed, A. Negev); *see also* FU07
Corpus Negev 1977 123

Inscription **1620**
Site Wadi Haggag, rock 3 area 1, #126
Technique scratched
Condition good
Content Greek inscription
ΓΕΟΡΓΙΣ
Access Negev 1977 fig. 90 (printed, A. Negev); *see also* FU07
Corpus Negev 1977 124

Inscription **1621**
Site Wadi Haggag, rock 3 area 1, #126
Technique incised
Condition fair
Content crosses with inscription
Access Negev 1977 fig. 90 (printed, A. Negev); *see also* FU07, FU08
Corpus Negev 1977 124

Inscription **1622**
Site Wadi Haggag, rock 3 area 1, #126
Technique scratched
Condition fair
Content Greek inscription
ΟΔΗΠΟΡ..ΛΕΡΕΚΕΕΚ ΧΟΥ ΥΠΕΡ
ΜΟΥΣ ΣΟΥ ΠΚΑ
ΤΟΣΠΑΥ
Access Negev 1977 fig. 90 (printed, A. Negev); *see also* FU07, FU08, Negev 1977 fig. 91
Corpus Negev 1977 125

Inscription **1623**
Site Wadi Haggag, rock 3 area 1, #126
Technique incised
Condition fair
Content Greek inscription
Limitation *Tentative decipherment only*
Access Negev 1977 fig. 90 (printed, A. Negev); *see also* ADg28, ADg31, BK56, BK57

Inscription **1624**
Site Wadi Haggag, rock 3 area 1, #126
Technique incised
Condition good
Content Greek inscription
ΔΙΑΝΝΟΣ Ο ΦΘΟΝΙΣ
Access Negev 1977 fig. 91 (printed, A. Negev); *see also* FU08
Corpus Negev 1977 126

Inscription **1625**
Site Wadi Haggag, rock 3 area 1, #126
Technique scratched
Condition good
Content Greek inscription
ΜΝΗΣΘΗ
ΙΟΥΛΙΟΣ
ΑΥΡΗΛΙΟΣ
Access Negev 1977 fig. 91 (printed, A. Negev); *see also* FU08
Corpus Negev 1977 127

Inscription **1626**
Site Wadi Haggag, rock 3 area 1, #126
Technique incised
Condition fair
Content crosses with inscription
Access Negev 1977 fig. 91 (printed, A. Negev)
Corpus Negev 1977 126

Inscription **1627**
Site Wadi Haggag, rock 3, #125
Technique incised
Condition good
Content Greek inscription
Χ Η Ν
Access Negev 1977 fig. 93 (printed, A. Negev)
Corpus Negev 1977 128

Inscription **1628**
Site Wadi Haggag, rock 3, #125
Technique incised
Condition good
Content crosses with inscription
Access Negev 1977 fig. 93 (printed, A. Negev)
Corpus Negev 1977 128

Inscription **1629**
Site Wadi Haggag, rock 3 area 4, #129
Technique incised
Condition good
Content Greek inscription
ΠΟΣΙΔΟΝ
Access Negev 1977 fig. 93 (printed, A. Negev)
Corpus Negev 1977 129

Inscription **1630**
Site Wadi Haggag, rock 3 area 4, #129
Technique incised
Condition good
Content crosses alone
Access Negev 1977 fig. 93 (printed, A. Negev)

Inscription **1631**
Site Wadi Haggag, rock 3 area 4, #129
Technique incised
Condition fair
Content Greek inscription
Limitation *Tentative decipherment only*
Access Negev 1977 fig. 93 (printed, A. Negev)

Inscription **1632**
Site Wadi Haggag, rock 3, #125
Technique scratched
Condition good
Content Greek inscription
ΜΝΗΣΘΗ
ΑΦΨΑΛΑΜΟΥ
ΟΣΑΓΟΥ
Access Negev 1977 fig. 94 (printed, A. Negev); *see also* Negev 1977 fig. 167
Corpus Negev 1977 130

Inscription **1633**
Site Wadi Haggag, rock 3, #125
Technique incised
Condition good
Content crosses with inscription
Access Negev 1977 fig. 94 (printed, A. Negev); *see also* Negev 1977 fig. 167
Corpus Negev 1977 130

Inscription **1634**
Site Wadi Haggag, rock 3 area 2, #127
Technique incised
Condition fair
Content Greek inscription
ΚΕ ΣΟΣΟΝ
Access Negev 1977 fig. 95 (printed, A. Negev); *see also* Negev 1977 figs. 163, 164, and 165
Corpus Negev 1977 131

Inscription **1635**
Site Wadi Haggag, rock 3 area 2, #127
Technique incised
Condition good
Content crosses alone
Access Negev 1977 fig. 95 (printed, A. Negev)
Corpus Negev 1977 131

Inscription 1636
Site Wadi Haggag, rock 3 area 2, #127
Technique scratched
Condition fair
Content Greek inscription
ΑΝΤΙΣΣΑ ΑΦ
ΣΑΡΑ
ΣΕΡΗΝΟΣ
ΑΛΑΦΟΝ
ΟΥΑΛΕΝΤΙΝΑ
ΤΕΚΝΑ
Access Negev 1977 fig. 95 (printed, A. Negev); *see also* Negev 1977 figs. 164 and165
Corpus Negev 1977 132

Inscription 1637
Site Wadi Haggag, rock 3 area 2, #127
Technique incised
Condition good
Content crosses alone
Access Negev 1977 fig. 95 (printed, A. Negev); *see also* Negev 1977 figs. 164 and165
Corpus Negev 1977 132

Inscription 1638
Site Wadi Haggag, rock 3, #125
Technique incised
Condition fair
Content Latin inscription
MART
Comment *language uncertain*
Access Negev 1977 fig. 96 (printed, A. Negev); *see also* Negev 1977 figs. 164 and 165
Corpus Negev 1977 133

Inscription 1639
Site Wadi Haggag, rock 3, #125
Technique incised
Condition good
Content Greek inscription
ΑΤΑΛΑΝΤΑ
ΦΣ.Τ ΣΥΜΕΛΟΕΣ
Access Negev 1977 fig. 96 (printed, A. Negev); *see also* Negev 1977 figs. 164 and 165
Corpus Negev 1977 134

Inscription 1640
Site Wadi Haggag, rock 3, #125
Technique incised
Condition good
Content crosses with inscription
Access Negev 1977 fig. 96 (printed, A. Negev)

Inscription 1641
Site Wadi Haggag, rock 3, #125
Technique scratched
Condition fair
Content Greek inscription
ΚΕ ΒΟΗΘΙ
. ΗΜΑ.
Access Negev 1977 fig. 96 (printed, A. Negev)
Corpus Negev 1977 135

Inscription 1642
Site Wadi Haggag, rock 3, #125
Technique incised
Condition good
Content unidentified signs
Comment *monogram*
Access Negev 1977 fig. 97 (printed, A. Negev); *see also* Negev 1977 fig. 164
Corpus Negev 1977 136

Inscription 1643
Site Wadi Haggag, rock 3, #125
Technique incised
Condition fair
Content varied crosses
Access Negev 1977 fig. 97 (printed, A. Negev)

Inscription 1644
Site Wadi Haggag, rock 3, #125
Technique incised
Condition poor
Content Greek inscription
Limitation *Tentative decipherment only*
Access Negev 1977 fig. 97 (printed, A. Negev)

Inscription 1645
Site Wadi Haggag, rock 3, #125
Technique scratched
Condition fair
Content Greek inscription
..ΗΣΘΗ ΑΧΒΑΡΟΣ
...
Access Negev 1977 fig. 98 (printed, A. Negev); *see also* Negev 1977 fig. 166
Corpus Negev 1977 137

Inscription 1646
Site Wadi Haggag, rock 3, #125
Technique incised
Condition good
Content crosses alone
Access Negev 1977 fig. 98 (printed, A. Negev)

Inscription 1647
Site Wadi Haggag, rock 3, #125
Technique incised
Condition fair
Content Greek inscription

ΜΝΗΣΘΗΤΙ Κ

ΙΕ . ΣΟΥ

ΝΟΝΝΑ

ΚΥΡΙΑΚΟΥ

Access Negev 1977 fig. 99 (printed, A. Negev)
Corpus Negev 1977 138

Inscription 1648
Site Wadi Haggag, rock 3, #125
Technique incised
Condition good
Content crosses with inscription
Access Negev 1977 fig. 99 (printed, A. Negev)
Corpus Negev 1977 138

Inscription 1649
Site Wadi Haggag, rock 3, #125
Technique incised
Condition fair
Content Greek inscription

ΚΕ ΕΥΛΟΓΗΣΟΝ ΤΟΝ ΔΟΥΛΟΝ ΣΟΥ

ΟΥΑΡΗΟΣ .ΚΑΙ ΑΣΟ.ΛΕΦΑΝ ΚΑΙ ΤΑ ΤΕ

ΚΝΑ ΑΥΤΟΙΣ

Access Negev 1977 fig. 100 (printed, A. Negev)
Corpus Negev 1977 139

Inscription 1650
Site Wadi Haggag, rock 3, #125
Technique incised
Condition fair
Content crosses with inscription
Access Negev 1977 fig. 100 (printed, A. Negev)
Corpus Negev 1977 139

Inscription 1651
Site Wadi Haggag, rock 3, #125
Technique incised
Condition good
Content Greek inscription

ΚΕ Ο ΘΣ

ΕΛΕΗΣΟΝ ΤΟΥΣ ΔΟΥΛΟΥΣ ΣΟΥ

ΑΝΑΣΤΑΣΙΟΝ ΚΑΙ ΠΡΟΚΟΠΙΟΝ

ΚΑΙ ΟΥΛΠΙΑΝΗΝ

ΚΕ.ΑΥΤΗΝ

Access Negev 1977 fig. 101 (printed, A. Negev)
Corpus Negev 1977 140

Inscription 1652
Site Wadi Haggag, rock 3, #125
Technique incised
Condition good
Content Arabic inscription
Limitation *Tentative decipherment only*
Access Negev 1977 fig. 100 (printed, A. Negev)

Inscription 1653
Site Wadi Haggag, rock 3, #125
Technique incised
Condition good
Content Arabic inscription
Limitation *Tentative decipherment only*
Access Negev 1977 fig. 101 (printed, A. Negev)

Inscription 1654
Site Wadi Haggag, rock 3 area 2, #127
Technique incised
Condition fair
Content Greek inscription

Ι ΧΕ

Ι ΧΣ

ΑΙΜΙΛΛΙΑ

...ΑΝΙΟΣ

...ΣΣΑ

ΜΕΤΑ

Access Negev 1977 fig. 102 (printed, A. Negev); *see also* Negev 1977 fig. 157
Corpus Negev 1977 141

Inscription 1655
Site Wadi Haggag, rock 3 area 2, #127
Technique incised
Condition fair
Content Greek inscription

Θ.Υ

Comment *monogram*
Access Negev 1977 fig. 102 (printed, A. Negev)
Corpus Negev 1977 142

Inscription 1656
Site Wadi Haggag, rock 3, #125
Technique incised
Condition good
Content Greek inscription

.ΛΙΧΟΣ

Access Negev 1977 fig. 103 (printed, A. Negev)
Corpus Negev 1977 143

Inscription 1657
Site Wadi Haggag, rock 3, #125
Technique incised
Condition fair
Content Greek inscription

ΚΕ ΒΟΗΘΙ

ΕΠΙΦΑ

ΝΙΑΝ ΚΑΙ ...

Access Negev 1977 fig. 104 (printed, A. Negev)
Corpus Negev 1977 144

Inscription **1658**
Site Wadi Haggag, rock 3, #125
Technique incised
Condition poor
Content crosses with inscription
Access Negev 1977 fig. 104 (printed, A. Negev)
Corpus Negev 1977 144

Inscription **1659**
Site Wadi Haggag, rock 3, #125
Technique incised
Condition poor
Content crosses alone
Access Negev 1977 fig. 104 (printed, A. Negev)

Inscription **1660**
Site Wadi Haggag, rock 3, #125
Technique incised
Condition poor
Content rock drawing
Access Negev 1977 fig. 104 (printed, A. Negev)

Inscription **1661**
Site Wadi Haggag, rock 3, #125
Technique incised
Condition fair
Content Greek inscription

ΚΕ ΒΟΗΘΗΣΟΝ
ΤΟΝ ΔΟΥΛΟΝ ΣΟΥ
ΑΝΑΣΤΑΣΙΣ Ω
ΡΙΟΝΟΣ ΑΜΗΝ

Access Negev 1977 fig. 104 (printed, A. Negev)
Corpus Negev 1977 145

Inscription **1662**
Site Wadi Haggag, rock 3, #125
Technique incised
Condition poor
Content crosses with inscription
Access Negev 1977 fig. 104 (printed, A. Negev)
Corpus Negev 1977 145

Inscription **1663**
Site Wadi Haggag, rock 3 area 2, #127
Technique incised
Condition fair
Content Greek inscription
Comment *Greek doubtful*
Access Negev 1977 fig. 105 (printed, A. Negev)
Corpus Negev 1977 146

Inscription **1664**
Site Wadi Haggag, rock 3, #125
Technique incised
Condition poor
Content Greek inscription
Access Negev 1977 fig. 105 (printed, A. Negev)
Corpus Negev 1977 147

Inscription **1665**
Site Wadi Haggag, rock 3, #125
Technique incised
Condition poor
Content Arabic inscription
Limitation *Tentative decipherment only*
Access Negev 1977 fig. 105 (printed, A. Negev)

Inscription **1666**
Site Wadi Haggag, rock 3, #125
Technique incised
Condition poor
Content crosses with inscription
Access Negev 1977 fig. 86 (printed, A. Negev)

Inscription **1667**
Site Wadi Haggag, rock 3, #125
Technique incised
Condition fair
Content varied crosses
Access Negev 1977 fig. 105 (printed, A. Negev)

Inscription **1668**
Site Wadi Haggag, rock 3 area 1, #126
Technique incised
Condition fair
Content Greek inscription

ΚΕ ΣΟΣΟΝ ΤΟΝ ΔΟΥ
ΛΟ ΣΟΥ ΚΛΑΥΔΙ
ΟΣ

Access Negev 1977 fig. 114 (printed, A. Negev)
Corpus Negev 1977 148

Inscription **1669**
Site Wadi Haggag, rock 3 area 1, #126
Technique incised
Condition good
Content crosses with inscription
Access Negev 1977 fig. 106 (printed, A. Negev); *see also* Negev 1977 fig. 114
Corpus Negev 1977 148

Inscription **1670**
Site Wadi Haggag, rock 3 area 1, #126
Technique incised
Condition fair
Content Greek inscription
Limitation *Tentative decipherment only*
Access Negev 1977 fig. 106 (printed, A. Negev)

Inscription **1671**
Site Wadi Haggag, rock 3 area 1, #126
Technique incised
Condition fair
Content varied crosses
Access Negev 1977 fig. 107 (printed, A. Negev)

Inscription **1672**
Site Wadi Haggag, rock 3 area 1, #126
Technique incised
Condition good
Content rock drawing
Comment *ibex*
Access Negev 1977 fig. 107 (printed, A. Negev)

Inscription 1673
Site Wadi Haggag, rock 3, #125
Technique incised
Condition fair
Content Greek inscription
ΚΕ ΙΥ ΧΕ ΜΝΗΣ
ΘΗΙ
ΤΟΝ ΓΡΑΨΑΝ
ΤΑ.. ΤΟΥΣ
...
...ΥΣ ΕΥΛΟΓΗ
Access Negev 1977 fig. 109 (printed, A. Negev)
Corpus Negev 1977 151

Inscription 1674
Site Wadi Haggag, rock 3, #125
Technique incised
Condition poor
Content crosses with inscription
Access Negev 1977 fig. 109 (printed, A. Negev)
Corpus Negev 1977 151

Inscription 1675
Site Wadi Haggag, rock 3, #125
Technique incised
Condition fair
Content Greek inscription
Limitation *Tentative decipherment only*
Access Negev 1977 fig. 109 (printed, A. Negev)

Inscription 1676
Site Wadi Haggag, rock 3, #125
Technique incised
Condition good
Content Greek inscription
ΚΕ ΒΟΗΘΙ
ΜΗΝΑΣ
Access Negev 1977 fig. 110 (printed, A. Negev)
Corpus Negev 1977 152

Inscription 1677
Site Wadi Haggag, rock 3, #125
Technique incised
Condition fair
Content crosses with inscription
Access Negev 1977 fig. 110 (printed, A. Negev)
Corpus Negev 1977 152

Inscription 1678
Site Wadi Haggag, rock 3, #125
Technique incised
Condition fair
Content Greek inscription
ΚΥΡ ΜΝΗΣΘΕ
Access Negev 1977 fig. 111 (printed, A. Negev)
Corpus Negev 1977 153

Inscription 1679
Site Wadi Haggag, rock 3, #125
Technique incised
Condition good
Content Greek inscription
ΛΕΟΝΤΙΣ
Access Negev 1977 fig. 112 (printed, A. Negev); *see also* FU12
Corpus Negev 1977 154

Inscription 1680
Site Wadi Haggag, rock 3, #125
Technique incised
Condition fair
Content Greek inscription
Limitation *Tentative decipherment only*
Access Negev 1977 fig. 112 (printed, A. Negev)

Inscription 1681
Site Wadi Haggag, rock 3, #125
Technique incised
Condition good
Content Greek inscription
ΔΙΑΣΟ
ΔΙΝΑΡΟΣ
Access Negev 1977 fig. 113 (printed, A. Negev)
Corpus Negev 1977 155

Inscription 1682
Site Wadi Haggag, rock 3, #125
Technique incised
Condition good
Content crosses with inscription
Access Negev 1977 fig. 113 (printed, A. Negev)
Corpus Negev 1977 155

Inscription 1683
Site Wadi Haggag, rock 3 area 1, #126
Technique incised
Condition good
Content Greek inscription
ΚΕ ΒΟΗΘΗΣΟΝ
ΤΟΝ ΔΟΥΛΟΝ ΣΟΥ
ΣΤΕΦΑΝΟΝ
Access Negev 1977 fig. 114 (printed, A. Negev); *see also* Negev 1977 fig. 115
Corpus Negev 1977 156

Inscription 1684
Site Wadi Haggag, rock 3 area 1, #126
Technique incised
Condition good
Content crosses with inscription
Access Negev 1977 fig. 114 (printed, A. Negev); *see also* Negev 1977 fig. 115
Corpus Negev 1977 156

Inscription **1685**
Site Wadi Haggag, rock 3 area 1, #126
Technique incised
Condition excellent
Content Greek inscription
ΧΟΥΡΑΣΑ
Access Negev 1977 fig. 114 (printed, A. Negev); *see also* FU07, Negev 1977 fig. 115
Corpus Negev 1977 157

Inscription **1686**
Site Wadi Haggag, rock 3 area 1, #126
Technique incised
Condition good
Content crosses with inscription
Access Negev 1977 fig. 114 (printed, A. Negev); *see also* FU07

Inscription **1687**
Site Wadi Haggag, rock 3 area 1, #126
Technique incised
Condition fair
Content Greek inscription
ΚΕ ΙΥ ΧΕ ΒΟΗΘΙ
...ΤΙΝΙΑΝΟΥ
ΚΑΙ ΙΩΑΝΝΟΥ
ΚΑΙ ΜΑΡΙΑ
...
...
Access Negev 1977 fig. 114 (printed, A. Negev); *see also* FU07, Negev 1977 fig. 115
Corpus Negev 1977 158

Inscription **1688**
Site Wadi Haggag, rock 3, #125
Technique incised
Condition good
Content crosses with inscription
Access Negev 1977 fig. 114 (printed, A. Negev); *see also* FU07, Negev 1977 fig. 115
Corpus Negev 1977 158

Inscription **1689**
Site Wadi Haggag, rock 3 area 1, #126
Technique incised
Condition good
Content Greek inscription
ΙΩΑΝΝ
..ΡΟΔΗ
ΑΝΑΣΤΑΣ
ΙΟΣ
Access Negev 1977 fig. 114 (printed, A. Negev); *see also* FU07, Negev 1977 fig. 115
Corpus Negev 1977 159

Inscription **1690**
Site Wadi Haggag, rock 3, #125
Technique incised
Condition fair
Content Greek inscription
..ΑΣΟΛΕΟΥ
ΚΑΙ ΟΜΡΙΑ
Access Negev 1977 fig. 114 (printed, A. Negev); *see also* Negev 1977 fig. 115
Corpus Negev 1977 160

Inscription **1691**
Site Wadi Haggag, rock 3, #125
Technique incised
Condition good
Content Greek inscription
ΧΕ ΣΟΣΟ ΝΟΝΝΟΣ Κ ΑΝΝΑ...
Access Negev 1977 fig. 100 (printed, A. Negev); *see also* Negev 1977 fig. 116
Corpus Negev 1977 161

Inscription **1692**
Site Wadi Haggag, rock 3, #125
Technique incised
Condition good
Content crosses with inscription
Access Negev 1977 fig. 100 (printed, A. Negev); *see also* Negev 1977 fig. 116
Corpus Negev 1977 161

Inscription **1693**
Site Wadi Haggag, rock 3, #125
Technique incised
Condition good
Content Greek inscription
ΚΕ ΣΟΣΟΝ ΤΟΝ
ΣΤΕΦΑΝΟΝ
Access Negev 1977 fig. 162 (printed, A. Negev)
Corpus Negev 1977 162

Inscription **1694**
Site Wadi Haggag, rock 3, #125
Technique incised
Condition good
Content crosses with inscription
Access Negev 1977 fig. 117 (printed, A. Negev)
Corpus Negev 1977 162

Inscription **1695**
Site Wadi Haggag, rock 3, #125
Technique incised
Condition fair
Content Greek inscription
ΣΘΕ ΚΥΡΙΚΟΣ
Access Negev 1977 fig. 118 (printed, A. Negev)
Corpus Negev 1977 163

Inscription **1696**
Site Wadi Haggag, rock 3, #125
Technique incised
Condition good
Content crosses with inscription
Access Negev 1977 fig. 118 (printed, A. Negev)
Corpus Negev 1977 163

Inscription **1697**
Site Wadi Haggag, rock 3, #125
Technique incised
Condition good
Content Greek inscription

ΠΡΟΚΟ

ΠΙΑΝΙΟΥ

ΜΑΓΔΙΣ

Access Negev 1977 fig. 119 (printed, A. Negev)
Corpus Negev 1977 164

Inscription **1698**
Site Wadi Haggag, rock 3, #125
Technique incised
Condition fair
Content crosses alone
Access Negev 1977 fig. 119 (printed, A. Negev)

Inscription **1699**
Site Wadi Haggag, rock 3, #125
Technique incised
Condition fair
Content Georgian inscription
Limitation *Tentative decipherment only*
Access Negev 1977 fig. 119 (printed, A. Negev)

Inscription **1700**
Site Wadi Haggag, rock 3, #125
Technique incised
Condition fair
Content Greek inscription
Limitation *Tentative decipherment only*
Access Negev 1977 fig. 119 (printed, A. Negev)

Inscription **1701**
Site Wadi Haggag, rock 3, #125
Technique scratched
Condition fair
Content Greek inscription

ΕΥΧΗ

Access Negev 1977 fig. 120 (printed, A. Negev)
Corpus Negev 1977 165

Inscription **1702**
Site Wadi Haggag, rock 3, #125
Technique scratched
Condition fair
Content Greek inscription

ΕΥΧΗ

Access Negev 1977 fig. 166 (printed, A. Negev)
Corpus Negev 1977 166

Inscription **1703**
Site Wadi Haggag, rock 3, #125
Technique scratched
Condition poor
Content Greek inscription
Limitation *Tentative decipherment only*
Access Negev 1977 fig. 121 (printed, A. Negev)

Inscription **1704**
Site Wadi Haggag, rock 3, #125
Technique incised
Condition fair
Content crosses with inscription
Comment *cross preceding insc. 1703*
Access Negev 1977 fig. 121 (printed, A. Negev)

Inscription **1705**
Site Wadi Haggag, rock 3, #125
Technique incised
Condition good
Content varied crosses
Comment *various crosses around insc. 1702*
Access Negev 1977 fig. 121 (printed, A. Negev)

Inscription **1706**
Site Wadi Haggag, rock 3, #125
Technique incised
Condition good
Content Greek inscription

ΜΝΗΣΘΕ ΑΦΡΗΑΚ

ΟΥ

Comment *corrected*
Access Negev 1977 fig. 122 (printed, A. Negev)
Corpus Negev 1977 167

Inscription **1707**
Site Wadi Haggag, rock 3, #125
Technique incised
Condition fair
Content crosses with inscription
Comment *cross between letters H and A of the inscription*
Access Negev 1977 fig. 122 (printed, A. Negev)
Corpus Negev 1977 167

Inscription **1708**
Site Wadi Haggag, rock 3, #125
Technique incised
Condition fair
Content Greek inscription

ΚΕ ΡΕΔΙΣΕ ΖΩ...

ΚΕ ΘΣ...ΣΚ

Access Negev 1977 fig. 123 (printed, A. Negev)
Corpus Negev 1977 168

Inscription **1709**
Site Wadi Haggag, rock 3, #125
Technique incised
Condition good
Content crosses with inscription
Comment *cross preceding insc. 1708*
Access Negev 1977 fig. 123 (printed, A. Negev)
Corpus Negev 1977 168

Inscription **1710**
Site Wadi Haggag, rock 3, #125
Technique incised
Condition fair
Content Greek inscription
ΑΛΦΙΟΣ ΧΑΣΕΤΟΥ
.. ΚΑΙ ΤΑ ΠΑΔΙΑ
Access Negev 1977 fig. 124 (printed, A. Negev)
Corpus Negev 1977 169

Inscription **1711**
Site Wadi Haggag, rock 3, #125
Technique incised
Condition fair
Content Greek inscription
ΜΝΗΣΘΗΤΙ ΚΕ Κ ΕΛΕΗΣΟΝ
ΤΟΙΣ ΔΟΥΛΟΙΣ ΣΟΥ ΠΕΤΡΟΝ
ΚΥΡ... Κ ΑΣΠΑΣΙΑ
Κ ΣΤΕΦΑΝΟΝ
Access Negev 1977 fig. 125 (printed, A. Negev)
Corpus Negev 1977 170

Inscription **1712**
Site Wadi Haggag, rock 3, #125
Technique incised
Condition good
Content crosses with inscription
Access Negev 1977 fig. 125 (printed, A. Negev)

Inscription **1713**
Site Wadi Haggag, rock 3, #125
Technique incised
Condition good
Content Greek inscription
Limitation *Tentative decipherment only*
Access Negev 1977 fig. 125 (printed, A. Negev)

Inscription **1714**
Site Wadi Haggag, rock 3, #125
Technique incised
Condition fair
Content crosses with inscription
Access Negev 1977 fig. 125 (printed, A. Negev)

Inscription **1715**
Site Wadi Haggag, rock 3, #125
Technique incised
Condition good
Content Greek inscription
ΚΕ ΒΟΗΘΙ ΤΟΝ ΔΟΥΛΟΝ
ΣΟΥ ΝΙΚΗΦΟΡΟΝ
ΚΟΝΚΑΤΕΩΣ
Access Negev 1977 fig. 126 (printed, A. Negev)
Corpus Negev 1977 171

Inscription **1716**
Site Wadi Haggag, rock 3, #125
Technique incised
Condition good
Content crosses with inscription
Access Negev 1977 fig. 126 (printed, A. Negev)
Corpus Negev 1977 171

Inscription **1717**
Site Wadi Haggag, rock 3, #125
Technique incised
Condition good
Content Greek inscription
ΜΝΗΣΘΗ
ΑΛΑΦΑΛΛΑ
ΑΣΑΔΟΥ
Access Negev 1977 fig. 126 (printed, A. Negev); *see also* Negev 1977 fig. 127
Corpus Negev 1977 172

Inscription **1718**
Site Wadi Haggag, rock 3, #125
Technique incised
Condition good
Content crosses with inscription
Access Negev 1977 fig. 127 (printed, A. Negev)

Inscription **1719**
Site Wadi Haggag, rock 3, #125
Technique incised
Condition good
Content Hebrew inscription
Limitation *Tentative decipherment only*
Access Negev 1977 fig. 127 (printed, A. Negev)

Inscription **1720**
Site Wadi Haggag, rock 3, #125
Technique incised
Condition fair
Content rock drawing
Access Negev 1977 fig. 127 (printed, A. Negev)

Inscription **1721**
Site Wadi Haggag, rock 3, #125
Technique incised
Condition good
Content Greek inscription
ΜΑΓΝΙΟΣ
ΑΙΑ
Access Negev 1977 fig. 128 (printed, A. Negev)
Corpus Negev 1977 173

Inscription **1722**
Site Wadi Haggag, rock 3, #125
Technique incised
Condition poor
Content unidentified inscription
Access Negev 1977 fig. 128 (printed, A. Negev)

Inscription 1723
Site Wadi Haggag, rock 3, #125
Technique incised
Condition good
Content Greek inscription
ΙΛΩΝ
Access Negev 1977 fig. 129 (printed, A. Negev)
Corpus Negev 1977 174

Inscription 1724
Site Wadi Haggag, rock 3, #125
Technique incised
Condition good
Content crosses with inscription
Access Negev 1977 fig. 129 (printed, A. Negev)
Corpus Negev 1977 174

Inscription 1725
Site Wadi Haggag, rock 3 area 3, #128
Technique incised
Condition good
Content rock drawing
Comment *See M. Stone, Armenian Inscriptions, Plate LXXXVI.*
Access Negev 1977 fig. 130 (printed, A. Negev)
Corpus Negev 1977 175

Inscription 1726
Site Wadi Haggag, rock 3 area 3, #128
Technique incised
Condition good
Content varied crosses
Comment *See M. Stone, Armenian Inscriptions, Plate LXXXVI.*
Access Negev 1977 fig. 130 (printed, A. Negev)
Corpus Negev 1977 175

Inscription 1727
Site Wadi Haggag, rock 3 area 3, #128
Technique scratched
Condition fair
Content Greek inscription
Limitation *Tentative decipherment only*
Access Negev 1977 fig. 130 (printed, A. Negev)

Inscription 1728
Site Wadi Haggag, rock 3 area 3, #128
Technique incised
Condition poor
Content Greek inscription
Limitation *Tentative decipherment only*
Access Negev 1977 fig. 130 (printed, A. Negev)

Inscription 1729
Site Wadi Haggag, rock 3, #125
Technique scratched
Condition fair
Content Greek inscription
ΚΕ Β
ΤΟΥ ΔΟΥ..
ΙΩΑΝΝΗ
ΤΑΒΙΝΙΤ.. ΚΑΙ
Access Negev 1977 fig. 131 (printed, A. Negev)
Corpus Negev 1977 176

Inscription 1730
Site Wadi Haggag, rock 3, #125
Technique incised
Condition fair
Content crosses with inscription
Access Negev 1977 fig. 131 (printed, A. Negev)
Corpus Negev 1977 176

Inscription 1731
Site Wadi Haggag, rock 3, #125
Technique incised
Condition good
Content Greek inscription
ΜΝΗΣΘΕ
ΜΟΥΡΑΙΣΙΟΣ
ΔΙΟΚΛΗ
Access Negev 1977 fig. 132 (printed, A. Negev)
Corpus Negev 1977 177

Inscription 1732
Site Wadi Haggag, rock 3, #125
Technique incised
Condition fair
Content Greek inscription
Limitation *Tentative decipherment only*
Access Negev 1977 fig. 132 (printed, A. Negev)

Inscription 1733
Site Wadi Haggag, rock 3, #125
Technique incised
Condition fair
Content Greek inscription
ΚΑΒΑΣ ΑΛ..
ΑΒΑΣ ΑΥΧΕ...
Comment *Negev's reading differs.*
Access Negev 1977 fig. 133 (printed, A. Negev)
Corpus Negev 1977 178

Inscription 1734
Site Wadi Haggag, rock 3, #125
Technique incised
Condition good
Content crosses with inscription
Access Negev 1977 fig. 133 (printed, A. Negev)

Inscription 1735
Site Wadi Haggag, rock 3, #125
Technique incised
Condition fair
Content Greek inscription
ΠΑΥΛΟΣ
Access Negev 1977 fig. 134 (printed, A. Negev)
Corpus Negev 1977 179

Inscription 1736
Site Wadi Haggag, rock 3, #125
Technique incised
Condition fair
Content Greek inscription
ΑΛΕΞΑΝΔΡΟΥ
..ΣΑΜΟΥΘΟΥ
Access Negev 1977 fig. 135 (printed, A. Negev)
Corpus Negev 1977 180

Inscription 1737
Site Wadi Haggag, rock 3, #125
Technique incised
Condition fair
Content Greek inscription
ΙΟ ΧΥ ΔΙΟΝΥ...
Comment *Negev's reading: ΙΟΧΑΙ*
Access Negev 1977 fig. 136 (printed, A. Negev)
Corpus Negev 1977 181

Inscription 1738
Site Wadi Haggag, rock 3, #125
Technique incised
Condition good
Content Greek inscription
ΝΑΤΙΡΑΣ
Access Negev 1977 fig. 137 (printed, A. Negev)
Corpus Negev 1977 182

Inscription 1739
Site Wadi Haggag, rock 3, #125
Technique incised
Condition good
Content Greek inscription
Limitation *Tentative decipherment only*
Access Negev 1977 fig. 137 (printed, A. Negev)

Inscription 1740
Site Wadi Haggag, rock 3, #125
Technique incised
Condition good
Content crosses with inscription
Access Negev 1977 fig. 137 (printed, A. Negev)

Inscription 1741
Site Wadi Haggag, rock 3, #125
Technique incised
Condition fair
Content Greek inscription
Limitation *Tentative decipherment only*
Access Negev 1977 fig. 137 (printed, A. Negev)

Inscription 1742
Site Wadi Haggag, rock 3, #125
Technique incised
Condition good
Content crosses with inscription
Access Negev 1977 fig. 137 (printed, A. Negev)

Inscription 1743
Site Wadi Haggag, rock 3, #125
Technique incised
Condition good
Content Greek inscription
Limitation *Tentative decipherment only*
Access Negev 1977 fig. 137 (printed, A. Negev)

Inscription 1744
Site Wadi Haggag, rock 3, #125
Technique scratched
Condition poor
Content Greek inscription
...ΣΜΑ
..Α
Access Negev 1977 fig. 138 (printed, A. Negev)
Corpus Negev 1977 183

Inscription 1745
Site Wadi Haggag, rock 3, #125
Technique incised
Condition poor
Content crosses with inscription
Access Negev 1977 fig. 138 (printed, A. Negev)

Inscription 1746
Site Wadi Haggag, rock 3, #125
Technique scratched
Condition poor
Content Greek inscription
Limitation *Tentative decipherment only*
Access Negev 1977 fig. 138 (printed, A. Negev)

Inscription 1747
Site Wadi Haggag, rock 3, #125
Technique scratched
Condition fair
Content Arabic inscription
Limitation *Tentative decipherment only*
Access Negev 1977 fig. 138 (printed, A. Negev)

Inscription 1748
Site Wadi Haggag, rock 3, #125
Technique scratched
Condition fair
Content Greek inscription
Limitation *Tentative decipherment only*
Access Negev 1977 fig. 139 (printed, A. Negev)

Inscription 1749
Site Wadi Haggag, rock 3, #125
Technique incised
Condition fair
Content Greek inscription
ΜΟΥΣΗ ΓΑΔΟΣ
Access Negev 1977 fig. 139 (printed, A. Negev)
Corpus Negev 1977 184

Inscription 1750
Site Wadi Haggag, rock 3, #125
Technique incised
Condition poor
Content Nabatean inscription
Limitation *Tentative decipherment only*
Access Negev 1977 fig. 139 (printed, A. Negev)

Inscription 1751
Site Jebel Maharun, #317
Technique scratched
Condition good
Content crosses alone
Comment *two crosses*
Access FS08 (photograph, Project)

Inscription 1752
Site Wadi Haggag, rock 3, #125
Technique incised
Condition good
Content crosses alone
Access Negev 1977 fig. 139 (printed, A. Negev)

Inscription 1753
Site Wadi Haggag, rock 3, #125
Technique scratched
Condition fair
Content Greek inscription
ΙΛΙΩΣ
Access Negev 1977 fig. 140 (printed, A. Negev)
Corpus Negev 1977 185

Inscription 1754
Site Wadi Haggag, rock 3, #125
Technique incised
Condition good
Content crosses with inscription
Access Negev 1977 fig. 140 (printed, A. Negev)

Inscription 1755
Site Wadi Haggag, rock 3, #125
Technique incised
Condition poor
Content Greek inscription
...ΚΙΔΙ
Access Negev 1977 fig. 102 (printed, A. Negev); *see also* Negev 1977 fig. 141
Corpus Negev 1977 186

Inscription 1756
Site Wadi Haggag, rock 3, #125
Technique incised
Condition fair
Content crosses with inscription
Access Negev 1977 fig. 102 (printed, A. Negev); *see also* Negev 1977 fig. 141

Inscription 1757
Site Wadi Haggag, rock 3, #125
Technique incised
Condition fair
Content Greek inscription
ΚΕ ΙΥ ΧΕ ΜΝΗΣΘ
ΑΙΣΙΚΙΟΣ ΜΟΥΣΑΙΟ
ΚΑΙ ΒΥ..ΙΑ.Χ.
ΚΑΙ
Access Negev 1977 fig. 141 (printed, A. Negev)
Corpus Negev 1977 187

Inscription 1758
Site Wadi Haggag, rock 3, #125
Technique incised
Condition good
Content Greek inscription
ΚΕ ΕΛ
ΔΩΜΝΑ
ΑΝΝΑΣ Ι
Access Negev 1977 fig. 142 (printed, A. Negev)
Corpus Negev 1977 188

Inscription 1759
Site Wadi Haggag, rock 3, #125
Technique scratched
Condition poor
Content crosses with inscription
Access Negev 1977 fig. 142 (printed, A. Negev)

Inscription 1760
Site Wadi Haggag, rock 3, #125
Technique incised
Condition fair
Content Greek inscription
ΔΩΜΝΑ
Access Negev 1977 fig. 143 (printed, A. Negev)
Corpus Negev 1977 189

Inscription 1761
Site Wadi Haggag, rock 3, #125
Technique incised
Condition fair
Content Greek inscription
ΦΑΘΕ
Comment *Negev's reading: ΦΑΣΕ[ΙΣ]*
Access Negev 1977 fig. 144 (printed, A. Negev)
Corpus Negev 1977 190

Inscription 1762
Site Wadi Haggag, rock 3, #125
Technique incised
Condition good
Content crosses with inscription
Access Negev 1977 fig. 144 (printed, A. Negev)
Corpus Negev 1977 190

Inscription **1763**
Site Wadi Haggag, rock 3, #125
Technique incised
Condition good
Content Greek inscription
ΑΛΦΙ
Access Negev 1977 fig. 145 (printed, A. Negev)
Corpus Negev 1977 191

Inscription **1764**
Site Wadi Haggag, rock 3, #125
Technique incised
Condition good
Content Greek inscription
ΟΛΙ
ΑΛΙΥΣ
Comment *fragment*
Access Negev 1977 fig. 146 (printed, A. Negev)
Corpus Negev 1977 192

Inscription **1765**
Site Wadi Haggag, rock 3, #125
Technique incised
Condition good
Content Greek inscription
XP
Comment *monogrammed cross*
Access Negev 1977 fig. 147 (printed, A. Negev)
Corpus Negev 1977 193

Inscription **1766**
Site Wadi Haggag, rock 3, #125
Technique incised
Condition good
Content crosses alone
Access Negev 1977 fig. 147 (printed, A. Negev)
Corpus Negev 1977 193

Inscription **1767**
Site Wadi Haggag, rock 3, #125
Technique incised
Condition good
Content Old North Arabic inscription
Limitation *Tentative decipherment only*
Access Negev 1977 fig. 147 (printed, A. Negev)

Inscription **1768**
Site Wadi Haggag, rock 3, #125
Technique incised
Condition fair
Content Greek inscription
ΙΣ XP
Access Negev 1977 fig. 148 (printed, A. Negev)
Corpus Negev 1977 194

Inscription **1769**
Site Wadi Haggag, rock 3, #125
Technique incised
Condition good
Content Greek inscription
NON
Comment *Negev's reading: NON[NA] (May be fragment of larger inscription).*
Access Negev 1977 fig. 148 (printed, A. Negev)
Corpus Negev 1977 195

Inscription **1770**
Site Sinai, unknown, #0
Technique scratched
Condition poor
Content Greek inscription
Limitation *Tentative decipherment only*
Access FU12 (photograph, A. Goren)

Inscription **1771**
Site Wadi Haggag, rock 3, #125
Technique incised
Condition fair
Content crosses with inscription
Access Negev 1977 fig. 149 (printed, A. Negev)
Corpus Negev 1977 196

Inscription **1772**
Site Ein Hudra, #117
Technique incised
Condition excellent
Dimensions 40 x 40 cm.
Content rock drawing
Comment *camel*
Access EX20 (photograph, Project)

Inscription **1773**
Site Wadi Haggag, rock 3, #125
Technique incised
Condition good
Content Greek inscription
ΕΙΣ ΘΕΟΣ
Ο ΒΟΗΘΩΝ
ΜΝΑΣΤΗ
..ΑΙΝΟΥ
ΟΜΜΕΝ
ΚΑΙ ΑΘΑΝ.
ΣΙΟΣ
Access Negev 1977 fig. 151 (printed, A. Negev)
Corpus Negev 1977 198

Inscription **1774**
Site Wadi Haggag, rock 3, #125
Technique incised
Condition good
Content crosses with inscription
Access Negev 1977 fig. 151 (printed, A. Negev)
Corpus Negev 1977 198

Inscription **1775**
Site Wadi Haggag, rock 3, #125
Technique incised
Condition fair
Content Greek inscription
NONNA
KYPA
Access Negev 1977 fig. 152 (printed, A. Negev)
Corpus Negev 1977 199

Inscription **1776**
Site Wadi Haggag, rock 3, #125
Technique incised
Condition fair
Content Greek inscription
NONNA
Access Negev 1977 fig. 153 (printed, A. Negev)
Corpus Negev 1977 200

Inscription **1777**
Site Wadi Haggag, rock 3, #125
Technique incised
Condition good
Content Greek inscription
MAPIA
ΘΡΕΟΡΙΣ
ΣΟΥΛΕΦΙΣ
Access Negev 1977 fig. 154 (printed, A. Negev); *see also* Negev 1977 fig. 176
Corpus Negev 1977 201

Inscription **1778**
Site Wadi Haggag, rock 3, #125
Technique incised
Condition good
Content crosses with inscription
Access Negev 1977 fig. 154 (printed, A. Negev); *see also* Negev 1977 fig. 176
Corpus Negev 1977 201

Inscription **1779**
Site Wadi Haggag, rock 3, #125
Technique incised
Condition good
Content Greek inscription
ΓΕΟΡΓΙΣ
Access Negev 1977 fig. 154 (printed, A. Negev); *see also* Negev 1977 fig. 176
Corpus Negev 1977 202

Inscription **1780**
Site Wadi Haggag, rock 3, #125
Technique incised
Condition good
Content crosses with inscription
Access Negev 1977 fig. 154 (printed, A. Negev); *see also* Negev 1977 fig. 176
Corpus Negev 1977 202

Inscription **1781**
Site Wadi Haggag, rock 3, #125
Technique incised
Condition good
Content Greek inscription
MAPIA
Access Negev 1977 fig. 154 (printed, A. Negev); *see also* Negev 1977 fig. 176
Corpus Negev 1977 203

Inscription **1782**
Site Wadi Haggag, rock 3, #125
Technique incised
Condition fair
Content Nabatean inscription
Limitation *Tentative decipherment only*
Access Negev 1977 fig. 154 (printed, A. Negev)

Inscription **1783**
Site Wadi Haggag, rock 3, #125
Technique incised
Condition good
Content Syriac inscription
Limitation *Tentative decipherment only*
Access Negev 1977 fig. 154 (printed, A. Negev)

Inscription **1784**
Site Sinai, unknown, #0
Technique incised
Condition good
Content Greek inscription
XP
Comment *monogram*
Access FU15 (photograph, Project)

Inscription **1785**
Site Wadi Haggag, rock 3, #125
Technique incised
Condition good
Content crosses alone
Access Negev 1977 fig. 155 (printed, A. Negev)

Inscription **1786**
Site Wadi Haggag, rock 3, #125
Technique incised
Condition fair
Content Greek inscription
ΛΟΥΛΙΑΝΟΣ
ΦΘΟΜΙΝ ΑΒΣ.ΕΛ..
...
Access Negev 1977 fig. 155 (printed, A. Negev); *see also* Negev 1977 fig. 176
Corpus Negev 1977 204

Inscription **1787**
Site Wadi Haggag, rock 3, #125
Technique incised
Condition fair
Content crosses with inscription
Comment *cross precedes each name*
Access Negev 1977 fig. 155 (printed, A. Negev); *see also* Negev 1977 fig. 176
Corpus Negev 1977 204

Inscription **1788**
Site Wadi Haggag, rock 3, #125
Technique incised
Condition fair
Content Greek inscription

A

Ω

N

K

OY

Comment *monogrammed cross*
Access Negev 1977 fig. 156 (printed, A. Negev)
Corpus Negev 1977 205

Inscription **1789**
Site Wadi Haggag, rock 3, #125
Technique incised
Condition fair
Content varied crosses
Access Negev 1977 fig. 156 (printed, A. Negev)

Inscription **1790**
Site Wadi Haggag, rock 3, #125
Technique incised
Condition fair
Content rock drawing
Access Negev 1977 fig. 156 (printed, A. Negev)

Inscription **1791**
Site Wadi Haggag, rock 3, #125
Technique incised
Condition poor
Content Greek inscription

KIY...HΣ

TAKEΦ . Γ...

Φ...

Access Negev 1977 fig. 100 (printed, A. Negev); *see also* Negev 1977 fig. 116
Corpus Negev 1977 206

Inscription **1792**
Site Wadi Haggag, rock 3, #125
Technique incised
Condition good
Content Nabatean inscription

šlm dʾbw

br ʾlz

ʿblyw

Access Negev 1977 fig. 84 (printed, A. Negev); *see also* Negev 1977 fig. 157
Corpus Negev 1977 207

Inscription **1793**
Site Wadi Haggag, rock 3, #125
Technique incised
Condition good
Content Nabatean inscription

šlm ḥlṣšt br

šʿwdt bṭb

Access Negev 1977 fig. 101 (printed, A. Negev); *see also* CIS II.2.202, Negev 1977 fig. 158
Corpus Negev 1977 208

Inscription **1794**
Site Wadi Haggag, rock 3, #125
Technique incised
Condition good
Content Nabatean inscription

dkyr bryʾw wšʿdʾlhy

bny klbw

Access Negev 1977 fig. 88 (printed, A. Negev)
Corpus Negev 1977 209

Inscription **1795**
Site Wadi Haggag, rock 3 area 4, #129
Technique scratched
Condition good
Content Nabatean inscription

dkyr ʿyydw

br bryʾw bṭb

Access Negev 1977 fig. 93 (printed, A. Negev)
Corpus Negev 1977 212

Inscription **1796**
Site Wadi Haggag, rock 3 area 4, #129
Technique scratched
Condition fair
Content Nabatean inscription

šlm zydw br šmrḥ bṭb

Access Negev 1977 fig. 93 (printed, A. Negev)
Corpus Negev 1977 213

Inscription **1797**
Site Wadi Haggag, rock 3 area 4, #129
Technique incised
Condition fair
Content Nabatean inscription

šlm wʾlw br ...

Access Negev 1977 fig. 93 (printed, A. Negev); *see also* Negev 1977 fig. 160
Corpus Negev 1977 214

Inscription **1798**
Site Wadi Haggag, rock 3 area 4, #129
Technique scratched
Condition good
Content Nabatean inscription

šlm tymw

Access Negev 1977 fig. 161 (printed, A. Negev)
Corpus Negev 1977 215

Inscription 1799
Site Wadi Haggag, rock 3 area 4, #129
Technique scratched
Condition good
Content Nabatean inscription
dkyr
ʿmyw br ...
Access Negev 1977 fig. 161 (printed, A. Negev)
Corpus Negev 1977 216

Inscription 1800
Site Wadi Haggag, rock 3 area 4, #129
Technique scratched
Condition good
Content Nabatean inscription
šlm šmrḥ br ʾbn ʾlqyny bṭb
Access Negev 1977 fig. 161 (printed, A. Negev)
Corpus Negev 1977 217

Inscription 1801
Site Wadi Haggag, rock 3 area 4, #129
Technique incised
Condition poor
Content Greek inscription
Limitation *Tentative decipherment only*
Access Negev 1977 fig. 161 (printed, A. Negev)

Inscription 1802
Site Wadi Haggag, rock 3 area 4, #129
Technique incised
Condition fair
Content varied crosses
Access Negev 1977 fig. 161 (printed, A. Negev)

Inscription 1803
Site Wadi Haggag, rock 3, #125
Technique incised
Condition good
Content Nabatean inscription
dkyr ʿyydw wʾbʾwšw
wbryʾw bny ḥryšw
Access Negev 1977 fig. 162 (printed, A. Negev)
Corpus Negev 1977 218

Inscription 1804
Site Wadi Haggag, rock 3, #125
Technique incised
Condition good
Content crosses alone
Access Negev 1977 fig. 162 (printed, A. Negev)

Inscription 1805
Site Wadi Haggag, rock 3 area 2, #127
Technique incised
Condition good
Content Nabatean inscription
mdkwr tymʾlhy
br šmrḥ bṭb
Access Negev 1977 fig. 163 (printed, A. Negev)
Corpus Negev 1977 219

Inscription 1806
Site Wadi Haggag, rock 3 area 2, #127
Technique scratched
Condition good
Content Nabatean inscription
šlm wʾlw br ʾbnʾlhy bṭb
Access Negev 1977 fig. 96 (printed, A. Negev); *see also* Negev 1977 figs. 164 and 165
Corpus Negev 1977 220

Inscription 1807
Site Wadi Haggag, rock 3 area 2, #127
Technique scratched
Condition fair
Content Nabatean inscription
šlm ʾlmwbqrw br
ʿmyw
Access Negev 1977 fig. 164 (printed, A. Negev); *see also* Negev 1977 fig. 165
Corpus Negev 1977 221

Inscription 1808
Site Wadi Haggag, rock 3 area 2, #127
Technique scratched
Condition fair
Content Nabatean inscription
dkyr bṭb wšlm
ʿwymw br wʾlw bṭb
Access Negev 1977 fig. 164 (printed, A. Negev); *see also* Negev 1977 fig. 165
Corpus Negev 1977 222

Inscription 1809
Site Wadi Haggag, rock 3 area 2, #127
Technique scratched
Condition good
Content Nabatean inscription
šlm ʾlm[bqrw?]
Access Negev 1977 fig. 98 (printed, A. Negev); *see also* Negev 1977 fig. 166
Corpus Negev 1977 223

Inscription 1810
Site Wadi Haggag, rock 3, #125
Technique scratched
Condition fair
Content Nabatean inscription
šlm yqwm br ʿmyw
ʿmrw
Access Negev 1977 fig. 167 (printed, A. Negev); *see also* Negev 1977 fig. 168
Corpus Negev 1977 224

Inscription **1811**
Site Wadi Haggag, rock 3, #125
Technique scratched
Condition good
Content Nabatean inscription
šlm tmlt br yqwm
Access Negev 1977 fig. 167 (printed, A. Negev); *see also* Negev 1977 fig. 168
Corpus Negev 1977 225

Inscription **1812**
Site Wadi Haggag, rock 3, #125
Technique incised
Condition fair
Content Nabatean inscription
bryk hnyʾw br ʿbdʾbʿly bṭb
Access Negev 1977 fig. 167 (printed, A. Negev)
Corpus Negev 1977 226

Inscription **1813**
Site Wadi Haggag, rock 3, #125
Technique incised
Condition fair
Content Nabatean inscription
dkyr ...
Access Negev 1977 fig. 167 (printed, A. Negev)
Corpus Negev 1977 227

Inscription **1814**
Site Wadi Haggag, rock 3, #125
Technique incised
Condition poor
Content Nabatean inscription
Access Negev 1977 fig. 167 (printed, A. Negev); *see also* Negev 1977 figs. 168 and 171
Corpus Negev 1977 228

Inscription **1815**
Site Wadi Haggag, rock 3, #125
Technique incised
Condition good
Content Arabic inscription
Limitation *Tentative decipherment only*
Access Negev 1977 fig. 169 (printed, A. Negev)

Inscription **1816**
Site Wadi Haggag, rock 3, #125
Technique incised
Condition good
Content crosses alone
Access Negev 1977 fig. 169 (printed, A. Negev)

Inscription **1817**
Site Wadi Haggag, rock 3, #125
Technique scratched
Condition fair
Content Nabatean inscription
šlm
Access Negev 1977 fig. 170 (printed, A. Negev)
Corpus Negev 1977 229

Inscription **1818**
Site Wadi Haggag, rock 3, #125
Technique incised
Condition fair
Content Nabatean inscription
Access Negev 1977 fig. 170 (printed, A. Negev)
Corpus Negev 1977 230

Inscription **1819**
Site Wadi Haggag, rock 3, #125
Technique incised
Condition fair
Content Nabatean inscription
šlm ... br grmlbʿly
Access Negev 1977 fig. 171 (printed, A. Negev); *see also* Negev 1977 fig. 172
Corpus Negev 1977 231

Inscription **1820**
Site Wadi Haggag, rock 3, #125
Technique incised
Condition fair
Content Nabatean inscription
šlm ḥlṣ br ʾwšw
Access Negev 1977 fig. 172 (printed, A. Negev); *see also* Negev 1977 fig. 173
Corpus Negev 1977 232

Inscription **1821**
Site Wadi Haggag, rock 3, #125
Technique incised
Condition good
Content Nabatean inscription
šlm pʾrn br
ʿbdʾlbʿly bṭb
Access Negev 1977 fig. 174 (printed, A. Negev)
Corpus Negev 1977 233

Inscription **1822**
Site Wadi Haggag, rock 3, #125
Technique incised
Condition fair
Content Nabatean inscription
šlm qymw br ʾ...
Access Negev 1977 fig. 94 (printed, A. Negev); *see also* Negev 1977 figs. 172 and 175
Corpus Negev 1977 234

Inscription **1823**
Site Wadi Haggag, rock 3, #125
Technique incised
Condition poor
Content Nabatean inscription
Access Negev 1977 fig. 176 (printed, A. Negev)
Corpus Negev 1977 235

Inscription **1824**
Site Wadi Haggag, rock 3, #125
Technique incised
Condition good
Content Nabatean inscription
šlm ʿbdʾlbʿly
br ʿbydw br ʿbdʾlbʿly
br wdw bṭb
Access Negev 1977 fig. 177 (printed, A. Negev)
Corpus Negev 1977 236

Inscription **1825**
Site Wadi Haggag, rock 3, #125
Technique incised
Condition fair
Content Nabatean inscription
šlm .. br
ḥnṭlw bṭb wšlm
Access Negev 1977 fig. 178 (printed, A. Negev)
Corpus Negev 1977 237

Inscription **1826**
Site Wadi Haggag, rock 3, #125
Technique incised
Condition fair
Content Nabatean inscription
[d]kyr ʾʿlʾ br
bṭb
Access Negev 1977 fig. 179 (printed, A. Negev)
Corpus Negev 1977 238

Inscription **1827**
Site Wadi Haggag, rock 3, #125
Technique incised
Condition good
Content Latin inscription
AVR VALERI
R ...
Access Negev 1977 fig. 110 (printed, A. Negev); *see also* Negev 1977 fig. 180
Corpus Negev 1977 239

Inscription **1828**
Site Wadi Haggag, rock 3, #125
Technique incised
Condition good
Content rock drawing
Comment *five-branched candelabrum*
Access Negev 1977 fig. 181 (printed, A. Negev)
Corpus Negev 1977 240

Inscription **1829**
Site Wadi Haggag, rock 3, #125
Technique incised
Condition good
Content rock drawing
Comment *pentagram within a rectangle*
Access Negev 1977 fig. 182 (printed, A. Negev)
Corpus Negev 1977 241

Inscription **1830**
Site Wadi Haggag, rock 5, #131
Technique incised
Condition good
Content Greek inscription
ΕΙΣ ΘΕΟΣ Υ Δ Θ
Ο ΒΟΗΘΩΝ
ΟΥΑΛΕΡΙΟΣ ΑΝΤΙ
ΓΟΥΝΟΥ ΣΤΡΑ
ΤΗΓΟΣ Γ ΙΝΔΙΚΤΙ
Access Negev 1977 fig. 183 (printed, A. Negev); *see also* CK08
Corpus Negev 1977 242

Inscription **1831**
Site Wadi Haggag, rock 5, #131
Technique incised
Condition good
Content Greek inscription
ΟΥ ΘΟΣ
Comment *Negev's reading: ΟΥΡΟΣ*
Access Negev 1977 fig. 184 (printed, A. Negev)
Corpus Negev 1977 243

Inscription **1832**
Site Wadi Haggag, rock 5, #131
Technique incised
Condition fair
Content rock drawing
Comment *two deer*
Access Negev 1977 fig. 184 (printed, A. Negev)

Inscription **1833**
Site Wadi Haggag, rock 5, #131
Technique incised
Condition poor
Content Greek inscription
Access Negev 1977 fig. 185 (printed, A. Negev)
Corpus Negev 1977 244

Inscription **1834**
Site Wadi Haggag, rock 5, #131
Technique incised
Condition fair
Content Greek inscription
ΧΑΡΙ ΜΝ
ΗΣΘΗ Σ...
Access Negev 1977 fig. 186 (printed, A. Negev)
Corpus Negev 1977 245

Inscription **1835**
Site Wadi Haggag, rock 5, #131
Technique incised
Condition good
Content *varied crosses*
Access Negev 1977 fig. 186 (printed, A. Negev)

Inscription **1836**
Site Wadi Haggag, rock 5, #131
Technique incised
Condition fair
Content Greek inscription
ΕΙΣ ΘΕΟΣ ΕΜΟ
Ο ΒΟΗΘΩΝ Δ...
...
Access Negev 1977 fig. 187 (printed, A. Negev)
Corpus Negev 1977 246

Inscription **1837**
Site Wadi Haggag, rock 5, #131
Technique incised
Condition fair
Content Arabic inscription
Limitation *Tentative decipherment only*
Comment *fragment*
Access Negev 1977 fig. 187 (printed, A. Negev)

Inscription **1838**
Site Wadi Haggag, rock 5, #131
Technique incised
Condition good
Content Greek inscription
ΧΑΡΙΣ ΜΝΗ
ΣΘΗ ΘΕΟΔΟΤΟΣ
Ο ΕΠΑΡΧΟΣ ΚΛ
ΑΥΔΙΟΥ
Access Negev 1977 fig. 188 (printed, A. Negev)
Corpus Negev 1977 247

Inscription **1839**
Site Sinai, unknown, #0
Technique scratched
Condition poor
Content Greek inscription
Limitation *Tentative decipherment only*
Access FU15 (photograph, A. Goren)

Inscription **1840**
Site Wadi Haggag, rock 5, #131
Technique incised
Condition fair
Content Greek inscription
ΣΩ
ΣΟΝ
ΤΟΝ ...
Access Negev 1977 fig. 191 (printed, A. Negev)
Corpus Negev 1977 249

Inscription **1841**
Site Wadi Haggag, rock 5, #131
Technique incised
Condition good
Content Greek inscription
ΜΝΗΣΘΗ
Access Negev 1977 fig. 191 (printed, A. Negev)
Corpus Negev 1977 250

Inscription **1842**
Site Wadi Haggag, rock 5, #131
Technique incised
Condition fair
Content Greek inscription
ΜΝΗΣΘΗ ΤΟΝ ΔΟΥΛΟΝ ΣΟΥ
ΕΧΗ ΩΗΝΟ...
Access Negev 1977 fig. 189 (printed, A. Negev)
Corpus Negev 1977 248

Inscription **1843**
Site Wadi Haggag, rock 5, #131
Technique incised
Condition good
Content crosses with inscription
Access Negev 1977 fig. 189 (printed, A. Negev)

Inscription **1844**
Site Wadi Haggag, rock 5, #131
Technique incised
Condition fair
Content Greek inscription
Limitation *Tentative decipherment only*
Access Negev 1977 fig. 189 (printed, A. Negev)

Inscription **1845**
Site Wadi Haggag, rock 5, #131
Technique incised
Condition fair
Content crosses with inscription
Access Negev 1977 fig. 189 (printed, A. Negev)

Inscription **1846**
Site Wadi Haggag, rock 5, #131
Technique incised
Condition good
Content Greek inscription
ΜΝΗΣΘΕ ΑΒΟ.ΑΛ.ΝΟΥ
ΕΙΣ ΘΕΟΣ Ο ΒΟΗΘΩΝ
Access Negev 1977 fig. 192 (printed, A. Negev)
Corpus Negev 1977 251

Inscription **1847**
Site Wadi Haggag, rock 5, #131
Technique incised
Condition good
Content varied crosses
Access Negev 1977 fig. 192 (printed, A. Negev)

Inscription **1848**
Site Wadi Haggag, rock 5, #131
Technique incised
Condition good
Content Arabic inscription
Limitation *Tentative decipherment only*
Access Negev 1977 fig. 192 (printed, A. Negev)

Inscription 1849
Site Wadi Haggag, rock 5, #131
Technique incised
Condition good
Content Nabatean inscription
šlm gdyw br wʾlw
Access Negev 1977 fig. 193 (printed, A. Negev); *see also* CP55
Corpus Negev 1977 252

Inscription 1850
Site Wadi Haggag, rock 5, #131
Technique scratched
Condition fair
Content Nabatean inscription
dkyr šlmw br tymʾlhy bṭb
Access Negev 1977 fig. 194 (printed, A. Negev)
Corpus Negev 1977 253

Inscription 1851
Site Wadi Haggag, rock 5, #131
Technique scratched
Condition good
Content Nabatean inscription
dkrwn ṭb lʿwdw br wʾlw
Access Negev 1977 fig. 194 (printed, A. Negev)
Corpus Negev 1977 254

Inscription 1852
Site Wadi Haggag, rock 5, #131
Technique scratched
Condition fair
Content Nabatean inscription
bryʾw br ḥryšw
Access Negev 1977 fig. 194 (printed, A. Negev)
Corpus Negev 1977 255

Inscription 1853
Site Wadi Haggag, rock 5, #131
Technique scratched
Condition good
Content Nabatean inscription
šlm ḥryšw br yʿly
Access Negev 1977 fig. 195 (printed, A. Negev); *see also* CP55
Corpus Negev 1977 256

Inscription 1854
Site Wadi Haggag, rock 5, #131
Technique scratched
Condition good
Content Nabatean inscription
šlm ḥršw
šlm ḥlṣw
Access Negev 1977 fig. 196 (printed, A. Negev)
Corpus Negev 1977 257

Inscription 1855
Site Wadi Haggag, rock 5, #131
Technique incised
Condition poor
Content Nabatean inscription
Comment *illegible*
Access Negev 1977 fig. 197 (printed, A. Negev)
Corpus Negev 1977 258

Inscription 1856
Site Wadi Haggag, rock 5, #131
Technique scratched
Condition fair
Content Nabatean inscription
šlm dʾbw br
ʾkbrw
Access Negev 1977 fig. 198 (printed, A. Negev); *see also* CP61
Corpus Negev 1977 259

Inscription 1857
Site Sinai, unknown, #0
Technique scratched
Condition poor
Content Greek inscription
Limitation *Tentative decipherment only*
Access FU15 (photograph, A. Goren)

Inscription 1858
Site Wadi Haggag, rock 5, #131
Technique incised
Condition fair
Content varied crosses
Access Negev 1977 fig. 198 (printed, A. Negev)

Inscription 1859
Site Wadi Haggag, rock 6, #135
Technique scratched
Condition good
Content Nabatean inscription
šlm ʿwdw br grmʾlbʿly
Access Negev 1977 fig. 199 (printed, A. Negev); *see also* CP59
Corpus Negev 1977 260

Inscription 1860
Site Wadi Haggag, rock 6, #135
Technique incised
Condition good
Content Nabatean inscription
dkyr bṭšw br wʾlw bṭb lʿlm
Access Negev 1977 fig. 200 (printed, A. Negev); *see also* CP57
Corpus Negev 1977 261

Inscription 1861
Site Wadi Haggag, rock 6, #135
Technique incised
Condition fair
Content rock drawing
Comment *boat? drawing is located above insc. 1860*
Access Negev 1977 fig. 200 (printed, A. Negev)

Inscription **1862**
Site Wadi Haggag, rock 6, #135
Technique incised
Condition good
Content Nabatean inscription
šlm ʾwšw br grmʾlbʿly
Access Negev 1977 fig. 201 (printed, A. Negev)
Corpus Negev 1977 262

Inscription **1863**
Site Wadi Haggag, rock 6, #135
Technique incised
Condition good
Content Nabatean inscription
šlm ʿmrw br klbw
Access Negev 1977 fig. 202 (printed, A. Negev)
Corpus Negev 1977 263

Inscription **1864**
Site Wadi Haggag, rock 6, #135
Technique incised
Condition fair
Content Nabatean inscription
šlm ... br wdw bṭb
Access Negev 1977 fig. 201 (printed, A. Negev)
Corpus Negev 1977 264

Inscription **1865**
Site Wadi Haggag, rock 6, #135
Technique incised
Condition poor
Content Nabatean inscription
grmw
Comment *doubtful reading*
Access Negev 1977 fig. 201 (printed, A. Negev)
Corpus Negev 1977 265

Inscription **1866**
Site Sinai, unknown, #0
Technique incised
Condition poor
Content Greek inscription
Limitation *Tentative decipherment only*
Access FU15 (photograph, A. Goren)

Inscription **1867**
Site Wadi Haggag, rock 6, #135
Technique incised
Condition fair
Content varied crosses
Access Negev 1977 fig. 201 (printed, A. Negev)

Inscription **1868**
Site Wadi Haggag, rock 6, #135
Technique incised
Condition poor
Content Nabatean inscription
Comment *illegible*
Access Negev 1977 fig. 201 (printed, A. Negev)
Corpus Negev 1977 266

Inscription **1869**
Site Wadi Haggag, rock 6, #135
Technique incised
Condition good
Content Nabatean inscription
šlm ʿwdw br
qrḥw
Access Negev 1977 fig. 202 (printed, A. Negev)
Corpus Negev 1977 267

Inscription **1870**
Site Wadi Haggag, rock 6, #135
Technique incised
Condition fair
Content rock drawing
Comment *cornucopia*
Access Negev 1977 fig. 202 (printed, A. Negev)

Inscription **1871**
Site Wadi Iqna, #74
Condition good
Content Nabatean inscription
šlm
grm'lbʿly
br w'lt
Access II.2.388 (printed, CIS)
Corpus CIS 706

Inscription **1872**
Site Wadi Iqna, #74
Condition good
Content Nabatean inscription
šlm mʿnw br
hnʾw bṭb
Access II.2.388 (printed, CIS)
Corpus CIS 707

Inscription **1873**
Site Wadi Iqna, #74
Condition poor
Content Nabatean inscription
...
... bṭb
Access II.2.388 (printed, CIS)
Corpus CIS 708

Inscription **1874**
Site Wadi Iqna, #74
Condition fair
Content Nabatean inscription
šlm wʾlw br ...
Access II.2.388 (printed, CIS)
Corpus CIS 709

Inscription 1875
Site Wadi Iqna, #74
Condition good
Content Nabatean inscription
šlm
ḥlṣšt br ʿbdʾbʿly
Access II.2.388 (printed, CIS)
Corpus CIS 710

Inscription 1876
Site Wadi Iqna, #74
Condition fair
Content Nabatean inscription
šlm ḥr...w
Access II.2.388 (printed, CIS)
Corpus CIS 711

Inscription 1877
Site Wadi Iqna, #74
Condition fair
Content Nabatean inscription
šlm ʾšʾdw
br ...
Access II.2.388 (printed, CIS)
Corpus CIS 712

Inscription 1878
Site Wadi Iqna, #74
Condition excellent
Content Nabatean inscription
šlm ʿbydw br ʿbdʾlbʿly bṭb
Access II.2.388 (printed, CIS)
Corpus CIS 713

Inscription 1879
Site Wadi Iqna, #74
Condition good
Content Nabatean inscription
šlm ʾṣlw br ʾ
klwšw bṭb
Access II.2.388 (printed, CIS)
Corpus CIS 714

Inscription 1880
Site Wadi Iqna, #74
Condition good
Content Nabatean inscription
šlm gdyw br w[ʾlw]
Access II.2.389 (printed, CIS)
Corpus CIS 715

Inscription 1881
Site Wadi Iqna, #74
Condition poor
Content Nabatean inscription
Comment *illegible*
Access II.2.389 (printed, CIS)
Corpus CIS 716

Inscription 1882
Site Wadi Iqna, #74
Condition poor
Comment *illegible*
Content Nabatean inscription
Access II.2.389 (printed, CIS)
Corpus CIS 717

Inscription 1883
Site Wadi Iqna, #74
Condition poor
Content Nabatean inscription
qrḥw
Access II.2.389 (printed, CIS)
Corpus CIS 718

Inscription 1884
Site Wadi Iqna, #74
Condition poor
Content Nabatean inscription
qrḥw
Access II.2.389 (printed, CIS)
Corpus CIS 719

Inscription 1885
Site Wadi Iqna, #74
Condition good
Content Nabatean inscription
ʾlmbqrw
Access II.2.389 (printed, CIS)
Corpus CIS 720

Inscription 1886
Site Wadi Iqna, #74
Condition poor
Content Nabatean inscription
..yʿly br ḥr...
Access II.2.389 (printed, CIS)
Corpus CIS 721

Inscription 1887
Site Wadi Iqna, #74
Condition poor
Content Nabatean inscription
Comment *illegible*
Access II.2.389 (printed, CIS)
Corpus CIS 722

Inscription 1888
Site Wadi Iqna, #74
Condition poor
Content Nabatean inscription
Comment *illegible*
Access II.2.389 (printed, CIS)
Corpus CIS 723

Inscription 1889
Site Wadi Iqna, #74
Condition poor
Content Nabatean inscription
Comment *illegible*
Access II.2.389 (printed, CIS)
Corpus CIS 724

Inscription **1890**
Site Wadi Iqna, #74
Condition poor
Content Nabatean inscription
Comment *illegible*
Access II.2.389 (printed, CIS)
Corpus CIS 725

Inscription **1891**
Site Wadi Iqna, #74
Condition poor
Content Nabatean inscription
Comment *illegible*
Access II.2.389 (printed, CIS)
Corpus CIS 726

Inscription **1892**
Site Wadi Iqna, #74
Condition poor
Content Nabatean inscription
Comment *illegible*
Access II.2.389 (printed, CIS)
Corpus CIS 727

Inscription **1893**
Site Wadi Iqna, #74
Condition poor
Content Nabatean inscription
Comment *illegible*
Access II.2.389 (printed, CIS)
Corpus CIS 728

Inscription **1894**
Site Wadi Iqna, #74
Condition poor
Content Nabatean inscription
Comment *illegible*
Access II.2.389 (printed, CIS)
Corpus CIS 729

Inscription **1895**
Site Wadi Iqna, #74
Condition poor
Content Nabatean inscription
Comment *illegible*
Access II.2.389 (printed, CIS)
Corpus CIS 730

Inscription **1896**
Site Wadi Iqna, #74
Condition poor
Content Nabatean inscription
Comment *illegible*
Access II.2.389 (printed, CIS)
Corpus CIS 731

Inscription **1897**
Site Wadi Iqna, #74
Condition poor
Content Nabatean inscription
.ʾwšw br w..
Access II.2.389 (printed, CIS)
Corpus CIS 732

Inscription **1898**
Site Wadi Iqna, #74
Condition poor
Content Nabatean inscription
Comment *illegible*
Access II.2.389 (printed, CIS)
Corpus CIS 733

Inscription **1899**
Site Wadi Iqna, #74
Condition fair
Content Nabatean inscription
šlm ʾʿlʾ
br š..
Access II.2.389 (printed, CIS)
Corpus CIS 734

Inscription **1900**
Site Wadi Iqna, #74
Condition fair
Content Nabatean inscription
škmlhy br ... m šlm
Access II.2.389 (printed, CIS)
Corpus CIS 735

Inscription **1901**
Site Wadi Iqna, #74
Condition fair
Content Nabatean inscription
brʾw br ʾkbry
Access II.2.390 (printed, CIS)
Corpus CIS 736

Inscription **1902**
Site Wadi Iqna, #74
Condition good
Content Nabatean inscription
šlm ʾlktyw br wʾlw
Access II.2.390 (printed, CIS)
Corpus CIS 737

Inscription **1903**
Site Wadi Iqna, #74
Condition good
Content Nabatean inscription
šlm šʿdʾlhy br yʿly bṭb wšlm
Access II.2.390 (printed, CIS)
Corpus CIS 738

Inscription **1904**
Site Wadi Iqna, #74
Condition good
Content Nabatean inscription
šlm ʾʿlʾ
br pšy
Access II.2.390 (printed, CIS)
Corpus CIS 739

Inscription 1905
Site Wadi Iqna, #74
Condition good
Content Nabatean inscription
šlm šdʾlhy
br yʿly bṭb
Access II.2.390 (printed, CIS)
Corpus CIS 740

Inscription 1906
Site Wadi Iqna, #74
Condition good
Content Nabatean inscription
šlm tymʿbdt br [pṣ]y
Access II.2.390 (printed, CIS)
Corpus CIS 741

Inscription 1907
Site Wadi Iqna, #74
Condition good
Content Nabatean inscription
šlm šʿdʾlhy
br pšy bṭb
Access II.2.390 (printed, CIS); *see also* DO19
Corpus CIS 742

Inscription 1908
Site Wadi Iqna, #74
Condition good
Content Nabatean inscription
šlm wdw br ʾšwdt
Access II.2.390 (printed, CIS); *see also* DO19
Corpus CIS 743

Inscription 1909
Site Wadi Iqna, #74
Condition good
Content Nabatean inscription
šlm ʾṣlḥw br ʾk
lwšw bṭb
Access II.2.391 (printed, CIS)
Corpus CIS 744

Inscription 1910
Site Wadi Iqna, #74
Condition good
Content Nabatean inscription
šlm ʿmyw br
ʿwdw
Access II.2.391 (printed, CIS)
Corpus CIS 745

Inscription 1911
Site Wadi Iqna, #74
Condition good
Content Nabatean inscription
šlm ʿmyw
Access II.2.391 (printed, CIS)
Corpus CIS 746

Inscription 1912
Site Wadi Iqna, #74
Condition good
Content Nabatean inscription
šlm ʿbdʾlbʿly
br ḥryšw bk[l ṭb]
Access II.2.391 (printed, CIS)
Corpus CIS 747

Inscription 1913
Site Wadi Iqna, #74
Condition good
Content Nabatean inscription
[šl]m wʾlw br hnyʾw bṭb
Access II.2.391 (printed, CIS)
Corpus CIS 748

Inscription 1914
Site Wadi Iqna, #74
Condition good
Content Nabatean inscription
šlm ʿbdʾlhy
Access II.2.391 (printed, CIS)
Corpus CIS 749

Inscription 1915
Site Wadi Iqna, #74
Condition good
Content Nabatean inscription
dkyr ʿmrw
br ʾbgrw
bšlm
Access II.2.391 (printed, CIS)
Corpus CIS 750

Inscription 1916
Site Wadi Iqna, #74
Condition good
Content Nabatean inscription
šlm ʿmyw
br wʾlt bṭb
Access II.2.391 (printed, CIS)
Corpus CIS 751

Inscription 1917
Site Wadi Iqna, #74
Condition good
Content Nabatean inscription
šlm ʿbydw
br wʾlt
Access II.2.392 (printed, CIS)
Corpus CIS 752

Inscription 1918
Site Wadi Iqna, #74
Condition good
Content Nabatean inscription
šlm ʿbdʾlhy br pʾrn
Access II.2.392 (printed, CIS)
Corpus CIS 753

Inscription 1919
Site Wadi Iqna, #74
Condition excellent
Content Nabatean inscription
šlm ḥryšw br wʾlw br
ʾlmbqrw
Access II.2.392 (printed, CIS)
Corpus CIS 754

Inscription 1920
Site Wadi Iqna, #74
Condition good
Content Nabatean inscription
šlm pšy br ʾʿlʾʿlʾ qšṭw bṭb
Access II.2.392 (printed, CIS)
Corpus CIS 755

Inscription 1921
Site Wadi Iqna, #74
Condition good
Content Nabatean inscription
šlm ʿbydw br ḥršw
Access II.2.392 (printed, CIS)
Corpus CIS 756

Inscription 1922
Site Wadi Iqna, #74
Condition excellent
Content Nabatean inscription
šlm pšy br ḥryšw br ʾʿlʾ qšṭw br ḥryšw
wʿbydw wgrmʾbʿlyw bṭb wbšlm blʾ
Access II.2.392 (printed, CIS)
Corpus CIS 757

Inscription 1923
Site Wadi Iqna, #74
Condition excellent
Content Nabatean inscription
šlm yʿly br pšyw br
bṭb wšlm
Access II.2.392 (printed, CIS)
Corpus CIS 758

Inscription 1924
Site Wadi Iqna, #74
Condition good
Content Nabatean inscription
šlm ʿmmw br
ʾbn ʾlqynw
ʾbn w...
Access II.2.392 (printed, CIS)
Corpus CIS 759

Inscription 1925
Site Wadi Iqna, #74
Condition good
Content Nabatean inscription
šlm ʾʿlʾ br
wʾlw
Access II.2.393 (printed, CIS)
Corpus CIS 760

Inscription 1926
Site Wadi Iqna, #74
Condition good
Content Nabatean inscription
šlm zydw br ʿbdw
Access II.2.393 (printed, CIS)
Corpus CIS 761

Inscription 1927
Site Wadi Sih, Jebel Muardjeh, #314
Condition good
Content Nabatean inscription
šlm ʾwšw br
ʿbdʾlbʿly bṭb
Access II.2.393 (printed, CIS)
Corpus CIS 762

Inscription 1928
Site Wadi Sih, Jebel Muardjeh, #314
Condition fair
Content Nabatean inscription
ʿmmw br [w]ʾl[w]
Access II.2.393 (printed, CIS)
Corpus CIS 763

Inscription 1929
Site Wadi Sih, Jebel Muardjeh, #314
Condition fair
Content Nabatean inscription
šlm grmʾlhy
br ...
Access II.2.393 (printed, CIS)
Corpus CIS 764

Inscription 1930
Site Wadi Sih, Jebel Muardjeh, #314
Condition fair
Content Nabatean inscription
šlm ʾlmb
qrw br nšy
g.w
Access II.2.393 (printed, CIS)
Corpus CIS 765

Inscription 1931
Site Wadi Sih, Jebel Muardjeh, #314
Condition fair
Content Nabatean inscription
dkyr ʿmrw br ḥryšw
khn tʾ ʾlh.ʾ.
Access II.2.394 (printed, CIS)
Corpus CIS 766

Inscription 1932
Site Wadi Sih, Jebel Muardjeh, #314
Condition fair
Content Nabatean inscription
šlm ḥ[l]yṣw br
[ʾ]tmw wʾtm[w] brh
bkl ṭb
Access II.2.394 (printed, CIS)
Corpus CIS 767

Inscription 1933
Site Wadi Sih, Jebel Muardjeh, #314
Condition poor
Content Nabatean inscription
šlm
wʾlw [ʾ]mynw
ʿmʾ ...
Access II.2.394 (printed, CIS)
Corpus CIS 768

Inscription 1934
Site Wadi Sih, Jebel Muardjeh, #314
Condition fair
Content Nabatean inscription
šlm zydw br ...
Access II.2.394 (printed, CIS)
Corpus CIS 769

Inscription 1935
Site Wadi Sih, Jebel Muardjeh, #314
Condition good
Content Nabatean inscription
[š]lm wʾlw br ʿwdw bṭb
Access II.2.394 (printed, CIS)
Corpus CIS 770

Inscription 1936
Site Wadi Sih, Jebel Muardjeh, #314
Condition good
Content Nabatean inscription
šlm wʾlw br šʿdʾlhy
Access II.2.394 (printed, CIS)
Corpus CIS 771

Inscription 1937
Site Wadi Sih, Jebel Muardjeh, #314
Condition fair
Content Nabatean inscription
šlm wʾlw
[b]r zydw br [ḥryšw]
Access II.2.395 (printed, CIS)
Corpus CIS 772

Inscription 1938
Site Wadi Sih, Jebel Muardjeh, #314
Condition poor
Content Nabatean inscription
Comment *illegible*
Access II.2.395 (printed, CIS)
Corpus CIS 773

Inscription 1939
Site Wadi Sih, Jebel Muardjeh, #314
Condition poor
Content Nabatean inscription
Comment *illegible*
Access II.2.395 (printed, CIS)
Corpus CIS 774

Inscription 1940
Site Wadi Mukatab, #64
Condition fair
Content Nabatean inscription
ḥlṣšt
Access II.2.395 (printed, CIS)
Corpus CIS 775

Inscription 1941
Site Wadi Mukatab, #64
Condition good
Content Nabatean inscription
šlm ʿwdw br ...
Access II.2.395 (printed, CIS)
Corpus CIS 776

Inscription 1942
Site Wadi Mukatab, #64
Condition good
Content Nabatean inscription
šlm k[l]bw br ʿmrw
bṭb
Access II.2.395 (printed, CIS)
Corpus CIS 777

Inscription 1943
Site Wadi Mukatab, #64
Condition good
Content Nabatean inscription
šlm ʿmyrt br zydw bṭb
Access II.2.395 (printed, CIS)
Corpus CIS 778

Inscription 1944
Site Wadi Mukatab, #64
Condition fair
Content Nabatean inscription
[š]lm [w]ʾlw br [ʾlm]bqrw
Access II.2.395 (printed, CIS)
Corpus CIS 779

Inscription 1945
Site Wadi Mukatab, #64
Condition good
Content Nabatean inscription
šlm šʿdʾlh br
wʾlw
Access II.2.396 (printed, CIS); *see also* CO18
Corpus CIS 780

Inscription 1946
Site Wadi Mukatab, #64
Condition excellent
Content Nabatean inscription
šlm pšy br bṭb
qšṭw wšlm
Access II.2.396 (printed, CIS); *see also* CO18
Corpus CIS 781

Inscription 1947
Site Wadi Mukatab, #64
Condition fair
Content Nabatean inscription
šlm ḥr
yšw br ...
Access II.2.396 (printed, CIS)
Corpus CIS 782

Inscription 1948
Site Wadi Mukatab, #64
Condition good
Content Nabatean inscription
šlm kʿmh
br ʾtmw
Access II.2.396 (printed, CIS)
Corpus CIS 783

Inscription 1949
Site Wadi Mukatab, #64
Condition poor
Content Nabatean inscription
šlm grmʾ
Access II.2.396 (printed, CIS)
Corpus CIS 784

Inscription 1950
Site Wadi Mukatab, #64
Condition good
Content Nabatean inscription
dkyr wʾlt br wdw
bṭb wšlm
Access II.2.396 (printed, CIS); *see also* CO13
Corpus CIS 785

Inscription 1951
Site Wadi Mukatab, #64
Condition good
Content Nabatean inscription
dkyrh ḥršw
brt šʿwdt
Access II.2.396 (printed, CIS); *see also* CO13
Corpus CIS 786

Inscription 1952
Site Wadi Mukatab, #64
Condition good
Content Nabatean inscription
šlm grmʾlbʿly
br ʾbn ʾlqyny bṭb
br šmrḥ
Access II.2.397 (printed, CIS)
Corpus CIS 787

Inscription 1953
Site Wadi Mukatab, #64
Condition good
Content Nabatean inscription
dkyr ʿlm
bṭb ʿmrw
ʾšbt
Access II.2.397 (printed, CIS)
Corpus CIS 788

Inscription 1954
Site Wadi Mukatab, #64
Condition good
Content Nabatean inscription
šlm dmgw
br ṭylt
Access II.2.397 (printed, CIS)
Corpus CIS 789

Inscription 1955
Site Wadi Mukatab, #64
Condition good
Content Nabatean inscription
šlm ʿbdḥrtt
hprkʾ wgrmw
ʿlymh
Access II.2.397 (printed, CIS)
Corpus CIS 790

Inscription 1956
Site Wadi Mukatab, #64
Condition good
Content Nabatean inscription
šlm prqw
Access II.2.397 (printed, CIS)
Corpus CIS 791

Inscription **1957**
Site Wadi Mukatab, #64
Condition good
Content Nabatean inscription
šlm
ʿwdw br ʿmrw
bṭb wšlm
Access II.2.398 (printed, CIS)
Corpus CIS 792

Inscription **1958**
Site Wadi Mukatab, #64
Condition good
Content Nabatean inscription
šlm yʿly
br ʾṣlḥw
bṭb
Access II.2.398 (printed, CIS)
Corpus CIS 793

Inscription **1959**
Site Wadi Mukatab, #64
Condition good
Content Nabatean inscription
šlm ḥryšw
šlm ḥršw br
ʿmrw bṭ[b]
Access II.2.398 (printed, CIS)
Corpus CIS 794

Inscription **1960**
Site Wadi Mukatab, #64
Condition good
Content Nabatean inscription
šlm ʿyydw
br ʾwšw
bṭb
Access II.2.398 (printed, CIS); *see also* CO27
Corpus CIS 795

Inscription **1961**
Site Wadi Mukatab, #64
Condition poor
Content Nabatean inscription
šlmh
Access II.2.398 (printed, CIS)
Corpus CIS 796

Inscription **1962**
Site Wadi Mukatab, #64
Condition fair
Content Nabatean inscription
šlm šʿdʾ[lhy]
br klbw bṭb
Access II.2.398 (printed, CIS); *see also* CO26
Corpus CIS 797

Inscription **1963**
Site Wadi Mukatab, #64
Condition good
Content Nabatean inscription
šlm ʿbdʾlhy br šmrḥ bṭb
Access II.2.398 (printed, CIS)
Corpus CIS 798

Inscription **1964**
Site Wadi Mukatab, #64
Condition good
Content Nabatean inscription
dkyr ḥrw b[r]
šbrh bṭb
Access II.2.399 (printed, CIS); *see also* CO26
Corpus CIS 799

Inscription **1965**
Site Wadi Mukatab, #64
Condition good
Content Nabatean inscription
dky[r] ʾlḥšpw
br ʿwdw
Access II.2.399 (printed, CIS); *see also* CO26
Corpus CIS 800

Inscription **1966**
Site Wadi Mukatab, #64
Condition fair
Content Nabatean inscription
šlm ʿbṭh br bryʾw
Access II.2.399 (printed, CIS); *see also* CO26
Corpus CIS 801

Inscription **1967**
Site Wadi Mukatab, #64
Condition good
Content Nabatean inscription
dkyr mʿyrw br
ʿbdʾlg[ʾ]
Access II.2.399 (printed, CIS); *see also* CO29
Corpus CIS 802

Inscription **1968**
Site Wadi Mukatab, #64
Condition good
Content Nabatean inscription
dkyr ʿyydw
ʾw[š]w
Access II.2.399 (printed, CIS)
Corpus CIS 803

Inscription 1969
Site Wadi Mukatab, #64
Condition excellent
Content Nabatean inscription
dkyr mgdyw
br ʿmrw bṭb
yʿly br slwns šlm
Access II.2.399 (printed, CIS)
Corpus CIS 804

Inscription 1970
Site Wadi Mukatab, #64
Condition good
Content Nabatean inscription
dkyr ʾʿlʾ
br zydw br ʾbw
qw[mw] bṭb
Access II.2.399 (printed, CIS)
Corpus CIS 805

Inscription 1971
Site Wadi Mukatab, #64
Condition good
Content Nabatean inscription
šlm ʿṣrw br yʿly
Access II.2.400 (printed, CIS)
Corpus CIS 806

Inscription 1972
Site Wadi Mukatab, #64
Condition good
Content Nabatean inscription
dkyr ʾšwdw
Access II.2.400 (printed, CIS)
Corpus CIS 807

Inscription 1973
Site Wadi Mukatab, #64
Condition good
Content Nabatean inscription
dkyr wʾl[w] br ʾl
mbqrw
Access II.2.400 (printed, CIS)
Corpus CIS 808

Inscription 1974
Site Wadi Mukatab, #64
Condition good
Content Nabatean inscription
šlm pšy br ʾʿlʾ
Access II.2.400 (printed, CIS)
Corpus CIS 809

Inscription 1975
Site Wadi Mukatab, #64
Condition fair
Content Nabatean inscription
šlm ʿl
šlm ḥ..
šlm ḥryšw
šlm yʿl[y]
šlm ʾlṭ[m]
w br
ʾbg
zydw
ḥryšw
lbʿly
dkyr
wbrḥ....
Access II.2.400 (printed, CIS)
Corpus CIS 810

Inscription 1976
Site Wadi Mukatab, #64
Condition good
Content Nabatean inscription
šlm šʿdʾlhy
br ʿlyw bṭb
šl[m]
Access II.2.400 (printed, CIS)
Corpus CIS 811

Inscription 1977
Site Wadi Mukatab, #64
Condition excellent
Content Nabatean inscription
dkyrn wʾ
lw wḥry
šw wʿyy
dw bny ʾbʾ
wšw bṭb
Access II.2.401 (printed, CIS)
Corpus CIS 812

Inscription 1978
Site Wadi Mukatab, #64
Condition good
Content Nabatean inscription
šlm ḥršw
br bḥgh
Access II.2.401 (printed, CIS)
Corpus CIS 813

Inscription 1979
Site Wadi Mukatab, #64
Condition good
Content Nabatean inscription
šlm gdyw br bḥgh bṭb šlm
grmʾlbʿly ʾḥwhy
Access II.2.401 (printed, CIS)
Corpus CIS 814

Inscription 1980
Site Wadi Mukatab, #64
Condition fair
Content Nabatean inscription
šlm ʾwšw br [klb]w
Access II.2.401 (printed, CIS)
Corpus CIS 815

Inscription 1981
Site Wadi Mukatab, #64
Condition good
Content Nabatean inscription
šlm šmrḥ br ʾwšʾlbʿly bṭb
Access II.2.401 (printed, CIS); *see also* CS59
Corpus CIS 816

Inscription 1982
Site Wadi Mukatab, #64
Condition good
Content Nabatean inscription
šlm šmrḥw
br ḥryšw
Access II.2.401 (printed, CIS); *see also* CS59
Corpus CIS 817

Inscription 1983
Site Wadi Mukatab, #64
Condition fair
Content Nabatean inscription
ʾldrdw wʾlm ...
Access II.2.402 (printed, CIS); *see also* CS59
Corpus CIS 818

Inscription 1984
Site Wadi Mukatab, #64
Condition fair
Content Nabatean inscription
...
pṣyʾw...
Access II.2.402 (printed, CIS)
Corpus CIS 819

Inscription 1985
Site Wadi Mukatab, #64
Condition good
Content Nabatean inscription
dkyr bṭb lʿlm ʿwdw br
grmʾlbʿly br gdyw bṭb
Access II.2.402 (printed, CIS)
Corpus CIS 820

Inscription 1986
Site Wadi Mukatab, #64
Condition fair
Content Nabatean inscription
šl[m] ʾ[w]šʾlbʿ[ly]
br grmʾlb[ʿly]
Access II.2.402 (printed, CIS)
Corpus CIS 821

Inscription 1987
Site Wadi Mukatab, #64
Condition fair
Content Nabatean inscription
ʿwdw wqym[w]
Access II.2.402 (printed, CIS)
Corpus CIS 822

Inscription 1988
Site Wadi Mukatab, #64
Condition good
Content Nabatean inscription
šlm grmʾlbʿly
br ʿbydw bṭb
Access II.2.402 (printed, CIS)
Corpus CIS 823

Inscription 1989
Site Wadi Mukatab, #64
Condition good
Content Nabatean inscription
šlm ḥnṭlw
br gʾnyw
Access II.2.402 (printed, CIS)
Corpus CIS 824

Inscription 1990
Site Wadi Mukatab, #64
Condition good
Content Nabatean inscription
dkyr ʾ šwdʾ bṭb
wʾltbqw br qymw ktbʾ
Access II.2.402 (printed, CIS)
Corpus CIS 825

Inscription 1991
Site Wadi Mukatab, #64
Condition fair
Content Nabatean inscription
šlm ʿnmw br
ʿbdšbw ...
Access II.2.403 (printed, CIS)
Corpus CIS 826

Inscription 1992
Site Wadi Mukatab, #64
Condition good
Content Nabatean inscription
šlm ʾlmbqrw
br wʾlw
Access II.2.403 (printed, CIS)
Corpus CIS 827

Inscription 1993
Site Wadi Mukatab, #64
Condition fair
Content Nabatean inscription
šlm ʾwšw br
š.bṭb
Access II.2.403 (printed, CIS)
Corpus CIS 828

Inscription 1994
Site Wadi Mukatab, #64
Condition good
Content Nabatean inscription
šlm wʾlw br ḥryšw
Access II.2.403 (printed, CIS)
Corpus CIS 829

Inscription 1995
Site Wadi Mukatab, #64
Condition poor
Content Nabatean inscription
šlm ʾlhmšw
br dbylt bṭb
Access II.2.403 (printed, CIS)
Corpus CIS 830

Inscription 1996
Site Wadi Mukatab, #64
Condition fair
Content Nabatean inscription
..wʾlw (?)
Access II.2.403 (printed, CIS)
Corpus CIS 831

Inscription 1997
Site Wadi Mukatab, #64
Condition good
Content Nabatean inscription
šlm pšy br ʾʿlʾ bṭb
Access II.2.403 (printed, CIS)
Corpus CIS 832

Inscription 1998
Site Wadi Mukatab, #64
Condition good
Content Nabatean inscription
šlm ḥryšw
br ʾṣrw [b]ṭb
Access II.2.403 (printed, CIS)
Corpus CIS 833

Inscription 1999
Site Wadi Mukatab, #64
Condition good
Content Nabatean inscription
dkyr ʿbdḥrtt
br ʿmrw br ʿrṭmw
Access II.2.404 (printed, CIS); *see also* CS51
Corpus CIS 834

Inscription 2000
Site Wadi Mukatab, #64
Condition good
Content Nabatean inscription
zydw br whb
Access II.2.404 (printed, CIS)
Corpus CIS 835

Inscription 2001
Site Wadi Mukatab, #64
Condition good
Content Nabatean inscription
ʿmyw br hnšnkyh br
wʾlt
Access II.2.404 (printed, CIS)
Corpus CIS 836

Inscription 2002
Site Wadi Mukatab, #64
Condition good
Content Nabatean inscription
šlm ʿmyw
br zbydt
Access II.2.404 (printed, CIS)
Corpus CIS 837

Inscription 2003
Site Wadi Mukatab, #64
Condition poor
Content Nabatean inscription
šlm ʿmmw br ʿl[ht]
[br] grmʾbʿly bṭ[b]
Access II.2.404 (printed, CIS)
Corpus CIS 838

Inscription 2004
Site Wadi Mukatab, #64
Condition good
Content Nabatean inscription
šlm ʿmmw br ʿlht
br grmʾlbʿly
Access II.2.404 (printed, CIS)
Corpus CIS 839

Inscription 2005
Site Wadi Mukatab, #64
Condition good
Content Nabatean inscription
šlm bḥgh br
ʿbdʾbʿly
Access II.2.404 (printed, CIS)
Corpus CIS 840

Inscription 2006
Site Wadi Mukatab, #64
Condition good
Content Nabatean inscription
šlm ḥnṭlw br ʿmyw bṭb
ʿmyw brh
Access II.2.405 (printed, CIS)
Corpus CIS 841

Inscription 2007
Site Wadi Mukatab, #64
Condition fair
Content Nabatean inscription
wdydw
Access II.2.405 (printed, CIS)
Corpus CIS 842

Inscription 2008
Site Wadi Mukatab, #64
Condition excellent
Content Nabatean inscription
šlm ʾwyšw br ʿydw
Access II.2.405 (printed, CIS); *see also* CS61
Corpus CIS 843

Inscription 2009
Site Wadi Mukatab, #64
Condition good
Content Nabatean inscription
šlm ʾptḥ br whbl[hy]
Access II.2.405 (printed, CIS); *see also* CS61
Corpus CIS 844

Inscription 2010
Site Wadi Mukatab, #64
Condition good
Content Nabatean inscription
šlm ḥryšw
br pṣ
yw
Access II.2.405 (printed, CIS); *see also* CS61
Corpus CIS 845

Inscription 2011
Site Wadi Mukatab, #64
Condition excellent
Content Nabatean inscription
šlm ḥyʾl
br šbty br
ʾḥyw
Access II.2.405 (printed, CIS)
Corpus CIS 846

Inscription 2012
Site Wadi Mukatab, #64
Condition good
Content Nabatean inscription
šlm ʿmyw br
grmʾlbʿly
Access II.2.406 (printed, CIS)
Corpus CIS 847

Inscription 2013
Site Wadi Mukatab, #64
Condition good
Content Nabatean inscription
šlm dʾbw
br ʾlzʿblyw
bṭb
Access II.2.406 (printed, CIS); *see also* CS54
Corpus CIS 848

Inscription 2014
Site Wadi Mukatab, #64
Condition fair
Content Nabatean inscription
šlm ḥlṣšt br
ḥnṭl[w]
Access II.2.406 (printed, CIS)
Corpus CIS 849

Inscription 2015
Site Wadi Mukatab, #64
Condition fair
Content Nabatean inscription
šlm ʿbdqwmw
[br gr]mʾlhy
Access II.2.406 (printed, CIS)
Corpus CIS 850

Inscription 2016
Site Wadi Mukatab, #64
Condition good
Content Nabatean inscription
šlm tymlhy br ʿbdʾlhy
Access II.2.406 (printed, CIS)
Corpus CIS 851

Inscription **2017**
Site Wadi Mukatab, #64
Condition good
Content Nabatean inscription
šlm ʿmyw br
šmrḥ
Access II.2.406 (printed, CIS)
Corpus CIS 852

Inscription **2018**
Site Wadi Mukatab, #64
Condition fair
Content Nabatean inscription
šlm ...dw br dwdw
Access II.2.406 (printed, CIS)
Corpus CIS 853

Inscription **2019**
Site Wadi Mukatab, #64
Condition poor
Content Nabatean inscription
dkyr ʾṣlḥw [br ʾ]
klw[š]w b[ṭb]
Access II.2.406 (printed, CIS)
Corpus CIS 854

Inscription **2020**
Site Wadi Mukatab, #64
Condition poor
Content Nabatean inscription
šlm šʿdʾlhy
....h
Access II.2.407 (printed, CIS)
Corpus CIS 855

Inscription **2021**
Site Wadi Mukatab, #64
Condition fair
Content Nabatean inscription
šlm ḥryšw
br wʾlw b[ṭb]
Access II.2.407 (printed, CIS)
Corpus CIS 856

Inscription **2022**
Site Wadi Mukatab, #64
Condition good
Content Nabatean inscription
šlm bṭšw
br bkrw
Access II.2.407 (printed, CIS)
Corpus CIS 857

Inscription **2023**
Site Wadi Mukatab, #64
Condition good
Content Nabatean inscription
dkyr ʿmrw br
pšyw bṭb
Access II.2.407 (printed, CIS)
Corpus CIS 858

Inscription **2024**
Site Wadi Mukatab, #64
Condition excellent
Content Nabatean inscription
dkyr ʿbydw br
wʾlw wwʾlw wḥryšw
wšʿdʾlhy bnyh
bṭb
Access II.2.407 (printed, CIS)
Corpus CIS 859

Inscription **2025**
Site Wadi Mukatab, #64
Condition good
Content Nabatean inscription
šlm ʿwdw br ʿmyw
Access II.2.407 (printed, CIS)
Corpus CIS 860

Inscription **2026**
Site Wadi Mukatab, #64
Condition good
Content Nabatean inscription
bryk wʾlw
Access II.2.408 (printed, CIS)
Corpus CIS 861

Inscription **2027**
Site Wadi Mukatab, #64
Condition fair
Content Nabatean inscription
dkyr wʾlw br ʾšdw
bṭb ..h
Access II.2.408 (printed, CIS)
Corpus CIS 862

Inscription **2028**
Site Wadi Mukatab, #64
Condition fair
Content Nabatean inscription
šlm ʿbd[ʾlbʿly] br
ʾtmw bṭb
Access II.2.408 (printed, CIS)
Corpus CIS 863

Inscription 2029
Site Wadi Mukatab, #64
Condition good
Content Nabatean inscription
šlm ʾlṭmw br
grmʾlbʿly
Access II.2.408 (printed, CIS)
Corpus CIS 864

Inscription 2030
Site Wadi Mukatab, #64
Condition good
Content Nabatean inscription
tntlw
Access II.2.408 (printed, CIS)
Corpus CIS 865

Inscription 2031
Site Wadi Mukatab, #64
Condition fair
Content Nabatean inscription
...yw
br zydw bṭb
Access II.2.408 (printed, CIS)
Corpus CIS 866

Inscription 2032
Site Wadi Mukatab, #64
Condition good
Content Nabatean inscription
šlm [g]mlw br
pndšw
Access II.2.408 (printed, CIS)
Corpus CIS 867

Inscription 2033
Site Wadi Mukatab, #64
Condition poor
Content Nabatean inscription
bryk [ʾp]t[ḥ]
br [b]ḥgh
Access II.2.409 (printed, CIS)
Corpus CIS 868

Inscription 2034
Site Wadi Mukatab, #64
Condition good
Content Nabatean inscription
ḥnṭlw
Access II.2.409 (printed, CIS)
Corpus CIS 869

Inscription 2035
Site Wadi Mukatab, #64
Condition good
Content Nabatean inscription
dkyr ʿbydw
br wʾlw bṭb
Access II.2.409 (printed, CIS)
Corpus CIS 870

Inscription 2036
Site Wadi Mukatab, #64
Condition good
Content Nabatean inscription
dkyr wʾlw
br ʿmyw bṭb
Access II.2.409 (printed, CIS)
Corpus CIS 871

Inscription 2037
Site Wadi Mukatab, #64
Condition good
Content Nabatean inscription
šlm ʾlmbqrw
Access II.2.409 (printed, CIS)
Corpus CIS 872

Inscription 2038
Site Wadi Mukatab, #64
Condition good
Content Nabatean inscription
dkyr ktryw
br hnyʾw
bṭb..
Access II.2.409 (printed, CIS)
Corpus CIS 873

Inscription 2039
Site Wadi Mukatab, #64
Condition poor
Content Nabatean inscription
brykh brt
...y..w...
Access II.2.409 (printed, CIS)
Corpus CIS 874

Inscription 2040
Site Wadi Mukatab, #64
Condition good
Content Nabatean inscription
bryk ʾptḥ
br bḥgh
Access II.2.409 (printed, CIS)
Corpus CIS 875

Inscription 2041
Site Wadi Mukatab, #64
Condition fair
Content Nabatean inscription
bryk
Access II.2.410 (printed, CIS)
Corpus CIS 876

Inscription 2042
Site Wadi Mukatab, #64
Condition poor
Content Nabatean inscription
brykh brt...
Access II.2.410 (printed, CIS)
Corpus CIS 877

Inscription 2043
Site Wadi Mukatab, #64
Condition good
Content Nabatean inscription
bryk rmʾl
br ʾwšw
Access II.2.410 (printed, CIS)
Corpus CIS 878

Inscription 2044
Site Wadi Mukatab, #64
Condition fair
Content Nabatean inscription
šlm ʾwšw br ʾ...
Access II.2.410 (printed, CIS)
Corpus CIS 879

Inscription 2045
Site Wadi Mukatab, #64
Condition good
Content Nabatean inscription
[b]ryk nšgw
br pšy
Access II.2.410 (printed, CIS)
Corpus CIS 880

Inscription 2046
Site Wadi Mukatab, #64
Condition good
Content Nabatean inscription
dkyr wʾlw br
šmrḥw bṭb
Access II.2.410 (printed, CIS)
Corpus CIS 881

Inscription 2047
Site Wadi Mukatab, #64
Condition fair
Content Nabatean inscription
šlm ʾ ...smw
br ʾwšyw
Access II.2.410 (printed, CIS)
Corpus CIS 882

Inscription 2048
Site Wadi Mukatab, #64
Condition excellent
Content Nabatean inscription
šlm pšyw w ḥryšw
bny zydw bṭb
Access II.2.410 (printed, CIS)
Corpus CIS 883

Inscription 2049
Site Wadi Mukatab, #64
Condition good
Content Nabatean inscription
bryk ḥryšw
[br] grmlbʿly
Access II.2.411 (printed, CIS)
Corpus CIS 884

Inscription 2050
Site Wadi Mukatab, #64
Condition good
Content Nabatean inscription
šlm ʿlyt
brt pšy
Access II.2.411 (printed, CIS); *see also* CM62
Corpus CIS 885

Inscription 2051
Site Wadi Mukatab, #64
Condition good
Content Nabatean inscription
šlm ʿmyw br
ʾbn ṣwbw wbrh
bṭb
Access II.2.411 (printed, CIS); *see also* CM62
Corpus CIS 886

Inscription 2052
Site Wadi Mukatab, #64
Condition good
Content Nabatean inscription
šlm yʿly br
prṣw
Access II.2.411 (printed, CIS); *see also* CM62
Corpus CIS 887

Inscription 2053
Site Wadi Mukatab, #64
Condition good
Content Nabatean inscription
šlm pšy br zydw
Access II.2.411 (printed, CIS)
Corpus CIS 888

Inscription 2054
Site Wadi Mukatab, #64
Condition good
Content Nabatean inscription
šlm wʾlw
Access II.2.411 (printed, CIS); *see also* CM62
Corpus CIS 889

Inscription 2055
Site Wadi Mukatab, #64
Condition good
Content Nabatean inscription
dnh swsyʾ dy
ʿbd šʿdlhy br ʾʿlʾ
Access II.2.411 (printed, CIS); *see also* CM2
Corpus CIS 890

Inscription 2056
Site Wadi Mukatab, #64
Condition excellent
Content Nabatean inscription
šlm šʿdlhy br
ʿmyw br šbʿw
wʿmyw brh bṭb
Access II.2.412 (printed, CIS)
Corpus CIS 891

Inscription 2057
Site Wadi Mukatab, #64
Condition good
Content Nabatean inscription
[šl]m šlmw br zydw
Access II.2.412 (printed, CIS); *see also* CM62
Corpus CIS 892

Inscription 2058
Site Wadi Mukatab, #64
Condition good
Content Nabatean inscription
šlm ʿbdʾlbʿly br ḥryšw
br gršw
Access II.2.412 (printed, CIS)
Corpus CIS 893

Inscription 2059
Site Wadi Mukatab, #64
Condition good
Content Nabatean inscription
šlm ʾʿllʾ br šmrḥ
bṭb
Access II.2.412 (printed, CIS); *see also* CM62
Corpus CIS 894

Inscription 2060
Site Wadi Mukatab, #64
Condition good
Content Nabatean inscription
[š]lm ʾʿlʾ br ʾwšw
Access II.2.412 (printed, CIS)
Corpus CIS 895

Inscription 2061
Site Wadi Mukatab, #64
Condition good
Content Nabatean inscription
šlm šgdyʾ
Access II.2.412 (printed, CIS)
Corpus CIS 896

Inscription 2062
Site Wadi Mukatab, #64
Condition fair
Content Nabatean inscription
šlm ʾw[šw] br pʾrn
Access II.2.412 (printed, CIS)
Corpus CIS 897

Inscription 2063
Site Wadi Mukatab, #64
Condition good
Content Nabatean inscription
šlm grmʾlbʿly br klbw
Access II.2.412-13 (printed, CIS)
Corpus CIS 898

Inscription 2064
Site Wadi Mukatab, #64
Condition excellent
Content Nabatean inscription
dkyr
wbryk
klbw br
ḥnʾw bṭb
Access II.2.413 (printed, CIS)
Corpus CIS 899

Inscription 2065
Site Wadi Mukatab, #64
Condition good
Content Nabatean inscription
šlm ʿbdʾlhy br pʾrn
Access II.2.413 (printed, CIS)
Corpus CIS 900

Inscription 2066
Site Wadi Mukatab, #64
Condition good
Content Nabatean inscription
šlm grmʾlbʿly br pʾrn
Access II.2.413 (printed, CIS)
Corpus CIS 901

Inscription 2067
Site Wadi Mukatab, #64
Condition poor
Content Nabatean inscription
Comment *illegible*
Access II.2.413 (printed, CIS)
Corpus CIS 902

Inscription 2068
Site Wadi Mukatab, #64
Condition good
Content Nabatean inscription
dkyr bṭšw
br zydw bṭb
Access II.2.413 (printed, CIS)
Corpus CIS 903

Inscription **2069**
Site Wadi Mukatab, #64
Condition poor
Content Nabatean inscription
šlm ʿbdšy . ʾ
...m.w
.y.h br ...
Access II.2.413 (printed, CIS)
Corpus CIS 904

Inscription **2070**
Site Wadi Mukatab, #64
Condition fair
Content Nabatean inscription
dkyr wʾlw br ʿ...
Access II.2.413 (printed, CIS)
Corpus CIS 905

Inscription **2071**
Site Wadi Mukatab, #64
Condition good
Content Nabatean inscription
šlm ʾlmbqrw br wʾlw
Access II.2.414 (printed, CIS)
Corpus CIS 906

Inscription **2072**
Site Wadi Mukatab, #64
Condition good
Content Nabatean inscription
šlm ʿwdw br ʿmyw
Access II.2.414 (printed, CIS)
Corpus CIS 907

Inscription **2073**
Site Wadi Mukatab, #64
Condition good
Content Nabatean inscription
dkyr ḥryšw
br ʿbydw
Access II.2.414 (printed, CIS)
Corpus CIS 908

Inscription **2074**
Site Wadi Mukatab, #64
Condition good
Content Nabatean inscription
dkyr ʿbdʾlbʿly br ḥryšw
Access II.2.414 (printed, CIS)
Corpus CIS 909

Inscription **2075**
Site Wadi Mukatab, #64
Condition good
Content Nabatean inscription
šlm yʿly br ḥryšw
Access II.2.414 (printed, CIS)
Corpus CIS 910

Inscription **2076**
Site Wadi Mukatab, #64
Condition poor
Content Nabatean inscription
....
ʿmmw
Access II.2.414 (printed, CIS)
Corpus CIS 911

Inscription **2077**
Site Wadi Mukatab, #64
Condition fair
Content Nabatean inscription
qrm dšrʾ wʾ[lw]...
ḥryšw br wʾlw
Access II.2.414 (printed, CIS)
Corpus CIS 912

Inscription **2078**
Site Wadi Mukatab, #64
Condition fair
Content Nabatean inscription
šlm wʾlw br
šʿd[ʾlhy] bṭb
Access II.2.415 (printed, CIS)
Corpus CIS 913

Inscription **2079**
Site Wadi Mukatab, #64
Condition fair
Content Nabatean inscription
dy ʿbd šʿdlhy
br ʾʿlʾ b...
Access II.2.415 (printed, CIS)
Corpus CIS 914

Inscription **2080**
Site Wadi Mukatab, #64
Condition fair
Content Nabatean inscription
dkyr ṣḥ[bw]
br grmʾ...
Access II.2.415 (printed, CIS)
Corpus CIS 915

Inscription **2081**
Site Wadi Mukatab, #64
Condition good
Content rock drawing
Comment *horse accompanying insc. 2055*
Access II.2.411 (printed, CIS)
Corpus CIS 890

Inscription **2082**
Site Wadi Mukatab, #64
Condition good
Content Nabatean inscription
šlm wʾlw wbryʾw
bny ʾlmbqrw
Access II.2.415 (printed, CIS)
Corpus CIS 916

Inscription **2083**
Site Wadi Mukatab, #64
Condition good
Content Nabatean inscription
šlm ʾlgmlw br
ʿmyw
Access II.2.415 (printed, CIS)
Corpus CIS 917

Inscription **2084**
Site Wadi Mukatab, #64
Condition good
Content Nabatean inscription
šlm zydw
br pʾrn
Access II.2.415 (printed, CIS)
Corpus CIS 918

Inscription **2085**
Site Wadi Mukatab, #64
Condition fair
Content Nabatean inscription
šlm ʿbdʾl[bʿly]
Access II.2.415 (printed, CIS)
Corpus CIS 919

Inscription **2086**
Site Wadi Mukatab, #64
Condition good
Content Nabatean inscription
šlm lbʾ. br tymʾlhy
Access II.2.415 (printed, CIS)
Corpus CIS 920

Inscription **2087**
Site Wadi Mukatab, #64
Condition good
Content Nabatean inscription
šlm ʿnmw br
ʿwymw
Access II.2.415 (printed, CIS)
Corpus CIS 921

Inscription **2088**
Site Wadi Mukatab, #64
Condition good
Content Nabatean inscription
šlm ḥršw
br dʾbw w
ʿmyw br ḥršw bṭb
Access II.2.416 (printed, CIS)
Corpus CIS 922

Inscription **2089**
Site Wadi Mukatab, #64
Condition good
Content Nabatean inscription
bryk wdw br
qwsʿdr
Access II.2.416 (printed, CIS); *see also* AEd48-49
Corpus CIS 923

Inscription **2090**
Site Wadi Mukatab, #64
Condition fair
Content Nabatean inscription
šlm ʿnmw wyʿly bny...
Access II.2.416 (printed, CIS)
Corpus CIS 924

Inscription **2091**
Site Wadi Mukatab, #64
Condition good
Content Nabatean inscription
pšy br yʿly
šlm ...wpšy
šʿdlhy brh
Access II.2.416 (printed, CIS)
Corpus CIS 925

Inscription **2092**
Site Wadi Mukatab, #64
Condition fair
Content Nabatean inscription
šlm ʿbdʾlbʿly br ...ʾ
Access II.2.416 (printed, CIS)
Corpus CIS 926

Inscription **2093**
Site Wadi Mukatab, #64
Condition good
Content Nabatean inscription
dkyr nmrw br
šʿdlhy
Access II.2.416 (printed, CIS)
Corpus CIS 927

Inscription **2094**
Site Wadi Mukatab, #64
Condition poor
Content Nabatean inscription
šlm ʿwdw br ḥ...
šlm ʾm....
Access II.2.416 (printed, CIS)
Corpus CIS 928

Inscription **2095**
Site Wadi Mukatab, #64
Condition good
Content Nabatean inscription
šlm
grmʾlbʿly br
mbršw
Access II.2.417 (printed, CIS)
Corpus CIS 929

Inscription **2096**
Site Wadi Mukatab, #64
Condition good
Content Nabatean inscription
bryk wdw br
zydw
Access II.2.417 (printed, CIS)
Corpus CIS 930

Inscription **2097**
Site Wadi Mukatab, #64
Condition good
Content Nabatean inscription
šlm wʾlw ʾlmbqrw
Access II.2.417 (printed, CIS)
Corpus CIS 931

Inscription **2098**
Site Wadi Mukatab, #64
Condition excellent
Content Nabatean inscription
dkyr ḥlṣšt wḥbrkn bny
šʿdʾlhy br ḥlṣšt
Access II.2.417 (printed, CIS)
Corpus CIS 932

Inscription **2099**
Site Wadi Mukatab, #64
Condition good
Content Nabatean inscription
šlm ʾbʾwšw
Access II.2.417 (printed, CIS)
Corpus CIS 933

Inscription **2100**
Site Wadi Mukatab, #64
Condition good
Content Nabatean inscription
šlm klbw br
ʿbdʾlbʿly bṭ[b]
Access II.2.417 (printed, CIS)
Corpus CIS 934

Inscription **2101**
Site Wadi Mukatab, #64
Condition poor
Content Nabatean inscription
[šlm] ʾtmw
[br ʿbd]ʾlhy
[šlm] wʾlw br
[ʾlmb]q[r]w bṭb
Access II.2.418 (printed, CIS)
Corpus CIS 935

Inscription **2102**
Site Wadi Mukatab, #64
Condition fair
Content Nabatean inscription
šlm ʿbdʾlh[y]
br tymʾlh[y]
bṭb
Access II.2.418 (printed, CIS)
Corpus CIS 936

Inscription **2103**
Site Wadi Mukatab, #64
Condition poor
Content Nabatean inscription
šlm ʿwdw br..
Access II.2.418 (printed, CIS)
Corpus CIS 937

Inscription **2104**
Site Wadi Mukatab, #64
Condition poor
Content Nabatean inscription
Comment *illegible*
Access II.2.418 (printed, CIS)
Corpus CIS 938

Inscription **2105**
Site Wadi Mukatab, #64
Condition good
Content Nabatean inscription
šlm ʾwšw
br ḥryšw b. šlm
Access II.2.418 (printed, CIS)
Corpus CIS 939

Inscription 2106
Site Wadi Mukatab, #64
Condition fair
Content Nabatean inscription
[g]rmʾlbʿly
Access II.2.418 (printed, CIS)
Corpus CIS 940

Inscription 2107
Site Wadi Mukatab, #64
Condition good
Content Nabatean inscription
zydw br ʿbdw
Access II.2.418 (printed, CIS)
Corpus CIS 941

Inscription 2108
Site Wadi Mukatab, #64
Condition fair
Content Nabatean inscription
šlm pšy br yʿ[ly]
šl[m] ʿyydw br ʾw[šw]
Access II.2.418 (printed, CIS)
Corpus CIS 942

Inscription 2109
Site Wadi Mukatab, #64
Condition good
Content Nabatean inscription
šlm ʾwšw [br]
mbršw
Access II.2.418 (printed, CIS)
Corpus CIS 943

Inscription 2110
Site Wadi Mukatab, #64
Condition good
Content Nabatean inscription
šlm wldw
br wʾlw
Access II.2.419 (printed, CIS)
Corpus CIS 944

Inscription 2111
Site Wadi Mukatab, #64
Condition good
Content Nabatean inscription
šlm ʾlmbqrw
br ʿwdw bṭb
Access II.2.419 (printed, CIS)
Corpus CIS 945

Inscription 2112
Site Wadi Mukatab, #64
Condition fair
Content Nabatean inscription
dkyr g..ʿlw
br ʿbdʾlʿzy bṭb
Access II.2.419 (printed, CIS)
Corpus CIS 946

Inscription 2113
Site Wadi Mukatab, #64
Condition good
Content Nabatean inscription
šlm ʿbdʾlbʿly br ʾlṣylt
Access II.2.419 (printed, CIS)
Corpus CIS 947

Inscription 2114
Site Wadi Mukatab, #64
Condition good
Content Nabatean inscription
šlm ʿbdʾhyw br
ʿwdw
Access II.2.419 (printed, CIS)
Corpus CIS 948

Inscription 2115
Site Wadi Mukatab, #64
Condition good
Content Nabatean inscription
dkyr ḥl
ṣt [b]r ʿbd
ʾlhy bṭb
Access II.2.419 (printed, CIS)
Corpus CIS 949

Inscription 2116
Site Wadi Mukatab, #64
Condition good
Content Nabatean inscription
šlm mʿnʾlhy
Access II.2.419 (printed, CIS)
Corpus CIS 950

Inscription 2117
Site Wadi Mukatab, #64
Condition poor
Content Nabatean inscription
šlm ..[w]ʾlw
Access II.2.419 (printed, CIS)
Corpus CIS 951

Inscription 2118
Site Wadi Mukatab, #64
Condition good
Content Nabatean inscription
šlm šlm šmr
šlm ḥw br ʾt
mw bṭb
Access II.2.420 (printed, CIS)
Corpus CIS 952

Inscription **2119**
Site Wadi Mukatab, #64
Condition good
Content Nabatean inscription
dkyr wʾlw
br bryʾww
bryʾw [brh]
Access II.2.420 (printed, CIS)
Corpus CIS 953

Inscription **2120**
Site Wadi Mukatab, #64
Condition good
Content Nabatean inscription
šlm šʿdʾlhy
Access II.2.420 (printed, CIS)
Corpus CIS 954

Inscription **2121**
Site Wadi Mukatab, #64
Condition poor
Content Nabatean inscription
šlm yʿly
dkyr ʾtm[w br ʿbdʾlhy]
Access II.2.420 (printed, CIS)
Corpus CIS 955

Inscription **2122**
Site Wadi Mukatab, #64
Condition fair
Content Nabatean inscription
[br]yk ḥr[yš]w br šʿdʾlhy
Access II.2.420 (printed, CIS)
Corpus CIS 956

Inscription **2123**
Site Wadi Mukatab, #64
Condition good
Content Nabatean inscription
šlm
tymʾlhy
br wdw
Access II.2.420 (printed, CIS)
Corpus CIS 957

Inscription **2124**
Site Wadi Mukatab, #64
Condition good
Content Nabatean inscription
šlm bryʾw br
yʿly [b]ṭb
Access II.2.420 (printed, CIS)
Corpus CIS 958

Inscription **2125**
Site Wadi Mukatab, #64
Condition good
Content Nabatean inscription
šlm ʿmmw br ʿbdʾl[b]ʿly
pʾrn bṭb
Access II.2.421 (printed, CIS)
Corpus CIS 959

Inscription **2126**
Site Wadi Mukatab, #64
Condition poor
Content Nabatean inscription
šlm .
br yʿly
Access II.2.421 (printed, CIS)
Corpus CIS 960

Inscription **2127**
Site Wadi Mukatab, #64
Condition fair
Content Nabatean inscription
šlm ʿwdw br
grmʾlbʿly
...
Access II.2.421 (printed, CIS)
Corpus CIS 961

Inscription **2128**
Site Wadi Mukatab, #64
Condition fair
Content Nabatean inscription
šlm ḥwrw br ʿbydw ʾ...
Access II.2.421 (printed, CIS)
Corpus CIS 962

Inscription **2129**
Site Wadi Mukatab, #64
dating 204
Condition excellent
Content Nabatean inscription
dkyr tymʾlhy br yʿly šnt mʾh ʿl
dmyn ʿl tltt qysryn
Access II.2.421-22 (printed, CIS); *see also* CM49
Corpus CIS 963

Inscription **2130**
Site Wadi Mukatab, #64
dating 189
Condition excellent
Content Nabatean inscription
bryk wʾlw br šʿdʾlhy
dʾ šnt 85 lhprkyh d[y]
bh ʾhrpw ʿnyʾ ʾrʿʾ
Access II.2.423 (printed, CIS)
Corpus CIS 964

Inscription 2131
Site Wadi Mukatab, #64
Condition excellent
Content Nabatean inscription
šlm ḥryšw wʿbdʾ
lbʿly bny ʿbydw
bṭb
Access II.2.424 (printed, CIS)
Corpus CIS 965

Inscription 2132
Site Wadi Mukatab, #64
Condition good
Content Nabatean inscription
šlm ʾwšw br
zwdy bṭb
Access II.2.424 (printed, CIS)
Corpus CIS 966

Inscription 2133
Site Wadi Mukatab, #64
Condition good
Content Nabatean inscription
šlm ʿwdw br šʿdʾlhy bṭb w[šlm]
Access II.2.424 (printed, CIS)
Corpus CIS 967

Inscription 2134
Site Wadi Mukatab, #64
Condition fair
Content Nabatean inscription
šlm ʿbdʾlbʿl[y br]
ʾlʾwytyw bṭb
Access II.2.424 (printed, CIS)
Corpus CIS 968

Inscription 2135
Site Wadi Mukatab, #64
Condition good
Content Nabatean inscription
šlm
ʿmyw br klbw ʾ...plʾ
wklbw wgrmʾlbʿly bnyh
Access II.2.424 (printed, CIS)
Corpus CIS 969

Inscription 2136
Site Wadi Mukatab, #64
Condition poor
Content Nabatean inscription
...
ḥry[šw]
Access II.2.425 (printed, CIS)
Corpus CIS 970

Inscription 2137
Site Wadi Mukatab, #64
Condition fair
Content Nabatean inscription
šlm ʿmyw br ʾ...
Access II.2.425 (printed, CIS)
Corpus CIS 971

Inscription 2138
Site Wadi Mukatab, #64
Condition good
Content Nabatean inscription
šlm dʾbw
br ʿmyw
bṭb
Access II.2.425 (printed, CIS)
Corpus CIS 972

Inscription 2139
Site Wadi Mukatab, #64
Condition fair
Content Nabatean inscription
šlm. ʾ
šlm bryʾw br mg[dyw]
Access II.2.425 (printed, CIS)
Corpus CIS 973

Inscription 2140
Site Wadi Mukatab, #64
Condition good
Content Nabatean inscription
dkyr ʾtmw br ʿbdʾlhy bṭb
Access II.2.425 (printed, CIS)
Corpus CIS 974

Inscription 2141
Site Wadi Mukatab, #64
Condition good
Content Nabatean inscription
ʾkbrw br pryzh bṭb
Access II.2.425 (printed, CIS)
Corpus CIS 975

Inscription 2142
Site Wadi Mukatab, #64
Condition good
Content Nabatean inscription
šlm zydw br wʾlw ʾbnqh bṭb
Access II.2.425 (printed, CIS)
Corpus CIS 976

Inscription 2143
Site Wadi Mukatab, #64
Condition good
Content Nabatean inscription
šlm ʾlḥšpw br ʾlmbqrw bṭb
Access II.2.425 (printed, CIS)
Corpus CIS 977

Inscription 2144
Site Wadi Mukatab, #64
Condition good
Content Nabatean inscription
dkyr ʾwšw br ʿbdʾlbʿly bṭb
Access II.2.426 (printed, CIS)
Corpus CIS 978

Inscription 2145
Site Wadi Mukatab, #64
Condition good
Content Nabatean inscription
šlm šʿdʾlhy br ʿbdʾlbʿly bṭb
Access II.2.426 (printed, CIS)
Corpus CIS 979

Inscription 2146
Site Wadi Mukatab, #64
Condition good
Content Nabatean inscription
šlm bḥgh br grmʾ
lbʿly bṭb
Access II.2.426 (printed, CIS)
Corpus CIS 980

Inscription 2147
Site Wadi Mukatab, #64
Condition good
Content Nabatean inscription
šlm yʿly br prṣw
Access II.2.426 (printed, CIS)
Corpus CIS 981

Inscription 2148
Site Wadi Mukatab, #64
Condition good
Content Nabatean inscription
šlm ḥršw br ʾnʿtw bkl ṭb
Access II.2.426 (printed, CIS)
Corpus CIS 982

Inscription 2149
Site Wadi Mukatab, #64
Condition fair
Content Nabatean inscription
šlmw br tymʾ[lhy]
Access II.2.426 (printed, CIS)
Corpus CIS 983

Inscription 2150
Site Wadi Mukatab, #64
Condition good
Content Nabatean inscription
šlm ʿwdw br wʾlw
[br] qrḥw
Access II.2.426 (printed, CIS)
Corpus CIS 984

Inscription 2151
Site Wadi Mukatab, #64
Condition good
Content Nabatean inscription
šlm ʾšdw br ʿmyw
bṭb
Access II.2.426 (printed, CIS)
Corpus CIS 985 (1)

Inscription 2152
Site Wadi Mukatab, #64
Condition good
Content Nabatean inscription
dkyr pšy br
tymdwšrʾ
Access II.2.427 (printed, CIS)
Corpus CIS 986

Inscription 2153
Site Wadi Mukatab, #64
Condition good
Content Nabatean inscription
dkyr wʾlw
br bryʾw w
bryʾw [brh]
Access II.2.427 (printed, CIS)
Corpus CIS 987

Inscription 2154
Site Wadi Mukatab, #64
Condition good
Content Nabatean inscription
šlm zydh br
tymʾlhy šlm
Access II.2.427 (printed, CIS)
Corpus CIS 988

Inscription 2155
Site Wadi Mukatab, #64
Condition good
Content Nabatean inscription
dkyr ṣḥbw
br grmʾlhy bṭb
Access II.2.427 (printed, CIS)
Corpus CIS 989

Inscription 2156
Site Wadi Mukatab, #64
Condition good
Content Nabatean inscription
dkyr mʿynw
br ḥry ḥnṭlw
bṭb
Access II.2.427 (printed, CIS)
Corpus CIS 990

Inscription 2157
Site Wadi Mukatab, #64
Condition fair
Content Nabatean inscription
dkyr wʾlw
br ʿbdʾ...
Access II.2.427 (printed, CIS)
Corpus CIS 991

Inscription 2158
Site Wadi Mukatab, #64
Condition good
Content Nabatean inscription
dkyr šlmw br ʾšwdw
bṭb
Access II.2.428 (printed, CIS)
Corpus CIS 992

Inscription 2159
Site Wadi Mukatab, #64
Condition good
Content Nabatean inscription
šlm qṭynw
br bkrw bṭb
Access II.2.428 (printed, CIS)
Corpus CIS 993

Inscription 2160
Site Wadi Mukatab, #64
Condition fair
Content Nabatean inscription
dkyr dʾbw
br ʿmyw...
Access II.2.428 (printed, CIS)
Corpus CIS 994

Inscription 2161
Site Wadi Mukatab, #64
Condition good
Content Nabatean inscription
dkyr ṣḥbw
br grmʾlh[y] bṭb
Access II.2.428 (printed, CIS)
Corpus CIS 995

Inscription 2162
Site Wadi Mukatab, #64
Condition good
Content Nabatean inscription
šlm ʾwšw br mʿnʾlhy
Access II.2.428 (printed, CIS)
Corpus CIS 996

Inscription 2163
Site Wadi Mukatab, #64
Condition fair
Content Nabatean inscription
šlm ʾwšw b...w br ʿwdw
Access II.2.428 (printed, CIS)
Corpus CIS 997

Inscription 2164
Site Wadi Mukatab, #64
Condition poor
Content Nabatean inscription
...
ʿmmw...ḥlṣw
Access II.2.429 (printed, CIS)
Corpus CIS 998

Inscription 2165
Site Wadi Mukatab, #64
Condition good
Content Nabatean inscription
šlm slwns
Access II.2.429 (printed, CIS)
Corpus CIS 999

Inscription 2166
Site Wadi Mukatab, #64
Condition poor
Content Nabatean inscription
bryk ...
Access II.2.429 (printed, CIS)
Corpus CIS 1000

Inscription 2167
Site Wadi Mukatab, #64
Condition poor
Content Nabatean inscription
šlm ʾbn ʾlqyn[y br]ʾ
tm[w]
Access II.2.429 (printed, CIS)
Corpus CIS 1001

Inscription 2168
Site Wadi Mukatab, #64
Condition poor
Content Nabatean inscription
šlm ...d...
wʾšbʿly
Access II.2.429 (printed, CIS)
Corpus CIS 1002

Inscription 2169
Site Wadi Mukatab, #64
Condition good
Content Nabatean inscription
dkyr ʿmyw
br kʿmh
bṭb
Access II.2.429 (printed, CIS)
Corpus CIS 1003

Inscription 2170
Site Wadi Mukatab, #64
Condition poor
Content Nabatean inscription
k]ʿmw br dn...
Access II.2.429 (printed, CIS)
Corpus CIS 1004

Inscription 2171
Site Wadi Mukatab, #64
Condition good
Content Nabatean inscription
šlm zydw br ḥnṭlw
wḥnṭlw br[h]
Access II.2.429 (printed, CIS)
Corpus CIS 1005

Inscription 2172
Site Wadi Mukatab, #64
Condition poor
Content Nabatean inscription
šlm ...ʾlh[y]
br zydw
Access II.2.429 (printed, CIS)
Corpus CIS 1006

Inscription 2173
Site Wadi Mukatab, #64
Condition poor
Content Nabatean inscription
šlm h. my.
b[r] zydw bṭ[b]
Access II.2.430 (printed, CIS)
Corpus CIS 1007

Inscription 2174
Site Wadi Mukatab, #64
Condition poor
Content Nabatean inscription
šlm .ʿdw...dyw bṭb
Access II.2.430 (printed, CIS)
Corpus CIS 1008

Inscription 2175
Site Wadi Mukatab, #64
Condition good
Content Nabatean inscription
šlm gšmw
Access II.2.430 (printed, CIS)
Corpus CIS 1009

Inscription 2176
Site Wadi Mukatab, #64
Condition poor
Content Nabatean inscription
...bw...bw ʿqw
Access II.2.430 (printed, CIS)
Corpus CIS 1010

Inscription 2177
Site Wadi Mukatab, #64
Condition good
Content Greek inscription
ΑΜΣΟΣ
ΡΥΘΕ
ΜΟΥ
Access II.2.427 (printed, CIS)
Corpus CIS 985 (2)

Inscription 2178
Site Wadi Mukatab, #64
Condition good
Content crosses with inscription
Access II.2.427 (printed, CIS)
Corpus CIS 985 (3)

Inscription 2179
Site Wadi Mukatab, #64
Condition poor
Content Nabatean inscription
ʿyw [br]
ʾwšw b[ṭb]
Access II.2.430 (printed, CIS)
Corpus CIS 1011

Inscription 2180
Site Wadi Mukatab, #64
Condition good
Content Nabatean inscription
dkyr wdyw
br ʾlmbqrw
Access II.2.430 (printed, CIS)
Corpus CIS 1012

Inscription 2181
Site Wadi Mukatab, #64
Condition good
Content Nabatean inscription
šlm wʾlw br
pydw bṭb
Access II.2.431 (printed, CIS)
Corpus CIS 1013

Inscription 2182
Site Wadi Mukatab, #64
Condition good
Content Nabatean inscription
šlm ʾwšw br ʾʿ[lʾ]
Access II.2.431 (printed, CIS)
Corpus CIS 1014

Inscription 2183
Site Wadi Mukatab, #64
Condition good
Content Nabatean inscription
dkyr ṣwbw bn nšygw
Access II.2.431 (printed, CIS)
Corpus CIS 1015

Inscription 2184
Site Wadi Mukatab, #64
Condition fair
Content Nabatean inscription
dkyr wd[w br] ytʿw
Access II.2.431 (printed, CIS)
Corpus CIS 1016

Inscription 2185
Site Wadi Mukatab, #64
Condition good
Content Nabatean inscription
šlm ʿbd
ʾlhy br
šmrḥ
Access II.2.431 (printed, CIS)
Corpus CIS 1017

Inscription 2186
Site Wadi Mukatab, #64
Condition good
Content Nabatean inscription
šlm
ʾʿlyw
br ṭy
lh bṭ[b]
Access II.2.431 (printed, CIS)
Corpus CIS 1018

Inscription 2187
Site Wadi Mukatab, #64
Condition fair
Content Nabatean inscription
šlm nš[gw] br pšy
Access II.2.431 (printed, CIS)
Corpus CIS 1019

Inscription 2188
Site Wadi Mukatab, #64
Condition fair
Content Nabatean inscription
šlm ʾw
šʾlbʿl[y] br
šmr[ḥ]
Access II.2.431 (printed, CIS)
Corpus CIS 1020

Inscription 2189
Site Wadi Mukatab, #64
Condition good
Content Nabatean inscription
dkyr wʾ
lw br
ʿyyd
w bṭb
Access II.2.431 (printed, CIS)
Corpus CIS 1021

Inscription 2190
Site Wadi Mukatab, #64
Condition good
Content Nabatean inscription
šlm wʾlw br
qrḥh bṭb
Access II.2.431 (printed, CIS)
Corpus CIS 1022

Inscription 2191
Site Wadi Mukatab, #64
Condition fair
Content Nabatean inscription
šlm .m. w br
wʾlw
Access II.2.432 (printed, CIS)
Corpus CIS 1023

Inscription 2192
Site Wadi Mukatab, #64
Condition good
Content Nabatean inscription
šlm ʾwšw
Access II.2.432 (printed, CIS)
Corpus CIS 1024

Inscription 2193
Site Wadi Mukatab, #64
Condition good
Content Nabatean inscription
[d]kyr wʾlw
br ʿwdw br
klbw
Access II.2.432 (printed, CIS)
Corpus CIS 1025

Inscription 2194
Site Wadi Mukatab, #64
Condition good
Content Nabatean inscription
dkyr yḥyw br ʿmrw
bkl ṭ[b]
bṭb
Access II.2.432 (printed, CIS)
Corpus CIS 1026

Inscription 2195
Site Wadi Mukatab, #64
Condition good
Content Nabatean inscription
šbrh br ḥrw
Access II.2.432 (printed, CIS)
Corpus CIS 1027

Inscription 2196
Site Wadi Mukatab, #64
Condition fair
Content Nabatean inscription
šlm ḥryšw
[br w]ʾlw
Access II.2.432 (printed, CIS)
Corpus CIS 1028

Inscription 2197
Site Wadi Mukatab, #64
Condition fair
Content Nabatean inscription
šlm ʾl...
dkyr ʿbdʾlbʿly
br ʾtmw
Access II.2.432 (printed, CIS)
Corpus CIS 1029

Inscription 2198
Site Wadi Mukatab, #64
Condition good
Content Nabatean inscription
šlm ṣwbw br
ʿmyw bṭb
Access II.2.432 (printed, CIS)
Corpus CIS 1030

Inscription 2199
Site Wadi Mukatab, #64
Condition good
Content Nabatean inscription
dkyr ṣwbw br ʿmyw
bṭb
Access II.2.433 (printed, CIS)
Corpus CIS 1031

Inscription 2200
Site Wadi Mukatab, #64
Condition fair
Content Nabatean inscription
dkyr ʿyydw br ʾwšw bṭb
[ʾw]šw br ʿyyd[w]
Access II.2.433 (printed, CIS)
Corpus CIS 1032

Inscription 2201
Site Wadi Mukatab, #64
Condition fair
Content Nabatean inscription
šlm ʿbdʾlbʿly br ʾwš[ʾlhy]
Access II.2.433 (printed, CIS)
Corpus CIS 1033

Inscription 2202
Site Wadi Mukatab, #64
Condition poor
Content Nabatean inscription
br ḥlṣšt
...šw br ...
Access II.2.433 (printed, CIS)
Corpus CIS 1034

Inscription 2203
Site Wadi Mukatab, #64
Condition good
Content Nabatean inscription
šlm wʾlw br
ʿmr[w]
Access II.2.433 (printed, CIS)
Corpus CIS 1035

Inscription 2204
Site Wadi Mukatab, #64
Condition fair
Content Nabatean inscription
dkyr ...yw
br nšygw
bṭb
Access II.2.433 (printed, CIS)
Corpus CIS 1036

Inscription 2205
Site Wadi Mukatab, #64
Condition fair
Content Nabatean inscription
šlm ʿbydw br
..dw bṭb
Access II.2.433 (printed, CIS)
Corpus CIS 1037

Inscription 2206
Site Wadi Mukatab, #64
Condition poor
Content Nabatean inscription
šlm .... br tymʾl[hy]
Access II.2.434 (printed, CIS)
Corpus CIS 1038

Inscription 2207
Site Wadi Mukatab, #64
Condition fair
Content Nabatean inscription
šlm ʿ[b]dʾhyw
Access II.2.434 (printed, CIS)
Corpus CIS 1039

Inscription 2208
Site Wadi Mukatab, #64
Condition good
Content Nabatean inscription
šlm wʾlw
br zydw bṭb
Access II.2.434 (printed, CIS)
Corpus CIS 1040

Inscription 2209
Site Wadi Mukatab, #64
Condition good
Content Greek inscription
ΜΝΗΣΘΗ ΑΥΣΟΣ ΕΡΣΟΥ
ΚΑΛ[Ε]ΙΤΑΙ ΟΥΜΑΡΟΥ
ΕΝ ΑΓΑΘΟΙΣ
Access II.2.438 (printed, CIS)
Corpus CIS 1044 (1)

Inscription 2210
Site Wadi Mukatab, #64
Condition good
Content Nabatean inscription
šlm ḥwbn br
ʾlmbqrw bṭb
Access II.2.434 (printed, CIS)
Corpus CIS 1041

Inscription 2211
Site Wadi Mukatab, #64
Condition poor
Content Nabatean inscription
....ṭb wšl[m]
dky[r] hnʾw
Access II.2.434 (printed, CIS)
Corpus CIS 1042

Inscription 2212
Site Wadi Mukatab, #64
Condition good
Content Nabatean inscription
dkyr hn[yʾw]
br ʾwšʾlh bṭb
Access II.2.434 (printed, CIS)
Corpus CIS 1043

Inscription 2213
Site Wadi Mukatab, #64
Condition good
Content Nabatean inscription
mdkyr ʾwšw br ḥršw ṭryw bṭb
Access II.2.434 (printed, CIS)
Corpus CIS 1044

Inscription 2214
Site Wadi Mukatab, #64
Condition good
Content Nabatean inscription
šlm wʾlw br ḥlṣšt
Access II.2.435 (printed, CIS)
Corpus CIS 1045

Inscription 2215
Site Wadi Mukatab, #64
Condition good
Content Nabatean inscription
šlm ʿyydw br ʾbʾwšw
Access II.2.435 (printed, CIS)
Corpus CIS 1046

Inscription 2216
Site Wadi Mukatab, #64
Condition good
Content Nabatean inscription
šlm ʿmyw
br grmʾlbʿly
Access II.2.435 (printed, CIS)
Corpus CIS 1047

Inscription 2217
Site Wadi Mukatab, #64
Condition good
Content Nabatean inscription
šlm šmrḥ br ḥrṣw
Access II.2.435 (printed, CIS)
Corpus CIS 1048

Inscription 2218
Site Wadi Mukatab, #64
Condition good
Content Nabatean inscription
šlm ḥ.
br ʾʿlʾ w
ʾʿlʾ brh
bṭb
Access II.2.435 (printed, CIS)
Corpus CIS 1049

Inscription 2219
Site Wadi Mukatab, #64
Condition good
Content Nabatean inscription
dkyr ʾtmw
br ʿbdʾlhy
br bryʾw bṭb
Access II.2.435-36 (printed, CIS)
Corpus CIS 1050

Inscription 2220
Site Wadi Mukatab, #64
Condition good
Content Nabatean inscription
šlm ḥryšw
br ʿwd[w]
Access II.2.436 (printed, CIS)
Corpus CIS 1051

Inscription 2221
Site Wadi Mukatab, #64
Condition good
Content Nabatean inscription
dkyr ʾbn qwmw
br pšyw bṭb
Access II.2.436 (printed, CIS)
Corpus CIS 1052

Inscription 2222
Site Wadi Mukatab, #64
Condition good
Content Nabatean inscription
šlm ʾwšw br šmrḥ bṭb
Access II.2.436 (printed, CIS)
Corpus CIS 1053

Inscription 2223
Site Wadi Mukatab, #64
Condition good
Content Nabatean inscription
šlm dʾybw br ʾwšw bṭb
Access II.2.436 (printed, CIS)
Corpus CIS 1054

Inscription 2224
Site Wadi Mukatab, #64
Condition good
Content Nabatean inscription
šlm ʿmrw
br ḥryšw bṭb
Access II.2.436 (printed, CIS)
Corpus CIS 1055

Inscription 2225
Site Wadi Mukatab, #64
Condition good
Content Nabatean inscription
šlm
ḥlṣšt
br ḥnṭlw
Access II.2.436 (printed, CIS)
Corpus CIS 1056

Inscription 2226
Site Wadi Mukatab, #64
Condition good
Content Nabatean inscription
dkyr šlmw br
tymʾlhy bṭb
Access II.2.436 (printed, CIS)
Corpus CIS 1057

Inscription 2227
Site Wadi Mukatab, #64
Condition good
Content Nabatean inscription
šlm ʾlḥšpw br
ʾlmbqrw bṭb
Access II.2.436 (printed, CIS)
Corpus CIS 1058

Inscription 2228
Site Wadi Mukatab, #64
Condition poor
Content Nabatean inscription
šlm ʿwdw br wʾlw bṭb
[šl]m [grm]ʾlbʿ[ly]
Access II.2.437 (printed, CIS)
Corpus CIS 1059

Inscription 2229
Site Wadi Mukatab, #64
Condition fair
Content Nabatean inscription
dkyr grmʾlb[ʿly]
br ḥnṭlw b[ṭb]
Access II.2.437 (printed, CIS)
Corpus CIS 1060

Inscription 2230
Site Wadi Mukatab, #64
Condition poor
Content Nabatean inscription
[ʿbd]ʾlbʿly br ʾwšʾ[lhy]
Access II.2.437 (printed, CIS)
Corpus CIS 1061

Inscription 2231
Site Wadi Mukatab, #64
Condition good
Content Nabatean inscription
bryk wʾlw
šlm wʾl[w]
br [ʾ]lmbqrw
Access II.2.437 (printed, CIS)
Corpus CIS 1062

Inscription 2232
Site Wadi Mukatab, #64
Condition fair
Content Nabatean inscription
šlm wʾlw [br ḥ]
ryšw
Access II.2.437 (printed, CIS)
Corpus CIS 1063

Inscription 2233
Site Wadi Mukatab, #64
Condition poor
Content Nabatean inscription
Comment *illegible*
Access II.2.437 (printed, CIS)
Corpus CIS 1064

Inscription 2234
Site Wadi Mukatab, #64
Condition good
Content Nabatean inscription
šlm dwdw br tymʾlhy bṭb
Access II.2.437 (printed, CIS)
Corpus CIS 1065

Inscription 2235
Site Wadi Mukatab, #64
Condition good
Content Nabatean inscription
šlm kʿmh
Access II.2.437 (printed, CIS)
Corpus CIS 1066

Inscription 2236
Site Wadi Mukatab, #64
Condition poor
Content Nabatean inscription
....w br ʿmyw
Access II.2.438 (printed, CIS)
Corpus CIS 1067

Inscription 2237
Site Wadi Mukatab, #64
Condition fair
Content Nabatean inscription
šlm ʿbydw.[br] ʿwdw.[b]ṭb
Access II.2.438 (printed, CIS)
Corpus CIS 1068

Inscription 2238
Site Wadi Mukatab, #64
Condition good
Content Nabatean inscription
dkyr ʾlḥ
špw br zydw
bṭb
Access II.2.438 (printed, CIS)
Corpus CIS 1069

Inscription 2239
Site Wadi Mukatab, #64
Condition fair
Content Nabatean inscription
dkyr ʾlḥšp[w br]
ʾlmbqr[w]
Access II.2.438 (printed, CIS)
Corpus CIS 1070

Inscription 2240
Site Wadi Mukatab, #64
Condition fair
Content Nabatean inscription
šlm .....
br ʾlmbqr[w]
Access II.2.438 (printed, CIS)
Corpus CIS 1071

Inscription 2241
Site Wadi Mukatab, #64
Condition fair
Content Nabatean inscription
šlm ḥgyrw [br]
šmrḥ bṭ[b]
Access II.2.438 (printed, CIS)
Corpus CIS 1072

Inscription 2242
Site Wadi Mukatab, #64
Condition good
Content Nabatean inscription
šlm ḥršw br dʾbw
Access II.2.435 (printed, CIS)
Corpus CIS 1044 (2)

Inscription 2243
Site Wadi Mukatab, #64
Condition good
Content Nabatean inscription
dkyr yʿly
[šlm] ḥgyrw br
šmrḥ bṭb
Access II.2.438 (printed, CIS)
Corpus CIS 1073

Inscription 2244
Site Wadi Mukatab, #64
Condition good
Content Nabatean inscription
dkyr ḥgyrw
br šmrḥ bṭb
Access II.2.438 (printed, CIS)
Corpus CIS 1074

Inscription 2245
Site Wadi Mukatab, #64
Condition fair
Content Nabatean inscription
[šl]m grmʾlbʿly br šʿdʾlhy
Access II.2.438 (printed, CIS)
Corpus CIS 1075

Inscription 2246
Site Wadi Mukatab, #64
Condition good
Content Nabatean inscription
dkyr wʾlw br šmrḥ wšlmh brth
Access II.2.438 (printed, CIS)
Corpus CIS 1076

Inscription 2247
Site Wadi Mukatab, #64
Condition fair
Content Nabatean inscription
šlm ḥršw
[br] ʿmyw
Access II.2.439 (printed, CIS)
Corpus CIS 1077

Inscription 2248
Site Wadi Mukatab, #64
Condition fair
Content Nabatean inscription
šlm ʾmtʾlhy brt...
ʿlyw br šdʾlhy bṭb
Access II.2.439 (printed, CIS)
Corpus CIS 1078

Inscription **2249**
Site Wadi Mukatab, #64
Condition good
Content Nabatean inscription
šlm gdyw br bḥgh
bṭb
Access II.2.439 (printed, CIS)
Corpus CIS 1079

Inscription **2250**
Site Wadi Mukatab, #64
Condition poor
Content Nabatean inscription
... br ʾʿlʾ
Access II.2.439 (printed, CIS)
Corpus CIS 1080

Inscription **2251**
Site Wadi Mukatab, #64
Condition fair
Content Nabatean inscription
[šl]m klbw br pʾrn
Access II.2.439 (printed, CIS)
Corpus CIS 1081

Inscription **2252**
Site Wadi Mukatab, #64
Condition good
Content Nabatean inscription
grmlhy
Access II.2.439 (printed, CIS)
Corpus CIS 1082

Inscription **2253**
Site Wadi Mukatab, #64
Condition fair
Content Nabatean inscription
dkyr zydw
br ʾwšw...
bṭb
Access II.2.439 (printed, CIS)
Corpus CIS 1083

Inscription **2254**
Site Wadi Mukatab, #64
Condition good
Content Nabatean inscription
šlm bryʾw br wʾlw
br qrḥw
Access II.2.439 (printed, CIS)
Corpus CIS 1084

Inscription **2255**
Site Wadi Mukatab, #64
Condition good
Content Nabatean inscription
šlm ʿmrw br pšyw wpšyw
bṭb wšlm
Access II.2.440 (printed, CIS)
Corpus CIS 1085

Inscription **2256**
Site Wadi Mukatab, #64
Condition good
Content Nabatean inscription
šlm wh[b]
lhy br wʾlw
Access II.2.440 (printed, CIS)
Corpus CIS 1086

Inscription **2257**
Site Wadi Mukatab, #64
Condition poor
Content Nabatean inscription
Comment *illegible*
Access II.2.440 (printed, CIS)
Corpus CIS 1087

Inscription **2258**
Site Wadi Mukatab, #64
Condition poor
Content Nabatean inscription
mgdyw...
Access II.2.440 (printed, CIS)
Corpus CIS 1088

Inscription **2259**
Site Wadi Mukatab, #64
Condition good
Content Nabatean inscription
šlm wʾlw
br ʿmmw
Access II.2.440 (printed, CIS)
Corpus CIS 1089

Inscription **2260**
Site Wadi Mukatab, #64
Condition good
Content Nabatean inscription
šlm ʾwšw br
mbršw
Access II.2.440 (printed, CIS)
Corpus CIS 1090

Inscription **2261**
Site Wadi Mukatab, #64
Condition poor
Content Nabatean inscription
dkyr wʾlw wʾw[šw bny]
ḥlṭlw [bṭb]
Access II.2.440 (printed, CIS)
Corpus CIS 1091

Inscription **2262**
Site Wadi Mukatab, #64
Condition fair
Content Nabatean inscription
šlm ʿlydw br .....
Access II.2.440 (printed, CIS)
Corpus CIS 1092

Inscription 2263
Site Wadi Mukatab, #64
Condition good
Content Nabatean inscription
šlm tymʾlhy
Access II.2.441 (printed, CIS)
Corpus CIS 1093

Inscription 2264
Site Wadi Mukatab, #64
Condition fair
Content Nabatean inscription
šlm ʿṣrw [br]
ʾlmbqrw bṭ[b]
Access II.2.441 (printed, CIS)
Corpus CIS 1094

Inscription 2265
Site Wadi Mukatab, #64
Condition good
Content Nabatean inscription
šlm ʾlmbqrw
br lšygw bṭb
Access II.2.441 (printed, CIS)
Corpus CIS 1095

Inscription 2266
Site Wadi Mukatab, #64
Condition fair
Content Nabatean inscription
dkyr wʾlw
br ʾlmbqrw b[ṭb]
Access II.2.441 (printed, CIS)
Corpus CIS 1096

Inscription 2267
Site Wadi Mukatab, #64
Condition good
Content Nabatean inscription
dkyr kʿmh br ḥrw b[ṭb]
Access II.2.441 (printed, CIS)
Corpus CIS 1097

Inscription 2268
Site Wadi Mukatab, #64
Condition good
Content Nabatean inscription
dkyr šmrḥ br ʿmnw
bṭb
Access II.2.441 (printed, CIS)
Corpus CIS 1098

Inscription 2269
Site Wadi Mukatab, #64
Condition poor
Content Nabatean inscription
... [b]r bryʾw bṭb
Access II.2.441 (printed, CIS)
Corpus CIS 1099

Inscription 2270
Site Wadi Mukatab, #64
Condition good
Content Nabatean inscription
ʿbdʾlhy br bryʾw
Access II.2.441 (printed, CIS)
Corpus CIS 1100

Inscription 2271
Site Wadi Mukatab, #64
Condition good
Content Nabatean inscription
dkyr ʾtmw
Access II.2.441 (printed, CIS)
Corpus CIS 1101

Inscription 2272
Site Wadi Mukatab, #64
Condition fair
Content Nabatean inscription
šlm ʿmyw br ....
Access II.2.441 (printed, CIS)
Corpus CIS 1102

Inscription 2273
Site Wadi Haggag, rock 3, #125
Technique scratched
Condition poor
Content Armenian inscription
Limitation *Tentative decipherment only*
Access Negev 1977 fig. 77 (printed, A. Negev)

Inscription 2274
Site Wadi Haggag, rock 3, #125
Technique scratched
Condition poor
Content Armenian inscription
Limitation *Tentative decipherment only*
Access Negev 1977 fig. 89 (printed, A. Negev)

Inscription 2275
Site Wadi Haggag, rock 6, #135
Technique scratched
Condition poor
Content Greek inscription
Limitation *Tentative decipherment only*
Access Negev 1977 fig. 200 (printed, A. Negev)

Inscription 2276
Site Wadi Mukatab, #64
Condition good
Content Nabatean inscription
šwdyw
Access II.2.441 (printed, CIS)
Corpus CIS 1103

Inscription 2277
Site Wadi Haggag, rock 3, #125
Technique incised
Condition fair
Content Greek inscription
Limitation *Tentative decipherment only*
Access Negev 1977 fig. 88 (printed, A. Negev)

Inscription	**2278**
Site	Wadi Haggag, rock 3, #125
Technique	incised
Condition	good
Content	varied crosses
Access	Negev 1977 fig. 88 (printed, A. Negev)

Inscription	**2279**
Site	Wadi Haggag, rock 3, #125
Technique	incised
Condition	good
Content	crosses with inscription
Access	Negev 1977 fig. 88 (printed, A. Negev)

Inscription	**2280**
Site	Wadi Mukatab, #64
Condition	fair
Content	Nabatean inscription šlm ʾwšw br ʾbn[qwmw]
Access	II.2.442 (printed, CIS); *see also* CM55
Corpus	CIS 1107

Inscription	**2281**
Site	Jebel Musa, Vale of Elijah, Chapel, #378
Technique	incised
Condition	good
Content	rock drawing
Comment	*camels with riders*
Access	Fm16 (photograph, Project)

Inscription	**2282**
Site	Jebel Musa, Vale of Elijah, Chapel, #378
Technique	incised
Condition	good
Content	rock drawing
Comment	*animals with riders*
Access	Fm17 (photograph, Project)

Inscription	**2283**
Site	Wadi Mukatab, #64
Condition	good
Content	Nabatean inscription šlm wʾlw br hnyʾw
Access	II.2.442 (printed, CIS); see also CM56
Corpus	CIS 1110

Inscription	**2284**
Site	Jebel Maharun, #317
Technique	painted
Condition	poor
Content	unidentified sign
Access	FS09 (photograph, Project)

Inscription	**2285**
Site	Wadi Mukatab, #64
Condition	fair
Content	Nabatean inscription dkyr wʾ lw br [ʿm]yw
Access	II.2.443 (printed, CIS)
Corpus	CIS 1112

Inscription	**2286**
Site	Jebel Maharun, #317
Technique	incised
Condition	poor
Content	Greek inscription
Limitation	*Tentative decipherment only*
Access	FS09 (photograph, Project)

Inscription	**2287**
Site	Jebel Maharun, #317
Technique	incised
Condition	poor
Content	Greek inscription
Limitation	*Tentative decipherment only*
Comment	*almost illegible*
Access	FS09 (photograph, Project)

Inscription	**2288**
Site	Jebel Maharun, #317
Technique	scratched
Condition	poor
Content	unidentified inscription
Comment	*illegible*
Access	FS09 (photograph, Project)

Inscription	**2289**
Site	Wadi Mukatab, #64
Condition	fair
Content	Nabatean inscription šlm ʾgmh bṭb
Access	II.2.443 (printed, CIS)
Corpus	CIS 1116

Inscription	**2290**
Site	Wadi Mukatab, #64
Condition	good
Content	Nabatean inscription šlm ʿbdʾlbʿly br ʿbdʾlbʿly bṭb
Access	II.2.443 (printed, CIS)
Corpus	CIS 1117

Inscription	**2291**
Site	Wadi Mukatab, #64
Condition	good
Content	Nabatean inscription dkyr wdw br nšygw
Access	II.2.443 (printed, CIS)
Corpus	CIS 1118

Inscription	**2292**
Site	Wadi Mukatab, #64
Condition	good
Content	Nabatean inscription šlm ʿytw br šʿdh
Access	II.2.444 (printed, CIS)
Corpus	CIS 1119

Inscription 2293
Site Wadi Mukatab, #64
Condition poor
Content Nabatean inscription
[ʾ]wyšw br š[ʿd]ʾl[hy]
Access II.2.444 (printed, CIS)
Corpus CIS 1120

Inscription 2294
Site Wadi Mukatab, #64
Condition good
Content Nabatean inscription
šlm zydw br ʾwšw
m. šw bṭ[b]
Access II.2.444 (printed, CIS)
Corpus CIS 1121

Inscription 2295
Site Wadi Mukatab, #64
Condition fair
Content Nabatean inscription
dy ʿbd bryʾw brʿ...
Access II.2.444 (printed, CIS)
Corpus CIS 1122

Inscription 2296
Site Wadi Mukatab, #64
Condition good
Content Nabatean inscription
dkyr ʿmyw br ʿbdʾlhy
Access II.2.444 (printed, CIS)
Corpus CIS 1123

Inscription 2297
Site Wadi Mukatab, #64
Condition fair
Content Nabatean inscription
dkyr ʾšw br ḥry[šw dy]
[m]qtry ʾšybw bṭb
Access II.2.444 (printed, CIS)
Corpus CIS 1124

Inscription 2298
Site Wadi Mukatab, #64
Condition fair
Content Nabatean inscription
šlm gdw br ʾlmbq[rw]
Access II.2.444 (printed, CIS)
Corpus CIS 1125

Inscription 2299
Site Wadi Mukatab, #64
Condition good
Content Nabatean inscription
dkyr bṭšw br zydw
Access II.2.444 (printed, CIS)
Corpus CIS 1126

Inscription 2300
Site Wadi Mukatab, #64
Condition good
Content Nabatean inscription
dkyr ʿbdʾlbʿly br
grmʾlhy
Access II.2.444 (printed, CIS)
Corpus CIS 1127

Inscription 2301
Site Wadi Mukatab, #64
Condition good
Content Nabatean inscription
[dky]r bṭšw br zydw bṭb
Access II.2.444 (printed, CIS)
Corpus CIS 1128

Inscription 2302
Site Wadi Mukatab, #64
Condition poor
Content Nabatean inscription
šlm ..rmṣw
br m wʾ[l]w
Access II.2.444 (printed, CIS)
Corpus CIS 1129

Inscription 2303
Site Wadi Mukatab, #64
Condition fair
Content Nabatean inscription
šlm ʿwdw br [bṭ]šw
Access II.2.445 (printed, CIS)
Corpus CIS 1130

Inscription 2304
Site Wadi Mukatab, #64
Condition poor
Content Nabatean inscription
šlm [ʿw]dw br
[grm]ʾlbʿly bṭb
Access II.2.445 (printed, CIS)
Corpus CIS 1131

Inscription 2305
Site Wadi Mukatab, #64
Condition good
Content Nabatean inscription
šlm tymw br grmʾlbʿly
Access II.2.445 (printed, CIS)
Corpus CIS 1132

Inscription 2306
Site Wadi Mukatab, #64
Condition poor
Content Nabatean inscription
šlm..m...šynʾ
Access II.2.445 (printed, CIS)
Corpus CIS 1133

Inscription **2307**
Site Wadi Mukatab, #64
Condition poor
Content Nabatean inscription
šlm qryzd
Access II.2.445 (printed, CIS)
Corpus CIS 1134

Inscription **2308**
Site Wadi Mukatab, #64
Condition good
Content Nabatean inscription
bryk
ʿwdw
Access II.2.445 (printed, CIS)
Corpus CIS 1135

Inscription **2309**
Site Wadi Mukatab, #64
Condition good
Content Nabatean inscription
šlm ʿmyw br ʿwdw
Access II.2.445 (printed, CIS)
Corpus CIS 1136

Inscription **2310**
Site Wadi Mukatab, #64
Condition good
Content Nabatean inscription
šlm ʿbdʾlbʿly br
ʿmrw bṭb
Access II.2.445 (printed, CIS)
Corpus CIS 1137

Inscription **2311**
Site Wadi Haggag, rock 3, #125
Technique scratched
Condition poor
Content Greek inscription
Limitation *Tentative decipherment only*
Access Negev 1977 fig. 91 (printed, A. Negev)

Inscription **2312**
Site Wadi Mukatab, #64
Condition poor
Content Nabatean inscription
šlm] [ʾw]šw [br] wdw
br bḥgh
Access II.2.446 (printed, CIS); *see also* CM53
Corpus CIS 1139

Inscription **2313**
Site Wadi Mukatab, #64
Condition fair
Content Nabatean inscription
šlm ʿbdʾlbʿly br ʿbdʾl[bʿly]
...ʾlbʿly ʿlym bṭb
Access II.2.446 (printed, CIS)
Corpus CIS 1140

Inscription **2314**
Site Wadi Mukatab, #64
Condition poor
Content Nabatean inscription
Comment *fragment*
Access II.2.446 (printed, CIS)
Corpus CIS 1141

Inscription **2315**
Site Wadi Haggag, rock 3, #125
Technique incised
Condition good
Content unidentified signs
Access Negev 1977 fig. 107 (printed, A. Negev)

Inscription **2316**
Site Wadi Haggag, rock 3, #125
Technique incised
Condition poor
Content Greek inscription
Limitation *Tentative decipherment only*
Access AC17 (photograph, M. Stone); *see also* AX20, AX21

Inscription **2317**
Site Wadi Haggag, rock 3, #125
Technique scratched
Condition poor
Content Greek inscription
Limitation *Tentative decipherment only*
Access Negev 1977 fig. 116 (printed, A. Negev)

Inscription **2318**
Site Wadi Mukatab, #64
Condition good
Content Nabatean inscription
šlm ʿmyw br ʾʿlʾ bṭb
Access II.2.446 (printed, CIS)
Corpus CIS 1145

Inscription **2319**
Site Wadi Mukatab, #64
Condition good
Content Nabatean inscription
dkyr ʾltbqw br qymw
Access II.2.446 (printed, CIS)
Corpus CIS 1146

Inscription **2320**
Site Wadi Mukatab, #64
Condition good
Content Nabatean inscription
šlm ʿmrw br klbw dy mqtry
kwšlm bkl ṭb
Access II.2.447 (printed, CIS)
Corpus CIS 1147

Inscription 2321
Site Wadi Mukatab, #64
Condition good
Content Nabatean inscription
šlm ʾwšlhy
Access II.2.447 (printed, CIS)
Corpus CIS 1148

Inscription 2322
Site Wadi Mukatab, #64
Condition poor
Content Nabatean inscription
mʿnlhy br w...
Access II.2.447 (printed, CIS)
Corpus CIS 1149

Inscription 2323
Site Wadi Mukatab, #64
Condition good
Content Nabatean inscription
bryk ntgw br [y]ʿly
wbnwhy bṭb wšlm
Access II.2.447 (printed, CIS)
Corpus CIS 1150

Inscription 2324
Site Wadi Mukatab, #64
Condition poor
Content Nabatean inscription
Comment *illegible*
Access II.2.447 (printed, CIS)
Corpus CIS 1151

Inscription 2325
Site Wadi Mukatab, #64
Condition good
Content Nabatean inscription
šlm mg[d]yw
br wʾlw bṭb
Access II.2.447 (printed, CIS)
Corpus CIS 1152

Inscription 2326
Site Wadi Mukatab, #64
Condition poor
Content Nabatean inscription
.w mgdʾ
.h....
Access II.2.447 (printed, CIS)
Corpus CIS 1153

Inscription 2327
Site Wadi Mukatab, #64
Condition good
Content Nabatean inscription
šlm ḥryšw
br ʾwšw
Access II.2.448 (printed, CIS)
Corpus CIS 1154

Inscription 2328
Site Wadi Mukatab, #64
Condition good
Content Nabatean inscription
šlm kyw
br ʾmrʾl
Access II.2.448 (printed, CIS)
Corpus CIS 1155

Inscription 2329
Site Wadi Mukatab, #64
Condition good
Content Nabatean inscription
dryk ʾywšw
br ʾmrw bṭb
Access II.2.448 (printed, CIS)
Corpus CIS 1156

Inscription 2330
Site Wadi Mukatab, #64
Condition good
Content Nabatean inscription
šʿdʾlh
br wdw bṭb
Access II.2.448 (printed, CIS)
Corpus CIS 1157

Inscription 2331
Site Wadi Mukatab, #64
Condition good
Content Nabatean inscription
šlm grmʾlhy
[br] ʿbydw
Access II.2.448 (printed, CIS)
Corpus CIS 1158

Inscription 2332
Site Wadi Mukatab, #64
Condition good
Content Nabatean inscription
dkyr zydw ʾwšw
ḥryšw wšʿdw
Access II.2.448 (printed, CIS)
Corpus CIS 1159

Inscription 2333
Site Wadi Mukatab, #64
Condition poor
Content Nabatean inscription
... br ʾʿlʾ bṭb
Access II.2.448 (printed, CIS)
Corpus CIS 1160

Inscription 2334
Site Wadi Mukatab, #64
Condition fair
Content Nabatean inscription
šlm ʾwšʾ[lhy]
Access II.2.448 (printed, CIS)
Corpus CIS 1161

Inscription 2335
Site Wadi Mukatab, #64
Condition good
Content Nabatean inscription
šlm ʿmyw br wdw
Access II.2.448 (printed, CIS)
Corpus CIS 1162

Inscription 2336
Site Wadi Mukatab, #64
Condition good
Content Nabatean inscription
šlm šmrḥ
br qwmw
Access II.2.449 (printed, CIS)
Corpus CIS 1163

Inscription 2337
Site Wadi Mukatab, #64
Condition fair
Content Nabatean inscription
dkyr ʿbdʾl[ʿ]ly br
ʿlht bṭ[b]
Access II.2.449 (printed, CIS)
Corpus CIS 1164

Inscription 2338
Site Wadi Mukatab, #64
Condition good
Content Nabatean inscription
bryk mʿnlh
br zydw
Access II.2.449 (printed, CIS)
Corpus CIS 1165

Inscription 2339
Site Wadi Mukatab, #64
Condition poor
Content Nabatean inscription
Comment *illegible*
Access II.2.449 (printed, CIS)
Corpus CIS 1166

Inscription 2340
Site Wadi Mukatab, #64
Condition good
Content Nabatean inscription
šlm ʿbydw br qšṭw bṭb
Access II.2.449 (printed, CIS)
Corpus CIS 1167

Inscription 2341
Site Wadi Mukatab, #64
Condition good
Content Nabatean inscription
šlm ḥwyḥw
Access II.2.449 (printed, CIS)
Corpus CIS 1168

Inscription 2342
Site Wadi Mukatab, #64
Condition good
Content Nabatean inscription
šlm ḥryšw
br ʾwšw
Access II.2.449 (printed, CIS)
Corpus CIS 1169

Inscription 2343
Site Wadi Mukatab, #64
Condition good
Content Nabatean inscription
šlm klbw br
grmʾlbʿly bṭb
Access II.2.449 (printed, CIS)
Corpus CIS 1170

Inscription 2344
Site Wadi Mukatab, #64
Condition fair
Content Nabatean inscription
dkyr šm[rḥ]
br ṣʿbw
Access II.2.450 (printed, CIS)
Corpus CIS 1171

Inscription 2345
Site Wadi Mukatab, #64
Condition fair
Content Nabatean inscription
dkyr ḥgw br š.ʾ...
zydw br šdʾlbʿly
Access II.2.450 (printed, CIS)
Corpus CIS 1172

Inscription 2346
Site Wadi Mukatab, #64
Condition fair
Content Nabatean inscription
bryk ḥrṣw br ....
Access II.2.450 (printed, CIS)
Corpus CIS 1173

Inscription 2347
Site Wadi Mukatab, #64
Condition fair
Content Nabatean inscription
dkyr bṭb šly br ....
Access II.2.450 (printed, CIS)
Corpus CIS 1174

Inscription 2348
Site Wadi Mukatab, #64
Condition fair
Content Nabatean inscription
šlm wṣ...
ʾšph bṭb
Access II.2.450 (printed, CIS)
Corpus CIS 1175

Inscription 2349
Site Wadi Mukatab, #64
Condition good
Content Nabatean inscription
šlm klbw br zydw
Access II.2.450 (printed, CIS)
Corpus CIS 1176

Inscription 2350
Site Wadi Mukatab, #64
Condition poor
Content Nabatean inscription
ḥrw br ....
Access II.2.450 (printed, CIS)
Corpus CIS 1177

Inscription 2351
Site Wadi Mukatab, #64
Condition poor
Content Nabatean inscription
šlm
rṣwʾ br m.ʾ...
Access II.2.450 (printed, CIS)
Corpus CIS 1178

Inscription 2352
Site Wadi Mukatab, #64
Condition poor
Content Nabatean inscription
... br zydqwm
Comment *uncertain reading*
Access II.2.450 (printed, CIS)
Corpus CIS 1179

Inscription 2353
Site Wadi Mukatab, #64
Condition good
Content Nabatean inscription
šlm šly br zydqwm
Access II.2.450 (printed, CIS)
Corpus CIS 1180

Inscription 2354
Site Wadi Mukatab, #64
Condition good
Content Nabatean inscription
š[l]m grmlbʿly
br ʿmyw
Access II.2.451 (printed, CIS)
Corpus CIS 1181

Inscription 2355
Site Wadi Mukatab, #64
Condition poor
Content Nabatean inscription
dkyr ṭb lʿš.w...w.nm
w blwhy
Access II.2.451 (printed, CIS)
Corpus CIS 1182

Inscription 2356
Site Wadi Mukatab, #64
Condition good
Content Nabatean inscription
bryk mgdyw br
šʿdlhy
Access II.2.451 (printed, CIS)
Corpus CIS 1183

Inscription 2357
Site Wadi Mukatab, #64
Condition good
Content Nabatean inscription
bryk grmʾlbʿly br ʿmyw
Access II.2.451 (printed, CIS)
Corpus CIS 1184

Inscription 2358
Site Wadi Mukatab, #64
Condition good
Content Nabatean inscription
šlm gdw
br mbqrw wbnyw bṭb
Access II.2.451 (printed, CIS)
Corpus CIS 1185

Inscription 2359
Site Wadi Mukatab, #64
Condition poor
Content Nabatean inscription
dkyr q..w...
...gmr...
ʾtm...
Access II.2.451 (printed, CIS)
Corpus CIS 1186

Inscription 2360
Site Wadi Mukatab, #64
Condition good
Content Nabatean inscription
šlm ʿbdʾl[b]ʿly
Access II.2.451 (printed, CIS)
Corpus CIS 1187

Inscription 2361
Site Wadi Mukatab, #64
Condition good
Content Nabatean inscription
dkyr ʿmyrt
br zydw
Access II.2.451 (printed, CIS)
Corpus CIS 1188

Inscription **2362**
Site Wadi Mukatab, #64
Condition good
Content Nabatean inscription
bryk zydw br
grmʾlbʿly
Access II.2.452 (printed, CIS)
Corpus CIS 1189

Inscription **2363**
Site Wadi Mukatab, #64
Condition good
Content Nabatean inscription
šlm ʿbydw br qšṭw bṭ[b]
Access II.2.452 (printed, CIS)
Corpus CIS 1190

Inscription **2364**
Site Wadi Mukatab, #64
Condition fair
Content Nabatean inscription
[dky]r wʾlw
br zydw
Access II.2.452 (printed, CIS)
Corpus CIS 1191

Inscription **2365**
Site Wadi Mukatab, #64
Condition poor
Content Nabatean inscription
dkyr ....
Access II.2.452 (printed, CIS)
Corpus CIS 1192

Inscription **2366**
Site Wadi Mukatab, #64
Condition good
Content Nabatean inscription
dkyr ʾtmw br
ʿbdʾlhy bṭb
Access II.2.452 (printed, CIS)
Corpus CIS 1193 (1)

Inscription **2367**
Site Wadi Mukatab, #64
Condition good
Content Nabatean inscription
šlm ʿwdw br ʾlmb
qrw ʿqry bṭb
Access II.2.452 (printed, CIS)
Corpus CIS 1194

Inscription **2368**
Site Wadi Mukatab, #64
Condition good
Content Nabatean inscription
dkyr ʿbdʾlbʿly
br ʿbydw bṭb
Access II.2.452-53 (printed, CIS)
Corpus CIS 1195 (1)

Inscription **2369**
Site Wadi Mukatab, #64
Condition good
Content Greek inscription
ΧΕ ΒΟΗΘΕ ΙΣΑΚ
ΧΕ ΒΟ[ΗΘΕ] ΣΤΕΦΑΝ[Ω]
Access II.2.452 (printed, CIS)
Corpus CIS 1193 (2)

Inscription **2370**
Site Wadi Mukatab, #64
Condition good
Content crosses with inscription
Access II.2.452 (printed, CIS)
Corpus CIS 1193 (3)

Inscription **2371**
Site Wadi Mukatab, #64
Condition good
Content Greek inscription
ΜΝΗΘΗ
ΑΥΔΟΣΑΛΜΟ
ΒΑΚΚΕΡΟΥ
Access II.2.452 (printed, CIS)
Corpus CIS 1194 (2)

Inscription **2372**
Site Wadi Mukatab, #64
Condition good
Content Greek inscription
ΜΝΗΣΘΗ
ΒΟΥΡΕΟΣ
ΣΑΔΑΛΛΟΥ
Access II.2.453 (printed, CIS)
Corpus CIS 1195 (2)

Inscription **2373**
Site Wadi Mukatab, #64
Condition good
Content Nabatean inscription
šlm hnʾw br zydw
Access II.2.453 (printed, CIS)
Corpus CIS 1196

Inscription **2374**
Site Wadi Mukatab, #64
Condition good
Content Nabatean inscription
dkyr ḥr[y]šw
br ʿmyw bṭb
Access II.2.453 (printed, CIS)
Corpus CIS 1197 (1)

Inscription 2375
Site Wadi Mukatab, #64
Condition good
Content Nabatean inscription
dkyr ʾbn qwmw
br ʿmrw bṭb
Access II.2.453 (printed, CIS)
Corpus CIS 1198

Inscription 2376
Site Wadi Mukatab, #64
Condition good
Content Nabatean inscription
šlm ʾwyšw br pšyw bṭb
Access II.2.453 (printed, CIS)
Corpus CIS 1199

Inscription 2377
Site Wadi Mukatab, #64
Condition good
Content Nabatean inscription
šlm zydw
br ʿmrw
Access II.2.453 (printed, CIS)
Corpus CIS 1200

Inscription 2378
Site Wadi Mukatab, #64
Condition good
Content Nabatean inscription
dkyr ʾlmbqrw
br ḥwbn bṭb
Access II.2.453 (printed, CIS)
Corpus CIS 1201

Inscription 2379
Site Wadi Mukatab, #64
Condition poor
Content Nabatean inscription
ʾw[yš]w br ...
Access II.2.453 (printed, CIS)
Corpus CIS 1202

Inscription 2380
Site Wadi Mukatab, #64
Condition good
Content Nabatean inscription
šlm bryʾw br ʿbdʾlbʿly
Access II.2.454 (printed, CIS)
Corpus CIS 1203

Inscription 2381
Site Wadi Mukatab, #64
Condition fair
Content Nabatean inscription
šlm ʾ... br
mgdyw bṭb wšlm
Access II.2.454 (printed, CIS)
Corpus CIS 1204

Inscription 2382
Site Wadi Mukatab, #64
Condition good
Content Nabatean inscription
šlm ʿbdʾlgʾ
br wʾlw dy ʿmr
bʾylt
Access II.2.454 (printed, CIS)
Corpus CIS 1205

Inscription 2383
Site Wadi Mukatab, #64
Condition good
Content Nabatean inscription
šlm ḥryšw wtymʿbd[t]
Access II.2.454 (printed, CIS)
Corpus CIS 1206

Inscription 2384
Site Wadi Mukatab, #64
Condition good
Content Nabatean inscription
šlm ʾbn ʾlqyn
br ʾwšw
Access II.2.454 (printed, CIS)
Corpus CIS 1207

Inscription 2385
Site Wadi Mukatab, #64
Condition poor
Content Nabatean inscription
šlm pšy br
....
Access II.2.454 (printed, CIS)
Corpus CIS 1208

Inscription 2386
Site Wadi Mukatab, #64
Condition good
Content Nabatean inscription
šlm ʿnmw br
pšy
Access II.2.454 (printed, CIS)
Corpus CIS 1209

Inscription 2387
Site Wadi Mukatab, #64
Condition good
Content Nabatean inscription
dkyr ʾlmbqrw
br mškw
Access II.2.455 (printed, CIS)
Corpus CIS 1210

Inscription **2388**
Site Wadi Mukatab, #64
Condition fair
Content Nabatean inscription
[dk]yr ʿmm[w]
br ʾʿly
Access II.2.455 (printed, CIS)
Corpus CIS 1211

Inscription **2389**
Site Wadi Mukatab, #64
Condition fair
Content Nabatean inscription
šlm gr[mʾ]lbʿly
Access II.2.455 (printed, CIS)
Corpus CIS 1212

Inscription **2390**
Site Wadi Mukatab, #64
Condition poor
Content Nabatean inscription
šlm ... zydw ...
Access II.2.455 (printed, CIS)
Corpus CIS 1213

Inscription **2391**
Site Wadi Mukatab, #64
Condition good
Content Nabatean inscription
wʾlw
Access II.2.455 (printed, CIS)
Corpus CIS 1214

Inscription **2392**
Site Wadi Mukatab, #64
Condition good
Content Nabatean inscription
šlm ʿbdʾlhy
br wʾl[w]
Access II.2.455 (printed, CIS)
Corpus CIS 1215

Inscription **2393**
Site Wadi Mukatab, #64
Condition poor
Content Nabatean inscription
šlm ...
grm...
ʾm...
Access II.2.455 (printed, CIS)
Corpus CIS 1216

Inscription **2394**
Site Wadi Mukatab, #64
Condition poor
Content Nabatean inscription
... ʾlktyw
Access II.2.455 (printed, CIS)
Corpus CIS 1217

Inscription **2395**
Site Wadi Mukatab, #64
Condition poor
Content Nabatean inscription
šlm ʿm[yw br ḥr]š[w]
Access II.2.455 (printed, CIS)
Corpus CIS 1218

Inscription **2396**
Site Wadi Mukatab, #64
Condition poor
Content Nabatean inscription
šlm d[ʾ]bw [bṭb]
Access II.2.455 (printed, CIS)
Corpus CIS 1219

Inscription **2397**
Site Wadi Mukatab, #64
Condition fair
Content Nabatean inscription
šlm [ḥry]šw
br qyzw
Access II.2.455 (printed, CIS)
Corpus CIS 1220

Inscription **2398**
Site Wadi Mukatab, #64
Condition good
Content Nabatean inscription
šlm ḥryšw br qyzw
Access II.2.456 (printed, CIS)
Corpus CIS 1221

Inscription **2399**
Site Wadi Mukatab, #64
Condition good
Content Nabatean inscription
šlm ʾlmbqrw
br ʿmyw
šʿyw bṭ[b]
Access II.2.456 (printed, CIS)
Corpus CIS 1222

Inscription **2400**
Site Wadi Mukatab, #64
Condition good
Content Nabatean inscription
šlm ḥnṭlw
br dʾbw bṭb
Access II.2.456 (printed, CIS)
Corpus CIS 1223

Inscription **2401**
Site Wadi Mukatab, #64
Condition good
Content Greek inscription
ΜΝΗΣ ΑΡΙΣΟΣ
ΘΗ ΑΜΜΑΙΟΣ
Access II.2.453 (printed, CIS)
Corpus CIS 1197 (2)

Inscription 2402
Site Wadi Mukatab, #64
Condition fair
Content Nabatean inscription
šlm ᵓtmw ᶜb[dᵓlhy]
Access II.2.456 (printed, CIS)
Corpus CIS 1224

Inscription 2403
Site Wadi Mukatab, #64
Condition good
Content Nabatean inscription
šlm ᶜbddwšrᵓ br tntlw
wᵓwšlbᶜly br grmlhy br t...mw
Access II.2.456 (printed, CIS)
Corpus CIS 1225

Inscription 2404
Site Wadi Mukatab, #64
Condition good
Content Nabatean inscription
ᶜbydw br
ḥrglw
Access II.2.456 (printed, CIS)
Corpus CIS 1226

Inscription 2405
Site Wadi Mukatab, #64
Condition good
Content Nabatean inscription
dkyr šᶜdᵓlhy br
ᶜlyw bṭb
Access II.2.457 (printed, CIS)
Corpus CIS 1227

Inscription 2406
Site Wadi Mukatab, #64
Condition good
Content Nabatean inscription
ᵓbᵓwšw br
ḥryšw
Access II.2.457 (printed, CIS)
Corpus CIS 1228

Inscription 2407
Site Wadi Mukatab, #64
Condition good
Content Nabatean inscription
dkyr grmᵓlhy
br ᶜbydw bṭb
Access II.2.457 (printed, CIS)
Corpus CIS 1229

Inscription 2408
Site Wadi Mukatab, #64
Condition fair
Content Nabatean inscription
[dky]r ᶜbdlbᶜly
[br ᵓw]šlhy
Access II.2.457 (printed, CIS)
Corpus CIS 1230

Inscription 2409
Site Wadi Mukatab, #64
Condition good
Content Nabatean inscription
šlm
dᵓbw br
grmᵓlbᶜly
ᶜmyw br klbw
Access II.2.457 (printed, CIS)
Corpus CIS 1231

Inscription 2410
Site Wadi Mukatab, #64
Condition good
Content Nabatean inscription
dkyr bṭb dᵓbw br
ᶜmyw
Access II.2.457 (printed, CIS)
Corpus CIS 1232

Inscription 2411
Site Wadi Mukatab, #64
Condition good
Content Nabatean inscription
dkyr wᵓlw br
ᵓlᵓbršw bṭ[b]
Access II.2.457 (printed, CIS)
Corpus CIS 1233

Inscription 2412
Site Wadi Mukatab, #64
Condition fair
Content Nabatean inscription
šlm lh..w br wᵓlw
Access II.2.457 (printed, CIS)
Corpus CIS 1234

Inscription 2413
Site Wadi Mukatab, #64
Condition fair
Content Nabatean inscription
šlm ᵓ
wšw br
ᶜbdᵓl
[bᶜ]ly b
ṭb
Access II.2.458 (printed, CIS)
Corpus CIS 1235

Inscription	**2414**
Site	Wadi Mukatab, #64
Condition	good
Content	Nabatean inscription dkyr ʿmyw br ḥryšw khn ʿzyʾ
Access	II.2.458 (printed, CIS)
Corpus	CIS 1236

Inscription	**2415**
Site	Wadi Mukatab, #64
Condition	good
Content	Nabatean inscription šlm ḥry šw br qyzw
Access	II.2.458 (printed, CIS)
Corpus	CIS 1237

Inscription	**2416**
Site	Wadi Mukatab, #64
Condition	fair
Content	Nabatean inscription šlm ḥryš w br yʿly..
Access	II.2.458 (printed, CIS)
Corpus	CIS 1238

Inscription	**2417**
Site	Wadi Mukatab, #64
Condition	poor
Content	Nabatean inscription ...šw br qynw
Access	II.2.458 (printed, CIS)
Corpus	CIS 1239

Inscription	**2418**
Site	Wadi Mukatab, #64
Condition	poor
Content	Nabatean inscription šlm .... [w]ʾlw
Access	II.2.458 (printed, CIS)
Corpus	CIS 1240

Inscription	**2419**
Site	Wadi Mukatab, #64
Condition	fair
Content	Nabatean inscription dkyr bkl ṭb ʾwšʾlhy br ....
Access	II.2.458 (printed, CIS)
Corpus	CIS 1241

Inscription	**2420**
Site	Wadi Mukatab, #64
Condition	good
Content	Nabatean inscription dkyr šʿdw br šgy
Access	II.2.458 (printed, CIS)
Corpus	CIS 1242

Inscription	**2421**
Site	Wadi Mukatab, #64
Condition	poor
Content	Nabatean inscription šlm ʾwšʾlbʿl[y] [br ḥr]yšw
Access	II.2.459 (printed, CIS)
Corpus	CIS 1243

Inscription	**2422**
Site	Wadi Mukatab, #64
Condition	poor
Content	Nabatean inscription šlm ṭr[py]w br wʾlw [bṭb]
Access	II.2.459 (printed, CIS)
Corpus	CIS 1244

Inscription	**2423**
Site	Wadi Mukatab, #64
Condition	good
Content	Nabatean inscription šlm ḥnṭlw br bṭšw
Access	II.2.459 (printed, CIS)
Corpus	CIS 1245

Inscription	**2424**
Site	Wadi Mukatab, #64
Condition	good
Content	Nabatean inscription šlm šʿdʾlhy br ʿlyw bṭb
Access	II.2.459 (printed, CIS)
Corpus	CIS 1246

Inscription	**2425**
Site	Wadi Mukatab, #64
Condition	good
Content	Nabatean inscription dkyr zydw br šmrḥ bṭb
Access	II.2.459 (printed, CIS)
Corpus	CIS 1247

Inscription 2426
Site Wadi Mukatab, #64
Condition good
Content Nabatean inscription
dkyr ʾwšʾlhy br hny
ʾw bṭb
Access II.2.459 (printed, CIS)
Corpus CIS 1248

Inscription 2427
Site Wadi Mukatab, #64
Condition poor
Content Nabatean inscription
dkyr ʿwdw..
Access II.2.459 (printed, CIS)
Corpus CIS 1249

Inscription 2428
Site Wadi Mukatab, #64
Condition good
Content Nabatean inscription
dkyr ḥryšw [br]
tymʾlhy
Access II.2.459 (printed, CIS)
Corpus CIS 1250

Inscription 2429
Site Wadi Mukatab, #64
Condition fair
Content Nabatean inscription
dkyr ...dw
br wʾlw bṭb w
šlm
Access II.2.459 (printed, CIS)
Corpus CIS 1251

Inscription 2430
Site Wadi Mukatab, #64
Condition good
Content Nabatean inscription
šlm ʿwtʾlhy
br ʿbdʿmrw
Access II.2.459 (printed, CIS)
Corpus CIS 1252

Inscription 2431
Site Wadi Mukatab, #64
Condition good
Content Nabatean inscription
dkyr wʾlw
br dʾ[b]w bṭb
Access II.2.460 (printed, CIS)
Corpus CIS 1253

Inscription 2432
Site Wadi Mukatab, #64
Condition good
Content Nabatean inscription
šlm ʾlṣdyw br
ʾwšʾlbʿly
dy mqtry ʾlʾḥ
ršw bṭb
Access II.2.460 (printed, CIS)
Corpus CIS 1254

Inscription 2433
Site Wadi Mukatab, #64
Condition good
Content Nabatean inscription
šlm ʿmyw br
dʾb[w]
Access II.2.460 (printed, CIS)
Corpus CIS 1255

Inscription 2434
Site Wadi Mukatab, #64
Condition good
Content Nabatean inscription
dkyr šʿdʾlhy
br br ʿlyw bṭb
Access II.2.460 (printed, CIS)
Corpus CIS 1256

Inscription 2435
Site Wadi Mukatab, #64
Condition good
Content Nabatean inscription
dkyr grmʾlbʿly
br klbw bkl ṭb
wšlm
Access II.2.460 (printed, CIS)
Corpus CIS 1257

Inscription 2436
Site Wadi Mukatab, #64
Condition good
Content Nabatean inscription
šlm grmʾlbʿly br
ʾwšʾlbʿly bṭb
Access II.2.460 (printed, CIS)
Corpus CIS 1258

Inscription 2437
Site Wadi Mukatab, #64
Condition good
Content Nabatean inscription
šlm ʿbdʾlbʿly
br slwns
Access II.2.461 (printed, CIS)
Corpus CIS 1259

Inscription 2438
Site Wadi Mukatab, #64
Condition good
Content Nabatean inscription
šlm ḥryšw br tymʾlhy bṭb
Access II.2.461 (printed, CIS)
Corpus CIS 1260

Inscription 2439
Site Wadi Mukatab, #64
Condition fair
Content Nabatean inscription
šlm s... br ḥrw bṭb
Access II.2.461 (printed, CIS)
Corpus CIS 1261

Inscription 2440
Site Wadi Mukatab, #64
Condition poor
Content Nabatean inscription
Comment *illegible*
Access II.2.461 (printed, CIS)
Corpus CIS 1262

Inscription 2441
Site Wadi Mukatab, #64
Condition poor
Content Nabatean inscription
... ʾyšw
Access II.2.461 (printed, CIS)
Corpus CIS 1263

Inscription 2442
Site Wadi Mukatab, #64
Condition poor
Content Nabatean inscription
Comment *illegible*
Access II.2.461 (printed, CIS)
Corpus CIS 1264

Inscription 2443
Site Wadi Mukatab, #64
Condition poor
Content Nabatean inscription
dkyr m..ʾ. br [bṭ]šw bṭb
Access II.2.461 (printed, CIS)
Corpus CIS 1265

Inscription 2444
Site Wadi Mukatab, #64
Condition good
Content Nabatean inscription
dkyr wʾlw br ʿmyw
Access II.2.461 (printed, CIS)
Corpus CIS 1266

Inscription 2445
Site Wadi Mukatab, #64
Condition good
Content Nabatean inscription
klbw br pʾrn bṭb
Access II.2.461 (printed, CIS)
Corpus CIS 1267

Inscription 2446
Site Wadi Mukatab, #64
Condition poor
Content Nabatean inscription
ḥryšw...ḥnṭ[l]w
Access II.2.461 (printed, CIS)
Corpus CIS 1268

Inscription 2447
Site Wadi Mukatab, #64
Condition poor
Content Nabatean inscription
šlm ...w...w bny ʿmrw
Access II.2.461 (printed, CIS)
Corpus CIS 1269

Inscription 2448
Site Wadi Mukatab, #64
Condition good
Content Nabatean inscription
šlm ṣʿbw
br šmrḥ ʾbn ʾ
lqyny
bṭb
Access II.2.462 (printed, CIS)
Corpus CIS 1270

Inscription 2449
Site Wadi Mukatab, #64
Condition fair
Content Nabatean inscription
šlm zydw br š[mrḥ]
bṭb
Access II.2.462 (printed, CIS)
Corpus CIS 1271

Inscription 2450
Site Wadi Mukatab, #64
Condition good
Content Nabatean inscription
šlm mgdyw b[r] šʿyw
Access II.2.462 (printed, CIS)
Corpus CIS 1272

Inscription 2451
Site Wadi Mukatab, #64
Condition good
Content Nabatean inscription
šlm ḥlṣšt br wʾlw
Access II.2.462 (printed, CIS)
Corpus CIS 1273

Inscription 2452
Site Wadi Mukatab, #64
Condition good
Content Nabatean inscription
šlm grmʾl
bʿly br klbw
Access II.2.462 (printed, CIS)
Corpus CIS 1274

Inscription 2453
Site Wadi Mukatab, #64
Condition good
Content Nabatean inscription
šlm šrpyw br
ʿrbyw bṭb
Access II.2.462 (printed, CIS)
Corpus CIS 1275

Inscription 2454
Site Wadi Mukatab, #64
Condition good
Content Nabatean inscription
šlm pšyw
br qypw bṭb
Access II.2.462 (printed, CIS)
Corpus CIS 1276

Inscription 2455
Site Wadi Mukatab, #64
Condition good
Content Nabatean inscription
šlm ʾʿlʾ
br ʿmyw šlm ʾ[ʿ]lʾ
Access II.2.462 (printed, CIS)
Corpus CIS 1277

Inscription 2456
Site Wadi Mukatab, #64
Condition fair
Content Nabatean inscription
[šl]m ḥryšw
[br] ʿbdʾlbʿly
br yʿly
Access II.2.463 (printed, CIS)
Corpus CIS 1278

Inscription 2457
Site Wadi Mukatab, #64
Condition good
Content Nabatean inscription
šbrh br ḥrw bṭb
Access II.2.463 (printed, CIS)
Corpus CIS 1279

Inscription 2458
Site Wadi Mukatab, #64
Condition fair
Content Nabatean inscription
mdkr ḥryšw br tym[ʾ]lhy
Access II.2.463 (printed, CIS)
Corpus CIS 1280

Inscription 2459
Site Wadi Mukatab, #64
Condition poor
Content Nabatean inscription
šlm [ṣ]wbw br
[wʾ]lw
Access II.2.463 (printed, CIS)
Corpus CIS 1281

Inscription 2460
Site Wadi Mukatab, #64
Condition good
Content Nabatean inscription
šmrḥ br ʿmmw
šl[m]
Access II.2.463 (printed, CIS)
Corpus CIS 1282

Inscription 2461
Site Wadi Mukatab, #64
Condition good
Content Nabatean inscription
šlm grmʾlbʿly br wd[w]
Access II.2.463 (printed, CIS)
Corpus CIS 1283

Inscription 2462
Site Wadi Mukatab, #64
Condition poor
Content Nabatean inscription
[š]lm ....
w... ḥryšw
Access II.2.463 (printed, CIS)
Corpus CIS 1284

Inscription 2463
Site Wadi Mukatab, #64
Condition poor
Content Nabatean inscription
šlm šmrḥ
šlm šlm m.. w..lbʿly bṭ[b]
Access II.2.463 (printed, CIS)
Corpus CIS 1285

Inscription 2464
Site Wadi Mukatab, #64
Condition fair
Content Nabatean inscription
šlm wʾlw br ʿ...
Access II.2.463 (printed, CIS)
Corpus CIS 1286

Inscription **2465**
Site Wadi Mukatab, #64
Condition poor
Content Nabatean inscription
.....
ʾlbʿly
Access II.2.463 (printed, CIS)
Corpus CIS 1287

Inscription **2466**
Site Wadi Mukatab, #64
Condition poor
Content Nabatean inscription
Comment *illegible*
Access II.2.464 (printed, CIS)
Corpus CIS 1288

Inscription **2467**
Site Wadi Mukatab, #64
Condition fair
Content Nabatean inscription
šlm ʿbydw br
ʾwšw
...lw
Access II.2.464 (printed, CIS)
Corpus CIS 1289

Inscription **2468**
Site Wadi Mukatab, #64
Condition good
Content Nabatean inscription
dkyr ʾlṣdyw br
ʾlʾḥršw bṭb
Access II.2.464 (printed, CIS)
Corpus CIS 1290

Inscription **2469**
Site Wadi Mukatab, #64
Condition good
Content Nabatean inscription
šlm ʿb
dʿmrw
br ʿwt
ʾlhy bṭb
Access II.2.464 (printed, CIS)
Corpus CIS 1291

Inscription **2470**
Site Wadi Mukatab, #64
Condition good
Content Nabatean inscription
šlm ʿmyw br
grmʾlbʿly
Access II.2.464 (printed, CIS)
Corpus CIS 1292

Inscription **2471**
Site Wadi Mukatab, #64
Condition good
Content Nabatean inscription
šlm ʿbdʾlhy
br ḥlypw
Access II.2.464 (printed, CIS)
Corpus CIS 1293

Inscription **2472**
Site Wadi Mukatab, #64
Condition good
Content Nabatean inscription
šlm ʿmyw br
dʾbw bṭb
Access II.2.464 (printed, CIS)
Corpus CIS 1294

Inscription **2473**
Site Wadi Mukatab, #64
Condition fair
Content Nabatean inscription
šlm wʾlw br ʿmmw...
Access II.2.464 (printed, CIS)
Corpus CIS 1295

Inscription **2474**
Site Wadi Mukatab, #64
Condition good
Content Nabatean inscription
šlm prdw br wʾlw br
šʿdt dy mqtry
br ḥry klbw
Access II.2.465 (printed, CIS)
Corpus CIS 1296

Inscription **2475**
Site Wadi Mukatab, #64
Condition good
Content Nabatean inscription
šlm ʾšw br ḥryšw bṭb
Access II.2.465 (printed, CIS)
Corpus CIS 1297

Inscription **2476**
Site Wadi Mukatab, #64
Condition good
Content Nabatean inscription
dkyr bryʾw br wʾlw bṭb
Access II.2.465 (printed, CIS)
Corpus CIS 1298

Inscription **2477**
Site Wadi Mukatab, #64
Condition fair
Content Nabatean inscription
šlm ʾ[b]n ...
br pšy
Access II.2.465 (printed, CIS)
Corpus CIS 1299

Inscription 2478
Site Wadi Mukatab, #64
Condition good
Content Nabatean inscription
šlm bryʾw br
klbw
Access II.2.465 (printed, CIS)
Corpus CIS 1300

Inscription 2479
Site Wadi Mukatab, #64
Condition good
Content Nabatean inscription
šlm ʿbydw br ṣḥbw bṭb
Access II.2.465 (printed, CIS)
Corpus CIS 1301

Inscription 2480
Site Wadi Mukatab, #64
Condition good
Content Nabatean inscription
šlm ḥlṣšt br
bryw bṭb
Access II.2.465 (printed, CIS)
Corpus CIS 1302

Inscription 2481
Site Wadi Mukatab, #64
Condition poor
Content Nabatean inscription
dkyr bṭb yʿly
bryk [š]ly br pšy bṭb
wš..g...ʿl..
Access II.2.466 (printed, CIS)
Corpus CIS 1303

Inscription 2482
Site Wadi Mukatab, #64
Condition good
Content Nabatean inscription
dkyr ʿbdʾlbʿly
Access II.2.466 (printed, CIS)
Corpus CIS 1304

Inscription 2483
Site Wadi Mukatab, #64
Condition good
Content Nabatean inscription
šlm ʾbn ʾlqyn
br wʾlw bṭb
wšlm
Access II.2.466 (printed, CIS)
Corpus CIS 1305

Inscription 2484
Site Wadi Mukatab, #64
Condition good
Content Nabatean inscription
šlm wʾlw br ʿwdw bṭb
Access II.2.466 (printed, CIS)
Corpus CIS 1306

Inscription 2485
Site Wadi Mukatab, #64
Condition good
Content Nabatean inscription
šlm nšygw
Access II.2.466 (printed, CIS)
Corpus CIS 1307

Inscription 2486
Site Wadi Mukatab, #64
Condition good
Content Nabatean inscription
šlm grmʾlhy
Access II.2.466 (printed, CIS)
Corpus CIS 1308

Inscription 2487
Site Wadi Mukatab, #64
Condition good
Content Nabatean inscription
ʿlym gdyrʾ brt ʿnmw
Access II.2.466 (printed, CIS)
Corpus CIS 1309

Inscription 2488
Site Wadi Mukatab, #64
Condition fair
Content Nabatean inscription
šlm ʿmrw br ʾbn ʾ
lqyny b[ṭb]
Access II.2.466 (printed, CIS)
Corpus CIS 1310

Inscription 2489
Site Wadi Mukatab, #64
Condition good
Content Nabatean inscription
dkyr ʾlḥšpw br
ʾlmbqrw bṭb
Access II.2.466 (printed, CIS)
Corpus CIS 1311

Inscription 2490
Site Wadi Mukatab, #64
Condition good
Content Nabatean inscription
dk[y]r ḥlṣšt br ḥryšw
Access II.2.467 (printed, CIS)
Corpus CIS 1312

Inscription **2491**
Site Wadi Mukatab, #64
Condition good
Content Nabatean inscription
šlm ʿwdw br ʿmyw
Access II.2.467 (printed, CIS)
Corpus CIS 1313

Inscription **2492**
Site Wadi Mukatab, #64
Condition good
Content Nabatean inscription
šlm wʾlw br šʿdʾlhy
Access II.2.467 (printed, CIS)
Corpus CIS 1314

Inscription **2493**
Site Wadi Mukatab, #64
Condition good
Content Nabatean inscription
šlm ḥrglw br
ʿbydw
Access II.2.467 (printed, CIS)
Corpus CIS 1315

Inscription **2494**
Site Wadi Mukatab, #64
Condition good
Content Nabatean inscription
mgdyw br
wʾlw
Access II.2.467 (printed, CIS)
Corpus CIS 1316

Inscription **2495**
Site Wadi Mukatab, #64
Condition good
Content Nabatean inscription
šlm wʾlw br hnyʾw bṭb
Access II.2.467 (printed, CIS)
Corpus CIS 1317

Inscription **2496**
Site Wadi Mukatab, #64
Condition good
Content Nabatean inscription
šlm ʾlhmšw
br dbylt
Access II.2.467 (printed, CIS)
Corpus CIS 1318

Inscription **2497**
Site Wadi Mukatab, #64
Condition good
Content Nabatean inscription
šlm wʾlw br
zydw br ḥryšw
Access II.2.467 (printed, CIS)
Corpus CIS 1319

Inscription **2498**
Site Wadi Mukatab, #64
Condition good
Content Nabatean inscription
dkyr bryʾw br
ḥryšw
Access II.2.467 (printed, CIS)
Corpus CIS 1320

Inscription **2499**
Site Wadi Mukatab, #64
Condition poor
Content Nabatean inscription
... br ʾbdʾlh
[dk]yr ʿbdʾlḥ br š...
Access II.2.467 (printed, CIS)
Corpus CIS 1321

Inscription **2500**
Site Wadi Mukatab, #64
Condition fair
Content Nabatean inscription
šlm bryʾw br y[ʿly]
Access II.2.468 (printed, CIS)
Corpus CIS 1322

Inscription **2501**
Site Wadi Mukatab, #64
Condition good
Content Nabatean inscription
šlm ʿwdw br qymw
Access II.2.468 (printed, CIS)
Corpus CIS 1323

Inscription **2502**
Site Wadi Mukatab, #64
Condition fair
Content Nabatean inscription
šlm ʿwdw br
ʿmyw...
Access II.2.468 (printed, CIS)
Corpus CIS 1324

Inscription **2503**
Site Wadi Mukatab, #64
dating 149
Condition good
Content Nabatean inscription
šlm šʿdʾlhy br grmʾlbʿly br
bḥgh bšnt ʾrbʿyn wḥmš
Access II.2.468 (printed, CIS)
Corpus CIS 1325

Inscription **2504**
Site Wadi Mukatab, #64
Condition poor
Content Nabatean inscription
šlm grmʾ
Access II.2.468 (printed, CIS)
Corpus CIS 1326

Inscription 2505
Site Wadi Mukatab, #64
Condition poor
Content Nabatean inscription
ʾwšw [ʿbd]ʾlh[y] br dmgw
Access II.2.468 (printed, CIS)
Corpus CIS 1327

Inscription 2506
Site Wadi Mukatab, #64
Condition good
Content Nabatean inscription
šlm ʿmrw br
ʾbn ʾlqyny bkl ṭ[b]
Access II.2.468 (printed, CIS)
Corpus CIS 1328

Inscription 2507
Site Wadi Mukatab, #64
Condition good
Content Nabatean inscription
š[l]m wʾlw br ḥryšw
Access II.2.468 (printed, CIS)
Corpus CIS 1329

Inscription 2508
Site Wadi Mukatab, #64
Condition good
Content Nabatean inscription
šlm wʾlw
Access II.2.469 (printed, CIS)
Corpus CIS 1330

Inscription 2509
Site Wadi Mukatab, #64
Condition good
Content Nabatean inscription
mdkwr
šʿdʾlhy br
klbw b...
Access II.2.469 (printed, CIS)
Corpus CIS 1331

Inscription 2510
Site Wadi Mukatab, #64
Condition fair
Content Nabatean inscription
dkyr ʾlḥšpw br ...
Access II.2.469 (printed, CIS)
Corpus CIS 1332

Inscription 2511
Site Wadi Mukatab, #64
Condition good
Content Nabatean inscription
dkyr yʿl[y] br ʿmyw
bṭb wšlm
Access II.2.469 (printed, CIS)
Corpus CIS 1333

Inscription 2512
Site Wadi Mukatab, #64
Condition good
Content Nabatean inscription
šlm šʿdʾlhy br ʿbd
ʾlbʿly
Access II.2.469 (printed, CIS)
Corpus CIS 1334

Inscription 2513
Site Wadi Mukatab, #64
Condition fair
Content Nabatean inscription
dkyr ʿm[yw]
Access II.2.469 (printed, CIS)
Corpus CIS 1335

Inscription 2514
Site Wadi Mukatab, #64
Condition fair
Content Nabatean inscription
dkyr ʿbdʾlbʿly
br ʾ....
Access II.2.469 (printed, CIS)
Corpus CIS 1336

Inscription 2515
Site Wadi Mukatab, #64
Condition fair
Content Nabatean inscription
š..mʾ
wʾlw
Access II.2.469 (printed, CIS)
Corpus CIS 1337

Inscription 2516
Site Wadi Mukatab, #64
Condition good
Content Nabatean inscription
šlm zydw
br ʿmyw bṭb
Access II.2.469 (printed, CIS)
Corpus CIS 1338

Inscription 2517
Site Wadi Mukatab, #64
Condition good
Content Nabatean inscription
šlm ʿwdw
br qymw
Access II.2.470 (printed, CIS)
Corpus CIS 1339

Inscription 2518
Site Wadi Mukatab, #64
Condition good
Content Nabatean inscription
šlm ḥršw br wʾlw bṭb
Access II.2.470 (printed, CIS)
Corpus CIS 1340

Inscription **2519**
Site Wadi Mukatab, #64
Condition good
Content Nabatean inscription
šlm gdyw
w[ʿ]bdw bny
ʾwšw
Access II.2.470 (printed, CIS)
Corpus CIS 1341

Inscription **2520**
Site Wadi Mukatab, #64
Condition good
Content Nabatean inscription
dky[r] wʾlw br ḥ
ryšw
Access II.2.470 (printed, CIS)
Corpus CIS 1342

Inscription **2521**
Site Wadi Mukatab, #64
Condition good
Content Nabatean inscription
šlm wʾlw br qrḥh
Access II.2.470 (printed, CIS)
Corpus CIS 1343

Inscription **2522**
Site Wadi Mukatab, #64
Condition good
Content Nabatean inscription
šlm ʾlkyw br
ḥryšw bṭb
Access II.2.470 (printed, CIS)
Corpus CIS 1344

Inscription **2523**
Site Wadi Mukatab, #64
Condition good
Content Nabatean inscription
šlm ḥr[yš]w br
klbw
wklbw br[h]
Access II.2.470 (printed, CIS)
Corpus CIS 1345

Inscription **2524**
Site Wadi Mukatab, #64
Condition good
Content Nabatean inscription
šlm ʾwšw
br gdyw bṭb
Access II.2.470 (printed, CIS)
Corpus CIS 1346

Inscription **2525**
Site Wadi Mukatab, #64
Condition fair
Content Nabatean inscription
šlm wʾlw
br t...
Access II.2.470 (printed, CIS)
Corpus CIS 1347

Inscription **2526**
Site Wadi Mukatab, #64
Condition poor
Content Nabatean inscription
šlm grm...
Access II.2.470 (printed, CIS)
Corpus CIS 1348

Inscription **2527**
Site Wadi Mukatab, #64
Condition poor
Content Nabatean inscription
šlm ʾʿlʾ
br wd...
Access II.2.471 (printed, CIS)
Corpus CIS 1349

Inscription **2528**
Site Wadi Mukatab, #64
Condition good
Content Nabatean inscription
šlm ʿbdyw br ʿbdʾlbʿly
Access II.2.471 (printed, CIS)
Corpus CIS 1350

Inscription **2529**
Site Wadi Mukatab, #64
Condition good
Content Nabatean inscription
šlm [d]ʾbw br ʿbydw
bṭb
Access II.2.471 (printed, CIS)
Corpus CIS 1351

Inscription **2530**
Site Wadi Mukatab, #64
Condition good
Content Nabatean inscription
šlm ʿmyrt br zydw bṭb
bṭb
Access II.2.471 (printed, CIS)
Corpus CIS 1352

Inscription **2531**
Site Wadi Mukatab, #64
Condition fair
Content Nabatean inscription
dkyr ʿ...
br wʾlw b[ṭb]
Access II.2.471 (printed, CIS)
Corpus CIS 1353

Inscription 2532
Site Wadi Mukatab, #64
Condition poor
Content Nabatean inscription
Comment *illegible*
Access II.2.471 (printed, CIS)
Corpus CIS 1354

Inscription 2533
Site Wadi Mukatab, #64
Condition good
Content Nabatean inscription
šlm mʿrqw br ʿnmw
Access II.2.471 (printed, CIS)
Corpus CIS 1355

Inscription 2534
Site Wadi Mukatab, #64
Condition fair
Content Nabatean inscription
šlm ʾʿlʾ
br ...t
Access II.2.471 (printed, CIS)
Corpus CIS 1356

Inscription 2535
Site Wadi Mukatab, #64
Condition fair
Content Nabatean inscription
ʿbydw br ʿbdʾ[lbʿly]
Access II.2.472 (printed, CIS)
Corpus CIS 1357

Inscription 2536
Site Wadi Mukatab, #64
Condition good
Content Nabatean inscription
šlm lḥryš
w br yʿly
Access II.2.472 (printed, CIS)
Corpus CIS 1358

Inscription 2537
Site Wadi Mukatab, #64
Condition fair
Content Nabatean inscription
šlm mlyḥw br ʾšwdw [b]ṭ[b]
.... ḥlṣšt
Access II.2.472 (printed, CIS)
Corpus CIS 1359

Inscription 2538
Site Wadi Mukatab, #64
Condition good
Content Nabatean inscription
šlm ʿbdʾlbʿly br ʾwšʾl[hy]
Access II.2.472 (printed, CIS)
Corpus CIS 1360

Inscription 2539
Site Wadi Mukatab, #64
Condition good
Content Nabatean inscription
šlm grmʾlbʿly
br bḥgh
Access II.2.472 (printed, CIS)
Corpus CIS 1361

Inscription 2540
Site Wadi Mukatab, #64
Condition good
Content Nabatean inscription
šlm bḥgh
Access II.2.472 (printed, CIS)
Corpus CIS 1362

Inscription 2541
Site Wadi Mukatab, #64
Condition good
Content Nabatean inscription
šlm ʾḥwl br wʾlt
Access II.2.472 (printed, CIS)
Corpus CIS 1363

Inscription 2542
Site Wadi Mukatab, #64
Condition good
Content Nabatean inscription
šlm ʾšph
Access II.2.472 (printed, CIS)
Corpus CIS 1364

Inscription 2543
Site Wadi Mukatab, #64
Condition good
Content Nabatean inscription
šlm [n]bhw
ʾlktyw
dy ʾbrqh
Access II.2.473 (printed, CIS)
Corpus CIS 1365

Inscription 2544
Site Wadi Mukatab, #64
Condition good
Content Nabatean inscription
šlm ʿmrw bṭb wš[d]
ʾlbʿly brh
Access II.2.473 (printed, CIS)
Corpus CIS 1366

Inscription 2545
Site Wadi Mukatab, #64
Condition fair
Content Nabatean inscription
šlm ʿbdʾlbʿl[y br]
šʿdʾlh[y]
Access II.2.473 (printed, CIS)
Corpus CIS 1367

Inscription 2546
Site Wadi Mukatab, #64
Condition fair
Content Nabatean inscription
šlm ʿyydw wʾbʾ[wšw]
wbryʾw bny ḥryšw bṭb
Access II.2.473 (printed, CIS)
Corpus CIS 1368

Inscription 2547
Site Wadi Mukatab, #64
Condition good
Content Nabatean inscription
šlm qšṭw
bn hny[ʾw]
Access II.2.473 (printed, CIS)
Corpus CIS 1369

Inscription 2548
Site Wadi Mukatab, #64
Condition poor
Content Nabatean inscription
šlm .dm. wʿlymʾlbʿ
Access II.2.473 (printed, CIS)
Corpus CIS 1370

Inscription 2549
Site Wadi Mukatab, #64
Condition good
Content Nabatean inscription
šlm ṭylh
br dmgw
Access II.2.473 (printed, CIS)
Corpus CIS 1371

Inscription 2550
Site Wadi Mukatab, #64
Condition good
Content Nabatean inscription
dkyr nšnkyh
br ʿṣrw
Access II.2.473 (printed, CIS)
Corpus CIS 1372

Inscription 2551
Site Wadi Mukatab, #64
Condition good
Content Nabatean inscription
tymw
dkyr
Access II.2.474 (printed, CIS)
Corpus CIS 1373

Inscription 2552
Site Wadi Mukatab, #64
Condition good
Content Nabatean inscription
šlm ʿyydw br wʾlw
wwʾl brh
Access II.2.474 (printed, CIS)
Corpus CIS 1374

Inscription 2553
Site Wadi Mukatab, #64
Condition good
Content Nabatean inscription
dkyr dmgw br
ṭylh bṭb w
šlm
Access II.2.474 (printed, CIS)
Corpus CIS 1375

Inscription 2554
Site Wadi Mukatab, #64
Condition good
Content Nabatean inscription
bryk [hn]ʾw
br zydw
Access II.2.474 (printed, CIS)
Corpus CIS 1376

Inscription 2555
Site Wadi Mukatab, #64
Condition good
Content Nabatean inscription
bryk
mqmʾlhy
br tymw...
Access II.2.474 (printed, CIS)
Corpus CIS 1377

Inscription 2556
Site Wadi Mukatab, #64
Condition good
Content Nabatean inscription
dkyr ʾlmbqrw br [ʿ]wymw
Access II.2.474 (printed, CIS)
Corpus CIS.1378

Inscription 2557
Site Wadi Mukatab, #64
Condition good
Content Nabatean inscription
dkyr nšnkyh
br ʿṣrw
Access II.2.474 (printed, CIS)
Corpus CIS 1379

Inscription 2558
Site Wadi Mukatab, #64
Condition good
Content Nabatean inscription
ḥnṭlw bṭb
Access II.2.474 (printed, CIS)
Corpus CIS 1380

Inscription 2559
Site Wadi Mukatab, #64
Condition good
Content Nabatean inscription
dkyr ʿbdʾlbʿly
bṭb wšlm
Access II.2.475 (printed, CIS)
Corpus CIS 1381

Inscription 2560
Site Wadi Mukatab, #64
Condition good
Content Nabatean inscription
šlm ʾldʾbw
br ḥršw
Access II.2.475 (printed, CIS)
Corpus CIS 1382

Inscription 2561
Site Wadi Mukatab, #64
Condition good
Content Nabatean inscription
šlm ʾwšw br pšyw bṭb
Access II.2.475 (printed, CIS)
Corpus CIS 1383

Inscription 2562
Site Wadi Mukatab, #64
Condition good
Content Nabatean inscription
šlm ʿrqbw br whbʾlhy
Access II.2.475 (printed, CIS)
Corpus CIS 1384

Inscription 2563
Site Wadi Mukatab, #64
Condition good
Content Nabatean inscription
bryk ʾʿlʾ br tnt[l]w
Access II.2.475 (printed, CIS)
Corpus CIS 1385

Inscription 2564
Site Wadi Mukatab, #64
Condition good
Content Nabatean inscription
dkyr šlmw br tym
ʾlhy bṭb wṣlm
Access II.2.475 (printed, CIS)
Corpus CIS 1386

Inscription 2565
Site Wadi Mukatab, #64
Condition good
Content Nabatean inscription
šlm ʾʿlʾ br zydw
Access II.2.475 (printed, CIS)
Corpus CIS 1387

Inscription 2566
Site Wadi Mukatab, #64
Condition fair
Content Nabatean inscription
dkyr ... w br pydw bṭb
Access II.2.475 (printed, CIS)
Corpus CIS 1388

Inscription 2567
Site Wadi Mukatab, #64
Condition fair
Content Nabatean inscription
[g]rmlbʿly
šlm zydw br
ʾwš
šlm yʿly br ḥryš[w]
Access II.2.476 (printed, CIS)
Corpus CIS 1389

Inscription 2568
Site Wadi Mukatab, #64
Condition good
Content Nabatean inscription
šlm šʿd
br ḥw
Access II.2.476 (printed, CIS)
Corpus CIS 1390

Inscription 2569
Site Wadi Mukatab, #64
Condition poor
Content Nabatean inscription
Comment *illegible*
Access II.2.476 (printed, CIS)
Corpus CIS 1391

Inscription 2570
Site Wadi Mukatab, #64
Condition fair
Content Nabatean inscription
dkyr whblhy br wʾlt nš..
Access II.2.476 (printed, CIS)
Corpus CIS 1392

Inscription 2571
Site Wadi Mukatab, #64
Condition good
Content Nabatean inscription
wdw br ytʿw
Access II.2.476 (printed, CIS)
Corpus CIS 1393

Inscription **2572**
Site Wadi Mukatab, #64
Condition good
Content Nabatean inscription
šlm tymʾlhy br yʿly
šlm šʿdʾlhy br bryʾw b[ṭb]
Access II.2.477 (printed, CIS)
Corpus CIS 1394

Inscription **2573**
Site Wadi Mukatab, #64
Condition poor
Content Nabatean inscription
Comment *illegible*
Access II.2.477 (printed, CIS)
Corpus CIS 1396

Inscription **2574**
Site Wadi Mukatab, #64
Condition poor
Content Nabatean inscription
Comment *illegible*
Access II.2.477 (printed, CIS)
Corpus CIS 1397

Inscription **2575**
Site Wadi Mukatab, #64
Condition poor
Content Nabatean inscription
Comment *illegible*
Access II.2.477 (printed, CIS)
Corpus CIS 1398

Inscription **2576**
Site Wadi Mukatab, #64
Condition poor
Content Nabatean inscription
...
wʾlw...mḥlmw
Access II.2.477 (printed, CIS)
Corpus CIS 1399

Inscription **2577**
Site Wadi Mukatab, #64
Condition poor
Content Nabatean inscription
Comment *illegible*
Access II.2.477 (printed, CIS)
Corpus CIS 1400

Inscription **2578**
Site Wadi Mukatab, #64
Condition poor
Content Nabatean inscription
Comment *illegible*
Access II.2.477 (printed, CIS)
Corpus CIS 1401

Inscription **2579**
Site Wadi Mukatab, #64
Condition poor
Content Nabatean inscription
šʿdw
Comment *fragment*
Access II.2.477 (printed, CIS)
Corpus CIS 1402

Inscription **2580**
Site Wadi Mukatab, #64
Condition fair
Content Nabatean inscription
...
grmʾlbʿly
ʿwdw
Access II.2.477 (printed, CIS)
Corpus CIS 1403

Inscription **2581**
Site Wadi Mukatab, #64
Condition fair
Content Nabatean inscription
dkyr ḥryš
w br [y]ʿ[ly]
Access II.2.477 (printed, CIS)
Corpus CIS 1404

Inscription **2582**
Site Wadi Mukatab, #64
Condition poor
Content Nabatean inscription
Comment *illegible*
Access II.2.477 (printed, CIS)
Corpus CIS 1405

Inscription **2583**
Site Wadi Mukatab, #64
Condition poor
Content Nabatean inscription
hnyʾw
Access II.2.477 (printed, CIS)
Corpus CIS 1406

Inscription **2584**
Site Wadi Mukatab, #64
Condition good
Content Nabatean inscription
šlm gdyw br
wʾlw
Access II.2.478 (printed, CIS)
Corpus CIS 1407

Inscription **2585**
Site Wadi Mukatab, #64
Condition fair
Content Nabatean inscription
šlm wʾlw wʾkbrw
[bny ḥ]ryšw b[ṭb]
Access II.2.478 (printed, CIS)
Corpus CIS 1408

Inscription 2586
Site Wadi Mukatab, #64
Condition good
Content Nabatean inscription
šlm
ʿbdʾlhy d
ʾbw br wʾlw
Access II.2.478 (printed, CIS)
Corpus CIS 1409

Inscription 2587
Site Wadi Mukatab, #64
Condition good
Content Nabatean inscription
šlm ʿ[w]dw br ʿmyw bṭb
Access II.2.478 (printed, CIS)
Corpus CIS 1410

Inscription 2588
Site Wadi Mukatab, #64
Condition good
Content Nabatean inscription
šlm ʾwšw
šlm w[ʾ]lw
Access II.2.478 (printed, CIS)
Corpus CIS 1411

Inscription 2589
Site Wadi Mukatab, #64
Condition good
Content Nabatean inscription
šlm nšgw
Access II.2.478 (printed, CIS)
Corpus CIS 1412

Inscription 2590
Site Wadi Mukatab, #64
Condition good
Content Nabatean inscription
šlm pšyw
Access II.2.479 (printed, CIS)
Corpus CIS 1413

Inscription 2591
Site Wadi Mukatab, #64
Condition good
Content Nabatean inscription
šlm gdyw br
wʾlw
Access II.2.479 (printed, CIS)
Corpus CIS 1414

Inscription 2592
Site Wadi Mukatab, #64
Condition fair
Content Nabatean inscription
šlm [ʿmn]w br ʿwdw
Access II.2.479 (printed, CIS)
Corpus CIS 1415

Inscription 2593
Site Wadi Mukatab, #64
Condition fair
Content Nabatean inscription
dkyr hn[yʾw]
br ʾwšʾlh[y] bṭb
Access II.2.479 (printed, CIS)
Corpus CIS 1416

Inscription 2594
Site Wadi Mukatab, #64
Condition good
Content Nabatean inscription
dkyr ʾʿlʾ br
pšyw bṭb wšlm
Access II.2.479 (printed, CIS)
Corpus CIS 1417

Inscription 2595
Site Wadi Mukatab, #64
Condition fair
Content Nabatean inscription
dkyr ḥryšw
br zydw bṭb
dky[r] wʾlw br
[ḥry]š[w]
Access II.2.479 (printed, CIS)
Corpus CIS 1418

Inscription 2596
Site Wadi Mukatab, #64
Condition fair
Content Nabatean inscription
dkyr br[yʾw]
br ʾ[w]šw
Access II.2.479 (printed, CIS)
Corpus CIS 1419

Inscription 2597
Site Wadi Mukatab, #64
Condition good
Content Nabatean inscription
šlm ʾwšw br grmʾlbʿly
Access II.2.479 (printed, CIS)
Corpus CIS 1420

Inscription 2598
Site Wadi Mukatab, #64
Condition good
Content Nabatean inscription
šlm ʿwdw br ʿmyw bṭb
šlm bryʾw
Access II.2.479 (printed, CIS)
Corpus CIS 1421

Inscription 2599
Site Wadi Mukatab, #64
Condition good
Content Nabatean inscription
šlm ʾwšw
Access II.2.480 (printed, CIS)
Corpus CIS 1422

Inscription 2600
Site Wadi Mukatab, #64
Condition poor
Content Nabatean inscription
.ʾkbrw
Comment *uncertain reading*
Access II.2.480 (printed, CIS)
Corpus CIS 1423

Inscription 2601
Site Wadi Mukatab, #64
Condition poor
Content Nabatean inscription
... br klbw wklbw brh
.bʾ brh bṭb
..bʿly b[ṭb]
Access II.2.480 (printed, CIS)
Corpus CIS 1424

Inscription 2602
Site Wadi Mukatab, #64
Condition fair
Content Nabatean inscription
šlm ʿmyw br ʿmrt šw
[ʾ]wšw
Access II.2.480 (printed, CIS)
Corpus CIS 1425

Inscription 2603
Site Wadi Mukatab, #64
Condition fair
Content Nabatean inscription
šlm grmʾ[l]hy [br] grmw
Access II.2.480 (printed, CIS)
Corpus CIS 1426

Inscription 2604
Site Wadi Mukatab, #64
Condition good
Content Nabatean inscription
lʾ dkyr [ʾ]bʾwšw wʿyy
dw wbryʾw bny ḥryšw
Access II.2.480 (printed, CIS)
Corpus CIS 1427

Inscription 2605
Site Wadi Mukatab, #64
Condition fair
Content Nabatean inscription
šlm m.w
br ʾʿlʾ bṭb
Access II.2.480 (printed, CIS)
Corpus CIS 1428

Inscription 2606
Site Wadi Mukatab, #64
Condition poor
Content Nabatean inscription
dkyr ʾšw br ḥry
šw dy mqtry ʾšy
bw bṭb
Access II.2.480 (printed, CIS)
Corpus CIS 1429

Inscription 2607
Site Wadi Mukatab, #64
Condition good
Content Nabatean inscription
šlm grmʾl
bʿly br
ʾwšw
Access II.2.480 (printed, CIS)
Corpus CIS 1430

Inscription 2608
Site Wadi Mukatab, #64
Condition fair
Content Nabatean inscription
šlm šmrḥ br ....
Access II.2.480 (printed, CIS)
Corpus CIS 1431

Inscription 2609
Site Wadi Mukatab, #64
Condition fair
Content Nabatean inscription
dkyr m.m.
ʿmnw
Access II.2.481 (printed, CIS)
Corpus CIS 1432

Inscription 2610
Site Wadi Mukatab, #64
Condition good
Content Nabatean inscription
dkyr šmrḥw br
ʿbdʾhyw bṭb
Access II.2.481 (printed, CIS)
Corpus CIS 1433

Inscription **2611**
Site Wadi Mukatab, #64
Condition good
Content Nabatean inscription
dkyr klbw br ʿwdw
Access II.2.481 (printed, CIS)
Corpus CIS 1434

Inscription **2612**
Site Wadi Mukatab, #64
Condition good
Content Nabatean inscription
šlm ʾlmbqrw
br nšygw
Access II.2.481 (printed, CIS)
Corpus CIS 1435

Inscription **2613**
Site Wadi Mukatab, #64
Condition fair
Content Nabatean inscription
šlm šlm pʾrn...
Access II.2.481 (printed, CIS)
Corpus CIS 1436

Inscription **2614**
Site Wadi Mukatab, #64
Condition good
Content Nabatean inscription
šlm mʿyrw [br] šlmw bṭb
Access II.2.481 (printed, CIS)
Corpus CIS 1437

Inscription **2615**
Site Wadi Mukatab, #64
Condition good
Content Nabatean inscription
šlm ḥlypw bryʾw brh
br ḥryšw bṭb
Access II.2.481 (printed, CIS)
Corpus CIS 1438

Inscription **2616**
Site Wadi Mukatab, #64
Condition good
Content Nabatean inscription
dky[r] hnʾw br ʿmyw
Access II.2.481 (printed, CIS)
Corpus CIS 1439

Inscription **2617**
Site Wadi Mukatab, #64
Condition good
Content Nabatean inscription
dkyr ʿbdʾlbʿly
šlm šʿdʾlhy br
ʿwdw
Access II.2.481 (printed, CIS)
Corpus CIS 1440

Inscription **2618**
Site Wadi Mukatab, #64
Condition good
Content Nabatean inscription
dkyr hnʾw br ʿmyw
Access II.2.481 (printed, CIS)
Corpus CIS 1441

Inscription **2619**
Site Wadi Firan, #53
Condition good
Content Nabatean inscription
šlm ʾwšw br
šmrḥ bṭb
Access II.2.482 (printed, CIS)
Corpus CIS 1442

Inscription **2620**
Site Wadi Firan, #53
Condition good
Content Nabatean inscription
dkyr hnʾw b
r ʿmyw
Access II.2.482 (printed, CIS)
Corpus CIS 1443

Inscription **2621**
Site Wadi Firan, #53
Condition good
Content Nabatean inscription
šlm wʾlw br
ʿmyw bṭb
Access II.2.482 (printed, CIS)
Corpus CIS 1444

Inscription **2622**
Site Wadi Firan, #53
Condition good
Content Nabatean inscription
šlm ʿyydw br wʾlw
wwʾl brh bṭ[b] wš[l]m
Access II.2.482 (printed, CIS)
Corpus CIS 1445

Inscription **2623**
Site Wadi Firan, #53
Condition poor
Content Nabatean inscription
Comment *illegible*
Access II.2.482 (printed, CIS)
Corpus CIS 1446

Inscription **2624**
Site Wadi Firan, #53
Condition good
Content Nabatean inscription
šlm bḥgh
Access II.2.482 (printed, CIS)
Corpus CIS 1447

Inscription 2625
Site Wadi Firan, #53
Condition good
Content Nabatean inscription
ʿbydw br
ḥrglw
Access II.2.482 (printed, CIS)
Corpus CIS 1448

Inscription 2626
Site Wadi Firan, #53
Condition good
Content Nabatean inscription
ḥlṣw br ʿmnw
Access II.2.482 (printed, CIS)
Corpus CIS 1449

Inscription 2627
Site Wadi Firan, #53
Condition fair
Content Nabatean inscription
šʿdʾlhy
Access II.2.482 (printed, CIS)
Corpus CIS 1450

Inscription 2628
Site Wadi Firan, #53
Condition good
Content Nabatean inscription
šlm ḥnṭlw br nšnkyh
Access II.2.483 (printed, CIS)
Corpus CIS 1451

Inscription 2629
Site Wadi Firan, #53
Condition good
Content Nabatean inscription
šlm ʿwdw
br ḥbrkn bṭb
Access II.2.483 (printed, CIS)
Corpus CIS 1452

Inscription 2630
Site Wadi Firan, #53
Condition poor
Content Nabatean inscription
Comment *illegible*
Access II.2.483 (printed, CIS)
Corpus CIS 1453

Inscription 2631
Site Wadi Firan, #53
Condition poor
Content Nabatean inscription
Comment *illegible*
Access II.2.483 (printed, CIS)
Corpus CIS 1454

Inscription 2632
Site Wadi Firan, #53
Condition poor
Content Nabatean inscription
....
... ʿmyw br klbw
Access II.2.483 (printed, CIS)
Corpus CIS 1455

Inscription 2633
Site Wadi Firan, #53
Condition poor
Content Nabatean inscription
Comment *illegible*
Access II.2.483 (printed, CIS)
Corpus CIS 1456

Inscription 2634
Site Wadi Firan, #53
Condition good
Content Nabatean inscription
ʾlʾ
tymʾlhy
ʿwdw
ṣʿbw br šmr[ḥ]
Access II.2.483 (printed, CIS)
Corpus CIS 1457

Inscription 2635
Site Wadi Firan, #53
Condition good
Content Nabatean inscription
... ʾbn ʾlqyny
ḥršw
br wʾlw
ḥryšw br yʿ[ly]
Access II.2.483 (printed, CIS)
Corpus CIS 1458

Inscription 2636
Site Wadi Firan, #53
Condition poor
Content Nabatean inscription
[ʿbd]ʾlbʿly
Access II.2.483 (printed, CIS)
Corpus CIS 1459

Inscription 2637
Site Wadi Firan, #53
Condition poor
Content Nabatean inscription
... [b]r ʾlmbqrw
zydw ... mʿnw
[š]lm ʾwšʾ[l]hy
br ʾtmw bṭb
Access II.2.483 (printed, CIS)
Corpus CIS 1460

Inscription 2638
Site Wadi Firan, #53
Condition good
Content Nabatean inscription
šlm šʿdʾlhy br bryʾ wbryk ʿmmw
ʾlmbqrw br wʾlw
Access II.2.484 (printed, CIS)
Corpus CIS 1461

Inscription 2639
Site Wadi Firan, #53
Condition poor
Content Nabatean inscription
... [ʿbd]ʾlbʿly
šlm grmʾlhy br ...
Access II.2.484 (printed, CIS)
Corpus CIS 1462

Inscription 2640
Site Wadi Firan, #53
Condition poor
Content Nabatean inscription
....
....
....
bryʾw
ʿmyw
Comment *fragments of various inscriptions*
Access II.2.484 (printed, CIS)
Corpus CIS 1463

Inscription 2641
Site Wadi Firan, #53
Condition fair
Content Nabatean inscription
šlm ʾlmbqrw br
[wʾ]l[w] bṭb
Access II.2.484 (printed, CIS)
Corpus CIS 1464

Inscription 2642
Site Wadi Firan, #53
Condition fair
Content Nabatean inscription
šlm ʿwdw br ḥršw
šlm ʿbṭh br
ʿmmw br ʿmrw
Comment *two inscriptions*
Access II.2.484 (printed, CIS)
Corpus CIS 1465

Inscription 2643
Site Wadi Firan, #53
Condition fair
Content Nabatean inscription
pšy
ʿbdʾlhy
br wʾlw
ʿydw
br wʾlw
Comment *three inscriptions*
Access II.2.485 (printed, CIS)
Corpus CIS 1466

Inscription 2644
Site Wadi Firan, #53
Condition poor
Content Nabatean inscription
.... ʿbdʾlbʿly
....
ʾwšʾlhy. šmrḥ
....
Comment *fragments of various inscriptions*
Access II.2.485 (printed, CIS)
Corpus CIS 1467

Inscription 2645
Site Wadi Firan, #53
Condition good
Content Nabatean inscription
dkyr wʾlw br
ʾwšw bṭb
Access II.2.485 (printed, CIS)
Corpus CIS 1468

Inscription 2646
Site Wadi Firan, #53
Condition fair
Content Nabatean inscription
bryk tntlw br
tymʾlhy
bryk šʿdlhy
ʾwšʾlhy b[ṭb]
šlm ʾlktyw
bryk bryʾw br ....
wʾlw. šʾ
ʾwšw br ....
Comment *fragments of various inscriptions*
Access II.2.485 (printed, CIS)
Corpus CIS 1469

Inscription **2647**
Site Wadi Firan, #53
Condition good
Content Nabatean inscription
šlm ʾwšw b[r]
šlm ḥršw br grmʾlbʿly
Access II.2.485 (printed, CIS)
Corpus CIS 1470

Inscription **2648**
Site Wadi Firan, #53
Condition fair
Content Nabatean inscription
bryk ʿmmw br ....
šlm ʾlmbqrw br wʾlw
ʿmmw br ....
šlm tymw
pšyw
ʿmrw br ....
šlm ʿmmw
ʾlmbqrw br ....
ʿwdw
šlm ḥrw
bryk bryʾw
Comment *fragments of various inscriptions*
Access II.2.486 (printed, CIS)
Corpus CIS 1471

Inscription **2649**
Site Wadi Firan, #53
Condition good
Content Nabatean inscription
šlm šlmw br ʾšwdw bṭb
Access II.2a.2 (printed, CIS)
Corpus CIS 1472

Inscription **2650**
Site Wadi Firan, #53
Condition poor
Content Nabatean inscription
...m ʿ...qrw.
Access II.2a.2 (printed, CIS)
Corpus CIS 1473

Inscription **2651**
Site Wadi Firan, #53
Condition good
Content Nabatean inscription
šlm grmʾlbʿly br ḥnṭlw
bṭb
bryk ....
Access II.2a.2 (printed, CIS)
Corpus CIS 1474

Inscription **2652**
Site Wadi Firan, #53
Condition good
Content Nabatean inscription
[ḥry]šw br ḥlšt bṭb
Access II.2a.3 (printed, CIS)
Corpus CIS 1475

Inscription **2653**
Site Wadi Firan, #53
Condition good
Content Nabatean inscription
dkyr zydw br
tymʾlhy bṭb
Access II.2a.3 (printed, CIS)
Corpus CIS 1476

Inscription **2654**
Site Wadi Firan, #53
Condition good
Content Nabatean inscription
dkyr ʾwyšw br pšyw bṭb
Access II.2a.3 (printed, CIS)
Corpus CIS 1477

Inscription **2655**
Site Wadi Firan, #53
Condition good
Content Nabatean inscription
šlm ʿmy[w]
Access II.2a.3 (printed, CIS)
Corpus CIS 1478

Inscription **2656**
Site Wadi Firan, #53
Condition good
Content Nabatean inscription
šlm wʾlw br ḥlṣšt qdm ʾlbʿly
Access II.2a.3 (printed, CIS)
Corpus CIS 1479

Inscription **2657**
Site Wadi Firan, #53
Condition good
Content Nabatean inscription
šlm ʾwšw
br ḥršw
Access II.2a.3 (printed, CIS)
Corpus CIS 1480

Inscription **2658**
Site Wadi Firan, #53
Condition good
Content Nabatean inscription
šlm ʿbydw br ʾwšw bṭb
Access II.2a.3 (printed, CIS)
Corpus CIS 1481

Inscription 2659
Site Wadi Firan, #53
Condition good
Content Nabatean inscription
šlm ḥlṣšt br
ʿbdʾlbʿly
Access II.2a.3 (printed, CIS)
Corpus CIS 1482

Inscription 2660
Site Wadi Firan, #53
Condition fair
Content Nabatean inscription
šlm grmʾlbʿly br ...
Access II.2a.4 (printed, CIS)
Corpus CIS 1483

Inscription 2661
Site Wadi Firan, #53
Condition good
Content Nabatean inscription
šlm qymw br ʿwdw
Access II.2a.4 (printed, CIS)
Corpus CIS 1484

Inscription 2662
Site Wadi Firan, #53
Condition good
Content Nabatean inscription
šlm pšy br šʿdʾlh
Access II.2a.4 (printed, CIS)
Corpus CIS 1485

Inscription 2663
Site Wadi Firan, #53
Condition good
Content Nabatean inscription
dkyr ʾlmbqrw bṭb
Access II.2a.4 (printed, CIS)
Corpus CIS 1486

Inscription 2664
Site Wadi Firan, #53
Condition fair
Content Nabatean inscription
šlm ʾwšw br ḥ...
ʿbdʾlbʿly
Access II.2a.4 (printed, CIS)
Corpus CIS 1487

Inscription 2665
Site Wadi Firan, #53
Condition good
Content Nabatean inscription
dkyr yʿly br tymʾlhy bkl [ṭb]
Access II.2a.4 (printed, CIS)
Corpus CIS 1488

Inscription 2666
Site Wadi Firan, #53
Condition good
Content Nabatean inscription
šlm ʾlmbqrw br ʿmyw
Access II.2a.4 (printed, CIS)
Corpus CIS 1489

Inscription 2667
Site Wadi Firan, #53
Condition good
Content Nabatean inscription
šlm ḥlṣšt br ḥryšw
Access II.2a.4 (printed, CIS)
Corpus CIS 1490

Inscription 2668
Site Wadi Firan, #53
dating 231
Condition good
Content Nabatean inscription
šlm ʿmyw br
šmrḥ mš[q]ʾ
šnt 126
Access II.2a.4 (printed, CIS)
Corpus CIS 1491

Inscription 2669
Site Wadi Firan, #53
Condition good
Content Nabatean inscription
ʿwdw br qrḥw
Access II.2a.5 (printed, CIS)
Corpus CIS 1492

Inscription 2670
Site Wadi Firan, #53
Condition good
Content Nabatean inscription
dkyr yʿly br tymʾ
Access II.2a.5 (printed, CIS)
Corpus CIS 1493

Inscription 2671
Site Wadi Firan, #53
Condition good
Content Nabatean inscription
šlm šʿdʾlhy br bryʾw
Access II.2a.5 (printed, CIS)
Corpus CIS 1494

Inscription 2672
Site Wadi Firan, #53
Condition good
Content Nabatean inscription
šlm ḥryš[w]
br ʿbydw
Access II.2a.5 (printed, CIS)
Corpus CIS 1495

Inscription 2673
Site Wadi Firan, #53
Condition poor
Content Nabatean inscription
šlm pšy br[ʾ]ʿl[ʾ]
Access II.2a.5 (printed, CIS)
Corpus CIS 1496

Inscription 2674
Site Wadi Firan, #53
Condition good
Content Nabatean inscription
šlm ḥwrw br
tymʾlhy
Access II.2a.5 (printed, CIS)
Corpus CIS 1497 (1)

Inscription 2675
Site Wadi Firan, #53
Condition fair
Content Greek inscription
ΑΥΣΑΛΛΑΣ
ΑΥΘΟ ...
Access II.2a.5 (printed, CIS)
Corpus CIS 1497 (2)

Inscription 2676
Site Wadi Firan, #53
Condition fair
Content Nabatean inscription
ʾbn ʾlqy[ny]
Access II.2a.5 (printed, CIS)
Corpus CIS 1498

Inscription 2677
Site Wadi Firan, #53
Condition good
Content Nabatean inscription
šlm wʾlw br
ʿwdw bḥyr
Access II.2a.5 (printed, CIS)
Corpus CIS 1499

Inscription 2678
Site Wadi Firan, Erzein el Gharain, #203
Condition fair
Content Nabatean inscription
šlm ḥgw br ...
Access II.2a.6 (printed, CIS)
Corpus CIS 1500

Inscription 2679
Site Wadi Firan, Erzein el Gharain, #203
Condition fair
Content Nabatean inscription
šlm ʿby
...ydw br
ṣḥbw
Access II.2a.6 (printed, CIS)
Corpus CIS 1501

Inscription 2680
Site Wadi Firan, Erzein el Gharain, #203
Condition poor
Content Nabatean inscription
šlm pšy
.yw..
Access II.2a.6 (printed, CIS)
Corpus CIS 1502

Inscription 2681
Site Wadi Firan, Erzein el Gharain, #203
Condition fair
Content Nabatean inscription
šlm wʾlw br ...
Access II.2a.6 (printed, CIS)
Corpus CIS 1503

Inscription 2682
Site Wadi Firan, Erzein el Gharain, #203
Condition good
Content Nabatean inscription
šlm ʿly ʿlht bṭb
Access II.2a.6 (printed, CIS)
Corpus CIS 1504

Inscription 2683
Site Wadi Firan, Erzein el Gharain, #203
Condition fair
Content Nabatean inscription
...
šlm zydw br
šlm
ḥry[šw]
šlm
Access II.2a.6 (printed, CIS)
Corpus CIS 1505

Inscription 2684
Site Wadi Firan, Erzein el Gharain, #203
Condition poor
Content Nabatean inscription
šlm ṣwbw ...
šlm ... bṭb šlm ḥ...
Access II.2a.6 (printed, CIS)
Corpus CIS 1506

Inscription 2685
Site Wadi Firan, Erzein el Gharain, #203
Condition poor
Content Nabatean inscription
šlm m.
..šw
..šw br
..šw
Access II.2a.6 (printed, CIS)
Corpus CIS 1507

Inscription 2686
Site Wadi Firan, Hesy el Khattatin, #204
Condition good
Content Nabatean inscription
šlm bryʾw
šmrḥ bṭb
Access II.2a.7 (printed, CIS)
Corpus CIS 1508

Inscription 2687
Site Wadi Firan, Hesy el Khattatin, #204
Condition fair
Content Nabatean inscription
ʿmyw br
šlm ʿ.. br ḥryšw
Access II.2a.7 (printed, CIS)
Corpus CIS 1509

Inscription 2688
Site Wadi Firan, Hesy el Khattatin, #204
Condition good
Content Nabatean inscription
šlm ʾlmbqrw
br ʿmrw
Access II.2a.7 (printed, CIS)
Corpus CIS 1510

Inscription 2689
Site Wadi Firan, Hesy el Khattatin, #204
Condition good
Content Nabatean inscription
šlm ʿnmw br p[ṣy]
wpšy brh
Access II.2a.7 (printed, CIS)
Corpus CIS 1511

Inscription 2690
Site Wadi Firan, Hesy el Khattatin, #204
Condition good
Content Nabatean inscription
šlm pʾrn
br ʿbdʾlbʿly bṭb
Access II.2a.7 (printed, CIS)
Corpus CIS 1512

Inscription 2691
Site Wadi Firan, Hesy el Khattatin, #204
Condition fair
Content Nabatean inscription
[ḥnṭ]lw br ....
gʾnyw
Access II.2a.7 (printed, CIS)
Corpus CIS 1513

Inscription 2692
Site Wadi Firan, Hesy el Khattatin, #204
Condition poor
Content Nabatean inscription
šlm ...
... ʿwdw ...
Access II.2a.7 (printed, CIS)
Corpus CIS 1514

Inscription 2693
Site Wadi Firan, Hesy el Khattatin, #204
Condition good
Content Nabatean inscription
šlm ʾwšw
br mbršw
Access II.2a.7 (printed, CIS)
Corpus CIS 1515

Inscription 2694
Site Wadi Firan, El Hesweh, #200
Condition good
Content Nabatean inscription
šlm
šlm z[y]dw
Access II.2a.8 (printed, CIS)
Corpus CIS 1516

Inscription 2695
Site Wadi Firan, El Hesweh, #200
Condition poor
Content Nabatean inscription
[šl]m ʾšw
br [ḥryš]w
Access II.2a.8 (printed, CIS)
Corpus CIS 1517

Inscription 2696
Site Wadi Firan, El Hesweh, #200
Condition poor
Content Nabatean inscription
ʾ... šlm t
ʿbydw br
Access II.2a.8 (printed, CIS)
Corpus CIS 1518

Inscription 2697
Site Wadi Firan, El Hesweh, #200
Condition fair
Content Nabatean inscription
šlm ʿm[yw br] wʾlw
Access II.2a.8 (printed, CIS)
Corpus CIS 1519

Inscription 2698
Site Wadi Firan, El Hesweh, #200
Condition fair
Content Nabatean inscription
šlm šʿdʾlh[y]
br [k]lbw
Access II.2a.8 (printed, CIS)
Corpus CIS 1520

Inscription 2699
Site Wadi Firan, El Hesweh, #200
Condition good
Content Nabatean inscription
dkyr bryʾw
br klbw bṭb
Access II.2a.8 (printed, CIS)
Corpus CIS 1521

Inscription 2700
Site Wadi Firan, El Hesweh, #200
Condition good
Content Nabatean inscription
dkyr ḥlṣšt br [bryʾw]
wbryʾw brh
bṭb wšlm
Access II.2a.8 (printed, CIS)
Corpus CIS 1522

Inscription 2701
Site Wadi Firan, El Hesweh, #200
Condition good
Content Nabatean inscription
whbʾlhy
br wʾlw bṭb
Access II.2a.9 (printed, CIS)
Corpus CIS 1523

Inscription 2702
Site Wadi Firan, El Hesweh, #200
Condition poor
Content Nabatean inscription
...ʾwšw br w ...
Access II.2a.9 (printed, CIS)
Corpus CIS 1524

Inscription 2703
Site Wadi Firan, El Hesweh, #200
Condition good
Content Nabatean inscription
dkyr ʿyṣw br
klbw bṭb
Access II.2a.9 (printed, CIS)
Corpus CIS 1525

Inscription 2704
Site Wadi Firan, El Hesweh, #200
Condition good
Content Nabatean inscription
šlm ʾkbrw br
ḥryšw bṭb
Access II.2a.9 (printed, CIS)
Corpus CIS 1526

Inscription 2705
Site Wadi Firan, El Hesweh, #200
Condition poor
Content Nabatean inscription
šl[m] wkylw
br ʾl.w..
[gby]lw
Access II.2a.9 (printed, CIS)
Corpus CIS 1527

Inscription 2706
Site Wadi Firan, El Hesweh, #200
Condition poor
Content Nabatean inscription
šlm d.. br
ʾwšw ʿbdʾlb[ʿly]
br ʿbdʾ[lhy]
Access II.2a.9 (printed, CIS)
Corpus CIS 1528

Inscription 2707
Site Wadi Firan, El Hesweh, #200
Condition fair
Content Nabatean inscription
šlm pšy br ...
Access II.2a.10 (printed, CIS)
Corpus CIS 1529

Inscription 2708
Site Wadi Firan, El Hesweh, #200
Condition poor
Content Nabatean inscription
dʾbw br
ʾl[zʿblyw]
Access II.2a.10 (printed, CIS)
Corpus CIS 1530

Inscription 2709
Site Wadi Firan, El Hesweh, #200
Condition poor
Content Nabatean inscription
ʾkbrw
Access II.2a.10 (printed, CIS)
Corpus CIS 1531

Inscription 2710
Site Wadi Firan, El Hesweh, #200
Condition fair
Content Nabatean inscription
šlm wʾlw
grmʾl[hy]
Access II.2a.10 (printed, CIS)
Corpus CIS 1532

Inscription 2711
Site Wadi Firan, #53
Condition poor
Content Nabatean inscription
šlm kʿmh
.m .
dkyr . ʾ ...
... šlm
Access II.2a.10 (printed, CIS)
Corpus CIS 1533

Inscription 2712
Site Wadi Firan, #53
Condition good
Content Nabatean inscription
šlm prqw šlm ʿly
Access II.2a.10 (printed, CIS)
Corpus CIS 1534

Inscription 2713
Site Wadi Firan, #53
Condition fair
Content Nabatean inscription
šlm
dʾbw br
p.w
Access II.2a.11 (printed, CIS)
Corpus CIS 1535

Inscription 2714
Site Wadi Firan, #53
Condition fair
Content Nabatean inscription
dʾbw br
ʾlzʿbl
yw
Access II.2a.11 (printed, CIS)
Corpus CIS 1536

Inscription 2715
Site Wadi Firan, #53
Condition fair
Content Nabatean inscription
dkyr ʿlyw
[br] šʿdʾl
hy
Access II.2a.11 (printed, CIS)
Corpus CIS 1537

Inscription 2716
Site Wadi Firan, #53
Condition poor
Content Nabatean inscription
šlm [ʿbd]ʾlʿly
br ʾ...
Access II.2a.11 (printed, CIS)
Corpus CIS 1538

Inscription 2717
Site Wadi Firan, #53
Condition poor
Content Nabatean inscription
ʿ.h. br ʿl...
Access II.2a.11 (printed, CIS)
Corpus CIS 1539

Inscription 2718
Site Wadi Firan, Wadi Umfus, #201
Condition good
Content Nabatean inscription
šlm ʾlmbqrw br ʿwdw
Access II.2a.11 (printed, CIS)
Corpus CIS 1540

Inscription 2719
Site Wadi Firan, Wadi Umfus, #201
Condition good
Content Nabatean inscription
šlm ʾlʾgmw br ḥlṣšt
Access II.2a.11 (printed, CIS)
Corpus CIS 1541

Inscription 2720
Site Wadi Firan, Wadi Umfus, #201
Condition good
Content Nabatean inscription
šlm tymw br ḥlṣšt
Access II.2a.12 (printed, CIS)
Corpus CIS 1542

Inscription 2721
Site Wadi Firan, Wadi Umfus, #201
Condition good
Content Nabatean inscription
šlm pʾrn br yʿly bṭb
Access II.2a.12 (printed, CIS)
Corpus CIS 1543

Inscription 2722
Site Wadi Firan, Wadi Umfus, #201
Condition poor
Content Nabatean inscription
Comment *illegible*
Access II.2a.12 (printed, CIS)
Corpus CIS 1544

Inscription 2723
Site Wadi Firan, Wadi Umfus, #201
Condition fair
Content Nabatean inscription
šlm ktryw [br]
ʿwdw
Access II.2a.12 (printed, CIS)
Corpus CIS 1545

Inscription 2724
Site Wadi Firan, Jebel el Jozeh, #195
Condition good
Content Nabatean inscription
šlm ḥršw
br ʿwdw br ʿmrw
Access II.2a.12 (printed, CIS)
Corpus CIS 1546

Inscription 2725
Site Wadi Firan, Jebel el Jozeh, #195
Condition poor
Content Nabatean inscription
šlm wʾlw b[r] ...
Access II.2a.12 (printed, CIS)
Corpus CIS 1547

Inscription 2726
Site Wadi Firan, Jebel el Jozeh, #195
Condition fair
Content Nabatean inscription
ʿwdw b[r]
ḥršw
Access II.2a.12 (printed, CIS)
Corpus CIS 1548

Inscription 2727
Site Wadi Firan, Jebel el Jozeh, #195
Condition good
Content Nabatean inscription
šlm ṭylh
br wʾlw
bṭb
Access II.2a.12 (printed, CIS)
Corpus CIS 1549

Inscription 2728
Site Wadi Firan, Jebel el Jozeh, #195
Condition fair
Content Nabatean inscription
šlm qrḥw br ...
Access II.2a.13 (printed, CIS)
Corpus CIS 1550

Inscription 2729
Site Wadi Firan, Jebel el Jozeh, #195
Condition fair
Content Nabatean inscription
wrydw
Access II.2a.13 (printed, CIS)
Corpus CIS 1551

Inscription 2730
Site Wadi Firan, Jebel el Jozeh, #195
Condition poor
Content Nabatean inscription
šlm prqw br .
šlm ʾ...
Access II.2a.13 (printed, CIS)
Corpus CIS 1552

Inscription 2731
Site Wadi Firan, Jebel el Jozeh, #195
Condition poor
Content Nabatean inscription
dkyr ʿbd...
Access II.2a.13 (printed, CIS)
Corpus CIS 1553

Inscription 2732
Site Wadi Firan, Jebel el Jozeh, #195
Condition fair
Content Nabatean inscription
.[d]ʾbw bṭb
šlm ʿmyw br
ʿbydw bṭb
Access II.2a.13 (printed, CIS)
Corpus CIS 1554

Inscription 2733
Site Wadi Firan, Jebel el Jozeh, #195
Condition good
Content Nabatean inscription
ʿmrw
br šʿdʾlh bṭb
Access II.2a.13 (printed, CIS)
Corpus CIS 1555

Inscription 2734
Site Wadi Firan, Jebel el Jozeh, #195
Condition fair
Content Nabatean inscription
dkyr w
[šlm] yʿly b[r]
Access II.2a.13 (printed, CIS)
Corpus CIS 1556

Inscription 2735
Site Wadi Firan, Jebel el Jozeh, #195
Condition fair
Content Nabatean inscription
šlm
grmʾlbʿly
br [ḥnṭ]lw
bṭb
Access II.2a.13 (printed, CIS)
Corpus CIS 1557

Inscription 2736
Site Wadi Firan, Jebel el Jozeh, #195
Condition good
Content Nabatean inscription
šlm wʾl[w]
Access II.2a.13 (printed, CIS)
Corpus CIS 1558

Inscription 2737
Site Wadi Firan, Jebel el Jozeh, #195
Condition good
Content Nabatean inscription
šlm ʿmyw br [ʿ]myw
Access II.2a.13 (printed, CIS)
Corpus CIS 1559

Inscription 2738
Site Wadi Firan, Jebel el Jozeh, #195
Condition good
Content Nabatean inscription
dkyr ʿlyw
bṭb
br šʿdʾlhy
bṭb
Access II.2a.14 (printed, CIS)
Corpus CIS 1560

Inscription 2739
Site Wadi Firan, Jebel el Jozeh, #195
Condition good
Content Nabatean inscription
dkyr bṭb wšlm ḥryšw br
ḥršw
Access II.2a.14 (printed, CIS)
Corpus CIS 1561

Inscription 2740
Site Wadi Firan, Jebel el Jozeh, #195
Condition good
Content Nabatean inscription
šlm ʿmrw
br ʿmyw b[ṭb]
Access II.2a.14 (printed, CIS)
Corpus CIS 1562

Inscription 2741
Site Wadi Firan, Jebel el Jozeh, #195
Condition good
Content Nabatean inscription
dkyr ḥryšw br tymʾlhy
Access II.2a.14 (printed, CIS)
Corpus CIS 1563

Inscription 2742
Site Wadi Firan, Jebel el Jozeh, #195
Condition good
Content Nabatean inscription
šlm ʿmmw br ʾbn ʾlqyny
Access II.2a.14 (printed, CIS)
Corpus CIS 1564

Inscription 2743
Site Wadi Firan, Jebel el Jozeh, #195
Condition fair
Content Nabatean inscription
ʿwdw br
[qr]ḥw
Access II.2a.14 (printed, CIS)
Corpus CIS 1565

Inscription 2744
Site Wadi Firan, Jebel el Jozeh, #195
Condition good
Content Nabatean inscription
šlm ʿmmw b[r]
ʾwšw
bṭb
Access II.2a.14 (printed, CIS)
Corpus CIS 1566

Inscription 2745
Site Wadi Firan, Jebel el Jozeh, #195
Condition poor
Content Nabatean inscription
Comment *illegible*
Access II.2a.14 (printed, CIS)
Corpus CIS 1567

Inscription 2746
Site Wadi Firan, Jebel el Jozeh, #195
Condition good
Content Nabatean inscription
šlm
ʿmyw br
[w]ʾlt
Access II.2a.14 (printed, CIS)
Corpus CIS 1568

Inscription 2747
Site Wadi Firan, Jebel el Jozeh, #195
Condition good
Content Nabatean inscription
šlm ʿwdw br wʾlw
[wqr]ḥw
Access II.2a.15 (printed, CIS)
Corpus CIS 1569

Inscription 2748
Site Wadi Firan, Jebel el Jozeh, #195
Condition good
Content Nabatean inscription
dkyr ʾwšʾlhy
br ʾwšw bkl ṭb
Access II.2a.15 (printed, CIS)
Corpus CIS 1570

Inscription **2749**
Site Wadi Firan, Jebel el Jozeh, #195
Condition good
Content Nabatean inscription
dkyr ʿwdw br mʿnw
Access II.2a.15 (printed, CIS)
Corpus CIS 1571

Inscription **2750**
Site Wadi Firan, Jebel el Jozeh, #195
Condition poor
Content Nabatean inscription
šlm .r
šlm nšnk[y]h ...
Access II.2a.15 (printed, CIS)
Corpus CIS 1572

Inscription **2751**
Site Jebel el Benat, #192
Condition fair
Content Nabatean inscription
ʿwdw br qrḥw
Access II.2a.15 (printed, CIS)
Corpus CIS 1573

Inscription **2752**
Site Jebel el Benat, #192
Condition good
Content Nabatean inscription
šl[m] ʿmyw br ʿmmw
Access II.2a.15 (printed, CIS)
Corpus CIS 1574

Inscription **2753**
Site Jebel el Benat, #192
Condition good
Content Nabatean inscription
šlm mʿdw br ʿnmw
Access II.2a.16 (printed, CIS)
Corpus CIS 1575

Inscription **2754**
Site Jebel el Benat, #192
Condition fair
Content Nabatean inscription
šlm grmʾlbʿly
[br ṣ]ʿbw
Access II.2a.16 (printed, CIS)
Corpus CIS 1576

Inscription **2755**
Site Jebel el Benat, #192
Condition fair
Content Nabatean inscription
d[k]yr bṭšw br ʿbydw dy [m]qtr[y]
ʿydw br ḥššw bkl ṭb
Access II.2a.16 (printed, CIS)
Corpus CIS 1577

Inscription **2756**
Site Jebel el Benat, #192
Condition fair
Content Nabatean inscription
d[k]yr grmʾlhy
br ʿbydw...
bṭb
Access II.2a.16 (printed, CIS)
Corpus CIS 1578

Inscription **2757**
Site Jebel el Benat, #192
Condition poor
Content Nabatean inscription
...lw br šlmw
Access II.2a.16 (printed, CIS)
Corpus CIS 1579

Inscription **2758**
Site Jebel el Benat, #192
Condition poor
Content Nabatean inscription
Comment *illegible*
Access II.2a.16 (printed, CIS)
Corpus CIS 1580

Inscription **2759**
Site Jebel el Benat, #192
Condition poor
Content Nabatean inscription
Comment *illegible*
Access II.2a.16 (printed, CIS)
Corpus CIS 1581

Inscription **2760**
Site Jebel el Benat, #192
Condition good
Content Nabatean inscription
šlm ʿbdʾlbʿly
Access II.2a.16 (printed, CIS)
Corpus CIS 1582

Inscription **2761**
Site Jebel el Benat, #192
Condition fair
Content Nabatean inscription
[ʿ]yṣw br
ʿbdʾlbʿly
Access II.2a.16 (printed, CIS)
Corpus CIS 1583

Inscription **2762**
Site Jebel el Benat, #192
Condition poor
Content Nabatean inscription
.šrpyw
[br ʿrby]w
Access II.2a.16 (printed, CIS)
Corpus CIS 1584

Inscription 2763
Site Jebel el Benat, #192
Condition good
Content Nabatean inscription
šlm ʾwšʾlhy
br ʿmyw
Access II.2a.17 (printed, CIS)
Corpus CIS 1585

Inscription 2764
Site Jebel el Benat, #192
Condition good
Content Nabatean inscription
šlm mlyḥw br ʾšwdw
Access II.2a.17 (printed, CIS)
Corpus CIS 1586

Inscription 2765
Site Jebel el Benat, #192
Condition good
Content Nabatean inscription
šlm ʿbdʾlbʿly br
klbw bṭb
Access II.2a.17 (printed, CIS)
Corpus CIS 1587

Inscription 2766
Site Jebel el Benat, #192
Condition good
Content Nabatean inscription
šlm ʿbdʾbʿly
br ʿbdʾlhy
bṭb
Access II.2a.17 (printed, CIS)
Corpus CIS 1588

Inscription 2767
Site Jebel el Benat, #192
Condition good
Content Nabatean inscription
ḥlṣšt br
ʾʿllʾ šlm
Access II.2a.17 (printed, CIS)
Corpus CIS 1589

Inscription 2768
Site Jebel el Benat, #192
Condition fair
Content Nabatean inscription
šlm ʿmrw br
ʿbdw w ....
Access II.2a.17 (printed, CIS)
Corpus CIS 1590

Inscription 2769
Site Jebel el Benat, #192
Condition good
Content Nabatean inscription
šlm ḥryšw br
ḥršw
Access II.2a.17 (printed, CIS)
Corpus CIS 1591

Inscription 2770
Site Jebel el Benat, #192
Condition good
Content Nabatean inscription
šlm ʾlkyw br ḥryšw
Access II.2a.17 (printed, CIS)
Corpus CIS 1592

Inscription 2771
Site Jebel el Benat, #192
Condition fair
Content Nabatean inscription
šlm ḥlṣw
br ʾ.pw...
Access II.2a.17 (printed, CIS)
Corpus CIS 1593

Inscription 2772
Site Jebel el Benat, #192
Condition good
Content Nabatean inscription
ʿbdʾl[b]ʿly
br ḥryšw
dkyr bṭb
Access II.2a.17 (printed, CIS)
Corpus CIS 1594

Inscription 2773
Site Jebel el Benat, #192
Condition good
Content Nabatean inscription
šlm šlmw br m[ʿy]rw
Access II.2a.18 (printed, CIS)
Corpus CIS 1595

Inscription 2774
Site Jebel el Benat, #192
Condition poor
Content Nabatean inscription
šlm ʾwšw
br ʾš...
Access II.2a.18 (printed, CIS)
Corpus CIS 1596

Inscription 2775
Site Jebel el Benat, #192
Condition fair
Content Nabatean inscription
ṣʿbw br
šmrḥ
Access II.2a.18 (printed, CIS)
Corpus CIS 1597

Inscription 2776
Site Jebel el Benat, #192
Condition good
Content Nabatean inscription
šlm ṭylh
br wʾlw
Access II.2a.18 (printed, CIS)
Corpus CIS 1598

Inscription 2777
Site Jebel el Benat, #192
Condition good
Content Nabatean inscription
šlm mgdyw
br tymw
Access II.2a.18 (printed, CIS)
Corpus CIS 1599

Inscription 2778
Site Jebel el Benat, #192
Condition good
Content Nabatean inscription
šlm ʾwšw br ḥnṭlw
Access II.2a.18 (printed, CIS)
Corpus CIS 1600

Inscription 2779
Site Jebel el Benat, #192
Condition fair
Content Nabatean inscription
dkyr ʾl.ʿw
br ʿlht
Access II.2a.18 (printed, CIS)
Corpus CIS 1601

Inscription 2780
Site Jebel el Benat, #192
Condition good
Content Nabatean inscription
šlm bryʾw
[br] mgdyw
Access II.2a.18 (printed, CIS)
Corpus CIS 1602

Inscription 2781
Site Jebel el Benat, #192
Condition good
Content Nabatean inscription
šlm ʿbdʾlhy
br bryʾw
Access II.2a.18 (printed, CIS)
Corpus CIS 1603

Inscription 2782
Site Jebel el Benat, #192
Condition good
Content Nabatean inscription
šlm wʾlw br šʿwdt
Access II.2a.18 (printed, CIS)
Corpus CIS 1604

Inscription 2783
Site Jebel el Benat, #192
Condition fair
Content Nabatean inscription
šlm ḥry[šw]
Access II.2a.19 (printed, CIS)
Corpus CIS 1605

Inscription 2784
Site Jebel el Benat, #192
Condition fair
Content Nabatean inscription
ʿwdw b[r]
šʿdʾl[h]y
Access II.2a.19 (printed, CIS)
Corpus CIS 1606

Inscription 2785
Site Jebel el Benat, #192
Condition poor
Content Nabatean inscription
šlm š...w br zydw
Access II.2a.19 (printed, CIS)
Corpus CIS 1607

Inscription 2786
Site Jebel el Benat, #192
Condition good
Content Nabatean inscription
šlm ḥršw br
ʾwšw
Access II.2a.19 (printed, CIS)
Corpus CIS 1608

Inscription 2787
Site Jebel el Benat, #192
Condition good
Content Nabatean inscription
šlm kwšlw br klbw
Access II.2a.19 (printed, CIS)
Corpus CIS 1609

Inscription 2788
Site Jebel el Benat, #192
Condition good
Content Nabatean inscription
dkyr yʿly br tymʾlhy
Access II.2a.19 (printed, CIS)
Corpus CIS 1610

Inscription 2789
Site Jebel el Benat, #192
Condition good
Content Nabatean inscription
šlm šmrḥ br klbw
Access II.2a.19 (printed, CIS)
Corpus CIS 1611

Inscription 2790
Site Jebel el Benat, #192
Condition good
Content Nabatean inscription
šlm ʿbdʾlbʿly br
ʿmyw [byt]yʾ
Access II.2a.19 (printed, CIS)
Corpus CIS 1612

Inscription 2791
Site Jebel el Benat, #192
Condition poor
Content Nabatean inscription
ʾlmbqrw
Access II.2a.19 (printed, CIS)
Corpus CIS 1613

Inscription 2792
Site Jebel el Benat, #192
Condition poor
Content Nabatean inscription
šlm
.nw br mʾw
Access II.2a.19 (printed, CIS)
Corpus CIS 1614

Inscription 2793
Site Jebel el Benat, #192
Condition poor
Content Nabatean inscription
ʿbdw
šl[m] š.ʾ ..
Access II.2a.20 (printed, CIS)
Corpus CIS 1615

Inscription 2794
Site Jebel el Benat, #192
Condition good
Content Nabatean inscription
šlm bryʾw br
klbw
Access II.2a.20 (printed, CIS)
Corpus CIS 1616

Inscription 2795
Site Jebel el Benat, #192
Condition poor
Content Nabatean inscription
šlm [grmʾlb]ʿl[y] br
[ʾbn] ʾl[qy]ny
Access II.2a.20 (printed, CIS)
Corpus CIS 1617

Inscription 2796
Site Jebel el Benat, #192
Condition good
Content Nabatean inscription
šlm wʾlw br
mgdyw
Access II.2a.20 (printed, CIS)
Corpus CIS 1618

Inscription 2797
Site Jebel el Benat, #192
Condition good
Content Nabatean inscription
šlm wʾlw br
ʾwyšw bṭb
Access II.2a.20 (printed, CIS)
Corpus CIS 1619

Inscription 2798
Site Jebel el Benat, #192
Condition good
Content Nabatean inscription
šlm
wʾlw br mgdyw
Access II.2a.20 (printed, CIS)
Corpus CIS 1620

Inscription 2799
Site Jebel el Benat, #192
Condition good
Content Nabatean inscription
šlm ʾbn ʾlqyny br ʿmrw
Access II.2a.20 (printed, CIS)
Corpus CIS 1621

Inscription 2800
Site Jebel el Benat, #192
Condition good
Content Nabatean inscription
šlm ḥršw br
ʾwšʾlhy bṭb
Access II.2a.20 (printed, CIS)
Corpus CIS 1622

Inscription 2801
Site Jebel el Benat, #192
Condition good
Content Nabatean inscription
šlm grymw br ḥršw
Access II.2a.20 (printed, CIS)
Corpus CIS 1623

Inscription **2802**
Site Jebel el Benat, #192
Condition good
Content Nabatean inscription
šlm ʾlmbqrw br wʾlw
Access II.2a.20 (printed, CIS)
Corpus CIS 1624

Inscription **2803**
Site Jebel el Benat, #192
Condition good
Content Nabatean inscription
šlm bryʾw br wʾlw
Access II.2a.21 (printed, CIS)
Corpus CIS 1625

Inscription **2804**
Site Jebel el Benat, #192
Condition good
Content Nabatean inscription
šlm wdʿw br ʾwyšw
ʾkbrw
Access II.2a.21 (printed, CIS)
Corpus CIS 1626

Inscription **2805**
Site Jebel el Benat, #192
Condition good
Content Nabatean inscription
šlm wʾlw ʾḥwhw
Access II.2a.21 (printed, CIS)
Corpus CIS 1627

Inscription **2806**
Site Jebel el Benat, #192
Condition poor
Content Nabatean inscription
šlm [ʿ]ydw br h...
Access II.2a.21 (printed, CIS)
Corpus CIS 1628

Inscription **2807**
Site Jebel el Benat, #192
Condition good
Content Nabatean inscription
šlm bryʾw
br mgdyw bṭb
Access II.2a.21 (printed, CIS)
Corpus CIS 1629

Inscription **2808**
Site Jebel el Benat, #192
Condition poor
Content Nabatean inscription
šlm šʿ...
Access II.2a.21 (printed, CIS)
Corpus CIS 1630

Inscription **2809**
Site Jebel el Benat, #192
Condition good
Content Nabatean inscription
šlm
wšw br
grmʾlb
ʿly
ḥyr bṭb
Access II.2a.21 (printed, CIS)
Corpus CIS 1631

Inscription **2810**
Site Jebel el Benat, #192
Condition good
Content Nabatean inscription
šlm ʿmnw br yʿly
Access II.2a.21 (printed, CIS)
Corpus CIS 1632

Inscription **2811**
Site Jebel el Benat, #192
Condition good
Content Nabatean inscription
šlm ʾwšw br ʿbdʾlbʿly šlm
Access II.2a.21 (printed, CIS)
Corpus CIS 1633

Inscription **2812**
Site Jebel el Benat, #192
Condition fair
Content Nabatean inscription
šlm grmʾl[bʿly]
Access II.2a.22 (printed, CIS)
Corpus CIS 1634

Inscription **2813**
Site Jebel el Benat, #192
Condition good
Content Nabatean inscription
šlm ḥryšw br ʿbdʾlbʿly
br wdw
Access II.2a.22 (printed, CIS)
Corpus CIS 1635

Inscription **2814**
Site Jebel el Benat, #192
Condition fair
Content Nabatean inscription
šlm wdʿw br ...
Access II.2a.22 (printed, CIS)
Corpus CIS 1636

Inscription 2815
Site Jebel el Benat, #192
Condition good
Content Nabatean inscription
šlm ʿlyt
br tpṣ[ʾ]
Access II.2a.22 (printed, CIS)
Corpus CIS 1637

Inscription 2816
Site Jebel el Benat, #192
Condition good
Content Nabatean inscription
šlm ḥlṣšt br
mʿnw
Access II.2a.22 (printed, CIS)
Corpus CIS 1638

Inscription 2817
Site Jebel el Benat, #192
Condition good
Content Nabatean inscription
šlm bryʾw br klbw
Access II.2a.22 (printed, CIS)
Corpus CIS 1639

Inscription 2818
Site Jebel el Benat, #192
Condition good
Content Nabatean inscription
ʿbdlbʿl[y]
br ʾwšw
Access II.2a.22 (printed, CIS)
Corpus CIS 1640

Inscription 2819
Site Jebel el Benat, #192
Condition poor
Content Nabatean inscription
dkyr wh[bʾlhy]
Access II.2a.22 (printed, CIS)
Corpus CIS 1641

Inscription 2820
Site Jebel el Benat, #192
Condition poor
Content Nabatean inscription
.... br ʾwšʾlhy
Access II.2a.22 (printed, CIS)
Corpus CIS 1642

Inscription 2821
Site Jebel el Benat, #192
Condition good
Content Nabatean inscription
šlm ḥryšw
br ʿmyw
Access II.2a.22 (printed, CIS)
Corpus CIS 1643

Inscription 2822
Site Jebel Sirbal, Wadi Ajaleh, #188
Condition fair
Content Nabatean inscription
šlm ʿbdʾlbʿl[y]
br ʿw[dw bṭb]
Access II.2a.23 (printed, CIS)
Corpus CIS 1644

Inscription 2823
Site Jebel Sirbal, Wadi Ajaleh, #188
Condition good
Content Nabatean inscription
šlm ʿmrt br ḥnṭlw
Access II.2a.23 (printed, CIS)
Corpus CIS 1645

Inscription 2824
Site Jebel Sirbal, Wadi Ajaleh, #188
Condition good
Content Nabatean inscription
šlm šlmw br ʿbdʾlbʿly
Access II.2a.23 (printed, CIS)
Corpus CIS 1646

Inscription 2825
Site Jebel Sirbal, Wadi Ajaleh, #188
Condition poor
Content Nabatean inscription
šlm ...swr
...wr
Access II.2a.23 (printed, CIS)
Corpus CIS 1647

Inscription 2826
Site Jebel Sirbal, Wadi Ajaleh, #188
Condition good
Content Nabatean inscription
šlm wʾlw br ḥlṣšt
Access II.2a.23 (printed, CIS)
Corpus CIS 1648

Inscription 2827
Site Jebel Sirbal, Wadi Ajaleh, #188
Condition good
Content Nabatean inscription
šlm ḥlṣšt br
wʾlw bṭb
Access II.2a.23 (printed, CIS)
Corpus CIS 1649

Inscription 2828
Site Jebel Sirbal, Wadi Ajaleh, #188
Condition poor
Content Nabatean inscription
šlm ʿmrw...
šlm ḥršw br
Access II.2a.24 (printed, CIS)
Corpus CIS 1650

Inscription 2829
Site Jebel Sirbal, Wadi Ajaleh, #188
Condition good
Content Nabatean inscription
šlm [m]ʿdw
Access II.2a.24 (printed, CIS)
Corpus CIS 1651

Inscription 2830
Site Jebel Sirbal, Wadi Ajaleh, #188
Condition poor
Content Nabatean inscription
Comment *fragment*
Access II.2a.24 (printed, CIS)
Corpus CIS 1652

Inscription 2831
Site Jebel Sirbal, Wadi Ajaleh, #188
Condition poor
Content Nabatean inscription
šlm wʾ[lw]
šlm ʿbd...
Access II.2a.24 (printed, CIS)
Corpus CIS 1653

Inscription 2832
Site Jebel Sirbal, Wadi Ajaleh, #188
Condition fair
Content Nabatean inscription
šlm mʿnw br h[nʾw]
Access II.2a.24 (printed, CIS)
Corpus CIS 1654

Inscription 2833
Site Jebel Sirbal, Wadi Ajaleh, #188
Condition good
Content Nabatean inscription
šlm wʾlw br bryʾw bṯb
Access II.2a.24 (printed, CIS)
Corpus CIS 1655

Inscription 2834
Site Jebel Sirbal, Wadi Ajaleh, #188
Condition fair
Content Nabatean inscription
šlm ʾwšʾlhy
br [n]š[gw]
Access II.2a.24 (printed, CIS)
Corpus CIS 1656

Inscription 2835
Site Jebel Sirbal, Wadi Ajaleh, #188
Condition poor
Content Nabatean inscription
šlm ʿmr[w]...
...ly
Access II.2a.24 (printed, CIS)
Corpus CIS 1657

Inscription 2836
Site Jebel Sirbal, Wadi Ajaleh, #188
Condition fair
Content Nabatean inscription
ʿbydw br
[ʿ]myw
Access II.2a.24 (printed, CIS)
Corpus CIS 1658

Inscription 2837
Site Jebel Sirbal, Wadi Ajaleh, #188
Condition good
Content Nabatean inscription
šlm ḥlṣšt br
ḥlṣšt
Access II.2a.24 (printed, CIS)
Corpus CIS 1659

Inscription 2838
Site Jebel Sirbal, Wadi Ajaleh, #188
Condition good
Content Nabatean inscription
šlm ʿbdʾlb[ʿly]
Access II.2a.24 (printed, CIS)
Corpus CIS 1660

Inscription 2839
Site Jebel Sirbal, Wadi Ajaleh, #188
Condition poor
Content Nabatean inscription
šlm ʾlktyw
br ... ʾ...
Access II.2a.25 (printed, CIS)
Corpus CIS 1661

Inscription 2840
Site Jebel Sirbal, Wadi Ajaleh, #188
Condition good
Content Nabatean inscription
šlm gdyw br
wʾlw
Access II.2a.25 (printed, CIS)
Corpus CIS 1662

Inscription 2841
Site Jebel Sirbal, Wadi Ajaleh, #188
Condition good
Content Nabatean inscription
šlm srpyw br
ʿrbyw
Access II.2a.25 (printed, CIS)
Corpus CIS 1663

Inscription 2842
Site Jebel Sirbal, Wadi Ajaleh, #188
Condition good
Content Nabatean inscription
šlm
kʿmh
br wʾ[l]w
Access II.2a.25 (printed, CIS)
Corpus CIS 1664

Inscription 2843
Site Jebel Sirbal, Wadi Ajaleh, #188
Condition good
Content Nabatean inscription
šlm ḥ ršw br
ḥgyrw
bṭb wšlm
Access II.2a.25 (printed, CIS)
Corpus CIS 1665

Inscription 2844
Site Jebel Sirbal, Wadi Ajaleh, #188
Condition good
Content Nabatean inscription
šlm ʿbdʾlbʿly br klbw
Access II.2a.25 (printed, CIS)
Corpus CIS 1666

Inscription 2845
Site Jebel Sirbal, Wadi Ajaleh, #188
Condition good
Content Nabatean inscription
šlm ʾlktyw br ʿbdʾlbʿly
Access II.2a.25 (printed, CIS)
Corpus CIS 1667

Inscription 2846
Site Jebel Sirbal, Wadi Ajaleh, #188
Condition poor
Content Nabatean inscription
šlm ʿmrw
br ....
Access II.2a.25 (printed, CIS)
Corpus CIS 1668

Inscription 2847
Site Jebel Sirbal, Wadi Ajaleh, #188
Condition fair
Content Nabatean inscription
šlm ....yw br wʾlw
Access II.2a.26 (printed, CIS)
Corpus CIS 1669

Inscription 2848
Site Jebel Sirbal, Wadi Ajaleh, #188
Condition fair
Content Nabatean inscription
ʿmrw br wʾlw
Access II.2a.26 (printed, CIS)
Corpus CIS 1670

Inscription 2849
Site Jebel Sirbal, Wadi Ajaleh, #188
Condition fair
Content Nabatean inscription
šlm ʿmrw br ...
Access II.2a.26 (printed, CIS)
Corpus CIS 1671

Inscription 2850
Site Jebel Sirbal, Wadi Ajaleh, #188
Condition good
Content Nabatean inscription
[š]lm ṣwbw br ʾtmw
Access II.2a.26 (printed, CIS)
Corpus CIS 1672

Inscription 2851
Site Jebel Sirbal, Wadi Ajaleh, #188
Condition good
Content Nabatean inscription
šlm ʿbdw br
[w]ʾlw
Access II.2a.26 (printed, CIS)
Corpus CIS 1673

Inscription 2852
Site Jebel Sirbal, Wadi Ajaleh, #188
Condition fair
Content Nabatean inscription
šlm ʾš... br
ʿmyw
Access II.2a.26 (printed, CIS)
Corpus CIS 1674

Inscription 2853
Site Jebel Sirbal, Wadi Ajaleh, #188
Condition good
Content Nabatean inscription
šlm wʾlw
br šmrḥ
Access II.2a.26 (printed, CIS)
Corpus CIS 1675

Inscription 2854
Site Jebel Sirbal, Wadi Ajaleh, #188
Condition poor
Content Nabatean inscription
Comment *illegible fragment*
Access II.2a.26 (printed, CIS)
Corpus CIS 1676

Inscription 2855
Site Jebel Sirbal, Wadi Ajaleh, #188
Condition good
Content Nabatean inscription
šlm wʾlw b[r]
šʿdʾlhy
Access II.2a.26 (printed, CIS)
Corpus CIS 1677

Inscription 2856
Site Jebel Sirbal, Wadi Ajaleh, #188
Condition good
Content Nabatean inscription
šlm ʿwdw br
z[yd]w
Access II.2a.26 (printed, CIS)
Corpus CIS 1678

Inscription 2857
Site Jebel Sirbal, Wadi Ajaleh, #188
Condition good
Content Nabatean inscription
šʿdʾlhy
br bryʾw
Access II.2a.26 (printed, CIS)
Corpus CIS 1679

Inscription 2858
Site Jebel Sirbal, Wadi Ajaleh, #188
Condition good
Content Nabatean inscription
šlm ʿwdw br klbw
Access II.2a.26 (printed, CIS)
Corpus CIS 1680

Inscription 2859
Site Wadi Haggag, rock 1, #160
Technique incised
Condition poor
Content unidentified inscription
Access Negev 1977 fig. 3 (printed, A. Negev)

Inscription 2860
Site Wadi Haggag, rock 1, #160
Technique incised
Condition fair
Content rock drawing
Comment *animal with rider*
Access Negev 1977 fig. 3 (printed, A. Negev)

Inscription 2861
Site Wadi Haggag, rock 1, #160
Technique incised
Condition poor
Content Greek inscription
Limitation *Tentative decipherment only*
Access Negev 1977 fig. 4 (printed, A. Negev)

Inscription 2862
Site Wadi Haggag, rock 1, #160
Technique incised
Condition poor
Content crosses with inscription
Access Negev 1977 fig. 4 (printed, A. Negev)

Inscription 2863
Site Wadi Haggag, rock 1, #160
Technique incised
Condition poor
Content rock drawing
Comment *ibexes*
Access Negev 1977 fig. 4 (printed, A. Negev)

Inscription 2864
Site Wadi Haggag, rock 1, #160
Technique incised
Condition poor
Content varied crosses
Access Negev 1977 fig. 4 (printed, A. Negev)

Inscription 2865
Site Wadi Haggag, rock 1, #160
Technique scratched
Condition poor
Content unidentified inscription
Comment *illegible*
Access Negev 1977 fig. 4 (printed, A. Negev)

Inscription 2866
Site Wadi Haggag, rock 1, #160
Technique scratched
Condition poor
Content Arabic inscription
Limitation *Tentative decipherment only*
Access Negev 1977 fig. 7 (printed, A. Negev)

Inscription 2867
Site Wadi Haggag, rock 1, #160
Technique incised
Condition poor
Content Greek inscription
Limitation *Tentative decipherment only*
Access Negev 1977 fig. 8 (printed, A. Negev)

Inscription 2868
Site Wadi Haggag, rock 1, #160
Technique incised
Condition poor
Content rock drawing
Comment *ibex*
Access Negev 1977 fig. 8 (printed, A. Negev)

Inscription 2869
Site Wadi Haggag, rock 1, #160
Technique incised
Condition poor
Content Arabic inscription
Limitation *Tentative decipherment only*
Access Negev 1977 fig. 9 (printed, A. Negev)

Inscription 2870
Site Wadi Haggag, rock 1, #160
Technique incised
Condition good
Content rock drawing
Comment *ibexes*
Access Negev 1977 fig. 9 (printed, A. Negev)

Inscription 2871
Site Wadi Haggag, rock 1, #160
Technique incised
Condition good
Content rock drawing
Comment *ibexes and camels*
Access Negev 1977 fig. 10 (printed, A. Negev)

Inscription **2872**
Site Wadi Haggag, rock 1, #160
Technique incised
Condition poor
Content rock drawing
Comment *ibexes*
Access Negev 1977 fig. 11 (printed, A. Negev)

Inscription **2873**
Site Wadi Haggag, rock 2, #119
Technique incised
Condition fair
Content crosses alone
Access Negev 1977 fig. 21 (printed, A. Negev)

Inscription **2874**
Site Wadi Haggag, rock 2, #119
Technique incised
Condition poor
Content unidentified signs
Access Negev 1977 fig. 21 (printed, A. Negev)

Inscription **2875**
Site Wadi Haggag, rock 2, #119
Technique incised
Condition poor
Content Greek inscription
Limitation *Tentative decipherment only*
Access Negev 1977 fig. 21 (printed, A. Negev)

Inscription **2876**
Site Wadi Haggag, rock 2, #119
Technique incised
Condition poor
Content unidentified inscription
Access Negev 1977 fig. 21 (printed, A. Negev)

Inscription **2877**
Site Wadi Haggag, rock 2, #119
Technique incised
Condition good
Content crosses alone
Access Negev 1977 fig. 22 (printed, A. Negev)

Inscription **2878**
Site Wadi Haggag, rock 2, #119
Technique incised
Condition fair
Content encircled crosses
Access Negev 1977 fig. 22 (printed, A. Negev)

Inscription **2879**
Site Wadi Haggag, rock 2, #119
Technique incised
Condition good
Content crosses with inscription
Access Negev 1977 fig. 24 (printed, A. Negev)

Inscription **2880**
Site Wadi Haggag, rock 2, #119
Technique incised
Condition fair
Content Arabic inscription
Limitation *Tentative decipherment only*
Access Negev 1977 fig. 38 (printed, A. Negev)

Inscription **2881**
Site Wadi Haggag, rock 2, #119
Technique incised
Condition good
Content rock drawing
Comment *ibex*
Access Negev 1977 fig. 39 (printed, A. Negev)

Inscription **2882**
Site Wadi Haggag, rock 2, #119
Technique incised
Condition good
Content crosses with inscription
Access Negev 1977 fig. 41 (printed, A. Negev)

Inscription **2883**
Site Wadi Haggag, rock 2, #119
Technique incised
Condition poor
Content rock drawing
Comment *two loops attached to a line*
Access Negev 1977 fig. 43 (printed, A. Negev)

Inscription **2884**
Site Wadi Haggag, rock 3 area 1, #126
Technique incised
Condition poor
Content Greek inscription
Limitation *Tentative decipherment only*
Access Negev 1977 fig. 56 (printed, A. Negev)

Inscription **2885**
Site Wadi Haggag, rock 3, #125
Technique incised
Condition good
Content crosses alone
Access Negev 1977 fig. 144 (printed, A. Negev)

Inscription **2886**
Site Wadi Haggag, rock 3, #125
Technique scratched
Condition poor
Content unidentified signs
Access Negev 1977 fig. 146 (printed, A. Negev)

Inscription **2887**
Site Jebel Sirbal, Wadi Ajaleh, #188
Condition good
Content Nabatean inscription
šlm klbw br wʾlw
Access II.2a.27 (printed, CIS)
Corpus CIS 1681

Inscription **2888**
Site Jebel Sirbal, Wadi Ajaleh, #188
Condition good
Content Nabatean inscription
šlm ʾlktyw br ʿbdʾlbʿly
Access II.2a.27 (printed, CIS)
Corpus CIS 1682

Inscription 2889
Site Jebel Sirbal, Wadi Ajaleh, #188
Condition good
Content Nabatean inscription
dkyr ʿlyw
br šʿdʾlhy
Access II.2a.27 (printed, CIS)
Corpus CIS 1683

Inscription 2890
Site Jebel Sirbal, Wadi Ajaleh, #188
Condition poor
Content Nabatean inscription
.... br ʾ...
šlm ḥb[rkn] br ...
Access II.2a.27 (printed, CIS)
Corpus CIS 1684

Inscription 2891
Site Jebel Sirbal, Wadi Ajaleh, #188
Condition good
Content Nabatean inscription
šlm ḥršw br ʿmrw
Access II.2a.27 (printed, CIS)
Corpus CIS 1685

Inscription 2892
Site Jebel Sirbal, Wadi Ajaleh, #188
Condition good
Content Nabatean inscription
šlm klbw br zydw bṭb
Access II.2a.27 (printed, CIS)
Corpus CIS 1686

Inscription 2893
Site Jebel Sirbal, Wadi Ajaleh, #188
Condition good
Content Nabatean inscription
šlm ʾwšw
br zydw
Access II.2a.27 (printed, CIS)
Corpus CIS 1687

Inscription 2894
Site Jebel Sirbal, Wadi Ajaleh, #188
Condition good
Content Nabatean inscription
šlm wʾlw br
ʿwdw
Access II.2a.27 (printed, CIS)
Corpus CIS 1688

Inscription 2895
Site Jebel Sirbal, Wadi Ajaleh, #188
Condition fair
Content Nabatean inscription
šlm wʾ šlm
sw b...
Access II.2a.27 (printed, CIS)
Corpus CIS 1689

Inscription 2896
Site Jebel Sirbal, Wadi Ajaleh, #188
Condition good
Content Nabatean inscription
šlm ʿwdw
bṭb
br wʾlw
bṭb
Access II.2a.28 (printed, CIS)
Corpus CIS 1690

Inscription 2897
Site Jebel Sirbal, Wadi Ajaleh, #188
Condition good
Content Nabatean inscription
šlm ʾlmb
qrw br zydw
Access II.2a.28 (printed, CIS)
Corpus CIS 1691

Inscription 2898
Site Jebel Sirbal, Wadi Ajaleh, #188
Condition good
Content Nabatean inscription
š[l]m dʾbw br ḥršw
ʿbdʾ[l]hy
Access II.2a.28 (printed, CIS)
Corpus CIS 1692

Inscription 2899
Site Jebel Sirbal, Wadi Ajaleh, #188
Condition good
Content Nabatean inscription
šlm zydw br wʾlw
Access II.2a.28 (printed, CIS)
Corpus CIS 1693

Inscription 2900
Site Jebel Sirbal, Wadi Ajaleh, #188
Condition fair
Content Nabatean inscription
šlm zydw br y...
Access II.2a.28 (printed, CIS)
Corpus CIS 1694

Inscription 2901
Site Jebel Sirbal, Wadi Ajaleh, #188
Condition good
Content Nabatean inscription
dkyr ʿlyw
br šʿdʾlhy
Access II.2a.28 (printed, CIS)
Corpus CIS 1695

Inscription 2902
Site Jebel Sirbal, Wadi Ajaleh, #188
Condition fair
Content Nabatean inscription
qynw
bryk
Access II.2a.28 (printed, CIS)
Corpus CIS 1696

Inscription 2903
Site Jebel Sirbal, Wadi Ajaleh, #188
Condition good
Content Nabatean inscription
šlm bryʾw
[br] ʿbdʾlbʿly
Access II.2a.28 (printed, CIS)
Corpus CIS 1697

Inscription 2904
Site Jebel Sirbal, Wadi Ajaleh, #188
Condition good
Content Nabatean inscription
šlm ʿbdʾlbʿl[y]
Access II.2a.28 (printed, CIS)
Corpus CIS 1698

Inscription 2905
Site Jebel Sirbal, Wadi Ajaleh, #188
Condition fair
Content Nabatean inscription
šlm ... br klbw
Access II.2a.28 (printed, CIS)
Corpus CIS 1699

Inscription 2906
Site Jebel Sirbal, Wadi Ajaleh, #188
Condition good
Content Nabatean inscription
šlm dʾbw br
ʿmyw
Access II.2a.29 (printed, CIS)
Corpus CIS 1700

Inscription 2907
Site Jebel Sirbal, Wadi Ajaleh, #188
Condition good
Content Nabatean inscription
šlm ḥršw
br ḥgyrw
Access II.2a.29 (printed, CIS)
Corpus CIS 1701

Inscription 2908
Site Jebel Sirbal, Wadi Ajaleh, #188
Condition good
Content Nabatean inscription
šlm ʾwšw br
zydw šlm
Access II.2a.29 (printed, CIS)
Corpus CIS 1702

Inscription 2909
Site Jebel Sirbal, Wadi Ajaleh, #188
Condition fair
Content Nabatean inscription
šlm grm...
Access II.2a.29 (printed, CIS)
Corpus CIS 1703

Inscription 2910
Site Jebel Sirbal, Wadi Ajaleh, #188
Condition fair
Content Nabatean inscription
šlm mgdyw [br]
wʾlw
Access II.2a.29 (printed, CIS)
Corpus CIS 1704

Inscription 2911
Site Jebel Sirbal, Wadi Ajaleh, #188
Condition good
Content Nabatean inscription
šlm mʿynw br
ḥry ḥnṭlw
bṭb
Access II.2a.29 (printed, CIS)
Corpus CIS 1705

Inscription 2912
Site Jebel Sirbal, Wadi Ajaleh, #188
Condition fair
Content Nabatean inscription
šlm ʿb[yd]w br
mḥmyw [b]ṭ[b]
Access II.2a.29 (printed, CIS)
Corpus CIS 1706

Inscription 2913
Site Jebel Sirbal, Wadi Ajaleh, #188
Condition good
Content Nabatean inscription
ʿbdʾlbʿly
Access II.2a.29 (printed, CIS)
Corpus CIS 1707

Inscription 2914
Site Jebel Sirbal, Wadi Ajaleh, #188
Condition good
Content Nabatean inscription
šlm šlmw br ʿbdʾlbʿl[y]
Access II.2a.29 (printed, CIS)
Corpus CIS 1708

Inscription 2915
Site Jebel Sirbal, Wadi Ajaleh, #188
Condition poor
Content Nabatean inscription
w... dkyr ḥryšw br ʿmyw b[ṭb]
[d]k[y]r nš[ygw br] ʿmyw
Access II.2a.29 (printed, CIS)
Corpus CIS 1709

Inscription 2916
Site Jebel Sirbal, Wadi Ajaleh, #188
Condition fair
Content Nabatean inscription
šlm klb[w]
br zydw b[ṭb]
Access II.2a.30 (printed, CIS)
Corpus CIS 1710

Inscription 2917
Site Jebel Sirbal, Wadi Ajaleh, #188
Condition fair
Content Nabatean inscription
šlm zydw [br]
ʾ[w]šw m[d]šw
Access II.2a.30 (printed, CIS)
Corpus CIS 1711

Inscription 2918
Site Jebel Sirbal, Wadi Ajaleh, #188
Condition good
Content Nabatean inscription
šlm tymʾlhy
br wdw
Access II.2a.30 (printed, CIS)
Corpus CIS 1712

Inscription 2919
Site Jebel Sirbal, Wadi Ajaleh, #188
Condition good
Content Nabatean inscription
šlm tymʾlhy br
zydw
Access II.2a.30 (printed, CIS)
Corpus CIS 1713

Inscription 2920
Site Jebel Sirbal, Wadi Ajaleh, #188
Condition fair
Content Nabatean inscription
šlm ʿbdʾlbʿly br
ḥ...
Access II.2a.30 (printed, CIS)
Corpus CIS 1714

Inscription 2921
Site Jebel Sirbal, Wadi Ajaleh, #188
Condition good
Content Nabatean inscription
šlm ʿwdw
br wʾlw
Access II.2a.30 (printed, CIS)
Corpus CIS 1715

Inscription 2922
Site Jebel Sirbal, Wadi Ajaleh, #188
Condition good
Content Nabatean inscription
šlm mʿnw br
hnʾw bṭ[b]
Access II.2a.30 (printed, CIS)
Corpus CIS 1716

Inscription 2923
Site Jebel Sirbal, Wadi Ajaleh, #188
Condition good
Content Nabatean inscription
šlm šʿdʾlhy br
h[nyʾw]
Access II.2a.30 (printed, CIS)
Corpus CIS 1717

Inscription 2924
Site Jebel Sirbal, Wadi Ajaleh, #188
Condition good
Content Nabatean inscription
šlm ʿbd
Access II.2a.30 (printed, CIS)
Corpus CIS 1718

Inscription 2925
Site Jebel Sirbal, Wadi Ajaleh, #188
Condition good
Content Nabatean inscription
šlm hnʾw
Comment *bilingual inscription; see insc. 2952 for the Greek*
Access II.2a.30 (printed, CIS)
Corpus CIS 1719

Inscription 2926
Site Jebel Sirbal, Wadi Ajaleh, #188
Condition good
Content Nabatean inscription
šlm ʿbdʾlbʿly br klbw
Access II.2a.31 (printed, CIS)
Corpus CIS 1720

Inscription 2927
Site Jebel Sirbal, Wadi Ajaleh, #188
Condition good
Content Nabatean inscription
šlm wʾlw
br mškw
Access II.2a.31 (printed, CIS)
Corpus CIS 1721

Inscription 2928
Site Jebel Sirbal, Wadi Ajaleh, #188
Condition good
Content Nabatean inscription
grmʾlh[y]
br ḥršw
Access II.2a.31 (printed, CIS)
Corpus CIS 1722

Inscription 2929
Site Jebel Sirbal, Wadi Ajaleh, #188
Condition good
Content Nabatean inscription
šlm ʿbdʾlbʿly br
šʿdʾlhy
bṭb
Access II.2a.31 (printed, CIS)
Corpus CIS 1723

Inscription 2930
Site Jebel Sirbal, Wadi Ajaleh, #188
Condition poor
Content Nabatean inscription
Comment *fragment*
Access II.2a.31 (printed, CIS)
Corpus CIS 1724

Inscription 2931
Site Jebel Sirbal, Wadi Ajaleh, #188
Condition poor
Content Nabatean inscription
Comment *fragment*
Access II.2a.31 (printed, CIS)
Corpus CIS 1725

Inscription 2932
Site Jebel Sirbal, Wadi Ajaleh, #188
Condition poor
Content Nabatean inscription
ʿmyw
Access II.2a.31 (printed, CIS)
Corpus CIS 1726

Inscription 2933
Site Jebel Sirbal, Wadi Ajaleh, #188
Condition good
Content Nabatean inscription
šlm šʿdʾlhy br wʾlw
Access II.2a.31 (printed, CIS)
Corpus CIS 1727

Inscription 2934
Site Jebel Sirbal, Wadi Ajaleh, #188
Condition good
Content Nabatean inscription
šlm šʿdʾlhy br wʾlw
Access II.2a.31 (printed, CIS)
Corpus CIS 1728

Inscription 2935
Site Jebel Sirbal, Wadi Ajaleh, #188
Condition poor
Content Nabatean inscription
[š]lm šʿdl[hy]
[br] ʿyydw
Access II.2a.31 (printed, CIS)
Corpus CIS 1729

Inscription 2936
Site Jebel Sirbal, Wadi Ajaleh, #188
Condition fair
Content Nabatean inscription
šlm ʾlḥyw br...yw šlm
Access II.2a.31 (printed, CIS)
Corpus CIS 1730

Inscription 2937
Site Jebel Sirbal, Wadi Ajaleh, #188
Condition good
Content Nabatean inscription
dkyr ʿlyw br
šʿdʾlhy
Access II.2a.31 (printed, CIS)
Corpus CIS 1731

Inscription 2938
Site Jebel Sirbal, Wadi Ajaleh, #188
Condition good
Content Nabatean inscription
šlm zydw
Access II.2a.32 (printed, CIS)
Corpus CIS 1732

Inscription 2939
Site Jebel Sirbal, Wadi Ajaleh, #188
Condition poor
Content Nabatean inscription
šlm zydw [br] ....
ʾ...
Access II.2a.32 (printed, CIS)
Corpus CIS 1733

Inscription 2940
Site Jebel Sirbal, Wadi Ajaleh, #188
Condition fair
Content Nabatean inscription
šlm wkylw
br [ʿbdʾlb]ʿly
Access II.2a.32 (printed, CIS)
Corpus CIS 1734

Inscription 2941
Site Jebel Sirbal, Wadi Ajaleh, #188
Condition poor
Content Nabatean inscription
.... wʾlw
Access II.2a.32 (printed, CIS)
Corpus CIS 1735

Inscription 2942
Site Jebel Sirbal, Wadi Ajaleh, #188
Condition good
Content Nabatean inscription
šlm ʿmyw br wʾlw
Access II.2a.32 (printed, CIS)
Corpus CIS 1736

Inscription **2943**
Site Jebel Sirbal, Wadi Ajaleh, #188
Condition good
Content Nabatean inscription
šlm klbw br wʾlw
Access II.2a.32 (printed, CIS)
Corpus CIS 1737

Inscription **2944**
Site Wadi Wata, #225
Technique incised
Condition fair
Content rock drawing
Comment *ibexes*
Access CZ62-63 (photograph, A. Goren); *see also* CZ66-67

Inscription **2945**
Site Wadi Wata, #225
Technique scratched
Condition poor
Content Arabic inscription
Limitation *Tentative decipherment only*
Access CZ66-67 (photograph, A. Goren)

Inscription **2946**
Site Wadi Haggag, rock 3, #125
Technique incised
Condition good
Content crosses alone
Access Negev 1977 fig. 119 (printed, A. Negev)

Inscription **2947**
Site Wadi Haggag, rock 3, #125
Technique incised
Condition good
Content crosses alone
Access Negev 1977 fig. 119 (printed, A. Negev)

Inscription **2948**
Site Wadi Haggag, rock 3, #125
Technique scratched
Condition poor
Content Armenian inscription
Comment *illegible*
Access Negev 1977 fig. 89 (printed, A. Negev)

Inscription **2949**
Site Wadi Haggag, rock 6, #135
Technique scratched
Condition poor
Content Arabic inscription
Limitation *Tentative decipherment only*
Access Negev 1977 fig. 200 (printed, A. Negev)

Inscription **2950**
Site Wadi Mukatab, #64
Condition fair
Content Greek inscription
ΑΜΜΑΙΟΣ ΑΤΤΑΛΟΥ
Access II.2.452 (printed, CIS)
Corpus CIS 1192

Inscription **2951**
Site Wadi Mukatab, #64
Condition good
Content Nabatean inscription
ḥššw
Access II.2.453 (printed, CIS)
Corpus CIS 1196

Inscription **2952**
Site Jebel Sirbal, Wadi Ajaleh, #188
Condition good
Content Greek inscription
ΑΝΕΟΣ
Comment *below Nabatean inscription; see insc. 2925 for the Nabatean*
Access II.2a.30 (printed, CIS)
Corpus CIS 1719

Inscription **2953**
Site Wadi Mukatab, #64
Technique incised
Condition good
Content Nabatean inscription
Limitation *Tentative decipherment only*
Access CM49 (photograph, Z. Radovan)

Inscription **2954**
Site Wadi Hesi, #180
Condition poor
Content Nabatean inscription
Comment *fragments*
Access II.2a.32 (printed, CIS)
Corpus CIS 1738

Inscription **2955**
Site Jebel Sirbal, Wadi Ajaleh, #188
Condition poor
Content Nabatean inscription
Comment *fragments*
Access II.2a.32 (printed, CIS)
Corpus CIS 1739

Inscription **2956**
Site Jebel Sirbal, Wadi Ajaleh, #188
Condition fair
Content Nabatean inscription
šlm ʿnm[w]
Access II.2a.32 (printed, CIS)
Corpus CIS 1740

Inscription **2957**
Site Jebel Sirbal, Wadi Ajaleh, #188
Condition good
Content Nabatean inscription
šlm ṣʿbw br
šmr[ḥ]
Access II.2a.32 (printed, CIS)
Corpus CIS 1741

Inscription 2958
Site Jebel Sirbal, Wadi Ajaleh, #188
Condition good
Content Nabatean inscription
šlm ʿbdʾlgyʾ
br wʾlw
Access II.2a.32 (printed, CIS)
Corpus CIS 1742

Inscription 2959
Site Jebel Sirbal, Wadi Ajaleh, #188
Condition poor
Content Nabatean inscription
[dk]yr ʿlyw br [šʿ]dʾlhy
Access II.2a.32 (printed, CIS)
Corpus CIS 1743

Inscription 2960
Site Jebel Sirbal, Wadi Ajaleh, #188
Condition fair
Content Nabatean inscription
šlm ʿwdw br
zydw...
Access II.2a.33 (printed, CIS)
Corpus CIS 1744

Inscription 2961
Site Jebel Sirbal, Wadi Ajaleh, #188
Condition good
Content Nabatean inscription
šlm ḥryšw
br zydw
Access II.2a.33 (printed, CIS)
Corpus CIS 1745

Inscription 2962
Site Jebel Sirbal, Wadi Ajaleh, #188
Condition fair
Content Nabatean inscription
šlm ʿlyw br šmrḥ[w]
dk[yr] ʿlyw br
šmrḥw
Access II.2a.33 (printed, CIS)
Corpus CIS 1746

Inscription 2963
Site Jebel Sirbal, Wadi Ajaleh, #188
Condition good
Content Nabatean inscription
ʿbdʾlh
šlm
br šʿdʾlh
Access II.2a.33 (printed, CIS)
Corpus CIS 1747

Inscription 2964
Site Jebel Sirbal, Wadi Ajaleh, #188
Condition good
Content Nabatean inscription
šlm ḥršw br
ʿmyw khn tʾ
Access II.2a.33 (printed, CIS)
Corpus CIS 1748

Inscription 2965
Site Jebel Sirbal, Wadi Ajaleh, #188
Condition good
Content Nabatean inscription
šlm wldw
br wʾlw
Access II.2a.33 (printed, CIS)
Corpus CIS 1749

Inscription 2966
Site Jebel Sirbal, Wadi Ajaleh, #188
Condition good
Content Nabatean inscription
šlm ʿmrw br
ḥryšw
kh[n] tʾ
Access II.2a.33 (printed, CIS)
Corpus CIS 1750

Inscription 2967
Site Jebel Sirbal, Wadi Ajaleh, #188
Condition good
Content Nabatean inscription
šlm ʿnmw br ʿbdʾlbʿly br hnyʾw bṭb
Access II.2a.34 (printed, CIS)
Corpus CIS 1751

Inscription 2968
Site Jebel Sirbal, Wadi Ajaleh, #188
Condition good
Content Nabatean inscription
šlm mʿnw br hnʾw [b]ṭb wšlm
Access II.2a.34 (printed, CIS)
Corpus CIS 1752

Inscription 2969
Site Jebel Sirbal, Wadi Ajaleh, #188
Condition good
Content Nabatean inscription
šlm ʿwdw br ʿmyw
Access II.2a.34 (printed, CIS)
Corpus CIS 1753 (1)

Inscription 2970
Site Jebel Sirbal, Wadi Ajaleh, #188
Condition good
Content Greek inscription
ΑΥΔΟΣ ΑΜΜΟΙΥ
Access II.2a.34 (printed, CIS)
Corpus CIS 1753 (2)

Inscription **2971**
Site Jebel Sirbal, Wadi Ajaleh, #188
Condition good
Content Nabatean inscription
šlm kʿmh
br ʿwdw
bṭb
Access II.2a.34 (printed, CIS)
Corpus CIS 1754

Inscription **2972**
Site Jebel Sirbal, Wadi Ajaleh, #188
Condition good
Content Nabatean inscription
šlm grmʾlʿly br whbʾlhy
Access II.2a.34 (printed, CIS)
Corpus CIS 1755

Inscription **2973**
Site Jebel Sirbal, Wadi Ajaleh, #188
Condition good
Content Nabatean inscription
šlm ʼwšw br
wʾlw bṭ...
Access II.2a.34 (printed, CIS)
Corpus CIS 1756

Inscription **2974**
Site Jebel Sirbal, Wadi Ajaleh, #188
Condition good
Content Nabatean inscription
dkyr ʾlkyw
br hnyʾw b[ṭ]b
Access II.2a.34 (printed, CIS)
Corpus CIS 1757

Inscription **2975**
Site Jebel Sirbal, Wadi Ajaleh, #188
Condition good
Content Nabatean inscription
pšy br ʾʿlʾ
Access II.2a.34 (printed, CIS)
Corpus CIS 1758

Inscription **2976**
Site Jebel Sirbal, Wadi Ajaleh, #188
Condition good
Content Nabatean inscription
šlm gdyw br bryʾw
ʿwdw br šʿdʾlhy
Access II.2a.34 (printed, CIS)
Corpus CIS 1759

Inscription **2977**
Site Jebel Sirbal, Wadi Ajaleh, #188
Condition good
Content Nabatean inscription
dkyr ʾwšw br
klbw bṭb
Access II.2a.35 (printed, CIS)
Corpus CIS 1760

Inscription **2978**
Site Jebel Sirbal, Wadi Ajaleh, #188
Condition good
Content Nabatean inscription
šlm mʿnʾlh
br hnʾw b[ṭb]
Access II.2a.35 (printed, CIS)
Corpus CIS 1761

Inscription **2979**
Site Jebel Sirbal, Wadi Ajaleh, #188
Condition good
Content Nabatean inscription
šlm ḥlṣšt
whbʾl[hy]
bṭb
Access II.2a.35 (printed, CIS)
Corpus CIS 1762

Inscription **2980**
Site Jebel Sirbal, Wadi Ajaleh, #188
Condition good
Content Nabatean inscription
šlm šlmw
Comment *fragments*
Access II.2a.35 (printed, CIS)
Corpus CIS 1763

Inscription **2981**
Site Jebel Sirbal, Wadi Ajaleh, #188
Condition poor
Content Nabatean inscription
šlm šlmw...
[br ʿb]dʾl[bʿly]
Access II.2a.35 (printed, CIS)
Corpus CIS 1764

Inscription **2982**
Site Jebel Sirbal, Wadi Ajaleh, #188
Condition poor
Content Nabatean inscription
dky[r] mydw br
ʾʿlh.w
bṭb
Access II.2a.35 (printed, CIS)
Corpus CIS 1765

Inscription 2983
Site Jebel Sirbal, Wadi Ajaleh, #188
Condition fair
Content Nabatean inscription
šl[m] klbw
br grmʾlbʿ[ly]
Access II.2a.35 (printed, CIS)
Corpus CIS 1766

Inscription 2984
Site Jebel Sirbal, Wadi Ajaleh, #188
Condition fair
Content Nabatean inscription
dkyr šʿdʾl[hy]
Access II.2a.35 (printed, CIS)
Corpus CIS 1767

Inscription 2985
Site Jebel Sirbal, Wadi Ajaleh, #188
Condition good
Content Nabatean inscription
šlm
dkyr ʿmyw br
ʾlʾ ʿwdw
bṭb
Access II.2a.35 (printed, CIS)
Corpus CIS 1768

Inscription 2986
Site Jebel Sirbal, Wadi Ajaleh, #188
Condition fair
Content Nabatean inscription
šlm .y.w
br pšyw
Access II.2a.36 (printed, CIS)
Corpus CIS 1769

Inscription 2987
Site Jebel Sirbal, Wadi Ajaleh, #188
Condition fair
Content Nabatean inscription
šlm zydw br ʿb[d]ʾl
[b]ʿly
Access II.2a.36 (printed, CIS)
Corpus CIS 1770

Inscription 2988
Site Jebel Sirbal, Wadi Ajaleh, #188
Condition poor
Content Nabatean inscription
ʿmy...šw
šlm
Access II.2a.36 (printed, CIS)
Corpus CIS 1771

Inscription 2989
Site Jebel Sirbal, Wadi Ajaleh, #188
Condition poor
Content Nabatean inscription
šlm mgdyw br ...š...
Access II.2a.36 (printed, CIS)
Corpus CIS 1772

Inscription 2990
Site Jebel Sirbal, Wadi Ajaleh, #188
Condition fair
Content Nabatean inscription
šlm wdw dy... ʿbdʾlbʿly
Access II.2a.36 (printed, CIS)
Corpus CIS 1773

Inscription 2991
Site Jebel Sirbal, Wadi Ajaleh, #188
Condition poor
Content Nabatean inscription
šlm ḥlṣšt br [ʿbdʾlbʿly]
Access II.2a.36 (printed, CIS)
Corpus CIS 1774

Inscription 2992
Site Jebel Sirbal, Wadi Ajaleh, #188
Condition good
Content Nabatean inscription
šlm pšy
br pʾrn
Access II.2a.36 (printed, CIS)
Corpus CIS 1775

Inscription 2993
Site Jebel Sirbal, Wadi Ajaleh, #188
Condition fair
Content Nabatean inscription
šlm ḥlṣšt br
.hʾh...
Access II.2a.36 (printed, CIS)
Corpus CIS 1776

Inscription 2994
Site Jebel Sirbal, Wadi Ajaleh, #188
Condition good
Content Nabatean inscription
šlm ʿbdʾlbʿly
br klbw bṭb
Access II.2a.36 (printed, CIS)
Corpus CIS 1777

Inscription 2995
Site Jebel Sirbal, Wadi Ajaleh, #188
Condition good
Content Nabatean inscription
šlm ʿdmw
Access II.2a.36 (printed, CIS)
Corpus CIS 1778

Inscription **2996**
Site Jebel Sirbal, Wadi Ajaleh, #188
Condition good
Content Nabatean inscription
šlm ḥnṭlw br
nšygw
Access II.2a.37 (printed, CIS)
Corpus CIS 1779

Inscription **2997**
Site Jebel Sirbal, Wadi Ajaleh, #188
Condition poor
Content Nabatean inscription
.... wgrmʾlbʿly ʾḥwh
Access II.2a.37 (printed, CIS)
Corpus CIS 1780

Inscription **2998**
Site Jebel Sirbal, Wadi Ajaleh, #188
Condition poor
Content Nabatean inscription
šlm zydw
Comment *fragment*
Access II.2a.37 (printed, CIS)
Corpus CIS 1781

Inscription **2999**
Site Jebel Sirbal, Wadi Ajaleh, #188
Condition poor
Content Nabatean inscription
ʾlbʿly šlm grm
...[ʾ]lbʿly
Access II.2a.37 (printed, CIS)
Corpus CIS 1782

Inscription **3000**
Site Jebel Sirbal, Wadi Ajaleh, #188
Condition good
Content Nabatean inscription
šlm ḥryšw br
ʾwšw
bṭb
Access II.2a.37 (printed, CIS)
Corpus CIS 1783

CATALOGUE OF SITES

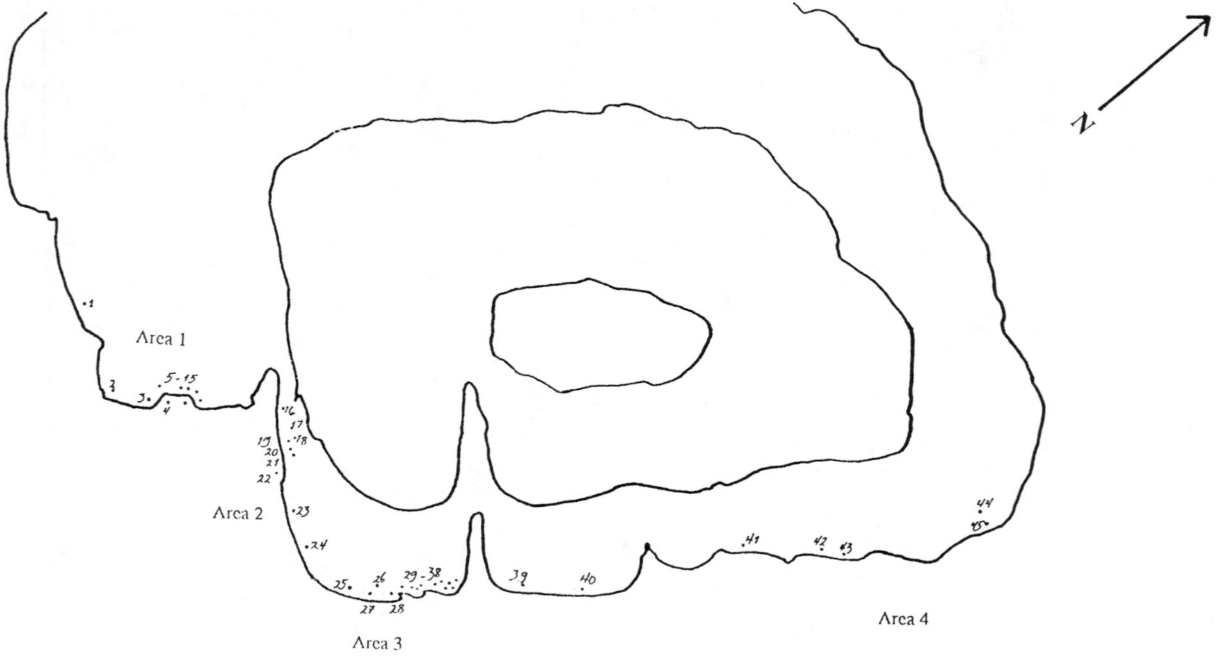

Rock III

Wadi Haggag

0 5 10 m.

(approximate scale)

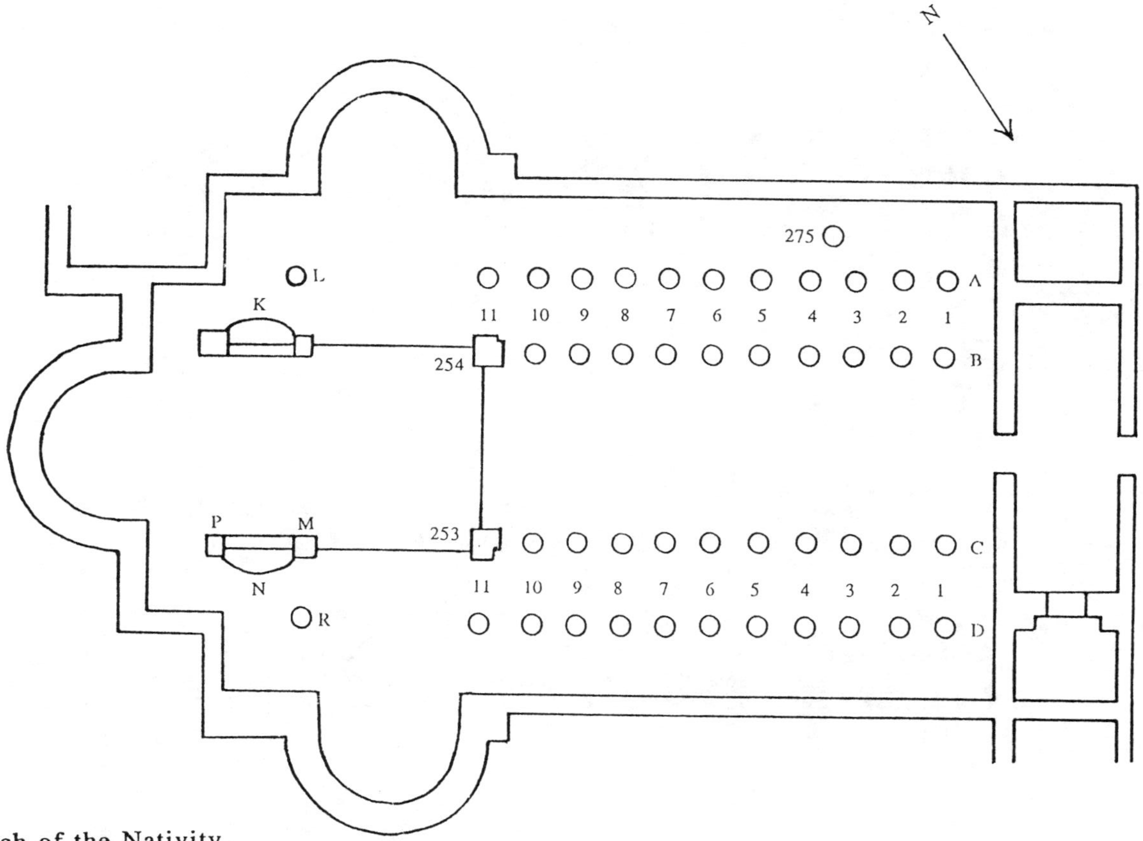

Church of the Nativity
Bethlehem

KEY TO LOCATION

Location	Site	Number
A-Tor	A-Tor	101
	Bir Abu Sueira	191
Church of the Nativity		
	north door to crypt	262
	pier P	263
	pillar A4	275
	pillar B3	268
	pillar B4	266
	pillar B6	264
	pillar B7	257
	pillar B9	256
	pillar C10	252
	pillar C11	253
	pillar C4	243
	pillar C5	244
	pillar C6	245
	south door to crypt	258
	well inside	267
Ein Hudra	Ein Hudra	117
Jebel Baraqa S	Jebel Baraqa S	139
Jebel el Benat	Jebel el Benat	192
Jebel Maharun	Jebel Maharun	317
Jebel Musa	Jebel Musa	19
	peak behind mosque	14
	peak flat rock	11
	peak grotto	12
	peak mosque	16
	stairs from upper gate	18
	steps above Elijah	15
	steps from lower gate	31
	Vale of Elijah	29
	Vale of Elijah, Chapel	378
Jebel Ṣafṣafa	Vale of John	379
Jebel Salmon	Khorbat Seadim	239
Jebel Sirbal	Wadi Ajaleh	188
	Wadi Alayat	187
	Wadi Rim	186
Jebel Tarbush	Jebel Tarbush	315
Jebel Umm Shumer	Bir Ramhan	5
Naqb Budra	Naqb Budra	99
Naqb Sara	Naqb Sara	309
Ostrakine	Ostrakine	208
Qunteilat Ajrud	Qunteilat Ajrud	211
Santa Katarina	Justinian doors rt	9
	Santa Katarina	10
Serabit el Khadem	Serabit el Khadem	86
Sinai	unknown	0
Wadi Abu Ghadhayyat	Ghadhayyat 1	36
	Wadi Abu Ghadhayyat	149

Location	Site	Number
Wadi Arade Lesser	Arade 1	140
Wadi Baba	Baba 1	190
	Wadi Baba	216
Wadi Biraq	Wadi Biraq	79
Wadi Firan	El Hesweh	200
	Erzein el Gharain	203
	Hesy el Khattatin	204
	Jebel el Jozeh	195
	Wadi Firan	53
	Wadi Umfus	201
Wadi Haggag	rock 1	160
	rock 13	202
	rock 2	119
	rock 3	125
	rock 3 area 1	126
	rock 3 area 2	127
	rock 3 area 3	128
	rock 3 area 4	129
	rock 5	131
	rock 6	135
	Wadi Haggag	118
Wadi Hesi	Wadi Hesi	180
Wadi Iqna	Wadi Iqna	74
Wadi Leja	Deir el Arbain	26
	Leja 1	22
	Leja 2	23
	Leja 3	24
	Leja 4	25
	Wadi Leja	27
Wadi Maghara	Wadi Maghara	72
Wadi Mukatab	Mukatab 1	65
	Mukatab 2	228
	Mukatab 3	229
	Mukatab 4	68
	Mukatab 5	69
	Mukatab 6	70
	Mukatab 7	71
	Wadi Mukatab	64
Wadi Sih	Jebel Muardjeh	314
Wadi Shellal	Shellal 1	91
	Shellal 2	92
	Shellal 5	96
	Wadi Shellal	90
Wadi Sih	Wadi Sih	80
Wadi Sreij	Wadi Sreij, ascent	381
Wadi Tueiba	Wadi Tueiba	226
Wadi Umm Sidra	Wadi Umm Sidra	174
Wadi Wata	Wadi Wata	225

Site Number 0
Site Name unknown
Location Sinai
Comment *General site designator, used as a convention for inscriptions whose exact location is unknown.*

Site Number 5
Site Name Bir Ramhan
Location Jebel Umm Shumer
Area Code J
UTM 59351379
ITM 04707537
Geology granite
Comment *Greek inscriptions and crosses en route to Santa Katarina via Wadi Rahba. Access to Wadi Rahba is gained from A-Tur via Wadi Isla or via Wadi Thanan.*

Site Number 9
Site Name Justinian doors rt
Location Santa Katarina
Area Code A
UTM 59561592
ITM 04937752
Geology wooden doors
Comment *Inscriptions incised on borders of panels of right valve of Justinian doors of the church of Santa Katarina. The wood is badly cracked. There are inscriptions on both valves, inside and outside. See Stone, Armenian Inscriptions, illustration 11.*

Site Number 10
Site Name Santa Katarina
Location Santa Katarina
Area Code A
UTM 59561592
ITM 04937752
Geology granite
Comment *General site designator.*

Site Number 11
Site Name peak flat rock
Location Jebel Musa
Area Code A
UTM 59551574
ITM 04927732
Geology granite
Comment *Flat rock to the left of the path leading to the chapel on the peak of Jebel Musa. Greek inscriptions and an Arabic inscription (Stone, Notebook, I 14).*

Site Number 12
Site Name peak grotto
Location Jebel Musa
Area Code A
UTM 59551574
ITM 04927732
Geology granite
Comment *Grotto of Moses beneath the mosque on the peak of Jebel Musa. The character of the rock permits cleaner incisions than those in Wadi Leja. Photography of the site is difficult since the Beduin hold ceremonies there on certain festivals and burn incense which has blackened the rock. For a description of this ritual see S. Levi, Beduin Religion in South Sinai. A number of inscriptions are hidden behind the rocks of the steps on a wall at the entrance to the grotto.*

Site Number 14
Site Name peak behind mosque
Location Jebel Musa
Area Code A
UTM 59551574
ITM 04927732
Geology granite
Comment *Series of flat rock faces to the side of and behind the mosque on the peak of Jebel Musa. The patina of the rock is very friable and large pieces have broken away carrying inscribed material with them.*

Site Number 15
Site Name steps above Elijah
Location Jebel Musa
Area Code A
UTM 59541577
ITM 04927735
Geology granite
Comment *Rocks to the right and left of the steps between the Vale of Elijah and the peak of the mountain. There are scattered inscriptions and crosses in area (Stone, Sinai Diary, 113).*

Site Number 16
Site Name peak mosque
Location Jebel Musa
Area Code A
UTM 59551574
ITM 04927732
Geology granite blocks
Comment *Inscriptions on the foundation stones of the mosque.*

Site Number 18
Site Name stairs from upper gate
Location Jebel Musa
Area Code A
UTM 59561582
ITM 04907743
Geology granite
Comment *Rock to the right of the path, below theupper Stephanos gate, at the beginning of the steps descending from the Vale of Elijah. These inscriptions are predominantly Greek (Stone, Sinai Dairy, 113).*

Site Number 19
Site Name Jebel Musa
Location Jebel Musa
Area Code A
UTM 59551574
ITM 04927732
Geology granite
Comment *General site designator.*

Site Number 22
Site Name Leja 1
Location Wadi Leja
Area Code A
UTM 59361580
ITM 04747738
Geology granite
Comment *Site 50 m. north of the Rock of Moses chapel.*

Site Number 23
Site Name Leja 2
Location Wadi Leja
Area Code A
UTM 59391577
ITM 04767734
Geology granite boulders
Comment *Site 300 m. north of the Rock of Moses chapel.*

Site Number 24
Site Name Leja 3
Location Wadi Leja
Area Code A
UTM 59401576
ITM 04777733
Geology granite
Comment *Site 700 m. north of the Rock of Moses chapel.*

Site Number 25
Site Name Leja 4
Location Wadi Leja
Area Code A
UTM 59381576
ITM 04767733
Geology granite
Comment *Site 300 m. north of the Rock of Moses chapel.*

Site Number 26
Site Name Deir el Arbain
Location Wadi Leja
Area Code A
UTM 59451570
ITM 04807727
Geology granite
Comment *The Monastery of the Forty Martyrs in Wadi Leja. Opposite the monastery on a rock there is a Greek inscription.*

Site Number 27
Site Name Wadi Leja
Location Wadi Leja
Area Code A
UTM 59421573
ITM 04807732
Geology granite
Comment *General site designator. Byzantine paving and footsteps throughout the wadi (Stone, Sinai Diary, 93). See Stone, Armenian Inscriptions, illustration 8.*

Site Number 29
Site Name Vale of Elijah
Location Jebel Musa
Area Code A
UTM 59541580
ITM 05927737
Geology granite

Site Number 31
Site Name steps from lower gate
Location Jebel Musa
Area Code A
UTM 59561584
ITM 04947742
Geology granite
Comment *Rocks by the stairs below the lower Stephanos gate on the descent from Jebel Musa.*

Site Number 36
Site Name Ghadhayyat 1
Location Wadi Abu Ghadhayyat
Area Code L
UTM 63931952
ITM 09378102
Geology sandstone
Comment *Bifurcated hadbe; Greek inscription, drawings, Arabic inscription, wasems (Stone, Notebook, I 88; Sinai Diary, 172). Also a group of crosses, including five large ones. See photograph in Stone, Armenian Inscriptions, illustration 45.*

Site Number 53
Site Name Wadi Firan
Location Wadi Firan
Area Code C
UTM 55401810
ITM 00807975
Geology granite
Comment *General site designator.*

Site Number 64
Site Name Wadi Mukatab
Location Wadi Mukatab
Area Code D
UTM 54201901
ITM 99628068
Geology sandstone
Comment *General site designator. The wadi contains numerous inscriptions in Nabatean, a few in Greek and Arabic. The sides of the wadi are of low sandstone. The southwest side, in particular, and to a lesser extent the northeast side, is covered with inscriptions.*

Site Number 65
Site Name Mukatab 1
Location Wadi Mukatab
Area Code D
UTM 54051932
ITM 99428098
Geology sandstone

Site Number 68
Site Name Mukatab 4
Location Wadi Mukatab
Area Code D
UTM 53981935
ITM 99438199
Geology sandstone
Comment *Latin inscriptions at the end of a cliff on the southwest side of the wadi (Stone, Sinai Diary, 41).*

Site Number 69
Site Name Mukatab 5
Location Wadi Mukatab
Area Code D
UTM 53861939
ITM 99288106
Geology sandstone
Comment *Two free-standing orange stones at the west end, southwestern side, of the wadi. The stones have Nabatean and other inscriptions, including Georgian (Stone, Sinai Diary, 40).*

Site Number 70
Site Name Mukatab 6
Location Wadi Mukatab
Area Code D
UTM 54151917
ITM 99568084
Geology sandstone
Comment *Drawing of 2 palms and crosses (Stone, Notebook, II 15).*

Site Number 71
Site Name Mukatab 7
Location Wadi Mukatab
Area Code D
UTM 54151915
ITM 99568082
Geology sandstone

Site Number 72
Site Name Wadi Maghara
Location Wadi Maghara
Area Code D
UTM 53601970
ITM 99058142
Geology sandstone
Comment *General site designator.*

Site Number 74
Site Name Wadi Iqna
Location Wadi Iqna
Area Code E
UTM 53701970
ITM 99168137
Geology sandstone
Comment *General site designator. This wadi's name is also pronounced "Gna" and appears in some sources as "Kene".*

Site Number 79
Site Name Wadi Biraq
Location Wadi Biraq
Area Code E
UTM 55901980
ITM 01358146
Geology sandstone
Comment *General site designator.*

Site Number 80
Site Name Wadi Sih
Location Wadi Sih
Area Code E
UTM 56102040
ITM 01568206
Geology granite, sandstone
Comment *General site designator.*

Site Number 86
Site Name Serabit el Khadem
Location Serabit el Khadem
Area Code F
UTM 55462123
ITM 99938291
Geology sandstone
Comment *General site designator.*

Site Number 90
Site Name Wadi Shellal
Location Wadi Shellal
Area Code F
UTM 53002020
ITM 98458180
Geology sandstone
Comment *General site designator. The following sites occur in this area are designated as sites Shellal 1-7: nos. 91, 92, 93, 94, 95, 96, 97.*

Site Number 91
Site Name Shellal 1
Location Wadi Shellal
Area Code F
UTM 53092023
ITM 98558195
Geology sandstone
Comment *Greek and Nabatean inscriptions, drawings (Stone, Notebook, III 27).*

Site Number 92
Site Name Shellal 2
Location Wadi Shellal
Area Code F
UTM 53082022
ITM 98538195
Geology sandstone
Comment *Fallen stones, below the road, with Nabatean inscriptions and drawings (Stone, Notebook, III 27).*

Site Number 96
Site Name Shellal 5
Location Wadi Shellal
Area Code F
UTM 52932018
ITM 98388189
Geology sandstone
Comment *Another rock behind Shellal 4. Nabatean inscriptions (Stone, Notebook, III 26).*

Site Number 99
Site Name Naqb Budra
Location Naqb Budra
Area Code F
UTM 52952011
ITM 98418182
Geology limestone

Site Number 101
Site Name A-Tor
Location A-Tor
Area Code G
UTM 56101230
ITM 01417396
Geology limestone
Comment *General site designator. Christian inscriptions in the plaster of monastic cells. See E. H. Palmer, Desert of Sinai, 1.222.*

Site Number 117
Site Name Ein Hudra
Location Ein Hudra
Area Code L
UTM 63881963
ITM 09358126
Geology sandstone
Comment *General site designator.*

Site Number 118
Site Name Wadi Haggag
Location Wadi Haggag
Area Code L
UTM 63701950
ITM 09148098
Geology sandstone
Comment *General site designator. See also Wadi Rum, Jebel Rum.*

Site Number 119
Site Name rock 2
Location Wadi Haggag
Area Code L
UTM 63741957
ITM 09198107
Geology sandstone
Comment *Syriac inscription on northern side, by odd rock formation (Stone, Sinai Diary, 19).*

Site Number 125
Site Name rock 3
Location Wadi Haggag
Area Code L
UTM 63761959
ITM 09208106
Geology sandstone
Comment *See Stone, Armenian Inscriptions, plan VI, p. 100.*

Site Number 126
Site Name rock 3 area 1
Location Wadi Haggag
Area Code L
UTM 63761956
ITM 09208106
Geology sandstone
Comment *Face at south corner of Rock 3. See Stone, Armenian Inscriptions, plan VI, p. 100.*

Site Number 127
Site Name rock 3 area 2
Location Wadi Haggag
Area Code L
UTM 63761956
ITM 09208106
Geology sandstone
Comment *South face adjoining area 1. See Stone, Armenian Inscriptions, plan VI, p. 100.*

Site Number 128
Site Name rock 3 area 3
Location Wadi Haggag
Area Code L
UTM 63761956
ITM 09208106
Geology sandstone
Comment *Southeast face at south end of Rock 3. See Stone, Armenian Inscriptions, plan VI, p. 100.*

Site Number **129**
Site Name rock 3 area 4
Location Wadi Haggag
Area Code L
UTM 63761956
ITM 09208106
Geology sandstone
Comment *Southeast face at north end of Rock 3. See Stone, Armenian Inscriptions, illustration 2 and plan VI.*

Site Number **131**
Site Name rock 5
Location Wadi Haggag
Area Code L
UTM 63891955
ITM 09368106
Geology sandstone
Comment *See Stone, Armenian Inscriptions, illustration 3.*

Site Number **135**
Site Name rock 6
Location Wadi Haggag
Area Code L
UTM 63731955
ITM 09178105
Geology sandstone

Site Number **139**
Site Name Jebel Baraqa S
Location Jebel Baraqa S
Area Code L
UTM 63731840
ITM 09177990
Geology sandstone

Site Number **140**
Site Name Arade 1
Location Wadi Arade Lesser
Area Code H
UTM 62631883
ITM 08048036
Geology sandstone
Comment *Near mouth of wadi, on Derech Ziva, rock face with drawings and Nabatean inscriptions.*

Site Number **149**
Site Name Wadi Abu Ghadhayyat
Location Wadi Abu Ghadhayyat
Area Code L
UTM 63951945
ITM 09388094
Geology sandstone
Comment *General site designator. Sandy area with many hadbes, surveyed in general direction from south to north (Stone, Notebook, I 89).*

Site Number **160**
Site Name rock 1
Location Wadi Haggag
Area Code L
UTM 63761956
ITM 09208106
Geology sandstone
Comment *Extremely large sandstone rock located south of Derekh Ziva in Wadi Haggag, known as "Hadbet Haggag". Nabatean, Arabic inscriptions, drawings (Stone, Notebook, II 34; Sinai Diary, 60).*

Site Number **174**
Site Name Wadi Umm Sidra
Location Wadi Umm Sidra
Area Code W
UTM 67702730
ITM 13358875
Geology sandstone
Comment *General site designator. Also called Canyon of Inscriptions. Special file assembled by B. Shulman of Eilat has been incorporated into the Project records.*

Site Number **180**
Site Name Wadi Hesi
Location Wadi Hesi
Area Code N
UTM 65262545
ITM 10818693
Geology sandstone
Comment *General site designator. A path turns south and connects with Wadi Watir at 10198552 ITM. This is a marked old route and there are further complexes of paths (Stone, Notebook, VI 23). See Wadi Watir.*

Site Number **186**
Site Name Wadi Rim
Location Jebel Sirbal
Area Code C
UTM 56651715
ITM 02057878
Geology granite
Comment *There are at least 20 Nabatean inscriptions. Dahari observes that the name on 1:50,000 map is wrong. See Rabinovitz, Mt. Sirbal 8. The coordinates are indicated in Rabinovitz, Mt. Sirbal 29.*

Site Number **187**
Site Name Wadi Alayat
Location Jebel Sirbal
Area Code C
UTM 56351738
ITM 01757898
Geology granite

Site Number **188**
Site Name Wadi Ajaleh
Location Jebel Sirbal
Area Code C
UTM 56051735
ITM 01457898
Geology granite

Site Number **190**
Site Name Baba 1
Location Wadi Baba
Area Code F
UTM 52852046
ITM 98338218
Geology granite
Comment *Isolated rock at entrance to Wadi Baba, near east wall, dirctly south of Bir Rakis.*

Site Number **191**
Site Name Bir Abu Sueira
Location ATor
Area Code G
UTM 55491305
ITM 00897472
Geology limestone
Comment *Site of monastery of Raithou near A-Tor.*

Site Number **192**
Site Name Jebel el Benat
Location Jebel el Benat
Area Code C
UTM 56161807
ITM 01557981
Geology sandstone
Comment *A. Negev, Ketovot Drom Sinai 335; see CIS II.3.2 (map); II.3.15 (description).*

Site Number **195**
Site Name Jebel el Jozeh
Location Wadi Firan
Area Code C
UTM 56351738
ITM 01757955
Geology sandstone
Comment *Negev, Ketovot Drom Sinai 350; CIS II.3.2 (map); II.3.12 (description).*

Site Number **200**
Site Name El Hesweh
Location Wadi Firan
Area Code C
UTM 55991759
ITM 01407926
Geology sandstone
Comment *See CIS II.3.2 (map); II.3.8 (description).*

Site Number **201**
Site Name Wadi Umfus
Location Wadi Firan
Area Code C
UTM 56001778
ITM 01417943
Geology sandstone
Comment *See CIS II.3.2 (map); II.3.11 (description). Another name is Wadi Nufus (on Hebrew maps).*

Site Number **202**
Site Name rock 13
Location Wadi Haggag
Area Code L
UTM 63721955
ITM 09168104
Geology sandstone
Comment *East of Rock 3. 51 degrees from top of Rock 3 and 97 degrees from top of Jebel Abu Ghadhayyat. See Stone, Armenian Inscriptions, illustration 4.*

Site Number **203**
Site Name Erzein el Gharain
Location Wadi Firan
Area Code C
UTM 55901782
ITM 01327937
Geology sandstone
Comment *See CIS II.3.2 (map); II.3.6 (description).*

Site Number **204**
Site Name Hesy el Khattatin
Location Wadi Firan
Area Code C
UTM 56651740
ITM 02077902
Geology sandstone
Comment *See CIS II.3.2 (map); II.3.6 (description) rock at east end of the Wadi Firan (Z. Meshel, Qadmoniot Sinai).*

Site Number **208**
Site Name Ostrakine
Location Ostrakine
Area Code U
ITM 00030598
Geology sand
Comment *See El Filusat (site code 207).*

Site Number **211**
Site Name Qunteilat Ajrud
Location Qunteilat Ajrud
Area Code V
ITM 09049506
Geology limestone

Site Number **216**
Site Name Wadi Baba
Location Wadi Baba
Area Code F
UTM 53342107
ITM 98808278
Geology granite
Comment *General site designator.*

Site Number **225**
Site Name Wadi Wata
Location Wadi Wata
Area Code F
UTM 53502297
ITM 99018465
Geology sandstone
Comment *At the foot of the escarpment of the Tih.*

Site Number **226**
Site Name Wadi Tueiba
Location Wadi Tueiba
Area Code W
UTM 68112641
ITM 13688782
Geology sandstone
Comment *South of Eilat. General site designator.*

Site Number **228**
Site Name Mukatab 2
Location Wadi Mukatab
Area Code D
UTM 54071930
ITM 99488098
Geology sandstone

Site Number **229**
Site Name Mukatab 3
Location Wadi Mukatab
Area Code D
UTM 54181916
ITM 99648083
Geology sandstone

Site Number **239**
Site Name Khorbat Seadim
Location Jebel Salmon
Area Code I

Site Number **243**
Site Name pillar C4
Location Church of the Nativity
Area Code IB
Comment *On the west side, an Arabic inscription. On the southwest, Armenian and Latin inscriptions.*

Site Number **244**
Site Name pillar C5
Location Church of the Nativity
Area Code IB
Comment *On the south side, Latin, Greek, unidentified inscriptions; on the east, English, Arabic; on the north, Arabic and unidentified.*

Site Number **245**
Site Name pillar C6
Location Church of the Nativity
Area Code IB

Site Number **252**
Site Name pillar C10
Location Church of the Nativity
Area Code IB
Comment *On the west side, Armenian and Greek inscriptions. On the south, an Arabic inscription.*

Site Number **253**
Site Name pillar C11
Location Church of the Nativity
Area Code IB
Comment *On the west side, a Greek inscription. On the southwest, Greek, Syriac and Armenian inscriptions.*

Site Number **256**
Site Name pillar B9
Location Church of the Nativity
Area Code IB
Comment *On the west and northwest sides, Armenian inscriptions. On the southwest, Arabic and Armenian inscriptions.*

Site Number **257**
Site Name pillar B7
Location Church of the Nativity
Area Code IB
Comment *On the north side, Armenian and Arabic inscriptions and cross. On the west, Arabic, Armenian, Greek inscriptions and cross. On the east, an Armenian inscription.*

Site Number **258**
Site Name south door to crypt
Location Church of the Nativity
Area Code IB
Comment *On the west side, Arabic and unidentified inscription. On the east, crosses, Armenian, Italian and Spanish inscriptions.*

Site Number **262**
Site Name north door to crypt
Location Church of the Nativity
Area Code IB
Comment *On the west side, Armenian and Arabic inscriptions and crosses. On the east, Armenian, Syriac, Arabic and European inscriptions and crosses.*

Site Number **263**
Site Name pier P
Location Church of the Nativity
Area Code IB
Comment *An Armenian inscription.*

Site Number **264**
Site Name pillar B6
Location Church of the Nativity
Area Code IB
Comment *On the north side, Armenian, Latin and Greek inscriptions. On the west, Latin, Armenian, Arabic inscriptions and crosses.*

Site Number **266**
Site Name pillar B4
Location Church of the Nativity
Area Code IB
Comment *On the north side, a Latin inscription. On the northeast, an Arabic inscription. On the northwest, an Armenian and an Arabic inscription. On the west, a Latin inscription.*

Site Number **267**
Site Name well inside
Location Church of the Nativity
Area Code IB
Comment *A Greek inscription.*

Site Number **268**
Site Name pillar B3
Location Church of the Nativity
Area Code IB
Comment *On the east side, an Arabic inscription.*

Site Number **275**
Site Name pillar A4
Location Church of the Nativity
Area Code IB
Comment *On the north side, many Arabic inscriptions.*

Site Number **309**
Site Name Naqb Sara
Location Naqb Sara
Area Code H
UTM 61201856
ITM 06628010
Geology sandstone
Comment *Near Derekh Ziva; stone removed to site off road by A. Goren.*

Site Number **314**
Site Name Jebel Muardjeh
Location Wadi Sih
Area Code E
UTM 54351947
ITM 99828112
Geology sandstone
Comment *See CIS II.2.358.*

Site Number **315**
Site Name Jebel Tarbush
Location Jebel Tarbush
Area Code B
UTM 58101634
ITM 03517798
Geology granite

Site Number **317**
Site Name Jebel Maharun
Location Jebel Maharun
Area Code H
Comment *Between Ein Hudra and Santa Katarina area. Not found on the map.*

Site Number **378**
Site Name Vale of Elijah, Chapel
Location Jebel Musa
Area Code A
UTM 59541580
ITM 05927737
Comment *Wall of chapel*

Site Number **379**
Site Name Vale of John
Location Jebel Ṣafṣafa
Area Code A
UTM 59481585
ITM 04837743
Geology granite

Site Number **381**
Site Name Wadi Sreij, ascent
Location Wadi Sreij
Area Code A
Comment *Ascent from Wadi Sreij to Ras Ṣafṣafa*

INDEXES

INDEX BY DATES

INDEX BY CONTENT

707 709 710 732 733 734 735 736 737 739 740 741 742 743 744 745 746 747 752 753
754 756 757 762 763 764 767 773 774 792 793 794 795 796 797 798 800 801 803 804
805 806 807 808 809 810 813 814 815 816 817 818 821 824 826 832 833 836 842 843
844 845 847 850 855 856 857 860 867 869 874 875 883 884 886 890 891 894 897 901
902 908 920 926 936 938 963 964 992 997 1007 1008 1107 1112 1117 1124 1125 1126
1129 1249 1250 1251 1252 1253 1254 1255 1256 1257 1258 1259 1260 1261 1262 1263
1264 1265 1266 1267 1268 1269 1270 1271 1272 1273 1274 1275 1276 1277 1278 1279
1280 1281 1282 1283 1284 1285 1286 1287 1288 1289 1290 1291 1292 1293 1294 1295
1296 1297 1298 1299 1300 1301 1302 1303 1304 1305 1306 1307 1308 1309 1310 1311
1312 1313 1314 1315 1316 1317 1318 1319 1320 1321 1322 1323 1324 1325 1326 1327
1328 1329 1330 1331 1332 1333 1334 1335 1336 1337 1338 1339 1340 1341 1342 1343
1344 1345 1346 1347 1348 1349 1350 1351 1352 1353 1354 1355 1356 1357 1358 1359
1360 1361 1362 1363 1364 1365 1366 1367 1368 1369 1370 1371 1372 1373 1374 1375
1376 1377 1378 1379 1380 1381 1382 1383 1384 1385 1386 1387 1388 1389 1390 1391
1392 1393 1394 1395 1396 1397 1398 1399 1400 1401 1402 1403 1404 1405 1406 1407
1408 1409 1410 1411 1412 1413 1414 1415 1416 1417 1418 1419 1420 1421 1422 1423
1424 1425 1426 1427 1428 1429 1430 1431 1432 1433 1434 1435 1436 1437 1438 1439
1440 1441 1442 1443 1444 1445 1446 1447 1448 1449 1450 1451 1452 1453 1454 1455
1456 1457 1458 1459 1460 1461 1462 1463 1464 1465 1467 1478 1479 1480 1481 1482
1483 1484 1485 1486 1750 1782 1792 1793 1794 1795 1796 1797 1798 1799 1800 1803
1805 1806 1807 1808 1809 1810 1811 1812 1813 1814 1817 1818 1819 1820 1821 1822
1823 1824 1825 1826 1849 1850 1851 1852 1853 1854 1855 1856 1859 1860 1862 1863
1864 1865 1868 1869 1871 1872 1873 1874 1875 1876 1877 1878 1879 1880 1881 1882
1883 1884 1885 1886 1887 1888 1889 1890 1891 1892 1893 1894 1895 1896 1897 1898
1899 1900 1901 1902 1903 1904 1905 1906 1907 1908 1909 1910 1911 1912 1913 1914
1915 1916 1917 1918 1919 1920 1921 1922 1923 1924 1925 1926 1927 1928 1929 1930
1931 1932 1933 1934 1935 1936 1937 1938 1939 1940 1941 1942 1943 1944 1945 1946
1947 1948 1949 1950 1951 1952 1953 1954 1955 1956 1957 1958 1959 1960 1961 1962
1963 1964 1965 1966 1967 1968 1969 1970 1971 1972 1973 1974 1975 1976 1977 1978
1979 1980 1981 1982 1983 1984 1985 1986 1987 1988 1989 1990 1991 1992 1993 1994
1995 1996 1997 1998 1999 2000 2001 2002 2003 2004 2005 2006 2007 2008 2009 2010
2011 2012 2013 2014 2015 2016 2017 2018 2019 2020 2021 2022 2023 2024 2025 2026
2027 2028 2029 2030 2031 2032 2033 2034 2035 2036 2037 2038 2039 2040 2041 2042
2043 2044 2045 2046 2047 2048 2049 2050 2051 2052 2053 2054 2055 2056 2057 2058
2059 2060 2061 2062 2063 2064 2065 2066 2067 2068 2069 2070 2071 2072 2073 2074
2075 2076 2077 2078 2079 2080 2082 2083 2084 2085 2086 2087 2088 2089 2090 2091
2092 2093 2094 2095 2096 2097 2098 2099 2100 2101 2102 2103 2104 2105 2106 2107
2108 2109 2110 2111 2112 2113 2114 2115 2116 2117 2118 2119 2120 2121 2122 2123
2124 2125 2126 2127 2128 2129 2130 2131 2132 2133 2134 2135 2136 2137 2138 2139
2140 2141 2142 2143 2144 2145 2146 2147 2148 2149 2150 2151 2152 2153 2154 2155
2156 2157 2158 2159 2160 2161 2162 2163 2164 2165 2166 2167 2168 2169 2170 2171
2172 2173 2174 2175 2176 2179 2180 2181 2182 2183 2184 2185 2186 2187 2188 2189
2190 2191 2192 2193 2194 2195 2196 2197 2198 2199 2200 2201 2202 2203 2204 2205
2206 2207 2208 2210 2211 2212 2213 2214 2215 2216 2217 2218 2219 2220 2221 2222
2223 2224 2225 2226 2227 2228 2229 2230 2231 2232 2233 2234 2235 2236 2237 2238
2239 2240 2241 2242 2243 2244 2245 2246 2247 2248 2249 2250 2251 2252 2253 2254
2255 2256 2257 2258 2259 2260 2261 2262 2263 2264 2265 2266 2267 2268 2269 2270
2271 2272 2276 2280 2283 2285 2289 2290 2291 2292 2293 2294 2295 2296 2297 2298
2299 2300 2301 2302 2303 2304 2305 2306 2307 2308 2309 2310 2312 2313 2314 2318
2319 2320 2321 2322 2323 2324 2325 2326 2327 2328 2329 2330 2331 2332 2333 2334
2335 2336 2337 2338 2339 2340 2341 2342 2343 2344 2345 2346 2347 2348 2349 2350
2351 2352 2353 2354 2355 2356 2357 2358 2359 2360 2361 2362 2363 2364 2365 2366
2367 2368 2373 2374 2375 2376 2377 2378 2379 2380 2381 2382 2383 2384 2385 2386
2387 2388 2389 2390 2391 2392 2393 2394 2395 2396 2397 2398 2399 2400 2402 2403
2404 2405 2406 2407 2408 2409 2410 2411 2412 2413 2414 2415 2416 2417 2418 2419
2420 2421 2422 2423 2424 2425 2426 2427 2428 2429 2430 2431 2432 2433 2434 2435
2436 2437 2438 2439 2440 2441 2442 2443 2444 2445 2446 2447 2448 2449 2450 2451
2452 2453 2454 2455 2456 2457 2458 2459 2460 2461 2462 2463 2464 2465 2466 2467
2468 2469 2470 2471 2472 2473 2474 2475 2476 2477 2478 2479 2480 2481 2482 2483
2484 2485 2486 2487 2488 2489 2490 2491 2492 2493 2494 2495 2496 2497 2498 2499
2500 2501 2502 2503 2504 2505 2506 2507 2508 2509 2510 2511 2512 2513 2514 2515
2516 2517 2518 2519 2520 2521 2522 2523 2524 2525 2526 2527 2528 2529 2530 2531
2532 2533 2534 2535 2536 2537 2538 2539 2540 2541 2542 2543 2544 2545 2546 2547
2548 2549 2550 2551 2552 2553 2554 2555 2556 2557 2558 2559 2560 2561 2562 2563
2564 2565 2566 2567 2568 2569 2570 2571 2572 2573 2574 2575 2576 2577 2578 2579
2580 2581 2582 2583 2584 2585 2586 2587 2588 2589 2590 2591 2592 2593 2594 2595
2596 2597 2598 2599 2600 2601 2602 2603 2604 2605 2606 2607 2608 2609 2610 2611
2612 2613 2614 2615 2616 2617 2618 2619 2620 2621 2622 2623 2624 2625 2626 2627
2628 2629 2630 2631 2632 2633 2634 2635 2636 2637 2638 2639 2640 2641 2642 2643

11 22 35 36 37 45 56 92 109 212 222 223 224 225 226 240 243 245 246 268 271 274 287 291 296 299 311 324 328 337 351 352 356 375 376 379 386 387 394 401 409 416 418 419 420 421 422 423 425 426 427 428 429 430 431 435 436 442 444 451 456 458 464 478 492 507 517 518 519 520 521 523 524 525 527 528 536 538 539 548 549 550 553 562 563 567 571 572 573 575 576 591 596 603 609 622 625 631 632 637 655 662 667 674 676 680 681 688 690 696 702 704 705 706 708 712 713 714 715 716 717 718 719 720 721 722 723 724 725 726 727 728 729 730 731 748 749 755 760 761 765 768 770 771 776 777 778 779 780 781 799 820 822 823 829 838 861 892 893 896 899 909 910 911 912 914 915 918 928 943 945 960 985 990 991 1044 1093 1096 1127 1128 1155 1171 1192 1556 1559 1563 1660 1672 1720 1725 1772 1790 1828 1829 1832 1861 1870 2081 2281 2282 2860 2863 2868 2870 2871 2872 2881 2883 2944

unidentified signs
24 31 54 55 108 259 270 339 385 393 440 443 445 469 522 566 574 593 626 628 633 711 758 846 851 868 885 905 913 935 1005 1006 1032 1072 1083 1114 1120 1123 1147 1182 1194 1245 1642 2315 2874 2886

wasems & other Bedouin marks
249 415 424 465 468 526 751 888

INDEX BY LOCATION

Sinai
609 707 708 709 710 712 713 714 715 716 717 718 719 720 721 722 723 724 725 726 727 728 729 730 731 848 849 854 855 856 857 858 859 860 861 862 863 864 893 894 897 898 908 909 910 911 912 913 914 915 916 991 996 997 1055 1124 1125 1126 1127 1128 1129 1130 1131 1228 1237 1239 1770 1784 1839 1857 1866

Vale of John
505 802

Wadi Abu Ghadhayyat
289 290 291 374 375 376 377 378 379 380 527

Wadi Arade Lesser
222 223 224 225 226 867

Wadi Baba
300 732 733 734 735 736 737 738 739 740 741 742 743 744 745 746 747 748 749 750 755 850 851 852 853

Wadi Biraq
45 46

Wadi Firan
465 466 467 468 469 663 664 841 1119 1120 1121 1122 1123 2619 2620 2621 2622 2623 2624 2625 2626 2627 2628 2629 2630 2631 2632 2633 2634 2635 2636 2637 2638 2639 2640 2641 2642 2643 2644 2645 2646 2647 2648 2649 2650 2651 2652 2653 2654 2655 2656 2657 2658 2659 2660 2661 2662 2663 2664 2665 2666 2667 2668 2669 2670 2671 2672 2673 2674 2675 2676 2677 2678 2679 2680 2681 2682 2683 2684 2685 2686 2687 2688 2689 2690 2691 2692 2693 2694 2695 2696 2697 2698 2699 2700 2701 2702 2703 2704 2705 2706 2707 2708 2709 2710 2711 2712 2713 2714 2715 2716 2717 2718 2719 2720 2721 2722 2723 2724 2725 2726 2727 2728 2729 2730 2731 2732 2733 2734 2735 2736 2737 2738 2739 2740 2741 2742 2743 2744 2745 2746 2747 2748 2749 2750

Wadi Haggag
1 2 4 5 6 7 8 9 10 12 13 14 15 16 17 18 19 20 21 22 23 24 25 26 27 28 29 30 31 38 39 40 41 42 43 44 47 48 49 50 51 52 53 54 55 56 57 58 59 60 61 62 63 64 65 66 67 68 69 70 71 72 73 74 75 76 77 78 81 82 83 84 85 86 87 88 89 90 91 92 93 94 95 96 97 98 99 100 101 102 103 104 105 106 107 108 109 110 111 112 113 114 115 116 117 119 120 121 122 123 124 125 126 127 128 129 130 131 132 133 134 135 136 137 138 139 140 141 142 143 144 145 146 147 148 149 150 151 152 153 154 155 156 157 158 159 160 161 162 213 214 215 216 217 218 220 221 229 230 231 232 233 234 235 242 243 244 245 246 247 248 251 252 253 254 256 257 258 259 260 261 262 263 264 265 266 267 268 269 270 271 272 273 274 281 282 283 286 287 288 296 299 301 302 305 338 340 345 353 363 364 386 387 388 391 392 393 394 395 410 411 412 413 414 415 416 417 418 419 420 421 422 423 424 425 426 427 428 429 430 431 440 578 579 580 582 583 584 585 586 587 588 589 590 591 592 593 594 595 596 597 598 599 600 601 602 603 604 605 606 607 608 610 646 647 765 766 782 783 784 785 786 787 792 793 794 799 827 828 829 830 831 832 833 834 835 865 866 868 869 872 873 875 876 877 878 879 880 881 882 928 929 930 931 932 933 934 935 942 968 998 1096 1106 1107 1108 1109 1110 1111 1112 1113 1114 1115 1116 1117 1466 1467 1468 1469 1470 1471 1472 1473 1474 1475 1476 1477 1478 1479 1480 1481 1482 1483 1484 1485 1486 1487 1488 1489 1490 1491 1492 1493 1494 1495 1496 1497 1498 1499 1500 1501 1502 1503 1504 1505 1506 1507 1508 1509 1510 1511 1512 1513 1514 1515 1516 1517 1518 1519 1520 1521 1522 1523 1524 1525 1526 1527 1528 1529 1530 1531 1532 1533 1534 1535 1536 1537 1538 1539 1540 1541 1542 1543 1544 1545 1546 1547 1548 1549 1550 1551 1552 1553 1554 1555 1557 1558 1559 1560 1562 1563 1564 1565 1566 1567 1568 1569 1570 1571 1572 1573 1574 1575 1576 1577 1578 1579 1580 1581 1582 1583 1584 1585 1586 1587 1588 1589 1590 1591 1592 1593 1594 1595 1596 1597 1598 1599 1600 1601 1602 1603 1604 1605 1606 1607 1608 1609 1610 1611 1612 1613 1614 1615 1616 1617 1618 1619 1620 1621 1622 1623 1624 1625 1626 1627 1628 1629 1630 1631 1632 1633 1634 1635 1636 1637 1638 1639 1640 1641 1642 1643 1644 1645 1646 1647 1648 1649 1650 1651 1652 1653 1654 1655 1656 1657 1658 1659 1660 1661 1662 1663 1664 1665 1666 1667 1668 1669 1670 1671 1672 1673 1674 1675 1676 1677 1678 1679 1680 1681 1682 1683 1684 1685 1686 1687 1688 1689 1690 1691 1692 1693 1694 1695 1696 1697 1698 1699 1700 1701 1702 1703 1704 1705 1706 1707 1708 1709 1710 1711 1712 1713 1714 1715 1716 1717 1718 1719 1720 1721 1722 1723 1724 1725 1726 1727 1728 1729 1730 1731 1732 1733 1734 1735 1736 1737 1738 1739 1740 1741 1742 1743 1744 1745 1746 1747 1748 1749 1750 1752 1753 1754 1755 1756 1757 1758 1759 1760 1761 1762 1763 1764 1765 1766 1767 1768 1769 1771 1773 1774 1775 1776 1777 1778 1779 1780 1781 1782 1783 1785 1786 1787 1788 1789 1790 1791 1792 1793 1794 1795 1796 1797 1798 1799 1800 1801 1802 1803 1804 1805 1806 1807 1808 1809 1810 1811 1812 1813 1814 1815 1816 1817 1818 1819 1820 1821 1822 1823 1824 1825 1826 1827 1828 1829 1830 1831 1832 1833 1834 1835 1836 1837 1838 1840 1841 1842 1843 1844 1845 1846 1847 1848 1849 1850 1851 1852 1853 1854 1855 1856 1858 1859 1860 1861 1862 1863 1864 1865 1867 1868 1869 1870 2273 2274 2275 2277 2278 2279 2311 2315 2316 2317 2859 2860 2861 2862 2863 2864 2865 2866 2867 2868 2869 2870 2871

INDEX BY CONTENT, PLACE AND DATE

8th-10th cent. 29
8th-9th cent. 26 76 153
971 97
9th-10th cent. 9 30 50 57 95 144
9th-11th cent. 38 39 40
10th cent. 142 148 155
10th-11th cent. 61 152 156 157
11th cent. 67
11th-12th cent. 129 130
unavailable 4 5 6 12 13 19 21 28 41 62 69 70 74 93 102 104 110 111 113 114 115 117 119 121 122 124 128 131 132 133 135 138 139 140 141 143 145 146 149 151 154 158 159 160 162 942 2273 2274 2948
Wadi Leja
9th-10th cent. 165
11th-12th cent. 163
unavailable 167 169
Wadi Maghara
unavailable 171
Wadi Mukatab
unavailable 172 173 175 176 917
Coptic inscriptions
Ostrakine
unavailable 660
Wadi Leja
unavailable 307
Egyptian hieroglyphs
Serabit el Khadem
unavailable 675
Wadi Maghara
unavailable 3 691 697 698 900
English inscriptions
Church of the Nativity
1601 1151
unavailable 1038 1134 1167
Jebel Musa
unavailable 200
Wadi Mukatab
unavailable 617 1002
French inscription
Serabit el Khadem
1872 895
Georgian inscriptions
Church of the Nativity
unavailable 1027 1138
Wadi Haggag
7th-8th cent. 234
7th-9th cent. 91 392
9th-10th cent. 27 42
9th-11th cent. 15 18
13th-14th cent. 213 229
14th cent. 215 232
unavailable 1699
Wadi Mukatab
8th-9th cent. 236
10th cent. 238
Greek inscriptions
A-Tor
1461 904
1766 643
1872 966
1889 907
unavailable 634 635 640 642 644 645 649 650 651 652 656 906 949 950 954 967 969 970 971 972 976 977
Church of the Nativity
1504 1024
unavailable 1009 1026 1033 1041 1046 1049 1061 1067 1069 1078 1097 1142 1166 1172 1196 1197 1205 1206 1221
Jebel Maharun
unavailable 2286 2287

18th cent. 1040
unavailable 1013 1035 1165 1208
Latin inscriptions
A-Tor
unavailable 946 955 975
Church of the Nativity
1051 1104
1528 1074
1641(?) 1240
unavailable 1020 1043 1092 1103 1135 1141 1144 1161 1177 1180 1181 1561
Santa Katarina
unavailable 389 390 397 400 402 432 433 434
Wadi Haggag
unavailable 49 364 1638 1827
Wadi Maghara
unavailable 276
Wadi Mukatab
unavailable 241 347
Wadi Tueiba
unavailable 658
Wadi Wata
unavailable 473
Nabatean inscriptions
A-Tor
unavailable 890 891
Jebel Baraqa S
unavailable 32 33 34
Jebel el Benat
unavailable 2751 2752 2753 2754 2755 2756 2757 2758 2759 2760 2761 2762 2763 2764 2765 2766 2767 2768 2769 2770 2771 2772 2773 2774 2775 2776 2777 2778 2779 2780 2781 2782 2783 2784 2785 2786 2787 2788 2789 2790 2791 2792 2793 2794 2795 2796 2797 2798 2799 2800 2801 2802 2803 2804 2805 2806 2807 2808 2809 2810 2811 2812 2813 2814 2815 2816 2817 2818 2819 2820 2821
Jebel Sirbal
unavailable 483 484 485 486 487 488 813 2822 2823 2824 2825 2826 2827 2828 2829 2830 2831 2832 2833 2834 2835 2836 2837 2838 2839 2840 2841 2842 2843 2844 2845 2846 2847 2848 2849 2850 2851 2852 2853 2854 2855 2856 2857 2858 2887 2888 2889 2890 2891 2892 2893 2894 2895 2896 2897 2898 2899 2900 2901 2902 2903 2904 2905 2906 2907 2908 2909 2910 2911 2912 2913 2914 2915 2916 2917 2918 2919 2920 2921 2922 2923 2924 2925 2926 2927 2928 2929 2930 2931 2932 2933 2934 2935 2936 2937 2938 2939 2940 2941 2942 2943 2955 2956 2957 2958 2959 2960 2961 2962 2963 2964 2965 2966 2967 2968 2969 2971 2972 2973 2974 2975 2976 2977 2978 2979 2980 2981 2982 2983 2984 2985 2986 2987 2988 2989 2990 2991 2992 2993 2994 2995 2996 2997 2998 2999 3000
Jebel Tarbush
unavailable 460
Naqb Budra
unavailable 1250 1251 1252
Naqb Sara
unavailable 446 447 448 449 450 452 453 454 455 457 459 461 462 463 756 757 810 847
Qunteilat Ajrud
unavailable 701 703
Serabit el Khadem
unavailable 670 671 672 673 842 843
Sinai
unavailable 707 709 710 855 856 857 860 894 897 908 997 1124 1125 1126 1129
Wadi Arade Lesser
unavailable 867
Wadi Baba
unavailable 300 732 733 734 735 736 737 739 740 741 742 743 744 745 746 747 850
Wadi Firan
231 2668
unavailable 466 467 663 664 2619 2620 2621 2622 2623 2624 2625 2626 2627 2628 2629 2630 2631 2632 2633 2634 2635 2636 2637 2638 2639

Unidentified inscriptions
A-Tor
unavailable 641 957 958 961 962 974
Church of the Nativity
unavailable 1028 1034 1037 1039 1050 1052 1056 1059 1071 1077 1079 1090 1094 1153 1178 1179 1183 1203 1213 1219 1224 1229 1230 1242
Jebel Maharun
unavailable 2288
Jebel Musa
unavailable 250 306 371 381 552 871
Naqb Sara
unavailable 811 812
Santa Katarina
unavailable 384
Sinai
unavailable 848 849 854 858 859 863 864 916
Wadi Abu Ghadhayyat
unavailable 378 380
Wadi Baba
unavailable 738
Wadi Biraq
unavailable 46
Wadi Firan
unavailable 841 1122
Wadi Haggag
unavailable 1 14 17 51 75 78 90 94 105 281 388 391 395 414 586 587 588 599 601 827 876 929 930 933 1116 1722 2859 2865 2876
Wadi Leja
unavailable 361
Wadi Maghara
unavailable 695
Wadi Mukatab
unavailable 304 540 551 558 559 624 819 825 887 889 919 921 922 923 924 944 993 994

CROSSES
crosses alone
A-Tor
unavailable 951 956
Church of the Nativity
1523 1226
unavailable 1014 1015 1025 1045 1060 1063 1064 1065 1073 1076 1082 1087 1098 1136 1146 1150 1152 1157 1159 1190 1193 1201 1211 1212 1216 1220 1231 1243 1246
Jebel Maharun
unavailable 1751
Jebel Musa
unavailable 366
Jebel Salmon
unavailable 988
Santa Katarina
unavailable 399 403 404
Sinai
unavailable 1131
Wadi Haggag
unavailable 44 52 58 59 60 63 64 72 77 96 123 127 136 147 150 231 251 252 263 265 282 594 604 606 608 787 828 931 934 1111 1115 1538 1544 1570 1583 1589 1590 1591 1594 1604 1616 1630 1635 1637 1646 1659 1698 1752 1766 1785 1804 1816 2873 2877 2885 2946 2947
Wadi Leja
unavailable 319
Wadi Mukatab
unavailable 174 279 295 303 348 350 937 941 965
Wadi Shellal
unavailable 406
crosses with inscription
A-Tor
unavailable 636 959 973 980
Church of the Nativity

Church of the Nativity
unavailable 1032 1072 1083 1147 1182 1194 1245
Jebel Tarbush
unavailable 443 445
Naqb Sara
unavailable 758
Qunteilat Ajrud
unavailable 711
Santa Katarina
unavailable 385
Sinai
unavailable 913
Wadi Baba
unavailable 750 851
Wadi Firan
unavailable 469 1120 1123
Wadi Haggag
unavailable 24 31 54 55 108 259 270 393 440 593 868 935 1114
1642 2315 2874 2886
Wadi Maghara
unavailable 846
Jebel Maharun
unavailable 2284
Wadi Mukatab
unavailable 522 566 574 626 628 633 885 1005 1006
Wadi Shellal
unavailable 339
wasems & other Bedouin marks
Wadi Firan
unavailable 465 468
Wadi Haggag
unavailable 415 424
Wadi Maghara
unavailable 249
Wadi Mukatab
unavailable 526 751 888

INDEX BY LOCATION, SITE AND CONTENT

A-Tor
- A-Tor
  - Armenian inscription 939
  - Greek inscriptions 904 906 907
  - unidentified signs 905
- Bir Abu Sueira
  - Arabic inscriptions 638 639 653 654 837 839 947 948 978 979 1118
  - crosses alone 951 956
  - crosses with inscriptions 636 959 973 980
  - encircled crosses 952 953
  - Greek inscriptions 634 635 640 642 643 644 645 649 650 651 652 656 949 950 954 966 967 969 970 971 972 976 977
  - Latin inscriptions 946 955 975
  - Nabatean inscriptions 890 891
  - rock drawings 838 892 960
  - unidentified inscriptions 641 957 958 961 962 974
  - varied crosses 648

Church of the Nativity
- north door to crypt
  - Arabic inscriptions 1075 1156 1158 1162 1164 1168
  - Armenian inscriptions 1160 1163
  - crosses alone 1076 1157 1159
  - crosses with inscription 1080
  - English inscription 1167
  - Greek inscriptions 1078 1166
  - Italian inscription 1165
  - Latin inscriptions 1074 1161
  - unidentified inscriptions 1077 1079
- pier P
  - Arabic inscription 1088
  - Armenian inscriptions 1084 1085 1089
  - crosses alone 1087
  - crosses with inscription 1086
  - unidentified inscription 1090
- pillar A4
  - Arabic inscriptions 1184 1189 1195
  - Armenian inscriptions 1186 1191
  - crosses alone 1190 1193
  - crosses with inscriptions 1185 1187
  - encircled crosses 1188
  - rock drawing 1192
  - unidentified signs 1194
- pillar B3
  - Arabic inscriptions 1091 1101 1102 1105 1173 1174 1175 1176
  - Armenian inscriptions 1057 1058 1100
  - crosses alone 1060 1063
  - crosses with inscription 1062
  - Greek inscriptions 1061 1172
  - Italian inscription 1054
  - Latin inscriptions 1092 1103 1104 1177 1180 1181
  - rock drawing 1093
  - unidentified inscriptions 1056 1059 1094 1178 1179 1183
  - unidentified signs 1182
- pillar B4
  - Arabic inscriptions 1099 1143
  - Armenian inscription 1095
  - crosses alone 1098
  - Greek inscriptions 1097 1142
  - Latin inscription 1141
- pillar B6
  - Arabic inscriptions 1137 1139
  - Armenian inscriptions 1132 1140
  - crosses alone 1136
  - crosses with inscription 1133
  - English inscription 1134
  - Georgian inscription 1138
  - Latin inscription 1135

	pillar B7	
	Arabic inscriptions	1217 1225 1232 1238
	Armenian inscriptions	1214 1215 1218 1222 1227 1234 1235 1236
	crosses alone	1216 1220 1226 1231 1243
	crosses with inscriptions	1223 1233
	Greek inscription	1221
	Latin inscription	1240
	Polish inscription	1241
	unidentified inscriptions	1219 1224 1229 1230 1242
	pillar B9	
	Armenian inscription	1244
	crosses alone	1246
	unidentified signs	1245
	pillar C10	
	crosses alone	1082
	Polish inscription	1081
	unidentified signs	1083
	pillar C11	
	Arabic inscriptions	1051 1200 1202 1248
	Armenian inscriptions	1199 1204 1209 1247
	crosses alone	1201 1211 1212
	crosses with inscriptions	1053 1210
	Greek inscriptions	1046 1049 1196 1197 1205 1206
	Italian inscriptions	1208
	Syriac inscriptions	1198 1207
	unidentified inscriptions	1050 1052 1203 1213
	varied crosses	1047 1048
	pillar C4	
	Arabic inscriptions	1145 1149
	crosses alone	1146 1150
	crosses with inscription	1148
	Latin inscription	1144
	unidentified signs	1147
	pillar C5	
	crosses alone	1152
	English inscription	1151
	unidentified inscription	1153
	pillar C6	
	Arabic inscription	1036
	English inscription	1038
	Italian inscription	1035
	Latin inscription	1561
	unidentified inscriptions	1037 1039
	south door to crypt	
	Arabic inscription	1066
	Armenian inscriptions	1017 1018 1029 1031
	crosses alone	1014 1015 1025 1045 1064 1065 1073
	crosses with inscriptions	1019 1030 1042 1070
	encircled crosses	1016
	Georgian inscription	1027
	Greek inscriptions	1024 1026 1033 1041 1067 1069
	Italian inscriptions	1013 1040
	Latin inscriptions	1020 1043
	rock drawing	1044
	Russian inscriptions	1011 1012 1021 1022 1023
	Syriac inscription	1068
	unidentified inscriptions	1028 1034 1071
	unidentified signs	1032 1072
	well inside	
	crosses with inscription	1010
	Greek inscription	1009
Ein Hudra		
	Hebrew inscription	437
	rock drawings	11 523 528 637 680 1556 1772
Jebel Baraqa S		
	Nabatean inscriptions	32 33 34
	rock drawings	35 36 37

rock drawings 442 444
unidentified signs 443 445
Jebel Umm Shumer
Bir Ramhan
Greek inscriptions 788 789 790 791
Naqb Budra
Nabatean inscriptions 1250 1251 1252
Naqb Sara
Nabatean inscriptions 446 447 448 449 450 452 453 454 455 457 459 461 462 463 756 757 810 847
rock drawings 451 456 458 464
unidentified inscriptions 811 812
unidentified signs 758
Ostrakine
Coptic inscription 660
crosses with inscription 666
Greek inscription 665
rock drawings 662 667
varied crosses 661
Qunteilat Ajrud
crosses with inscription 700
Greek inscription 699
Nabatean inscriptions 701 703
rock drawings 702 704 705 706
unidentified signs 711
Santa Katarina
Justinian doors rt
Armenian inscriptions 219 227 228
crosses with inscription 382
Greek inscription 383
unidentified inscription 384
unidentified signs 385
Santa Katarina
Armenian inscriptions 79 80
crosses alone 399 403 404
crosses with inscription 398
encircled crosses 1154 1170
Greek inscriptions 396 1169
Latin inscriptions 389 390 397 400 402 432 433 434
masons' marks 405
rock drawings 401 435 1155 1171
varied crosses 118
Serabit el Khadem
crosses with inscription 669
Egyptian hieroglyphs 675
encircled crosses 759
French inscription 895
Greek inscription 668
Nabatean inscriptions 670 671 672 673 842 843
rock drawings 674 676 760 896
Sinai
Arabic inscriptions 898 996 1239
crosses alone 1131
Greek inscriptions 1130 1228 1237 1770 1784 1839 1857 1866
Nabatean inscriptions 707 709 710 855 856 857 860 894 897 908 997 1124 1125 1126 1129
Old North Arabic inscriptions 862 1055
rock drawings 609 708 712 713 714 715 716 717 718 719 720 721 722 723 724 725 726 727 728 729 730 731 861 893 909 910 911 912 914 915 991 1127 1128
unidentified inscriptions 848 849 854 858 859 863 864 916
unidentified signs 913

Vale of John
Greek inscriptions 505 802
Wadi Abu Ghadhayyat
Ghadhayyat 1
crosses with inscription 290
Greek inscriptions 289 377

Nabatean inscriptions 320 874
rock drawings 324 328 655
Shellal 2
footsteps 408
rock drawing 337
unidentified signs 339
Shellal 5
crosses with inscriptions 358 360
Greek inscriptions 341 357 359
rock drawings 356 409
Wadi Shellal
footsteps 293
Greek inscription 292
Nabatean inscription 1249
Wadi Sih
Nabatean inscriptions 1253 1254 1255 1256 1257 1258 1259 1260 1261 1262 1263 1264 1265 1266 1267 1268 1269 1270 1271 1272 1273 1274 1275 1276 1277 1278 1279 1280 1281 1282 1283 1284 1285 1286 1287 1288 1289 1290 1291 1292 1293 1294 1295 1296 1297 1298 1299 1300 1301 1302 1303 1304 1305 1306 1307 1308 1309 1310 1311 1312 1313 1314 1315 1316 1317 1318 1319 1320 1321 1322 1323 1324 1325 1326 1327 1328 1329 1330 1331 1332 1333 1334 1335 1336 1337 1338 1339 1340 1341 1342 1343 1344 1345 1346 1347 1348 1349 1350 1351 1352 1353 1354 1355 1356 1357 1358 1359 1360 1361 1362 1363 1364 1365 1366 1367 1368 1369 1370 1371 1372 1373 1374 1375 1376 1377 1378 1379 1380 1381 1382 1383 1384 1385 1386 1387 1388 1389 1390 1391 1392 1393 1394 1927 1928 1929 1930 1931 1932 1933 1934 1935 1936 1937 1938 1939
Wadi Sreij
Greek inscriptions 500 694
varied crosses 693
Wadi Tueiba
Arabic inscription 840
Greek inscriptions 657 659
Latin inscription 658
Wadi Umm Sidra
Arabic inscription 581
Greek inscription 630
Nabatean inscription 629
rock drawing 631
Wadi Wata
Arabic inscription 2945
Greek inscription 479
Latin inscription 473
Nabatean inscriptions 470 471 472 474 475 476 477 480 481 482 795 796 797
rock drawings 478 2944